AF572132

Critical Realism

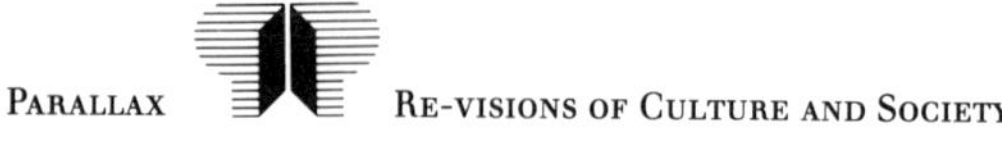

Parallax Re-visions of Culture and Society

Stephen G. Nichols, Gerald Prince, and Wendy Steiner,

Series Editors

Dagmar Barnouw

Critical Realism

History, Photography, and the Work of Siegfried Kracauer

The Johns Hopkins University Press
Baltimore and London

For Jeff and all the times and places

© 1994 The Johns Hopkins University Press
All rights reserved
Printed in the United States of America on acid-free paper
03 02 01 00 99 98 97 96 95 94 5 4 3 2 1

The Johns Hopkins University Press
2715 North Charles Street
Baltimore, Maryland 21218-4319
The Johns Hopkins Press Ltd., London
ISBN 0-8018-4753-2
0-8018-4754-0 (pbk.)

Library of Congress Cataloging-in-Publication Data will be found at the end of this book.

A catalog record for this book is available from the British Library.

Book design by Wesley B. Tanner

Photographs 1 through 38 are from the collection of the J. Paul Getty Museum, Malibu, California.
Photograph 39 is from the Museum Folkwang Essen in Essen, Germany.

Contents

Photographs

FOLLOWING PAGE 188

Time Travel

In a recent American review of her autobiographical writings, a Russian intellectual exile is sternly reminded of the "thoroughly familiar subject" of "existential exile." She is told that her refusal to accept it is most "unusual"; that she is "whistling in the dark," pretending to herself.[1] The twentieth century has seen much violently imposed intellectual migration, and intellectuals as a group have tended to view their condition in the modern world in terms of existential exile, which imposes a particularly difficult quest for identity. Isolation, whether literal or figurative, caused by separation from one's own culture and history, has illuminated the quest and given it a curious distinctness. In contrast, writers more absorbed in their interaction with different–and changing–cultural environments, less given to worrying about the boundaries of identity, have seemed more remote or diffuse, and their intellectual presence somehow less brilliant. One of them was Siegfried Kracauer, a German exile in France and in the United States, where, after a time, he felt temporarily at home. When I started this project, I was interested in the preoccupation of many intellectual exiles with redefining themselves through rewriting a cultural history that had been traumatically ruptured. It was the connection made by Kracauer between his work on photography (film) and on historiography–a connection explicitly skeptical of such self-authorized rewriting–that alerted me most effectively to the different meanings of exile and the different spaces of cultural memory.

In the fall of 1962, Kracauer the New Yorker wrote to Arnold Hauser that he was happily working on his history book while traveling in Europe: "The mixture of working in hotels, strolling in the streets, looking at pictures and talking to people is exactly what we like."[2] Living in hotels had been a grim necessity for the exile, who was very much isolated in the Paris of the late thirties. Now it was a pleasure that enabled the older and ever more curious writer to observe people in their different environments and to make contacts. Then a metaphor for the extreme uncertainties and the precariousness of life, it now held in balance life's poignant riches.

Kracauer had always been a traveler and a looker; traveling and looking were, in a sense, synonymous for the writing process. Again and again he found himself in the position of the stranger to whom strange people and objects would become (more) familiar in time—a position of negotiation he would ascribe to the time-traveling historian in his posthumous *History: Last Things before the Last.* Together with the analogy, also drawn there, between the historian and the utopian traveler, this ascription shows the influence of Kracauer's particular experience of exile: the historian's expectation of encountering strangeness in other places and times, her intense selective attention, the possibility of seeing some things more clearly, the probability of learning something of value—not nothing, not everything.

In *History* Kracauer reflects on the difficulties of historical perspective as the entanglement of both observer and observed in the experience of historicity and temporality. This experience concerns time shifts not only beyond, but also within, the historian's lifetime as they give shape to the reading and writing of history. Ideally, then, modern historiography demonstrates an awareness of the historian's temporally (and culturally) mobile self and changing identity. This entails an acknowledgment of the composite and unstable mode of historiographical discourse: by necessity interpretive, it subverts a concept of strict objectivity. Kracauer had become intrigued by these questions during the Weimar period, when, as a critic and commentator, he had been concerned with the complex temporal actuality of a modern culture, which importantly included photographic technology, in flux.

Reviewing films for *Frankfurter Zeitung* in the twenties and thirties, he was struck by their potential to enlarge viewers' visual capabilities in relation to a rapidly expanding natural-cultural world. In *Theory of Film* (1960) he would argue that the cultural contribution of photo images, still or moving, is to show new phenomena and, suspending an assumed familiarity with the world, to extend and preserve its visibility. If they are true to the medium, photo images show the pictured. Elucidating the particularity of the pictured, they metamorphose the visual "raw material." They do not, as does art, consume it, because as images they are not self-authorized: in her surrender to the experience of the natural-cultural world the photographer cannot suppress the presence of unseen things. Kracauer's focus has been on the potential preserved in photo images for multiple and different acts of viewing, simultaneously and over time.

The analogy between photography and historiography, which is central to Kracauer's argument in *History*, is based on this potential. Photography and film can achieve a clarifying reclamation of often inconspicuous but important phenomena of the modern life-world. Such reclamation does not deny the tension, inherent in any artificial image, between the picture and the pictured. Like the temporally composite perspective of the historian, the visually composite perspective of the photographer is interpretive and produces many different shapes of objectivity. But also like historiography, photography is "art with a difference." In both cases we look for authentication; we have come to expect, from photographical and historiographical practice, shared and sharable acts of seeing and of reading.

The problems–as well as the fascinations and satisfactions–for the historian and the photographer are grounded in the particularities of these acts, which are shaped by different degrees of temporal distance and of acculturation in perception. The intimacy between the challenges of authentication and interpretation, and the tension between the picture and the pictured, account for what Kracauer called the "anteroom" status of both photography and historiography: here are located the different shapes of objectivity predicated on partial, provisional, relative truths. The reaffirmed or restored pull of the elucidated presence of (past) reality depends on visual and historical discrimination and judgment, which is culturally learned. Photography and historiography as the recovery into the present of past experience preserve the otherness and strangeness of the world and also reflect the viewer's–the photographer's, the historian's–acculturated perception.

For Kracauer the looker and traveler visible things (events, acts, actors, objects) of the present or the past are real in that their presence is sharable. Visible things penetrate the viewer's self-absorption and thus reshape, in surprising ways, the spaces of (cultural) memory. In his work on *History*, the exile was to find consolation in the unforeseeable and unpredictable capaciousness of cultural memory, which accommodates changes in time. The temporary state of exile, the state of the stranger, revealed itself to be a useful spatial and temporal "extraterritoriality" for the intellectual. It enabled Kracauer to question his own witnessing and to appreciate the extended future of past events–an appreciation that enlarged, in changing it, his own memory.

Kracauer's concerns are central to our history-based modern culture. Reflecting his capacity for connection and transformation, the most thought-provoking aspect of his work may very well be its curiously adaptive contemporaneity. Products of his probings and reconsiderations, his texts encourage the reader's negotiation of their meanings and thus resist the emergence of a sharply defined intellectual gestalt. My book is not about Kracauer but about the significance of his critical realism for cultural modernity. Thinking along with and against his arguments, I have extrapolated from them, argued around them, and expanded them. But I have also attempted to stay engaged with his thought as much as possible on his terms, since they reflect an intellectual development shaped by a critical interest and pleasure in the thought of others.

I have used Kracauer's work to think about some of the more puzzling interdependencies of representation and knowledge in two eminently modern cultural activities–historiography and photography–starting with the analogies between them that he himself drew. In order to do justice to these analogies I have placed his texts in different intellectual contexts: his critical interaction with Adorno, Benjamin, and Bloch, especially during the Weimar period (chap. 2); the criticism and history of photography and film (chaps. 3, 4, and 6); the criticism and history of historiography and the status of exile (chaps. 5 and 6). The Epilogue extends the argument of the book to some current debates in historiography in which, I assume, Kracauer would have been keenly interested. Reconstructing these different contexts meant trespassing into different areas of inquiry, which required a great deal of documentation, some of it of archival material. Much of this documentation is contained in the notes, which in a number of cases provide a neccessary additional perspective on the arguments developed in the text. If you read the text, please also read the notes.

Kracauer's frequent references to the historian's time travel suggest the role of the imagination in the search for historical knowledge. It is a search driven by the modern desire to "get it right," to assume responsibility for knowing our natural and cultural environment. At issue are the shifting multiple shapes of objectivity that this search has produced and that have motivated it. Approximations rather than certainties, they have been circumscribed by the inevitable acculturation and historicity of perception, the then and there of both observer and observed. And they have both defied and made possible the accumulation of historical knowledge. Time travel, then, is a metaphor for the obstacles and the enrichment experienced by the historian who tries to be concretely interested in the temporal reality of other lives. Aware of their uses for the present but never certain of their meanings in the past, the historian needs to continue time travel in different directions and, coming and going, to be a stranger and an attentive looker whose knowledge changes as the past retreats and approaches.

Unless otherwise stated, all translations from the German are mine and all emphases are those of the author quoted.

For his intellectual and practical support of the research and writing of this book I thank Marshall Cohen, Dean of Humanities of the University of Southern California. I have had generous help from the staffs of the photo collection at the Getty Center for the History of Art and the Humanities in Santa Monica, the Literaturarchiv Marbach, the Archives of the Hoover Institution in Stanford, and the German Department of the University of Southern California. I am grateful to the friends who looked at the arguments and the photographs.

Critical Realism

Outside

outside myself

there is a world

the rumbled subject to my incursions

—a world (to me) at rest

which I approach

concretely—

William Carlos Williams

Chapter One

Time and Knowledge

1 Kracauer's reflections on historiography, *History: Last Things before the Last*, were published posthumously in 1969.[1] They have had virtually no impact on the history profession,[2] despite the ongoing debates in the last two decades on the fallacies of objectivism, a problem central to *History*. This is in some sense surprising, since his discussion of the relation between cultural and epistemological questions in historiography is both "down to earth"–a quality many professional historians have liked to identify with–and suggestively speculative. One practising historian described the effect of Kracauer's "mixed" approach as "a startling combination of the sort of deep analysis of history that has characterized the best German writing on the subject with the sort of solid common sense one expects but does not often find in Anglo-American writing."[3] Kracauer would have been very happy with this generous assessment, which shows appreciation precisely for what he wanted to achieve. He also would have been much less certain about the success of his enterprise.

American readers interested in film have been familiar with two other books that Kracauer wrote in exile in the United States, *From Caligari to Hitler: A Psychological History of the German Film* (1947) and *Theory of Film: The Redemption of Physical Reality* (1960). It was late in life that he came to the study of historiography. Born in 1889 into a middle-class German Jewish family, he was trained as an architect and earned a doctorate in engineering with a thesis (1915) on the development of the art of forging metal in seventeenth to nineteenth century Prussia. After the war he left the unloved profession, which had kept him out of military service, and in 1921 joined the left-liberal, widely read *Frankfurter Zeitung*, which published almost everything he wrote during the Weimar period, including the autobiographical novel, *Ginster*. Explorations, in writing, of the contemporary life-world had always been his real interest. He had studied sociology and philosophy with Georg Simmel and Max Scheler, among others, and by the end of the Weimar period had become a well-known and respected cultural critic posing historical-philosophical questions in a variety of contexts and discourses. He never saw himself in one particular role, even where that might have helped the recognition of his work. Thus he expressly asked the critic Wolfgang Weyrauch not to present him to a post–World War II German audience as "a film man . . . but rather as a cultural philosopher or sociologist and also as a poet."[4]

Between the two wars, Kracauer maintained conflicted cultural alliances with Marxist critics such as Theodore W. Adorno, Ernst Bloch, Max Horkheimer, and Walter Benjamin; in exile, these changed into uneasy friendships. The attractiveness of these writers to intellectuals in postwar Germany was based to a large extent on the allegorically clear, indeed poetic "purity" of their outsider position. Even before the traumatic cultural rupture brought about by a totalitarian regime that had caused total war and genocide, they had stated emphatically their distance from their cultural environment. Kracauer's attractiveness has been of a very different kind. In contrast to Adorno, Bloch, Benjamin, and Horkheimer, whose texts he occasionally published, he was known during the Weimar period to large numbers of liberal educated readers. Yet, in contrast to their work, his Weimar texts have been rediscovered only gradually in West Germany and are largely unavailable in English.

As a professional journalist, Kracauer was broadly informed about the modern world. He was also attuned to general questions of the intellectual's contemporaneity, which were posed with increasing urgency during the Weimar period. Though interested in Marxian thought as an epistemological tool, he did not share his friends' fascination with the Lukacsian concept, presented in *History and Class Consciousness*, of an intellectual vanguard that would redeem a culture in crisis. From the beginning, Kracauer was critical of Lukacs's "totality" as well as Adorno's *emphatische Theorie.*[5] He was highly critical, too, of Bloch's, Benjamin's, and Adorno's self-consciously esoteric writing: the intricately idiosyncratic enciphering of (their own) and deciphering of (others') arguments. In his view, neither truth nor language was his to define from a position of authorial autonomy. His journalistic practice had taught him to acknowledge, even delight in, the complexly constructed pluralistic nature of cultural modernity. He found it impossible to share in Adorno and Horkheimer's single-minded fictions of a modern, suppressive logocentricity, which they could then "deconstruct."[6] Working with a concept of culture as an open-ended, shared, and therefore contradictory and inconclusive state of affairs, Kracauer did not wish, as did Benjamin, to be the first and only critic-creator of German literature.[7] Nor did he think it meaningful, as did Adorno and Horkheimer, to rewrite the entire history of Western thought in order to create a fiction of bourgeois totalitarian reason. Nor was he interested in suspending this history in Bloch's "Not Yet" of a utopia of Hope (or in Marcuse's using such suspension as the basis for a total rejection of post–World War II Western culture).

In contradistinction to his friends' idiosyncratic Marxisms, Kracauer's interest in Marxian thought was not admixed with neoidealism, especially not with Freudianism.[8] Unlike them, too, he was interested neither in a significantly predestined course of history nor in the cultural critic's "calling" to produce primary texts, that is, to rewrite texts of others in acts of self-authorized construction. As a reader of texts, and in writing about them, he was interested–in the literal sense of "entering", "being among"–in the recorded thought of others. He tried to understand them on their own terms, that is also their relatedness to other writers' texts and to their own cultural contexts.

Such thoughtfulness and hermeneutic caution was arguably strengthened by his early curiosity about the cultural meanings of the new, modern medium of photography and film, which was significantly a nonverbal medium, as he never ceased to emphasize.[9] His visual talent and professional training had made him particularly sensitive to the postwar experience as shaped by rapid technological advances, including photo images, and new urban spaces. In recording it, film contributed to and formed contemporary experience and thus quickly assumed, as Kracauer recognized early, an extraordinary cultural importance. Starting in the midtwenties, he moved away from a (partly Simmel-influenced) metacultural critique of the modern loss of a meaningfully centered world toward a broadly conceived, nuanced, sophisticated cultural empiricism.[10] Arguably, this development was connected as much with his becoming in 1924 the film critic for *Frankfurter Zeitung* as with his attention to the accelerating social impact of changing production methods between 1925 and 1928. He observed and analyzed these changes in detail in his 1929 study of the new and politically important class of white collar workers, *Die Angestellten*,[11] who were also avid moviegoers.

The importance of this text, one of the best examples of the new genre of literary documentary and investigative reporting, lies in its recording and explaining, with exasperation and sympathy, the many different voices of the petty bourgeoisie–the bête noir of intellectuals. Since the turn of the century, German intellectuals had been in the habit of speaking for this allegedly silent majority. They had deplored their language without taking the trouble to listen to their language use and decried their support for a status quo politics of power without considering the realities of exercising power.[12] Kracauer did listen to their stories. Even if he retold them as case histories of the despair caused by a chaotic economy and the virulent phobias caused by despair, he sought to circumvent the temptation, difficult for the intellectual to resist, to appropriate prematurely the other's experience into *his* stories.

It would be difficult to overestimate the significance of Kracauer's professional experience for the formation of his independent position in cultural politics, which was to inform his concept of historiography so profoundly. He was used to writing for a plurality of readers with different backgrounds and interests and was thus sharply aware of the entangled motivations behind language use. In his role as editor, Kracauer objected to Bloch's mysticist opacity and Adorno's and Benjamin's often impenetrable self-illuminating brilliance. He thought their emphasis on a critical discourse that was at the same time self-consciously "original" and normative would be a further contribution to cultural polarization.[13] In spite of the hopes placed on such critical discourse and the claims made for it, it would not, as he rightly saw, be able to unmask power. In its emphasis on the distance and obscurity of contemporary social and cultural phenomena, cultural critique in this form was helpless when confronted with the variety of their meanings. By paying close attention to his contemporary world, Kracauer had developed an intimate sensitivity to the new, the unexpected aspects of the process of modernity. Thus he came to understand that it was precisely these unpredictable developments, exhilarating or troubling, which could not be accommodated in the discourse of self-reflexivity that had become more and more characteristic of intellectual vanguard positions. Because it was eclectically resonant, in its grammar and semantics, of contemporary cultural fragmentation, this discourse provided only distorted mirrorings of a shared, difficult modern world. It failed conspicuously to provide intelligible analyses.

In exile, after experiencing the rupture of the cultural tradition that had formed him and to which he had made important contributions, Kracauer came to focus his interest on the cultural meanings of history. He shared this interest with many other exiles but, unlike them, was particularly impressed by the epistemological and hermeneutic difficulties posed by history. The reasons for his attitude can be found in his particular intellectual temperament, which seemed to have made more easily acceptable the critical insight that all perception is perspectivist. But while temperament is a crucial, if elusive, force in the formation of intellectual sympathies and alliances, there were also his experiences during the Weimar period, when, as critical commentator on cultural developments, he was in fact involved in the writing of what is curiously termed "contemporary history," *Zeitgeschichte.* If, in the arguments at that time with Bloch, Adorno, and Benjamin, Kracauer emphasized the importance of a more informed and self-critical questioning of the intellectual's position in cultural space and time, he did so out of his concern, on a daily basis, with the complex temporal actuality of a modern culture in flux. An awareness of the observer's historicity was in his view central to modern knowledge. Increasingly, he saw the fallacies in the unchecked propensity of a Marxist intellectual vanguard to make vastly generalized statements on the particular experience of temporality and historicity in which the observer and the observed alike are entangled.[14] It is, of course, precisely this entanglement that resists complete theoretical clarification because it resists transcending the particularities of place, time, and temperament. Within this entanglement is located the question of historical evidence—*the* argument of most practicing, evidence-gathering historians with respect to a "poverty of theory."[15] Kracauer's last work, *History*, would be distinguished from the other exiles' attempts at rewriting (intellectual) history after a profound cultural break by the explicitly reflected, fully accessible incompleteness of solutions.[16]

In her reply to Eric Voegelin's critical review of *Origins of Totalitarianism*, Hannah Arendt described her approach as "analysis in terms of history."[17] This descriptive definition illuminates an important shared property of the counterhistories of exile. While Arendt's analysis differs sharply from

Adorno and Horkheimer's *Dialectic of Enlightenment* in regard to the historian's responsibility toward past actuality, it shares with that analysis the primacy of construction over reconstruction. The "terms of history" are more assertively her own than professional historians might think desirable or acceptable. The reason she gave for this approach reflects instructively the impact of the experience of exile on historical understanding: "All historiography is necessarily salvation and frequently justification; it is due to man's fear that he may forget and to his striving for something which is even more than remembrance" (77). Arendt shared with many other exiles this striving fed by the traumatic rupture of tradition and of remembrance. It moved her to construct, in *The Human Condition*, spaces of human interaction in which the likes of Eichmann would have no place or time. These spaces of humanly meaningful, temporary permanence are too historically concrete to be dismissed as "merely" utopian. But they are also too clearly constructed from the present into the past to be historical. Even–especially–in exile, Kracauer was reluctant to give in to such yearnings. The contribution of historiography was for him the articulated presence of things past, the recovery of the past into the present. Notwithstanding his emphasis on the "poetic," the creatively constructive dimension of his work, by intellectual temperament and professional experience he was unable to disregard the powerfully disruptive diversity of present and past actuality. Thus he was more easily persuaded by the argument of evidence and less easily seduced by the shortcuts promised by "theory" in whatever guise.

Yet–and this is important–he still was familiar with the motivations behind such promises and understood their rootedness in very real and indeed troubling epistemological questions that were also, in a larger sense, political. At the same time he analyzed the tendency of theory to isolate and inflate individual problems and consequently to level rather than articulate the complexity of cultural historical phenomena. The declared aim of his reflections on the writing of history was to restore "legitimacy and independence" to historical understanding by explicitly acknowledging its fragmentary, uncertain nature. But he knew, from long experience, how difficult it was to protect from the belief systems of theories especially those areas of inquiry in which different discourses and different epistemological assumptions intersect and thereby create lacunae and indeterminacies that, in turn, create the need for boundaries and certainties.

Historiography–including his own reflections on its difficulties–as Kracauer presents it in *History* is located in such an "intermediary area" or "anteroom" of partial, conditional truths.[18] Entering it, he had also entered a critical community of historical thought since the Enlightenment. Kracauer navigated it as circumspectly and imaginatively as he had done in the case of the culture of Weimar Berlin, of the Paris of Jacques Offenbach, of European and American film. His ability to become fully immersed in very different subjects of inquiry was largely responsible for the fact, too, that exile, whether in Paris or in New York, was for him a practical, not an existential, question. In contrast to Benjamin, Adorno, and Bloch, he did not feel significantly exiled in either his "own" or any other culture because he had always maintained a negotiable distance with respect to preestablished conceptual grids as well as cultural spaces and periods.[19] (The others' elaborately articulated and firmly maintained distance from most of Weimar culture was arguably interdependent with their sense that it should rightly have been theirs.) But where Kracauer did not participate in the exile's state of mind as one of lasting alienating disjunction, he saw that it could produce a distorting as well as a usefully ordering perspective. And in that respect it was not unlike the perspective of the utopian traveler, to whom he compared the historian in her explorations of the different times and spaces of the past. The temporary suspension of temporality and historicity causes the voluntary visitor of nowhere to be absorbed in the strangeness of people in relation to their cultural spaces and objects. Usefully, it also causes him to reflect on the significance of his own dissociation from familiar places of his past. For the exile, however, such suspension and dissociation are not temporary and cannot be negotiated. Shaped by the experience of lasting cultural rupture, the exile's perspective on the tradition as well as the new place is and remains foreshortened. Kracauer understood this situation in its literal and figurative meanings and finally sought to overcome it by reflecting on the richly recalcitrant problems of historical understanding.

2

Kracauer's goal–and his greatest problem–in *History* was to show his readers how to find their way in the "anteroom" of historical inquiry. A workable concept of truth would have to be tolerant of, even emphasize, its partial, conditional, provisional, and relational properties. Such explicit cognitive modesty might seem too plain to historians hard at work in search of evidence to support their respective "objective" approaches to the past. Yet it does speak to questions that have been central to historiography from its beginnings and much discussed among modern historians. With the first sentence of his *History*, Herodotus stated the nature of his project as *istorie*, inquiry into the past as that which was human reality and therefore could be questioned. Among several available Greek terms, he chose *istorie*, a word that referred to questioning in general and the questioning of witnesses in particular, probably because he thought the stories of witnesses an important source of historical information. The word *istorie* signifies "with research into things past also the account, narration [*Erzählung*] of things past . . . , as we find it first in Aristotle's *Poetics*."[20]

History as account or narration of the past: are we speaking about narration as the mode of presentation, namely the communication of (historical) information, the result of inquiry? Or do we mean narration as the mode of inquiry itself, narration as guiding the gathering, the evaluation, and the ordering of information? Or are my questions here based on a too rigid distinction rooted in a too narrow concept of narration? What Aristotle said was

> that the poet's function is to describe, not the thing that has happened, but a kind of thing that might happen, i.e. what is possible as being probable or necessary. The distinction between historian and poet is not in the one writing prose and the other verse—you might put the work of Herodotus into verse, and it would be a species of history; it consists really in this, that the one describes the thing that has been, and the other a kind of thing that might be. Hence poetry is something more philosophic and of graver import than history, since its statements are of the nature rather of universals, whereas those of history are singulars. By a universal statement I mean one as to what such or such a kind of man will probably or necessarily say or do—which is the aim of poetry, though it affixes proper names to the characters; by a singular statement one as to what, say, Alcibiades did or had done to him.[21]

In describing the "thing that has been," history "tells the particulars of an event or an act."[22] It narrates in the original sense of the word: Latin "*narrare* to relate, account, supposed to be for **gnarare*, related to *gnarus* knowing, skilled, and thus ultimately allied to KNOW" (compact OED). Both poetic and historical narration contribute to knowledge, but with a different emphasis.[23] Francis Bacon, shrewdly elaborating on the famous Aristotelian distinction, describes the difference in the following way:

> Because the acts or events of true history have not that magnitude which satisfieth the mind of man, poesy feigneth acts and events greater and more heroical; because true history propoundeth the successes and issues of action not so agreeable to the merits of virtue and vice, therefore poesy feigns them more just in retribution, and more according to revealed providence; because true history representeth actions and events more ordinary and less interchanged, therefore poesy endueth them with more rareness, and more unexpected alternative variations. So as it appeareth that poesy serveth and conferreth to magnaminity, morality, and to delectation.[24]

History, alas, does not, because it sticks to "what was" or "what happened" rather than what "might be" or what "might happen"–those alluring "unexpected alternative variations." And "what was" has seldom been congenial to "magnaminity," "morality," or "delectation." Poetry improves on historical narration because it creates order and thereby reveals meaning, which seems to remain hidden in ordinary lives. But Bacon, clearly, is not excited by the possibility of such revelation. A skilled historian himself, he stressed the dignity and authority of the historian as compiler and narrator.

> For to carry the mind in writing back into the past, and bring it into sympathy with antiquity; diligently to examine, freely and faithfully to report, and by the light of words to place as it were before the eyes, the revolutions of times, the characters of persons, the fluctuations of councels, the courses and currents of actions, the bottoms of pretences, and the secrets of governments; is a task of great labour and judgment–the rather because in ancient transactions the truth is difficult to ascertain, and in modern it is dangerous to tell.[25]

Bacon, author of *The History of the Reign of King Henry the Seventh*, was of course also aware of the problems of documentation and evidence in more recent history since he was aware of the entanglement and open-endedness of human affairs. But in his statements about history–perhaps not so much in his role as historiographer–he separated the historian who compiled information to answer the question "What was?" from the historically interested thinker who commented on gathered historical materials. And posing here questions of causation and larger patterns, he did not ask about the limitations or distortions of the compiler.[26] Bacon's early modern concept of historical narration, then, did not take into consideration the considerable problem of the historian's perspectivist perception. This perception shapes the question "Why was it?" which, in turn, shapes historical narration, carrying the mind back to the past–a recounting that shapes the reconstruction of "what was," the placing it "before the eyes" as evidence.

To the practicing modern historian these are obvious interdependencies, though, not infrequently, their very obviousness has obscured certain important fallacies. These fallacies have been more glaring, more easily visible (if not always less attractive for that reason), where in the stricter sense ideological sympathies and goals are involved. They then tend to collapse the distinction between poetic and historical narration which separates the "has been" from the "might be." But while loss of this distinction hinders the process of historical knowledge, the separation is possible only up to a point; it signifies a difference in degree, not in kind. In practice, historical narration has been a mixed mode of discourse in more than one sense and for many purposes, and in that, too, it has reflected past experience, including the historian's.

Kracauer experienced a variety of ideological threats to historical understanding during the Weimar period. But, again, such threats came in different shapes, and though in some cases dangerous, they pointed to a general problem that they exacerbated. In its many and complex interdependencies, not the least of which concerns the cumulative nature of historical inquiry, historical narration has been particularly open–especially at certain times and in certain cultural situations–to the temptation to relate what might or ought to be. Implicitly or even explicitly, the attraction of those feigned "acts and events greater and more heroical" would assert itself against "the successes and issues of action not so agreeable to the merits of virtue and vice" propounded by "true history," the (ideally) unadulterated actuality of the past. When Kracauer argued for the recognition of an independent status of historiography, he sought to clarify precisely these aspects of historical narration. His giving photography and film such an important place in his argument is intimately connected with this goal.

In the last chapter of *History*, "The Anteroom," which would have been the first had it not given him so much trouble and therefore remained the most fragmentary part of the book, Kracauer tries to define what is, in the terms of his argument, undefinable: the independent status of historiography and photography.

> One may define the area of historical reality, like that of photographic reality, as an anteroom area. Both realities are of a kind which does not lend itself to

> being dealt with in a definite way. The peculiar material in these areas eludes the grasp of systematic thought; nor can it be shaped in the form of a work of art. Like the statements we make about physical reality with the aid of the camera, those which result from our preoccupation with historical reality may certainly attain to a level above mere opinion; but they do not convey, or reach out for, ultimate truths, as do philosophy and art proper. They share their inherently provisional character with the material they record, explore and penetrate. . . . In this treatise, I consider it my task to do for history what I have done for the photographic media in *Theory of Film*–to bring out and characterize the peculiar nature of an intermediary area which has not yet been fully recognized and valued as such. (191f)

But the "as such" is the problem, because the perception of the area is shifting, as he himself argues–and demonstrates in the very shape of his argument. Photography is neither art nor "mere" recording; it is both. Historiography is neither art nor philosophy nor science; it is all these things. But how exactly is it? How, in photography, does the art component affect the recording component, or vice versa? How, in historical narration, does the question after causes and patterns, posed from hindsight, inform, shape the re-presentation of lived lives? In both cases, the answer is in the detailed account of the interaction, not in a "theory," and the analogy serves to emphasize the irrepressible and irresistible presence of details[27] as of the things before the last:

> I have pointed out in *Theory of Film* that the photographic media help us to overcome our abstractness by familiarizing us, for the first time as it were, with "this earth which is our habitat" (Gabriel Marcel); they help us to think *through* things, not above them. Otherwise expressed, the photographic media make it much easier for us to incorporate the transient phenomena of the outer world, thereby redeeming them from oblivion. Something of this kind will also have to be said of history. (192)

Like photography and film, historiography reclaims for our attention the earth as our habitat, our natural-cultural world in which we think and act, for a time. More perhaps even than by the entangled plurality and diversity of these thoughts and acts, Kracauer was impressed by their transience. Photo images and historical narration defy, for a time, oblivion. It had not taken exile and old age to see that this was their "ultimate" cultural legitimation, though both experiences made him appreciate more deeply the preciousness of memory as the presence of things past. In this (his last) book, Kracauer was intensely aware of the composite historicity of the historian's perspective: the experiences of time shifts beyond but also within her lifetime that motivate and shape historical knowledge. The profound impact of time passing on historiographical objectivity was his central concern and, arguably, the book's most illuminating aspect. Palpably fascinated by the implications of historians' travel in time, he invoked, again and again, their imaginative mobility–a mobility that called up deep resonances in his own experience of temporality.

An old man in exile, Kracauer was known to guard jealously information about the actual date of his birth. Immersed in his work on *History*, trying to cope with its considerable organizational difficulties, he bitterly complained to the historian Hans Kohn about the German newspaper that foolishly had published the date of his seventy-fifth birthday: "Of course I am aware of the dates, which become increasingly ominous. But in the interest of the continuation of my work, my whole inner economy, it is infinitely important that they not be startled and then confront me publicly so that everyone, myself included, is forced to look at them constantly. My kind of existence depends on the preservation of a state of extraterritoriality with regard to chronological time."[28] It is significant that it was work on the issue of time in historiography which affirmed the independence he found so essential: "For a certain purpose," he wrote to Adorno in 1963, "I have started writing, out of turn, a chapter of my history book on the historical concept of time. I am passionately involved with it, a sign that I still feel quite young."[29]

With age, Kracauer had become more and more preoccupied with the question of change and continuity in time, in himself and others. But the much younger man had already been fascinated with the cultural and personal meanings of lifetime, that is, perspectivist perception created by the individual's temporality. If photography and historiography familiarize us with our world, they also modify, reshape, question familiarization. The historian's and the photographer's position is well served by the state of "extraterritoriality," an awareness of change and transience that calls for mobility in space and time.[30] The actual visual co-temporality shared by the observer and the observed that was made possible by the new technology of photography and particulary of film was a source of deep fascination for Kracauer–an analogy to the historian's more precarious attempts at becoming, temporarily, a contemporary of past events and acts. Time travel with historical narration and photo images is seen as a usefully distancing experience that might clarify aspects of the past and thereby of the present: "History resembles photography in that it is, among other things, a means of alienation." This statement in the introduction to *History* (5) does not claim essentially alienating properties for either photography or historiography. It points out certain shared areas that can be activated, depending on the situation and the observer.

Working on *History*, Kracauer established important continuities with his previous work in the mapping of certain "mixed" modes of knowledge production which are still largely unexplored and in which both photography and historiography participate. As he points out in the introduction to *History*, the epistemological "anteroom" that they share is defined by historiography's responsibility to "historical reality" and by photography's dependence on "camera reality" (4). It reflects, that is, the "contingent and indeterminant" traits of human reality which appear in the patterns of both photo images and historiography (181). But Kracauer does not therefore equate historiography and photography with an arbitrary concept and pursuit of knowledge; nor does the asystemic nature of historiography and photography signify to him "artistic freedom," that is self-authorizing decisions and strategies. His aim is, rather, to explore the "mixed" approach of the photographer and the historian in terms of a combined surrender to and control of their "material," the complex natural-cultural worlds of the present and the past.

History is explicitly not a philosophy or theory of historiography,[31] nor is the thesis proposed in the (I think misnamed) *Theory of Film* developed into anything resembling a theory in the stricter sense of the term, which Kracauer had never considered useful in this kind of inquiry. In *History*, he offers reflections on the cultural place of modern historical understanding, which, he thought, was defined by an experiential dimension deliberately distinguished, separated, from the last truths of–in a stricter or conventional sense–theoretical or philosophical speculations.

In its absorbed consideration of others' thought on historical writing, *History*, with its sharp awareness of passing time and changing identity, is very much a late work. Meditating on the temporality of his own position as a composite of different stages, Kracauer is revisited by his own earlier insights, which now appear transformed and more clearly recognizable, justified even, in that backward glance, and then in turn justify the later work. Since he is now so centrally focused on the inevitably and complexly historical alignment of his as of any inquirer's perspective, he is less thesis oriented here than in *From Caligari to Hitler* and more loosely organized than in *Theory of Film*. He has crossed over into a large, complex, and very old discipline, where he can be, at best, a thoughtfully cautious, curious, and fascinated visitor. He rightly perceived his work on film, however, as an important contribution to a new field of inquiry. But much of his more broadly directed and therefore more reflected curiosity, his circumspect syn- and diachronic gathering of information on historiography, was based on his feeling exhilarated by the intellectual wealth of the new enterprise he had dared to embark on late in life. If his work on film had meant establishing conceptual accessibility for a new field of inquiry, his study of history and historiography meant entering one of the best-established and seemingly most accessible areas of inquiry. However, if the study turned out to produce encounters with new thoughts, his previous experiences had, as he saw it, not only been the preparation for them but a precondition.

In his writings on film, especially in *Theory of Film: The Redemption of Physical Reality*, Kracauer had been very much aware both of the new medium's distinct mode of perception and knowledge and of the difficulties involved in determining such distinctiveness. Attempting to describe and evaluate the photographer's responsibility to the potential of the medium, he looked at it from his own position as critic commenting on an ongoing contemporary culture but also as historian of the recent past, most clearly so in *From Caligari to Hitler*. In this role he had not been aware of some of the more intriguing and treacherous intricacies of historical perspective, but this was to change with the inclusion of time in the cultural acts of "redeeming" or recovering "reality" as the (elusively) shared experience of an (elusively) shared world.

This change did not, in Kracauer's view, weaken the link between photographic or filmic and historiographic discourse, and much of what he says in this context is indeed helpfully suggestive. To Leo Lowenthal he wrote, at an early stage of his work on *History*:

> My historical studies–excerpts and many notes of my own–are progressing. I have made a discovery that affirms my choice of topic. This essay on history, I suddenly understood, is the direct continuation of my *Theory of Film*: der [*sic*] *historian has traits of the photographer, and historical reality resembles camera reality*. The similarities are really startling; I had taken this route completely unconsciously."[32]

What Kracauer stresses here is not so much the fact of a certain continuity in his own position as cultural historian or the perhaps even more important fact that much of his journalism during the Weimar period had been placed in the context, important for all cultural critique, of contemporary history. What he stresses is, rather, the epistemological question of historical evidence. And it is here, in that question, that the media of photography and historiography intersect. His reflections on a film-specific empiricist epistemology had led him "unconsciously" to extend his inquiry to the meaning of past experience. As the cultural contribution of historiography is articulated cultural memory, in the sense of the cultural presence of things past, so film and photography enable the future presence, as "redemption,"[33] of the phenomena of ordinary, everyday life, "physical reality." These are the questions he struggled with in *Theory of Film*: how could, how should, finally, how does the (individual) photographer balance ordering and shaping impulses with a medium-specific ability to record, for the future, the presence of objects, agents, acts, and events that constitute present-tense reality? For Kracauer such recording ability clearly signified a particular responsiblity to an always only partially accessible experience of a world both natural and cultural, in need of being made present in its polysemic elusiveness for other viewers in different places and times: a world that in the moment of being pictured is always already past in relation to the picture.

In the introduction to *History*, written in the beginning stages of the work, 1961–62, Kracauer stated that he had already connected the development of nineteenth-century historism and the invention of photography in an early essay, "Die Photographie" (1927).[34] In preparatory notes for the study and in a series of drafts, he frequently discussed analogous examples from both media. He pointed out, for instance, that the presence, in the historical material itself, of "intelligible patterns" could be seen as comparable to the "'found story' in documentaries."[35] And, using a counter example, he likened the "artist-historian," the historian with explicitly formal interests who imposes patterning on the material, to the "artist-photographer" who confronts the phenomenon with an explicitly ordering, creative perspective (9). In his view, neither succeeds in fully realizing the potential of his medium, because–in contrast to the artist, painter, or poet–neither can freely abstract from the phenomenal world. In the case of the historian's responsibility to "historical reality," the past demands to be retrieved as it once *was*, namely as a shared experience, into which the historian, too, has to be immersed in order to tell its story. In the case of the photographer's dependence on "camera reality," the present (which will always be already the past in relation to its photographic image) demands to be recorded as fully as possible, namely retaining, for multiple viewers, that which has not been (consciously) seen by the photographer. This was not, for Kracauer, an issue of the richness of the artwork enabling an "infinite" variety of interpretations; it was, rather, the importance of being true to the combined accidentality and deliberateness of perspective in response to randomness in experience. If the camera records more than the photographer controls, if there are more or different things to be seen than the photographer thought or knew, this is a challenge to shape objectivity so that it accommodates both control and submission.

Kracauer used these analogies to clarify the specific status of "historical reality" in order to "rehabilitate" it, to restore to it "legitimacy and independence" (9, 20): "The intermediary areas have been overshadowed by misconceptions founded on the traditional prejudice that there exists no field of knowledge in its own right between the hazy expanses of opinion and the lofty realms of philosophy and theology. . . . Perhaps the most important function of history is to gather fragments of the past in an uncertain light and for uncertain ends" (9).

"Rehabilitation" of historical understanding depends on recognizing, on explicitly acknowledging, the fragmentary, uncertain nature of historical knowledge. Many contemporary historians would admit to an existing general problem of uncertainty and fragmentation in their field of inquiry. As practitioners of a discipline no longer clearly distinguished from the social sciences, they might find it difficult to see the need for Kracauer's insistence that such uncertainty and fragmentation had to be explicitly acknowledged, and, moreover, more importantly, that the legitimation of the field would have to be based on precisely such acknowledgment. There are indeed quite radical implications in Kracauer's proposition to explore the specific cultural contribution of historical understanding and historiography as mediation between "hazy" mere opinion, that is, subjective ad hoc value judgments, and "the lofty realms of philosophy and theology," that is, systematizing, generalizing predictive statements of cultural values concerning knowledge and representation. In our current ideologically charged situation of cultural diversity, history has again become more intensely "questionable," *fragwürdig* in the double sense of the word: needing to be questioned and worthy of questions. Kracauer's preoccupation with the partial, provisional, relative truths of cultural memory goes to the heart of our understanding modernity at the end of the twentieth century. Reflecting his capacity for connection and transformation, the most useful aspect of his work may very well be its curiously adaptive contemporaneity.

Chapter Two

Contemporaneity and the Concept of History

1 Kracauer's interest in the modalities of historical knowledge goes back to his increasingly skeptical participation in postwar debates among intellectuals about the contemporary significance of their position as critics in a history-based modern culture. Self-consciously modernist, these debates were shaped by a German intellectual tradition largely derived from and echoing Hegel, including his eschatological impulses, which made for a curious mixture of utopianism and pessimism.

In the Weimar period intellectuals saw their cultural status as more and more marginalized by the rapidly accelerating interdependence of technological advancements and social change, on the one hand, and increasing political polarization, on the other. The now broadly diffused experience of modernity eliminated traditional cultural demarcations. But it encouraged the enormously expanding business of culture, that is, the distribution of cultural activities, which achieved a new visibility, social accessibility, and political exploitability. Intellectual positions during the Weimar period were defined in terms of alliances that reflected this situation in various ways. Terms like *left* (meaning progressive) and *right* (meaning conservative) are too entangled in composite perspectives to be of much use to a historical understanding of the meanings of these alliances. Frequently extended or resumed in exile and absorbed, to an extent, into the host culture, they underwent shifts in meaning and composition that have to be taken into consideration.

Historical hindsight here has tended to blur rather than sharpen the picture, and Kracauer's position in the twenties and early thirties has been linked too simplistically to the position of Adorno, Benjamin, and Bloch. It is true that he himself explicitly encouraged the connection in his later years in exile, when the resumed reader reception of his earlier texts was an issue.[1] And the placement has undeniably been influenced by the fact that the Frankfurt School, highly visible and vaguely understood, seemed a convenient label to help along the rather belated rediscovery of Kracauer's post–World

War I work in Germany after World War II. However, the comparisons drawn, especially with Benjamin, are not borne out by the texts. Rather, they have been imposed on them by critics who were following preestablished intellectual sympathies, and here the influence of Adorno on the West German cultural scene of the 1960s and 1970s cannot be exaggerated. Kracauer's work, both during the Weimar period and in exile, does not fit easily into the German critical tradition, which has not placed much value on "the common reader"; that is, on a discourse aware of the implications of plural language use and of the importance of accessibility.[2]

In the ongoing, changing actuality of the Weimar years, Kracauer's position differed profoundly from that of Adorno, Benjamin, and Bloch. Differing strongly among themselves with respect to ideological details, these three shared a fundamental openness to the seductions of metaempirical, transhistorical meaning, which he increasingly questioned. When, in a letter to Bloch, Kracauer referred to his "unfathomable realism," the attribute made sense in relation to his friends, who could not "fathom," appreciate, this position.[3] Adorno's essay, "Der wunderliche Realist" ("The Odd Realist"), written in the midsixties on the occasion of Kracauer's seventy-fifth birthday and ostensibly meant to help Kracauer's reputation in West Germany, was in actuality a deeply ambiguous (d)evaluation of his friend's intellectual position and achievement. Too easily ("exorably," Adorno's coinage reversing "inexorable," "*unerbittlich*")–persuaded by what actually happened–Kracauer had not been able to rise above the lowlands of empiricism.[4] To the reader who thinks less inexorably, Kracauer's realism appears not so much "unfathomable" as beneficently rational. Mediating between concept and sensation, Kracauer's cultural criticism shared with Benjamin's, Bloch's, and Musil's an ideational-sensual focus on the endlessly fascinating "ordinary" phenomena of the contemporary life-world.[5] And even where the influence of Simmel was explicitly denied, their essayistic bridging of the particular with the general owed much to Simmel's explorations of modern urban life, especially in *The Philosophy of Money* (1900).[6]

Despite certain similarities in their poetico-philosophical mode of cultural criticism–a mode of discourse that is perhaps the most important literary contribution to twentieth-century modernism–Kracauer's style of thought and language use was markedly different from Benjamin's and

Bloch's, and particularly from Adorno's.[7] In its peculiarly circumspect search for precision and clarity it was symbiotically linked to his rejection of all-embracing historical-philosophical theories. Increasingly, he came to see the place of the present in history (a crucially important question after the trauma of World War I) as interdependent with the place of history in the present. And together with that growing skepticism regarding belief systems, especially in the guise of neo-Hegelian abstractionism, went an insistence on the importance of intelligibility. Intellectuals needed to shape their arguments in such a way that, reproducing them, the reader could question rather than just repeat (or reject) them. Kracauer's sophisticated cultural essayism of the late twenties and thirties suggests affinities to Musil's writing precisely in this emphasis on the social and communicative rather than the individualist and hermetic value of natural language as artefact. This holds true despite Musil's extraordinary verbal talent and much greater familiarity with modern scientific thought. It holds true, too, despite the hopes Kracauer still had then for his version of "*Theorie*": that a "*reale Dialektik*" might provide an epistemological tool with which to pose authoritatively the question of cultural meaning. Philosophizing made sense only if it took place within the life-world–for him eminently the visible world. Characteristically, Kracauer used a visual metaphor to describe what he admired as Simmel's phenomenological approach: "He always traces what he has seen [*Gesehenes*]. Basically, all his thought is nothing but a grasping [*Erfassen*] of objects by looking at them [*durch das Hinblicken auf sie*]."[8]

"*Theorie*" for Kracauer was never Adorno's "*emphatische Theorie*," which, in interpretation, "has to penetrate through its objects to the most extreme if it wants to be true to its concept of itself."[9] Adorno was quite right to point out Kracauer's aversion to such totalism, "*das Hundertprozentige*" (393). He simply could not understand that this aversion signified not so much an a priori hostility to all theoretical statements (398–400) as a different attitude toward that "connecting tension between [verbal] expression and [philosophy's] binding force" that he, Adorno, had always thought absolutely central to intellectual activity (389). Kracauer did not think it useful, as did Adorno, to locate claims to validity in the intricately idiosyncratic enciphering of an argument. In the process of writing for a plurality of readers with very different experiences and interests, he had learned that such emphasis on enciphering–arguably the praxis of Adorno's "*emphatische Theorie*"–tended to produce many and serious, if "interesting," misunderstandings rather than the one single-mindedly sought, uniquely revelatory insight. Worse, it presupposed, on the side of the reader, mindless mirroring rather than critical understanding. The issue was not, as Adorno saw it, Kracauer's "pure [mere] individualism," which resisted solidarity with the "like-minded"–by which Adorno meant the initiated (393). Rather, it was Kracauer's experiential insight that his subject matter concerned a reality in whose construction other minds had had a share, and a considerable one. He did not assume that he alone was equipped to ferret out and cut through the ever-multiplying deceptions of a manipulated surface simplicity that, for all others, obscured the "real" truths of their culture. Adorno, on the other hand, would never outgrow the sense of his own intellectual singularity, which was to have an enduring influence on the highly self-conscious writing style that controlled his thinking.

The central problem for the cultural critic as well as the historian, Kracauer came to realize, is the relation of the general to the particular, which changes with the disposition and the position of the observer. Both are largely defined by the observer's cultural place and time, including time of life. He thought *History* the culmination of his work because here, reflecting on the composite historicity of the historian-as-observer's perspective, he found himself able to appreciate the magnitude of the difficulties. His explicit motivation for writing the book was to explore the implications of the question, How can one generalize concerning particular experiences of temporality and historicity that entangle observer and observed alike? Over the years–a lifetime spent observing the rapid and traumatic changes that have signified twentieth-century cultural modernity–Kracauer had learned to focus more sharply on this entanglement because he had come to understand more fully the incompleteness of answers in this area of inquiry.

2 In his essays of the Weimar period, Kracauer articulated his attempts to understand the bewildering complexity of cultural changes in tentative observations of "surfaces," the densely interrelated phenomena of shared everyday life. Where his analyses contain ambiguities–especially in the texts that strain for more general definitions of the modernity of Weimar culture–they were largely caused by a perspective

still insufficiently probing and self-critical. One of the most instructively troubled essays in this respect is "Das Ornament der Masse" (1927) which Adorno chose as the title essay for the 1963 collection *Das Ornament der Masse.* (Adorno placed this volume with his own publisher in order to help reintroduce Kracauer's Weimar texts to West German audiences). His choice is understandable for several reasons. Not only is the essay focused on the significance of the insignificant, easily overlooked surface expressions of a culture, which were so important to Benjamin, Bloch, and Adorno; it also puts particular emphasis on the dynamics of the crowd, and in ways congenial to these writers' Marxian-Freudian scenarios. In their "unselfconsciousness" (*Unbewusstheit*) these surface expressions allow access to the "fundamental content" of an epoch. Kracauer asserts that "the fundamental content of an epoch and its unnoticed impulses are linked in mutual elucidation."[10] For whom? From what position of observation? This projected "automatic" mediation between some fundamental truth underlying cultural phenomena and an observer's (correct) consciousness points to one of the more problematic aspects of Kracauer's concept of "*reale Dialektik.*" Developed during the earlier years of the Weimar period as his alternative to his friends' insistence on the redemptive power of Marxian "*emphatische Theorie,*" this concept retained vestiges of the latter's potent fallacies.

The opaqueness of the argument in "Das Ornament der Masse" has its source in a concept of the masses which anticipated certain aspects of the Frankfurt School's rigid perspective on mass culture, notably the global range and the conceptual patterning of its total rejection of it. His openly critical attitude toward "the masses" notwithstanding, Kracauer stated explicitly that his aim was to understand rather than reject. But for an experienced observer of a contemporary social and political environment he appears curiously ill attuned here to the phenomenon of crowd behavior, which played such an important role in Weimar's modern mass democracy. For one, he failed to distinguish between "the masses" and the crowd, alternating between the terms *Masse* and *Menge* (crowd). His curiosity was not provoked by the diverse forms and purposes of actual crowd gatherings: large groups gathering spontaneously for demonstrations, crowding around a charismatic leader, drawn by various directives of political organizations; large numbers of people attracted by the new phenomenon of spectator sports. He also showed little interest in the significance of the places where crowds gathered: the streets, squares, halls, sport fields, stadiums. Rather, he focused on selective attributes of modern mass man and woman–their desire for distraction,[11] their becoming anonymous particles contained in abstract ornamental patterns–and then adduced this eclectic collection "dialectically" as general attributes of modernity.

Invoking the ambiguity of the phenomenon as he had constructed it, he did not permit himself to be really puzzled by it. Rather, he relied on formulaic arrangements of concepts in setting up general cultural correspondences. Thus he proposed a significant resemblance between the crowd fitting itself into an abstract ornament and the abstractness of capitalism–a resemblance located precisely in a shared ambiguity: capitalism, Kracauer wrote, is a stage on the way to "disenchantment,"[12] a process set in motion by the Enlightenment that, following Weber, he regarded as central to modernity. He also pointed out that capitalism in the Weimar period exhibited not too much but rather too little "abstractness," relying too little on rationality.

How are we supposed to judge the meanings of capitalism? For long parts of his argument, Kracauer just shuffles around the term "abstractness," linking capitalism to Taylorist production methods, to the Tiller girls' dancing, to the "ornamental" configurations of crowds in the modern metropolis. This energetic associationism foreshadows in some ways Adorno's and Horkheimer's approach in *Dialectic of Enlightenment* ("The Culture Industry: Enlightenment as Mass Deception"). And yet, Kracauer's perspective on mass culture also clearly differs from the Frankfurters' in that he seems to be seriously trying to get closer to the phenomenon. Significantly, he would discuss it in probing detail and much more intelligently in his classic study of white-collar workers, *Die Angestellten* (1929), Hitler's most impressionable mass audience.

Kracauer found a puzzling symbiotic tension between the social impact of scientific and technological developments and the desire to locate, (re-)construct, look back to one's roots. (This tension, I think, turned out to be the single most important reason for the success of rightist extremism at the end of the Weimar period). Contemporary thought, he remarked here shrewdly, is confronted with the question whether it ought to accommodate reason or just go on drifting with the wave of "It's coming." Together with the increasing abstractness and rationalization of high capitalist industry, this wave carries the ever more threatening power of "dark nature" which prevents the "arrival of man," whose roots are in reason.[13] A more useful variation of the "New Man" pathos dating back to the radical intellectual left shortly before and immediately after World War I,[14] Kracauer's assessment of the situation to some degree resonates Bloch's cultural utopianism, Benjamin's cultural despair, and Adorno's estheticism. But it also differs dramatically from these positions (which are very postmodernist now) in its strong affirmation of the rational mind's cultural significance and the modern necessity of disenchantment.[15]

There are instructive conflicts in Kracauer's use of the terms *rational* and *rationality* when he characterizes the abstractness of contemporary thought as literally "*doppeldeutig*," of double meaning, relating it to the ornamental configurations of modern crowds. On the one hand–and rightly so in view of the growing importance of fascism–he chides contemporary intellectuals for too easily dismissing the crowd phenomenon as just another aspect of regressive mass culture. It is, he asserts, a more important phenomenon than most other contemporary cultural expressions. On the other hand, he attributes the importance of the crowd phenomenon to the fact that under "rational questioning" it is revealed as a "*mythologischer Kult*" in the disguise of abstractness. Because in the ornament of the crowd is presented the "*rationale Leerform*," the rational empty form, of the cult (60f.).

Here is the core of Kracauer's ambivalence and of his argument's unresolved contradiction–not in the remarks made in passing about a greater worthiness of the "*Volk*" rooted in concrete community than of the masses dispersed in abstract collectivity (51). *Rational* and *abstract* are play concepts in these passages. The "empty form of the cult" may be empty of meaning in the terms set by Kracauer, the intellectual as observer who perceives from the outside the ornamental configuration. It is not so for the crowd in the climactic affirmation of its own elusive significance. People coming together at athletic fields to watch ball games and merging into crowds in the prolonged moments of victory or defeat experience a vicarious, but not therefore less intense, participation in communal striving for excellence. People gathered for a political demonstration are similarly united in shouts of affirmation or rejection. The intellectual, viewing and listening, may think both

nity, and tradition and increasingly destroyed by modernity. In the context of pointing out Baudelaire's highly ambivalent feelings about photography as an attack on his sensibility associated with modernity, Benjamin quotes Valéry on the inexhaustibility of the work of art, adding the comment: "The painting we look at reflects back at us that of which our eyes will never have their fill. What it contains that fulfills the original desire would be the very same stuff on which the desire continuously feeds." The photograph, in contrast, would fulfill and thereby still and deaden the desire. Precisely this satiation produces the "crisis of artistic reproduction" in which the beautiful has no place. Here the decline of the aura is nothing but impoverishment, and the loss of beauty caused by it is the most potent metaphor for the loss of humanity in the modern world. And now a passage that might be considered astonishing in its combined estheticism and mysticism, if one wished to see Benjamin as a cultural critic thinking *within* (instead of above) a modern world of increasingly complex technology:

> What was inevitably felt to be inhuman, one might even say deadly, in the daguerreotype was the prolonged looking into the camera, since the camera records our likeness without returning our gaze. But looking at someone carries the implicit expectation that our look will be returned by the object of our gaze. Where this expectation is met . . . there is an experience of the aura to the fullest extent. . . . Experience of the aura thus rests on the transposition of a response common in human relationships to the relationship between the inanimate or natural object and man. The person we look at or who feels he is being looked at, looks at us in turn. To perceive the aura of an object we look at means to invest it with the ability to look at us in return.[23]

By virtue of its artistic aura, the painted portrait looks back at us, and in fulfilling our desire keeps it alive. The photographed portrait, which lacks the auratic element, stills and deadens our desire and thereby removes, irretrievably, the viewed from the viewer. Modern technology, which has immeasurably facilitated the recording of human life, has also contributed to the devaluation of such recording.

Kracauer, in his 1927 essay on photography, which was influenced by Proust and was to influence Benjamin, was by no means so certain about these negative cultural meanings of photography. Where Benjamin's argument circles around the relation between the new visual technology and the always and in each case valuable tradition of the visual arts (in the eyes of an ideal viewer), Kracauer focuses on the tension, inherent in any artificial image, between the picture and the pictured. The important question for Kracauer, then, is not what is the nature of the image but, rather, what is the contribution of the image to bringing out the nature of that of which it is an image. And in posing that question he does not refer to an ideal viewer (about whom he can only speculate) but to the photographer's use of the medium. The contribution of the image depends on the photographer's making the fullest possible use of the medium specific technique that assures the preservation of real phenomena in space and time. Wary of a self-consciously interfering "creative" perspective, Kracauer argues that artistic photography is an anachronism, a throwback to nineteenth-century staging and draping, a premodern disregard for the important inconspicuous details of daily life.

As a whole, the argument in "Die Photographie" is conflicted and ambiguous. In some passages Kracauer works with the same contrast between the storing, deadening properties of the recording photo image (33–35) and the life-restoring, life-enhancing power of the work of art (26–28) which we find, more than a decade later, in Benjamin's Baudelaire essay. Where the photograph achieves mere likenesses, Kracauer writes, the work of art allows substance to shine through.[24] "The work of art can be compared to a magic mirror that reflects the person questioning it not as he appears but as he wishes to be or as he substantially is. The work of art, too, decomposes in time; but from its crumbling particles emerges what it was meant to signify, while photography stores away the particles" (27).

Most significant and telling: the image presented by the work of art is linked to an image that is alive in memory, whereas the reality represented in the images produced by photography becomes "ghostly," "unredeemed," *unerlöst* (32). It is not clear whether the responsibility for this change rests more with the viewer or with the photo image. Kracauer invokes the laughter of young girls looking at photographs of their grandmothers. They ridicule the cumbersome fashions of the past–clothes their grandmothers have left behind–and yet they are awed by that glimpse at a moment of time gone by, time that flows on inexorably and without return. "Time, it is true, has not been photographed together with the smiles and the chignons, but photography itself, so it seems to them [the young girls], is a representation of time. If it was only photography that granted them [the pictured smiles, etc.] duration, they would not be preserved beyond mere [chronological] time—rather, time would create images of them" (23).

Such images, in contrast to memory images, falsify experience. It is in these portions of his argument that Kracauer shows most clearly the influence of Proust's stories of time and memory. Later, in exile, in his *Theory of Film* and, more decisively, in *History*,[25] Kracauer was to revise his evaluation of Proust's negative comparison between the photo picture that, storing it, freezes the pictured at a moment in time and thereby alienates (from) it, and the memory image that, restoring that moment to life, brings it close again. In the later texts he would emphasize precisely the enabling power of the recording medium that helped the viewer (reader) to gain access to past lives. However, already in this early essay the term *unredeemed* is not resonant with Benjamin's concept of redemption through significant messianic rupture of insignificant lived time. Here, too, Kracauer expresses his desire to preserve and bring back (or forward) into the living present the mundane phenomena of the lived time of the past. Unlike Benjamin, he had no use for the hope of transcendent salvation. His reflections on the human experience of time stress its secular contingencies. Memory images are precious because they anchor the present tense of things past so that their cultural meanings can be explored. In time, that is, through experience, he came to see that such anchoring can indeed be supported rather than undermined by photography and film, and this insight led him to establish the connection of this medium to history as cultural memory.[26]

It is instructive for our context to look at the difference in Kracauer's reaction to two Benjamin texts that he discussed in a collective review written about seven months after "Die Photographie": *Ursprung des deutschen Tauerspiels* ("The Origin of German Tragic Drama") and *Einbahnstrasse* ("One-Way Street"), a collection of aphoristic descriptions or, as Benjamin preferred to see them, decipherings of modern urban phenomena. *Origins*, a most curious mosaic of quotes from esoteric baroque dramas intended to obtain for Benjamin an advanced academic degree,[27] seemed praiseworthy to Kracauer for its "immense knowledge" combined with profound philosophical insight. Kracauer knew next to nothing about that field of inquiry, but he was evidently intrigued by Benjamin's "dialectical" linkage of allegory with the baroque understanding of nature as delivered into the power of death and of history as surrendered to eschatological suffering. Kracauer misread Benjamin (though his German in this part of the review is almost as opaque and slippery as Benjamin's in the reviewed text) as showing how the theological approach "obstructs" the (meanings of the) world so that he himself would attempt the redemption that befitted theology.[28]

For Benjamin the term *redemption* signifies a total and transcending cultural salvation that is indeed theological. Kracauer, however, normally uses the word in the sense of salvaging from cultural oblivion the seemingly insignificant phenomena of daily life by looking at them closely and making them visible[29]–hence his interest in the photographic media and his critical involvement with film during the Weimar period. He deliberately read *Origins* through a perspective shaped by his interests, and while no reviewer (or critic, or historian) can ever entirely avoid such distortion, it is too powerful here. The reason for Kracauer's emphatic if vacuous generosity in this case may have been partly the pressure exerted on him to show solidarity with Benjamin, who had had difficulties placing his work and getting it reviewed sympathetically, especially the (then as much as today) largely inpenetrable *Origins*.[30] But in addition, Kracauer was no doubt open to the suggestiveness of thought images clustered around Benjamin's use of allegory, which echoed, if faintly, his own understanding at the time of the effects of photography, namely the stiffening, deadening of the depicted person or object, which dissociated them from the viewer.

Instructively, Kracauer viewed this preoccupation in Benjamin's work quite differently in that part of his essay where he dealt with *Einbahnstrasse*, that is, where he was on his own territory.[31] There is a remarkable change here with respect to both language and evaluation. Gone are the grammatical contortions and semantic obscurities, and the scales of evaluation are now, as it were, in constant (contradictory) motion. Kracauer praises the occasionally profound insights of Benjamin's meditations and sums up his "philosophical" position as holding in the middle "between the researcher and the artist," even where it is extreme or one-sided. Influenced by Proust, whom he translated, Benjamin in Kracauer's opinion shares with Karl Kraus, whom he interpreted, the ability to perceive the "chthonic depth of language."[32] His achievement is summed up in the last sentence of the review: "He may not sojourn in the realm of the living, but he fetches from the storehouse of lived life the meanings deposited there which are waiting for the receiver" (255).

Even this uplifting conclusion is by no means unambiguously positive. When and where will the receivers appear? Are they contemporaries? Are not these "deposited meanings" ("storehouse" has a negative connotation resonant with the photography essay) characteristic of Benjamin's essentially noncontemporaneous position? And does not such noncontemporaneity seriously impede his perspective on the ordinary surfaces of modern life? The rest of the review suggests that Benjamin, yielding cultural critique to frequently arbitrary, private impression, however brilliantly put, fails to reach an audience in this world. His method of dissociation, developed in the book on baroque drama, may explode modern surfaces, but the detonations render only disconnected particles with little interpretive power (253). Benjamin, Kracauer points out rightly, directs his gaze exclusively to the past, and the dialectic of the uncovered meanings is oriented to the realm of the esthetic. That past, then, is of his own making. He is not interested in the "redemption of the living world," because he is not engaged in the "*reale Dialektik*" between "the elements of its objects and their configurations, between the concrete and the abstract, between the meaning of form and form itself."[33] Though the statement of Kracauer's reservations is too formulaic to be of much use as a directive for changing approaches in cultural criticism, it does suggest the focus of his attempts at locating the trouble.

3 Despite certain intellectual sympathies and affinities with Benjamin's texts, Kracauer did not think useful to cultural criticism the rupturing gaze on a contemporary world into which Benjamin felt exiled, inexorably and from the beginning. But, culminating in Adorno's *Negative Dialektik*, it was precisely this experience of the intellectual's irrevocable status of exile that was so important for the Frankfurt group.[34] The differences among these writers, who were all, at the time, trying to develop highly individualistic variations on a Marxian position (rather than philosophy) cannot be easily paraphrased, much less ascribed with a few key terms. In each case, conceptual strategies were so intimately tied up with self-consciously original "poetic" language use that intellectual exchange tended to rely more on a shared sympathy of thinking rather than rationally accessible critical discourse.[35]

In this situation I have found useful the more informal debates carried on in letters, precisely because they retain, up to a point, the correspondents' instinctive impulses to make sense to each other. These informal epistolary debates were informed by the realization that the contingencies of understanding as well as misunderstanding ought not be made to disappear too smoothly into elaborate, custom-made "language games." Here the letters exchanged between Kracauer and Bloch during the twenties and thirties are particularly useful documents because they bring out, with great clarity, the culturally significant distances between their intellectual positions. The fact that for a long time Kracauer tried to negotiate these distances, persuaded by Bloch's lively utopianism, and that Bloch tried to simply argue them away, supports rather then hinders this process of clarification. It is precisely the give and take in these personal epistolary debates which allows the different positions to emerge as complex compositions of temperamental inclinations, personal loyalities, cultural-political motivations, and economic necessity. The relative informality of the medium is helpful here, even if the arguments were still presented in a discourse of "high seriousness." It is especially helpful in the case of Bloch, who during these years saw himself as keeping together the intellectual vanguard and whose notoriously luxuriant wordiness tended to be less self-conscious here, where he did not address eternity but just another person as partner in the correspondence.[36]

The addressee of an argument is a significant if often overlooked contributing factor to the development of intellectual positions in the context of ongoing cultural activities. Simply but importantly, Bloch needed to make sense to Kracauer because he wished him to understand where he had, in the role of reviewer, misunderstood the intentions (achievements) of Bloch's books or why, in the role of editor, he ought to publish Bloch's essays. These motivations could not but intensify his efforts to shore up Kracauer's interest in Marxism as a cultural power and win him over as an ally for his, Bloch's, particular (and indeed most peculiar) excavations in the quarry of Marxian thought. The correspondence is instructive because it was carried on within, not above, the daily business of culture with its frustrations and rewards, concrete lacunae and closures. In this context general ideas of cultural responsibility were put in terms of feasibility–explicitly by Kracauer, implicitly by Bloch. The exchanges were to have lasting influence on Kracauer's work, both in *Theory of Film* and in *History*. His reflections in exile about the contributions of photography and historiography to cultural memory would be crucially informed by the insights he had gained through his pragmatic, probing involvement, in these heady and difficult years, with the making of a contemporary intellectual culture.[37]

The most sustained discussion of the viability of contemporary intellectual positions took place in an exchange of letters in the summer of 1926 about Lukacs's *History and Class Consciousness*. Bloch had taken the initiative in resuming contact after their 1922 disagreement over Kracauer's critical review entitled "Prophetentum" of his *Thomas Münzer als Theologe der Revolution*. Kracauer had attacked, in no uncertain terms, Bloch's characteristic mixture of Marxian arguments and chiliastic mysticism.[38] The occasion for Bloch's interest in renewing contact with Kracauer was ostensibly Kracauer's elegantly and masterfully argued critical review of the first volume of Martin Buber and Franz Rosenzweig's translation of the Old Testament. Kracauer had mentioned with respect Rosenzweig's rejection of decaying idealist philosophy in his *Stern der Erlösung* (1921; *Star of Redemption*), a Weimar underground classic that influenced, among others, Heidegger and Benjamin.[39] Respectfully, too, he had drawn attention to the religious *Lebenspraxis* as source and support for the translators' linguistic decisions.[40] But exploring the cultural connotations of their "*archaisierend*" language (180), Kracauer works with a concept of "*Aktualität*," an explicitly contemporary actuality, which refers to the reality of an economically motivated mass society rather than of a community centered in shared religious meaning.

In Buber and Rosenzweig's view, Luther's translation did not reflect the revolutionary impulses of twentieth-century culture and needed to be updated by retaining, in the translation, the more ancient energies of the original texts. Kracauer, however, pointed out that Luther's language, its revolutionary forcefulness firmly anchored in theology, had forsworn the language of feudal high culture and thus been truly contemporaneous to its intended audience, the commmon people of the sixteenth century. Buber and Rosenzweig's language, with its mixture of a currently chic–in contrast to contemporaneous–mythologism,[41] and late nineteenth-century neoromantic archaism, could not in Kracauer's view stand up to Luther's German

(180f). Trying to stretch German back into the language of Scripture in order to restore to the text its legitimate power, the translators landed not (as intended) in the vicinity of the old epic Hebrew but of Wagnerian alliterations. The Ur-German they strove for was not of the dark and distant past but of the murky last decades. Language has taken its revenge for having been pressed too forcefully into representing as reality what is no longer real (179–81).

The examples quoted by Kracauer are hilarious; but he was himself too high-minded and too concerned about the volkish echoes of such language to be amused. The translation, he argued, was both "private" and "reactionary" because in repressing modern profane language it left behind the realm of necessity, modern social and economic conditions. Its most troubling aspects were located in the general issue of religious rejuvenation. Buber's "Thou-world" with its assumptions of human immediacy, playing off the (so-called) real against the unreal, the concrete against the nonconcrete, seemed to Kracauer easily exploitable by a reactionary political leadership that claimed the authority of deeper than rational truths. Referring here to Marxian thought, Kracauer came down strongly on the side of rationality as the more truly contemporaneous position in intellectual matters because it acknowledges the modern usefulness of abstract thought.[42] His argument in support of reason was decidedly more straightforward here than in other essays of (roughly) the same time, for instance "Das Ornament der Masse" or his Benjamin review. The more obvious the semantic and conceptual obscurities, the more urgently he stated the need for logical clarity–if not always where his friends' texts were concerned.

A forcefully eclectic reader, Bloch professed to find some kindred ideas in this review, unaware, it seems, of the implications of Kracauer's argument for his own language, which was in many respects quite close to Buber and Rosenzweig's. He declared himself partly reconciled to Kracauer's Münzer review because he understood now that by stressing the "path of the seemingly external, practical, lustreless . . . which is exactly the path taken by Marxism," Kracauer, too, measured all truth in terms of this "needy" contemporary actuality and therefore was indeed quite close to a concept of the totality of truth in Lukacs's sense.[43]

Notwithstanding the syntactic opacity of these passages, it is clear that

Bloch was trying here to make a fundamental statement about essential intellectual affinities between himself and Kracauer which included Lukacs. For Kracauer, though he was pleased, even moved by Bloch's conciliatory gesture, such affinities were fictitious. He accepted Bloch's agreement that the concept of "*Aktualität*" was central to his argument with the Buber circle, though it was surprising after the Münzer book, but he emphatically dissociated himself from Lukacs's formalist-idealist position. In his opinion, Lukacs's concept of totality, so attractive to Bloch, was a defensive move. His philosophy was reactionary, he explained, because it failed to reclaim for Marxism "materialism," that is, the natural and socioeconomic conditions and contingencies of everyday life.

Kracauer was very well aware that *History and Class Consciousness* was under attack from the Communist party for seemingly similar reasons,[44] and he made it clear to Bloch that he would not state his own reservations publicly to avoid having them used against Lukacs. But he insisted strongly on the need for reclamation of materialism so that Marxian theory could be activated as the most significantly contemporaneous revolutionary theory. Consequently, he still found Bloch's attempt to link theology and Marxism deeply troubling and suggested that he "confront theology in the realm of the profane" so that he could get to and make use of its anthropological insights. The most important contemporary issue, Kracauer pointed out to Bloch, was the rooting of revolutionary theory in "material and external" conditions,[45] not in private, inward needs and desires.

Bloch, in his answer, presented Lukacs's position in *History and Class Consciousness* in the same religio-Hegelian terms in which he had persuaded Benjamin to accept its redemptive energies.[46] A short analysis is in order here of the remarkable effect this 1923 collection of essays had on the group of intellectuals who saw themselves as the vanguard of Weimar culture. In his review essay, "Jewish Mysticism" (1911), on two books by Buber, *Baal Shem* and *Rabbi Nachman*, Lukacs had shown himself very much attracted to the "irrationalism" of Hasidism and its achievement of true community. He found here a refutation of accusations that Jews as a group had been excessively rational and therefore particularly responsible for the rapid and destructive advance of calculating, mechanizing, alienating modernity. Under the influence of Buber and Bloch, Lukacs had moved from his tragic vision in *Die Seele und die Formen* (1910) to a position that stressed utopian hope, mysticism, and the importance of nontragic literature. The importance for him during these years of Bloch's intellectual presence or gestalt, rather than argumentation, cannot be exaggerated. It confirmed him in his conversion to a "new philosophy" of messianism built on Bloch's belief in an evolving antirational, ascetic type of Jew, "the opposite of everything that today is customarily called 'Jewish.'"[47]

Marxian thought–of a peculiarly stretchable kind–was to be the more durable extension of this messianism and a lasting solution for Lukacs's personal dilemma.[48] He began with an eclectic re-Hegelianization of Marx or, as he himself described it aptly half a century later in the preface to the 1967 edition of *History and Class Consciousness*, an "attempt to out-Hegel Hegel."[49] (In his 1924 review of the book, Bloch had already argued admiringly that Lukacs had traced Marx back to Hegel and had vigorously pushed Hegel beyond himself.)[50] The "decisive difference" between Marxian and bourgeois thought was located, for the Lukacs of *History and Class Consciousness*, not in the "primacy of economic motives in historical explanation" but in "the point of view of totality."

> The category of totality, the all-pervasive supremacy of the whole over the parts, is the essence of the method which Marx took over from Hegel and brilliantly transformed into the foundation of a wholly new science. . . . Proletarian science is revolutionary not just by virtue of its revolutionary ideas which it opposes to bourgeois society, but above all because of its method. *The primacy of the category of totality is the bearer of the principle of revolution in science.*[51]

The metaphorical reference to (natural) science is significant. Marx, according to Lukacs, has transformed the revolutionary aspects of Hegelian dialectics into a "science of revolution . . . into what Herzen described as the 'algebra of revolution'" (27). Of prime importance for Lukacs is the very totality of a system–its total constructedness and therefore its power to control–not the question of its explanatory adequacy. Closed to "external" evidence, such constructedness can come to mean a clearly defined, enduring cultural significance for intellectuals confronted with the marginality of their position. After the failed attempts at revolution in Germany and Hungary, Lukacs, like many other intellectuals, found it even more difficult to consider the potential usefulness of such marginality in terms of a composite, multiperspectivist view of contemporary culture in flux.[52]

However, if Lukacs shared with other early twentieth-century intellectuals the need for utopian visions of totality, his realization of his desire contrasted sharply with their vacuous if well-intentioned prerevolutionary messianic-Marxian yearnings. He constructed, in the postrevolutionary *History and Class Consciousness*, a system of totality by setting into "theoretical," frictionless motion the dialectics of the processes of history and of the consciousness of the proletariat. This level of abstraction was new in intellectual speculations about the proletarian masses, as Bloch made a point of mentioning in his review (473). The insistence on the dialectical unity, in totality, of theory and practice was the conceptual leitmotiv that connected the essays making up the book. It proved to be highly attractive to Weimar intellectuals in their attempts to rethink their cultural position after the proletarian masses as well as their intellectual leaders had failed to meet the challenges of the revolution. Such abstract unity could adapt itself quite easily to absorbing as well as stressing the differences and the distance between the position of the intellectual and that of the proletariat. Even more importantly, it fit a significantly predestined course of history.

The dialectician has no need to take into consideration the realities of proletarian lives because he is "concerned always with the same problem: knowledge of the historical process in its entirety." Ideological and economic problems "merge into one another. . . . The approach of *literary* history is the one best suited to the problems of history. The history of philosophy becomes the philosophy of history"[53]—in the hands of a theoretician whose primary concern is neither historical evidence nor the social existence of the proletariat but the significant form of his own cultural and intellectual autonomy.

The dialectics of an "objective" and "imputed" (*zugerechnet*) consciousness of the proletariat[54] conveniently supported the role of the party as "the concrete principle of mediation between man and history" (321). The party could then be "distinguished from the rest of the proletariat by the fact that it has a clear understanding of the historical path to be taken by the proletariat as a whole" (325). Consequently the intellectual Lukacs, who had also taken a leadership role in the cultural politics of the aborted Hungarian revolution, viewed party discipline as "one of the most exalted and important *intellectual* problems in the history of revolution. This discipline can only come into being as the free and conscious deed of the most conscious element, of the vanguard of the revolutionary class [the party]. Without the intellectual foundations of that class it cannot be realised" (320).

This strongly affirmative "theoretical" argument in support of the "objective" importance of an intellectual elite for the coming into being of an "objective" (construct of) totality proved to be highly attractive to intellectuals who thought it their mission to establish a cultural vanguard. Of particular interest was the fact that it allowed considerable flexibility of interpretation regarding the concrete details of that mission. Bloch had shared with Lukacs, since their first meeting in Budapest in 1910, the concept of a "new philosophy" of greater intellectual immediacy vis-à-vis the life-world. He sought to articulate this immediacy in his emphatically earthy and idiosyncratic poeticophilosophical discourse. But Lukacs, differently talented, promptly translated it into the high abstractionism of neoidealist philosophizing. More than half a century later, when both were celebrating an eightieth birthday, Lukacs remembered the "vehemence" of the "impulses" coming out of that meeting and its lasting importance regardless of the different directions their lives had taken.[55]

There were differences. Bloch stressed them during the years 1949–55, when he taught philosophy at Leipzig University and had good professional contact with Lukacs.[56] They concerned emotional response, situation, opportunity, and also attitude toward political power.[57] There were, too, enduring intellectual affinities that went deeper and were indeed based on the shared ability to abstract their thought from the complexities and contingencies of the life-world. Exhilarated and troubled by what he referred to as "reality," Kracauer did not share this ability; Adorno did.[58]

Bloch saw his vanguard role, under Lukacs's influence, in general, "theoretical" terms of Marxian cultural politics. This was too general for Benjamin, who needed to anchor his personal concept of cultural truth, that is, his role in bringing it about. He imitated Lukacs's opponent, Brecht, in his personal religiointellectual subjection to party discipline.[59] Adorno proceeded more independently and creatively. He gratefully accepted from Lukacs the "theoretically" demonstrated "objective" importance of the intellectual elite in relation to an "objective" totality. But he was most impressed by the interpretative usefulness of dialectical mediation itself. It enabled him to conclude that theory and political practice are not identical but stand in a highly mediated relationship that necessitates a clear and permanent division between manual and intellectual workers. As he informed the composer Ernst Krenek in the 1930s, "in reified society, all progress occurs via continued specialization,"[60] and he defined his role in the intellectual vanguard accordingly.

Like Lukacs, Adorno was interested above all in the question of the intellectual's control over his position as one of culturally significant intellectual autonomy. Lukacs, in presenting the discipline of the party as an *intellectual* issue, suggested a solution on the proverbially, now dialectically, higher level. If for Lukacs the intellectual's place was in the vanguard of the revolution, for Adorno it was in the revolutionary artistic avant-guarde. In actuality, both positions were equally removed from reflected connection with any class consciousness—most of all with that of the proletariat. Bloch, trying to make palatable to Kracauer Lukacs's philosophical view of the intellectual's position as articulated in *History and Class Consciousness*, already saw that much. But where Lukacs sublated this fact dialectically—his many essays on the literary tradition would claim that "somehow" prerevolutionary writers had subconsciously produced postrevolutionary insights—[61] Adorno arrested it. He found the importance for him of Lukacs's argument precisely in the fact that it enabled him to construct on his own terms the intellectual's general cultural marginality. Moreover, he could further elevate it to the significance of negativity, which had been revealed to him in Benjamin's arresting and rupturing gaze. Distancing his position sharply from that of the concrete, nonphilosophical proletariat, the amorphous unwashed masses, did not prevent him from blaming them for their false consciousness with respect to High Culture. At the same time, his attempts at asserting an intellectually autonomous and culturally authoritative elite could draw on Lukacs's "theoretically" fortified argument for the historically "objective" necessity of an *intellectual* vanguard.

Adorno's priorities, then, had nothing to do with trying to define the intellectual's (artist's) role and contribution in social-historical terms, and everything with carving out and legitimizing a place for his creative autonomy.[62] It was in socially independent, artistically creative work that the intellectual could best achieve and maintain a good conscience vis-à-vis the proletariat, that is, a correct consciousness in terms of "objective" dialectic historical development. As he wrote to Ernst Krenek, "Precisely in his solitariness and isolation the composer carries out social demands; . . . society dwells in the inmost cells of the self-enclosed technical problems, and he registers its demands all the more legitimately the less he is prompted from the outside, arbitrarily, and in constraint of the rule of form ["*Formgesetz*"].[63]

Bloch, typically, tried to solve the troublesome (cultural) political issue of the intellectual's connection with the (self-)consciousness of the proletariat by extending it into the realm of the religious: he proposed linkage between a political sphere of the "*Selbstergreifung des Proletariats*" and a religious sphere of the "*Selbstergreifung des 'Volk Gottes.'*" And in a remarkably generous attempt to reassure the "realist" Kracauer, he asserted that Lukacs was no longer interested in the idealist philosophy of self-consciousness, that even the term *class consciousness* could be eliminated now.[64] But Kracauer's answer to Bloch's most urgent attempt to make him change his mind about Lukacs immediately clarified the fact that the importance for Lukacs of the "objective" subject-object relation, idealist or not, was not at issue. The question was the contemporary intellectual's position, which Kracauer, in contrast to Lukacs, understood to be one of responsible openness to cultural change brought about by a multitude of cultural activities. Lukacs's "theoretical" totalizing definition–as construction–of the intellectual vanguard was unacceptable to him because he had learned, from experience, that his cultural contribution as an intellectual was neither unique nor totally defined by a group.

Precisely this view motivated Kracauer to clarify the place from which he spoke by describing, with critical sympathy, the position of the other, in this case Bloch's, not in general terms but as it appeared to him. Such clarification, particularly if it uncovered some similarities, was not meant to be a declaration of solidarity of the kind Bloch wanted to extract from him: "In the last analysis," Kracauer wrote, "I am an anarchist, to be sure sufficiently skeptical to think actual anarchism, too, a distortion."[65] Nevertheless, in Bloch he found the desire, close to his own, to reveal and to preserve, which he thought central to a meaningfully contemporary philosophy of history based on the postulate that "nothing may be forgotten and nothing remembered may remain unchanged. The motive of transformation plays a decisive role for me" (281).

Transformation was the reason why Kracauer disagreed with Lukacs, and with Bloch on Lukacs. Lukacs had concealed, in his reception of Hegel, the "real source" of fundamental Marxian concepts of man and morals in the French Enlightenment and in writers like Locke, Helvetius, and Holbach; moreover, in Kracauer's view, these concepts appeared much more clearly in Kant than in Hegel.[66] The question did not simply concern idealism or nonidealism, or the importance or nonimportance of class consciousness. At issue was the kind of idealism, which in Kracauer's view was a historical question. He would have thought the situation different if Lukacs's neo-Hegelianism had indeed transformed idealism by showing which of its assumptions needed to be changed, because such responsibly critical reading would have preserved the undoubtable achievement of historical idealism. But with his formal dialectics moving into empty totality, into constructing for its own sake, Lukacs as reader of Hegel had gone back behind Marx: "I would really like to know," Kracauer was finally moved to ask Bloch, "where you would place Lukacs's material intentions?" (283).

4 Bloch dropped the matter rather than attempting an answer. His letters to Kracauer during the ideologically less heated midtwenties focused on his own work, which he wished to have published in *Frankfurter Zeitung*, and here he showed himself to be remarkably flexible, offering to make changes in the direction of greater accessibility, even where they concerned the "mysticisms" so dear to his heart.[67] But in late 1929, with intensified social and economic pressures and political polarization, the issue of Lukacs reemerged, and with it the question of the intellectual's cultural role in increasingly dark times. In a masterfully opaque letter, Bloch summed up recent conversations with Lukacs, urging Kracauer again to consider seriously the affinities between himself, Bloch, Benjamin, and Lukacs—framed, as it were, by the concept of totality. Lukacs's "doctrine" stated that totality was "presently being realized by/in the proletariat" and contained "everything that was not 100 percent false consciousness in the false consciousness of the past or of several (classical, feudal, capitalist) pasts."[68]

Bloch's reservations were by no means about the viability of a "doctrine" of totality but about certain processual, "somewhat social democratic" implications in Lukacs's present scheme which suggested the notion, deeply disturbing to him, of having to postpone temporarily the realization of totality (323). But Bloch's desire for the reliable solidarity of an intellectual vanguard was so powerful that it prevented him from appreciating the actual diversity of what he considered vanguard cultural politics. If his utopianism differed from Benjamin's theologism and from Lukacs's absolutism, it differed much more from Kracauer's empiricism. His attempts to persuade Kracauer to take seriously Lukacs's "doctrine" in the political situation of late 1929 were blatantly incongruous with his praising, in the same letter, the first part of *Die Angestellten*, which Kracauer had just sent him. It is hard to believe that Bloch could have overlooked the fact that this text was based not on utopian speculations but on considerable information and shrewd insights into the actual social and political dynamics of these years. In the spring of 1931 Bloch would complain to Adorno, with reference to *Die Angestellten*, that Kracauer had always exhibited false consciousness in the question of economics; he had been too "materialist," not sufficiently Marxist, in his lack of interest in "mediation."[69] But by that time intellectual differences for Bloch had become enlarged into concrete political hostilities, and the ideal of solidarity applied less to a self-selected intellectual vanguard than to a group of like-minded persons receiving Communist directives.

In his answer to Bloch's call for solidarity, Kracauer focused characteristically on intellectual affinities that Bloch, discussing Lukacs, had found in Kracauer's and Benjamin's reviews of Julien Green's recently published *Leviathan* (324). His emphatic rejection of such kinship was meant to distinguish sharply his general cultural and critical position from Benjamin's. Kracauer located the main difference between them in the degree to which the reality of another writer's work was acknowledged in the critic's response. For Benjamin that work

> is only the occasion for a more or less brilliant interpretation. Thus the world in its reality escapes him. He has no relation to it. I have looked at that work in esthetic terms, discussing critically its construction. Furthermore I have dealt with the phenomenon of the province, with the role that it plays in Green's work. Finally I have not been content to glorify, as does Benjamin, Soviet Russia in one corner of my conscience and Green's mythology in the other—to

> keep them apart in this way is pure estheticism—but I have tried to force these two phenomena into the *reale Dialektik* that is due them. So you see, every sentence carries an intention that is different from Benjamin's, and it was not without reason that I firmly rejected his essay.[70]

These distinctions focus nicely the fallacies inherent in the critic's assumed autonomy, be it regarding a shared cultural environment or another writer's cultural contribution. Kracauer argues that his review is "*realer*" (more real) than Benjamin's since it is conscious of, attuned to the object of, the critique—the other author's text. It is not arrested in a priori sated and therefore static, self-creating textual self-consciousness, as Benjamin's is, notwithstanding its agile, often "brilliant" verbality.

Lukacs, Kracauer remarked in this context, had remained stuck in the same introverted idealism: "It is pure and bad idealism to locate [truth] contents and genuine concretizations exclusively in the postrevolutionary period." Pointing out Lukacs's contorted and deeply ahistorical second-guessing of prerevolutionary literature and art to make it politically correct, Kracauer referred to his own "*abgrundtief*" ("unfathomable") realism. He could not, as Bloch had advised him to do, join Lukacs temporarily in the "prison of his premises" and then take out with him whatever seemed useful.[71] Not that he was not troubled, in these increasingly difficult years, by the very real social and political implications of the intellectuals' cultural marginality. It was precisely for this reason that he found it impossible to defer to an authority that smoothly and vacuously sublated these implications. He could not know, at that point, that in their self-centered Stalinism Bloch and Lukacs would continue in the same characteristic mixture of rigidity and flexibility, even though they drew further and further apart with respect to the style of their discourse.

5

The concrete political implications of intellectual positions in relation to power games emerged in the spring of 1931, when Bloch started attacking Kracauer openly for his lack of unquestioning solidarity with "the left."[72] The occasion was Kracauer's critical report on a lecture that the Soviet writer Sergei Tretiakov had recently given in Berlin on the worker and peasant writers' movements. Bloch blamed Kracauer for his rejection of Tretiakov's (in Kracauer's view) dogmatically simple-minded glorification of the collective. His criticism had disregarded the fact that

Tretiakov was also attacked in *Linkskurve*, the organ of the radical political Left, for his avant-garde notions and his liquidation of true proletarian literature.[73] In Kracauer's view, such dilemmas were common among leftist intellectuals during the last years of Weimar, but precisely for this reason unquestioning solidarity was not the answer.

Bloch's accusations are a good case in point. He lamented Kracauer's changes, noticed by himself and "without exception and in disbelief" by "all our common friends," toward a reformist, aphilosophical, revisionist, merely personal position. Bloch's not so subtle exclusionary gesture was accompanied by an apodictic statement that Bolsheviks must not be criticized in a journal like the bourgeois *Frankfurter Zeitung*. If there was to be any critique at all, it could be only from an "*innermarxistisch*" position "through which world-historical developments have passed" (355f.), that is, a position defined by history "itself."

The fiction of inevitable, inexorable historical developments had always provided a ready-made authority for vanguard Marxian argumentation, but Bloch infused it with more passionate group dynamics. His accusatory complaints were to become much harsher a year later, when he took Kracauer to task for his critical review of the film, *Kuhle Wampe*, made by an independent collective that included Brecht.[74] The film had originally been censored but was released after considerable cutting. Kracauer's review was strongly critical of the censor but expressed clear reservations about the film's celebration of (all) proletarian Communist youth and its dismissal of older, mostly social democratic workers. Bloch's assertions here are predictable but nevertheless instructive: "I am not saying anything about the film, which I have not seen; it does not matter whether it is good or bad. But in view of *your past* and *our friendship*, it is *difficult* to accept that you expressed a blind and ugly hatred of Brecht *on this occasion*, arm in arm with censorship, in a newspaper that has been increasingly anti-Marxist."

Bloch was not interested in the question of whether the movie would or would not further "the cause," as it had never been a question of judging "the cause" but rather of upholding the discipline imposed by it and for the sake of it. Kracauer, in his view, had "*left our common cause* by mixing so irresponsibly the *ideologies* of your *private feelings* with the cause," at a time when "our small circle *is in need of a more trustworthy solidarity*" (357).

Upset by the insinuation that his review had supported censorship, Kracauer reminded Bloch of an earlier accusation that his decision against publishing one of Benjamin's celebratory essays on Brecht was indicative of his, Kracauer's, private feelings against Brecht.[75] When he stressed the (to him) very important issue of separating personal feelings from facts he touched, of course, on the critic's most troubling problem. As was his tendency, he asserted his own more and more difficultly balanced perspective in terms that were too certain but also too concrete to protect him from Bloch's attack.[76] Kracauer, citing his well-known position to the left of his paper's, argued that his statements in *Frankfurter Zeitung* had been read according to his intentions, namely as *his* and not the newspaper's. He also charged Bloch with having disregarded the continuity of his work and distorted its meaning; Bloch had ignored, among other things, Kracauer's insistence on the right to change his mind in deference to factual evidence. But Bloch saw only the inertia of social democracy, or of a Marxism that preferred a planned economy to revolution. Thus Kracauer's criticism of contemporary culture was now too well adjusted, no longer "exiled," "in despair," "inexorable." Yielding to rationalist revisionist reservations vis-à-vis Hegel and lacking in "demonic power and, above all, explosiveness," Kracauer's critical discourse had sadly lowered the level of Marxism.[77]

If Bloch located the source of Kracauer's (alleged) former explosive demonic intensity of thought in the intellectual's inevitable mental state of exile, he had never understood, much less appreciated, his friend's work. His response was characteristic of the carefully nurtured spontaneity and authenticity with which he legitimized his notoriously elliptic verbosity. His extraordinary self-centeredness was reflected not the least in the fact that his texts had always been willfully hermetic, relying on connotative verbal 'thickness' rather than conceptual complexity.[78]

Unlike Kracauer, Bloch had remained convinced of his own significant uniqueness, which extended to a circle of the chosen few and fed his categorical demands for solidarity.[79] Such conviction, normal for talented young people, is usually shed in the process of maturation. But in the years after World War I this process was retarded, especially for vanguard intellectuals. Brilliant sons, they emphasized, with their own uniqueness, the sharp generational conflict and cultural-political polarization of their time. And Bloch was just a particularly energetic example of the reluctance to understand that people, including himself, are like other people. Kracauer had tried to correct this inability in his role as critical reader of Bloch's texts. But Bloch's elaborately composite persona of creative heretic applying his explosive verbal powers to inauthentic modern mass society resisted change. It was a combination of Marxian critic, theologian, utopist, Stalinist, philosopher, Romantic *vates* (seer), and authentically innocent poet, in which many of the political and intellectual dilemmas and epistemological dead ends characteristic of twentieth-century modernity coexisted suggestively. Finally, having remained the same self-centered and self-created original all his life,[80] Bloch became a German university professor, officially honored in both East and West Germany. Telling Lukacs in 1911 that he "would like to direct life toward the devil as pure principle (the devil's arse is restlessness), since form has to be directed toward God as its principle (boredom is God's arse)," he wanted to present himself as demonically subversive, the devil's advocate. But the devil, addicted to transformation and the pluralism of power, proved too restless for him.[81]

Kracauer, not the oldest but arguably the most adult member of that vanguard group, was sharply aware of human sameness and diversity and therefore was especially attuned to the disturbing contemporary social and cultural polarization. If people shared most anxieties and desires, they lived different lives, and they were receptive to and shaped by different values. Both the familiarity and the strangeness of these lives were accessible, at least partly, to the observer who was willing to take seriously their actuality and to adjust his points of observation accordingly. In his answer to Bloch's pleas for solidarity, Kracauer explained that he changed his observational position as situations and facts changed, not in accordance with an alleged move toward establishment social democracy.[82] Changing his point of observation, which, in turn, changes the observer, had also moved him to reject the demand for solidarity at any cost (365). It was an imposition that he feared would paralyze the powerfully concrete "motive of transformation."[83] Not that it was impossible for a group of intellectuals to strive for solidarity when trying to evaluate a situation in terms that could be shared, that is, agreed on as adequate to its perceived temporal actuality. But, knowing from his journalistic experience how difficult it could be to arrive at such an agreement, Kracauer neither expected nor demanded solidarity. Moreover, he was not willing to contribute to it when he saw the issue obscured and controlled by fuzzy reasoning and unexamined motivations–a form of control commonly used by the more aggressive members of any given group (366).

This distinction signifies Kracauer's profound respect for "*die Sache*," facts constructed in critical consultation with others, which was central to his critical arguments against a dangerous intellectual propensity for ideology and solidarity. His conceptual strategies and judgments could not be based on some hazy, a priori "objective" moment in the course of world history as defined by a small, isolated group of intellectuals, no matter how "brilliantly." *Relatively* objective at best, they would have to be informed by his attempts to understand historical evidence. When Bloch countered automatically with Freudian unconscious motivations that had tainted his belief in "objective realiability" (362f.), Kracauer simply reminded him again that "passion for factuality" was his nature, implying that this included the unconscious dimension of his thought (365). This passion moved him toward objectivity, but was not synonymous with and did not guarantee it. The distance between the friends was indeed unbridgeable, because Bloch was unable to appreciate that Kracauer's critical realism excluded a belief in the individual's full access to "objective reliability." When he insisted on the relational, therefore relative, power of factuality to keep in check and guide the personal perspective, he did so precisely because acknowledgment of factuality signified acknowledgment of the perspectives and the voices of others. It was not possible for someone of his intellectual temperament and experience to disregard the articulation of plural, multivocal positions of observation.

Thus understood, factuality works as an antidote to the belief systems of ideology and to impositions of solidarity. Bloch's dialectic connection between revolutionary Marxism and the transcendental is personal, not "objective," because it evades the check of factuality, namely the test of admitting the voices of others. The issue was not, Kracauer wrote in this context, that he did not think important, or was no longer interested in Marxism. Rather, he tried to understand its significance by involving it in a "*reale Dialektik*" on the basis of factuality as shared experience (367). Working with Marxism, he wanted it to work: to make sense of, explain, give meaning to a contemporary experience dangerously entangled and conflicted. But he also knew from that experience that serious attempts at a dialectic which would acknowledge rather than abstract from such concrete conflict were a painfully difficult enterprise.

Kracauer had indeed undergone transformation during the Weimar period in response to rapid social and political changes;[84] he was to go on changing in exile. It was difficult for Bloch to consider the meanings of this change, which consisted of continuities and discontinuities. When Adorno reacted critically to his *Heritage of Our Times* (1934), Bloch accused him, too, of having changed for the worse. Adorno was now an "evil and therefore bad reader" whose "metaphysical philology" and "writing fetishes" (Bloch's phrase for Adorno's exclusive focus, developed under Benjamin's influence, on allegorical configurations of signs) deadened the language of philosophy.[85] In some ways this is a perceptive description of Adorno's self-consciously difficult encipherings based on his idiosyncratic decipherings of others' texts. But Bloch did not touch on the fact that Adorno, too, had responded, if in his own enduringly abstracting manner, to the increasing polarization and marginality of intellectual positions. (Nor did he touch on the fact that he, Bloch, had simply and exuberantly talked himself out of recognizing the situation.)

Against Adorno's objections to the impressionistic, pointillist, undialectic style of the pieces collected in *Heritage* and his (in Bloch's view) "dogmatic" opinion that the book needed a denser, "unmediated, immanent analysis of contemporary ideological contents," Bloch argued that it was necessary to be "diabolically engaged with these ideological movements."[86] In contrast, Adorno's and Kracauer's praxis was not sufficiently "demonic," "red," "warm," mysterious, dynamic. Published in 1934 and meant to deal with the "symptomatically effective" phenomena of a "late bourgeois period" (426, 424), the collection consists of reviews and essays written over the previous ten years. (For a writer who preached the liberating spontaneity of the "rough draft," Bloch was curiously eager to collect and republish as often as possible every line as he was writing it and to guard most jealously his copyrights to the "brilliant" phrases he coined.)[87] These pieces do not show much awareness that the times were constantly changing but reflect, again,

Bloch's familiar (self)-expressionist concerns and self-referential formulations spanning half a century, from the early *Spirit of Utopia* (1918) to *The Principle of Hope* (1938–47), which he went on revising. His writing is indeed, as Adorno said of *Heritage*, like a transcript of an endless and endlessly meandering conversation at night.[88] It circles around what Bloch stated in 1934 as "the *Specifica* of my philosophical thought: the darkness of the lived moment, the shape of the question that cannot be construed, not-yet conscious knowledge, a new substance for utopia."[89] Sometimes there were indeed "brilliant" formulations, momentary flashes of insight. But most characteristic was a neoromantic suggestive mood of intellectual penetration, complete with images of the bright eroticism and the dark caves of higher or deeper knowledge.

From the position of the intellectual in the heart of a uniquely significant exile rather than on the margins of a shared, increasingly difficult social and political reality, Bloch had never understood Kracauer's critical realism. That would have required measuring Kracauer's insights against his own contemporary experience. But he was straining too much toward the not-yet, which "inexorably" limited his spontaneous monologues on the world. He saw it, if in the bold outlines of hope, through his chiliastic perspective darkly. His projections of the world as it was to become were too ignorant of the world as it had become. The seemingly spontaneous earthiness and vitality of his style, which fed on the exoticism of archaic language and on often private games with proverbs and idioms, were not, as he thought, a powerfully concrete antidote to modern abstracting reification. They were, rather, expressive of the same nostalgic "*Ungleichzeitigkeit*," noncontemporaneity, of which he accused the Weimar petty bourgeois: the desire to go back to the roots, regardless of the cost.

Anachronism and vanguard can be interconnected, even interdependent, in intellectual positions; it is a question not so much of the fact but of the manner of bridging past and future. Bloch's version shows his unwillingness to deal with the historicity of cultural modernity, that is, the interplay of continuities and discontinuities which was indeed very confusing during the Weimar period. Forced to exchange his comfortably controlled choice of cultural exile for the imposed contingencies of political exile, he promptly translated them into another custom-made "objective" moment in the course of history. Kracauer's growing awareness of the fallacies inherent in this position would direct his development in exile toward a more concrete and more imaginative understanding of history as an open-ended, ongoing cultural construction with different and often contradictory meanings. Dependent on the presence and participation of many different voices, history resists, as he saw, "objective" interpretations because the differences are real, not finally reconcilable.

Chapter Three

Representation as Reclamation

1

The similarities Kracauer established, from the vantage point of his work on *History*, between the kinds of knowledge produced by photography and modern historiography have so far been unexplored. Yet they are central to the development of his composite concept of objectivity which found its clearest articulation in his attempts to describe (rather than define) the "mixed" mode of historical understanding.[1] He used extensive analogies between photographic and historiographic procedures when he explored the validity of perspectivism in historical inquiry, which leads to the coexistence of different shapes of objectivity. The lively presence of photographic examples in the argument of *History*, most of them from *Theory of Film*, served to elucidate the particularity of these shapes, which is at the roots of the obstacles faced by the historian in writing history. But these obstacles also suggest the exhilarating richness of past cultural activities: the historian's particular sensual and intellectual pleasures of seeing and knowing something, rather than a general melancholic resignation to being unable to see and know everything. If Kracauer appears to draw on the analogies between photography and historiography especially in those moments when he seems overwhelmed by the choices that the historian faces, he does so for the sake of emphasizing a shared interest in preserving things past for memory. They serve to clarify the historiographical enterprise, which depends on the ability to negotiate, in agreeing and disagreeing, a shifting, provisional concept of objectivity.

Theory of Film is not a theory in the sense of a stringently constructed argument or model. Rather, it is a viewer-oriented poetics of filmmaking with interspersed reflections on the cultural meanings and status of the photo image. It is based on a wealth of material gathered by the viewer and reader Kracauer, who selected it according to his views on the nature of the photo image. As the arrangement shows, he also developed, expanded, refined, and questioned these views within the accumulating material. Kracauer's concentration and generosity as viewer and reader was rooted in his notion of reality as the presence of others in their cultural activities, contemporary or past. In *Theory of Film* he repeatedly refers to the (ideal) photographer as an insatiable reader who, driven by an ever-increasing curiosity, roams far and wide in the knowable, visible world.[2] There is another instructive example of the metaphorical use of *reader* in *Theory of Film.* The experimental filmmaker who approaches the product of another artist "creatively" –that is, uses it for his own creation–refuses to assume the role of the reader. Having "atomized" (deconstructed) the other's work, it is for him nothing but raw material, disposable. Kracauer hastens to add that this is not an argument against the experimental film in general, whether it deals with art or not. Individual films would have to be judged by their "cinematic" quality. But, clearly, Kracauer thinks it important that the reader's role be taken seriously. My argument, then, is based on careful and critical readings of Kracauer's writings on photography and film; as in the previous chapter, I move slowly, referring to the text in order to establish the context of terms and the qualifying connections between different parts of an argument. Since Kracauer's argumention is never linearly developed, I, too, must come back to arguments from different angles and in different contexts.

The problems readers have had with *Theory of Film* start with the claims made in the title and the potentially misleading message of the subtitle, *The Redemption of Physical Reality* (the German version is also misleading: *Die Errettung der äusseren Wirklichkeit*). *Redemption* in Kracauer's use tends in the direction of the German "*einlösen*"–to save, redeem, or reclaim pawned objects or objects wrongly thought useless, or to fulfill promises–rather than "*erlösen*"–to save, redeem a person in an existentially difficult situation; the latter is a word with strong religious connotations and a key term in Benjamin's work. *Redemption* in Kracauer's meaning applies to the potential knowledge (made possible by photo images) of a world outside the individual observer, a world that is not automatically his. In contrast to the autofictive, autoassertive perspective of critics like Adorno, Benjamin, and Bloch, Kracauer's perspective reflects an increasing openness to the difficulties of access posed by his contemporary cultural and natural environment. Reading Benjamin on photography and film, one looks at Benjamin looking; reading Kracauer, one sees what he is looking at. This comparison is obviously overstated; such control is always a question of degree. Besides, as we will see, some of Kracauer's early "position papers" on the photographic media share Benjamin's perspective to some extent. But on the whole, and increasingly in exile, Kracauer is concerned with photographic reclamation as retrieving, by making visible, what is (was) present and should not therefore be lost. His interest, unlike Benjamin's, is focused not on an a priori significance of the insignificant but rather on restoring to its proper significance what has become, through human inattention and forgetting, insignificant.

Kracauer's own activities as a viewer and critic of films contributed to such nonforgetting. He had looked at a large number of films in Frankfurt, Berlin, Paris, and New York and attempted to situate them in relation to the experiences of their audiences. What was it exactly that films did for their viewers? Was there a unique contribution? And if so, what was it? Kracauer explicitly posed these questions in the concluding part, "Film in Our Time," of *Theory of Film*—a passage that, he complained repeatedly, had been very difficult to write. He worked on the Epilogue from the late spring to the early fall of 1959 "with fear and trembling," he wrote to Lowenthal, because he found it quite impossible to articulate in generalizing evaluative statements the many highly individual filmic solutions to the challenge of recording the motions of daily living: "In this chapter, the trick is to communicate the historical and philosophical insights so concretely that the reader does not notice their generality. Oh, how I hate generalities." Still, he thought the exercise necessary because such an analysis of the meanings of film would serve him as a "decisive analysis of our contemporary intellectual situation."[3]

It is instructive that Kracauer placed so much weight on the cultural contribution of film after he had experienced the profound *Zivilisationsbruch* caused by national socialism. If *From Caligari to Hitler* was meant to explain through the analysis of filmic images the social psychological dynamics that made possible the rise of political extremism, *Theory of Film* goes back behind such an analysis with the question of how the photographic media produce knowledge; it contrasts photography with painting, film with theater. Kracauer was struck by the fact that photo images, still or moving, pose epistemological questions concerning visibility in peculiarly literal terms.

> The truly decisive reason for the elusiveness of physical reality is the habit of abstract thinking we have acquired under the reign of science and technology. No sooner do we emancipate ourselves from the "ancient beliefs" than we are led to eliminate the qualities of things. So the things continue to recede. And, assuredly, they are all the more elusive since we usually cannot help setting them in the perspective of conventional views and purposes which point beyond their self-contained being. Hence, were it not for the intervention of the film camera, it would cost us an enormous effort to surmount the barriers which separate us from our everyday surroundings.
>
> Film renders visible what we did not, or perhaps even could not, see before its advent. It effectively assists us in discovering the material world with its psychophysical correspondences. We literally redeem this world from its dormant state, its state of virtual nonexistence, by endeavoring to experience it through the camera. And we are free to experience it because we are fragmentized. The cinema can be defined as a medium particularly equipped to promote the redemption of physical reality. Its imagery permits us, for the first time, to take away with us the objects and occurrences that comprise the flow of material life. (299f.)

I will disregard the reservations stated here with respect to science and technology, which are, in any case, contradicted by Kracauer's analysis of the cultural importance of the new *technology* of film. The passage is instructive, rather, for its emphasis on the visual potential of film. Film can help us enter a new dimension of experience from which we have been barred by impoverished perception. And it can do so precisely because our modern daily experience is fragmented and in temporal flux. The technology that made film possible, then, enables and opens rather than closes; its modernity signifies an extension of our visual capabilities.[4] It does not create a new world; it enables another part of the old familiar world to become ours because with the help of the camera we see new and different parts of it. In 1940, waiting nervously for the visa that would enable him to leave Marseille for America, Kracauer wrote the richly detailed outline of a book on film that fills three large copybooks in his tiny architectural handwriting and touches on almost all the important issues with which he was to deal with, many years later, in *Theory of Film*.[5] The questions he puts to the photographic medium here show him straining to see more clearly the fragility and endurance, concretely and sensuously intertwined, of the world of cultural and natural things, which was all the more precious because it had become so endangered. It is this text that establishes the link between Kracauer's pre- and postwar writing, not the study of Jacques Offenbach written in Paris in the midthirties or the exploration of the symbiotically entangled filmic images and social and political energies in *From Caligari to Hitler*, written in New York in the forties. Like those of any intelligent productive person, Kracauer's life and work exhibit continuities and discontinuities.[6] But his awareness of the effects of time passing and of a changing self was unusually intense. Against the losses he set the plea for anamnesis, both in photography and in historiography. Yet he realized that "nothing remembered may remain unchanged"[7] and accepted, from the beginning, the contingencies of transformation. In his last work he was to compare the historian's perspective to that of the exile who is particularly challenged by such contingencies.[8]

Kracauer's concern was the cultural significance of photography in general rather than of film in particular. He was of course aware of the important differences regarding perception, interpretation, and meaning which separated film from photography. But reviewing films in the 1920s and 1930s, and trying to work out a poetics of film in the 1950s, he stressed as the most fundamental contribution of film its ability to represent the natural and cultural world *photographically*.[9] He was profoundly impressed by the fact that in the case of the photo image, still or moving, representation signified *re-production*, if only for one of the senses, in stunningly literal terms. That is to say, the differences, no matter how intricate, were for him secondary in importance to that shared photographic "essence." Where *Theory of Film* explores the epistemological questions posed by the photo image, references are to photography rather than film. Kracauer's principal examples are images by American photographers like Robinson, Stieglitz, Strand, Sheeler, Steichen, Weston, Adams, which he found in the photo collection of the New York Museum of Modern Art, in photo journals, and in the 1949 history of photography by MOMA's photography curator Beaumont Newhall. (The current cultural interest in photography, which has stimulated a wealth of historical monographs, is of fairly recent date). In tracing back to the "area of photography itself" the cinematic conflict between "documentary tendency" and "story tendency," Kracauer seems to have followed suggestions made by Erwin Panofsky, with whom he corresponded about his planned "study of film esthetics" in 1948 and 1949.[10]

Kracauer's emphasis was not, then, on the meanings of a mimetic image flow in cinematic representation. Rather, his deepest interest was in the act of seeing now, having present in the photo image, still or moving, what had been there all along in the visible world but was not seen before.[11] In an essay of 1960 which explores the "The Creative Use of Reality" in film, the experimental filmmaker Maya Deren provides an instructive contrast. Kracauer referred to her work repeatedly in *Theory of Film* and enlisted her help when discussing avant-garde film.[12] However, I cannot see him accepting her distinction, made in the later article, between the photo image as a creation of the object itself by the action of light (and light-sensitive materials) and the painterly image as the likeness of a mental concept. For Deren a graphic image can be realistic, but the photograph is "*a form of reality itself.*"[13] For Kracauer, the photo image reflects, as a matter of course, the photographer's mental image of the object. And the painterly image is, in most cases, a likeness of a mental image developed in interactive response to a visible shape or color. Significantly, after making extraordinary claims for the photo image, Deren is interested mainly in its "transfiguration" in the editing of a film, "which gives particular or new meaning to the images *according to their function.*" The creative action in film, in her view, occurs in its "time dimension; and for this reason the motion picture, though composed of spatial images, *is primarily a time form*" (61f.).

It is the very "objectivity" of the image which makes it omni-disposable in the eye of the filmmaker. Significantly, Deren separates the "witnessing" camera from the film artist's "creating," and the "vocabulary of filmic images" from the "syntax of filmic techniques" (62, 65). Kracauer is not interested in the homogeneous objectivity of the photo image or in the camera as the perfect, "pure" instrument of witnessing. In his understanding, photo image and witnessing are composite, reflecting the use made of the instrument by the human eye, that is, subjected to the shapings and colorings of perception, of mental images. Such compositeness includes, with position in time and space, the temporality of the pictured. In a sense, the commonly invoked cinematic spatialization of time is, for Kracauer, a property of the photo image.[14] Writing a "theory of film," unlike Deren, he explicitly does not treat the photo image as "only the beginning, the basic material of the creative process."[15] Because he is interested above all in the epistemological implications and cultural status of the composite nature of the photo image: a kind of knowledge that is interdependent with the shaping and shading of objectivity.

Depending on the pictured, the picture, and the viewer, photographic reproduction can enlarge and enrich the perception of what has been reproduced: looking at the photo image, the viewer (including the photographer) can recall so far obscured, therefore new, phenomena into the present. It was precisely this potential that for Kracauer constituted the link between photography and historiography. After the completion of *Theory of Film*, when he was in the beginning stages of writing *History*, Kracauer explicitly stated this connection, which, as he saw rightly, had been underlying his work for many decades: "This essay on history, I suddenly saw, is the direct continuation of my *Theory of Film*: der [!] *historian has traits of the photographer, and historical reality resembles camera reality*."[16] The implications of such "camera reality" for the historian are clear: to bring back what was means to reconstruct the experienced quality of events, acts, agents, and things so that they can be re-called into the present. And such recalling involves, too, revealing new, because thus far obscure dimensions of past experience—obscure both to the past contempory participators in that experience and to its past historians looking at it from its past future.

The cultural status of photography and film, then, is not defined by autonomous creation. Film is "art with a difference" because in order "to make us experience physical reality, films must show what they picture."[17] This is the central and indeed, as Kracauer knew, subversive message of the book.[18] The "requirement" that films show what they picture "is so little self-evident that it raises the issue of the medium's relation to the traditional arts."[19] His argument for a special artistic status of photographic in contrast to painterly images seemed deeply irritating to those critics who wished photography to be appreciated as a serious, "truly" artistic medium. In their eyes, Kracauer had unduly limited photographic vision to a world anchored in everyday life. He had thereby invoked the trivial experiences shared by many and very diverse viewers rather than the educated sensibilities of serious art lovers. From a position of naive or idealistic realism, he had not allowed the new medium to create its own authority and thus had robbed it of its art status.[20]

Actually, Kracauer had done something very different, namely argued that there are different epistemological conditions for photographic and painterly images. This had been his argument, too, in the 1927 essay "Die Photographie." But his discussion of these conditions in *Theory of Film* shows how far he had left behind many of the notions articulated in the earlier piece, which now appear largely uninformed and obfuscating generalities.[21] We will look at his argument in the earlier text once more because its neo-Platonic resonances are so instructively linked to the attempts to make *authoritative* statements about the cultural status of the new medium. "Die Photographie" was influenced by Proust's reservations about photography, and it in turn was to influence Benjamin's currently (and curiously) canonical essays, "The Work of Art in the Age of Mechanical Reproduction" (1936) and "On Some Motifs in Baudelaire" (1939). Like Benjamin's, Kracauer's argumentation in this piece is neither coherent nor consistent–quite apart from the (for him) relatively unusual tortuous language, which echoes Adorno's and Benjamin's.[22]

In *The Guermantes Way* Proust distinguishes between seeing a loved face through the perspective of familiarity, shaped by many repeated acts of perception in time, and seeing the same face through the perspective of a camera lens, which, instantaneous and mechanical, causes alienation. In some portions of his argument (24–28), Kracauer's response to Proust is enlarged imitation. His juxtapositions between the collecting, fragmenting, storing, arresting, even deadening properties of the photograph and the "somehow" sublating, meaningfully preserving, enlivening properties of the work of art are very close to what we find, more than a decade later, in Benjamin's essays. For Benjamin, reproducibility, the product of the new visual technology, is a problem rather than an achievement of cultural modernity, even where he seems to celebrate it. His argument moves erratically around the relation, as it appears in the eyes of the viewer whose gaze ruptures (mere) surfaces, between the inauthenticity of the photo image and the authenticity of the work of art. For Kracauer the crucial issue is not authenticity. In fact, there is no one crucial issue but a number of conflicted attempts to probe the meanings of photography for identity construction and for the "truth content" of memory images.[23] There also are distinct traces of the familiar hierarchical lineup of the painterly and the photographic portrait based on the neo-Platonic dichotomy of essence versus appearance.

> For in the work of art the significance of the object becomes its spatial appearance, while in photography the spatial appearance of an object is its significance. The two spatial appearances, the "natural" one and that of the recognized, known object are not congruent. By sublating the former for the sake of the latter, the work of art condenses at the same time the *similarity* produced by the photograph. It [photographic similarity] refers to the appearance of the object, which does not easily betray in what way it can be known; but the transparency[24] of the object is mediated solely by the work of art. In that it [the work of art] is like a magic mirror that reflects the person questioning it not as he appears but as he wishes to be or as he substantially is. The work of art, too, decomposes in time; but from its crumbling particles emerges what it was meant to signify, while photography stores away the particles. (27)

This cumbersome argument puts Kracauer, too, in the armchair metaphysics of difference. He shows remarkably little interest in the aesthetic and epistemological questions that were increasingly put to photo images by the practitioners of photography in the twenties. Yet–and here lies the importance of his in many ways troubled "theoretical" argument–Kracauer has not lost sight of the problem central to the cultural meaning of the new medium: the relation between the picture and the pictured. He shows less concern about the photo image "itself" than about its potential for bringing out the nature of the pictured. There is the shadow of an insight into a desirable multiplicity of viewings. Importantly, critical consideration of different acts of viewing the picture and the pictured would diffuse the position and imposition of an ideal viewer, usually a clone of the critic. This establishes a connection to Kracauer's argument, in another part of the essay, against self-consciously artistic photography as both dilettantish and anachronistic. Unwilling (unable) to fit its object to the specific photographical conditions, it is a throwback to nineteenth-century staging and draping. It obscures rather than clarifies the *shared* surfaces of daily life shaped by modern technology (35–39).

2 "Die Photographie," like Benjamin's essays on reproducibility, was written in a curious cultural vacuum as far as both critics' knowledge of the contemporary practice of photography was concerned. From hindsight, this seems more remarkable in Kracauer's case because of his concrete engagement with the ongoing business of culture and his activities as a film critic. (He would explicitly grant to films the knowledge poten-

tial of a now more clearly secularized "transparency" in his 1940 German draft of *Theory of Film* and in the 1947 *From Caligari to Hitler.* In his film reviews of the late twenties and early thirties, he implicitly attributed a similar potential to those films that documented successfully a contemporary social-psychological reality). By 1927 the "new photography," reflecting a growing sophistication of photo technology, had begun to provoke lively debates on the different methods and meanings of photographic representation. In 1925, the year of the seminal *Neue Sachlichkeit* art exhibition in Mannheim, Lászl6 Moholy-Nagy published in the Bauhaus series his *Malerei, Photographie, Film* based on three years of experimenting with photograms. Kracauer drew on it repeatedly in *Theory of Film* but not in the essay "Die Photographie." Moholy-Nagy declared here his unbounded enthusiasm for the potential of the medium: "When the true qualities of photography are recognized, the process of representation by mechanical means will be brought to a level of perfection never before attained. Modern illustrated magazines are still lagging behind, considering their enormous potential! And to think what they could and must achieve in the field of education and culture."[25]

The debate carried over into the magazines. In 1927, *Deutsches Lichtbild* published Moholy-Nagy's and Albert Renger-Patzsch's statements on the significance of the new medium, both emphasizing strongly its artistically independent status. For Moholy-Nagy, photography's special place among the visual arts was defined by its sensitivity to light, which made for its experimental qualities (fig. 28). Renger-Patzsch, on the other hand, found the secret of a good photograph, its aesthetic qualities, in its particular kind of realism. He pleaded to "leave art to the artist, and let us try–with photographic means–to create photographs that can stand alone because of their very *photographic* character–without borrowing from art."[26]

A good example of such photographic (super)realism was Renger-Patzsch's book on nature photography, *Das Photographieren von Blüten* (1924). He described "the excitement" of the photographic experience as making visible, with the help of the camera, aspects of the natural world normally invisible to the human eye. Looking through a lens, the photographer's eye, adjusting to a relatively small organism like a flower, "must see, as it were, through the eyes of an insect."[27] In *Die Welt ist schön* (1928; first entitled *Die Dinge*), Renger-Patzsch juxtaposed, without captions, natural and industrial objects in order to exhibit their inherent beauty and the formal connections that could be made between them. This photo book was so successful that Thomas Mann reviewed "this astonishing picturebook" in *Berliner Illustrirte Zeitung*.[28] He found the photographs to be "exact statements drawn from the whole–and that's the way it usually is with this man who is, in his way, impassioned. The detail, the objective is removed from the world of appearances, isolated, sharpened, made meaningful, animated. What more, I would like to ask, has art or the artist done?"[29] Admitting some uneasiness with respect to the "technification" of the artistic, Mann characteristically concluded with an uplifting suggestion: "But what if, since the spiritual has been superseded by the technical, the technical proves to be spiritualizing?"[30] The issue for Thomas Mann and (many of) his contemporary readers was not whether or how that could happen. It was, rather, the insinuation of a powerful combined demonization and domestication of technology that was attractive to a broad spectrum of audiences, including Hitler's, at the end of the Weimar period. Renger-Patzsch's indeed stunning images of landscapes (fig. 18) and of natural and technical objects were vulnerable to this kind of interpretive viewing precisely because their technical excellence and emotional reticence suggested "objectivity" as availability. There are images of trees which anticipate in certain ways Ansel Adams's "Aspens," made in the 1950s, and some of his formally explorative plant images (fig. 20) evoke Paul Strand's and Laura Gilpin's work of about the same time.[31] Renger-Patzsch's shapely, even decorative, and yet powerful photographs of industrial objects (figs. 17, 19, 21) show visual and conceptual focus (fig. 16) similar to Charles Sheeler's and Strand's in the 1920s, and 1930s.[32] Neither Sheeler nor Strand, however, juxtaposed images of nature and technological culture so dramatically; more importantly, they worked in a culture less dramatically torn by the modern conflict between the experience of nature and technology. Renger-Patzsch's technical excellence and his delight, stated repeatedly, in the potential of photographic technology opened his images to viewings that emphasized either the spiritual or the formalistic aspects of his work. The issue was not his "idealistic concept of realism" but his great technical dedication to the making of visually pleasurable images in politically troubled times.[33]

The great commercial success of the excellently printed book encouraged the savvy publisher Kurt Wolff to come out with another photo book the following year, August Sander's *Antlitz der Zeit*, a critical if not a commercial success.[34] Alfred Döblin, author of *Berlin Alexanderplatz* (1929), wrote an intelligent introduction to the collection, which he described as "a kind of cultural history, even a sociology of the last thirty years."[35] Those last thirty years, of course, had brought extraordinary social and political changes, and it was the documentation of these changes which Döblin admired and thought particularly useful:

> Men are shaped by their livelihood, the air and light they move in, the work they do or do not do, and moreover the special ideology of their class. . . . The class structure is undergoing a revolution, the cities have grown enormously, some originals are still there but new types are already developing. . . . The divisions between youth and adulthood have become less clear, the dominance of youth, the urge for rejuvenation and for renewal, which has even biological effects, has become obvious. Whole stories could be told about quite a lot of these photographs; they invite us to tell stories. As subject matter, they are more stimulating and they yield more than many newspaper reports. These are my suggestions. He who knows how to look will be enlightened more effectively by them than by lectures and theories. Through these clear and conclusive photographs he will discover something of himself and others. (59)

Döblin, a socially engaged writer, thought particularly important the accessibility of the portraits. Sander's photos had a curious power to show both pastness and contemporaneity, enabling the viewer at the end of the Weimar period to share a past with the presences created in the images. Fittingly, the more or less contemporary presences, recorded in the 1920s and reflecting an advanced photographic technology, were more forcefully distinct. Sander explicitly photographed individuals as representing professions and occupations. But these images of nameless "peasants," "artists," "aristocrats," "artisans," "civil servants," "students," and "clerks" also show, through the many different shades of acculturation, the individuality of the sitters, because their pictures were not so much taken as offered. Literally self-composed, they looked back at the photographer, presenting themselves naturally as social beings. Sander strove for the fullest possible documentary completion. His remarkable ability to "happen" on representative subjects, to penetrate "the type" without intruding, resulted in a precise and suggestive social portraiture that has indeed become an important contribution to the social history of Germany in the first half of the twentieth century.[36]

Like Renger-Patzsch, Sander was highly conscious of the specifically modern potential of the medium he worked in. John Szarkowski, whose history of photography aims to "sketch out a history of photographic pictures, organized according to patterns of technological change," notes a revision of style in the twenties, citing the images of photographers like Alfred Stieglitz, August Sander, and Edward Weston. They were all well known for their earlier work, and their adoption of a new "technical vocabulary" reflected the influence of the rapidly developing commercial photography of the twenties: "full-scale negatives that yielded brilliant prints on smooth, hard-finished papers that revealed maximum detail and tonal nuance. The change of direction exemplified in the work of these exceptional artists was international and apparently intuitive, with theoretical rationales trailing behind the fact of change."[37]

One would expect that Kracauer saw reviews of Sander's volume, if he did not actually see the photos (figs. 5–10). Sander's images share qualities–a reflected imaginative realism–that Kracauer sought out and praised in his film reviews of the late twenties, if not in "Die Photographie."[38] In the introduction to *Theory of Film*, "Photography," where he explicitly dealt with the question of knowledge specific to the photographic media, Kracauer recapitulated the nineteenth-century debate between realism and pictorialism, pointing out the "naive realism" on both sides. The debate concerned the use of the camera as either a reproducing, recording device (and, as such, a potential source of inspiration for the artist) or a means of artistic photography which, in the effort to beautify the reproduced object, relied on manipulation of the negative. This debate was naive, Kracauer thought, because it did not take into consideration the "kind and degree of creativeness that may go into a photographic record" (7). Modern realists, in contrast, no longer assume that we can see reality as it is, but "that reality is as we see it" (8).

This is an important point, of course; still, such summary assessment of modern notions of perception glosses over a great many difficulties that are still hotly argued, and Kracauer himself repeatedly acknowledges the ongoing problem. Moreover, he asserts an important connection between modern and ninteenth-century realists in that both emphasize the reproducing and revealing properties of the camera. In Kracauer's scenario, both the "naive" and the modern realist appreciate, above all, the camera's help in seeing the natural cultural world. And here he (mis)quotes the American painter and photographer Charles Sheeler, who defined the photograph's achievement as making the "best statement of facts" (8). The reference to Sheeler raises a set of intriguing problems with respect to the visual potential of photography on which Kracauer touches here. But he leaves them unresolved, and they will come up again in *History*. Sheeler's remark has to be seen in its context, an explanation of his professional experience that he gave to his biographer, Constance Rourke, in the late thirties. Looking back on his development, he said:

> I have come to value photography more and more for those things which it alone can accomplish, rather than discredit it for the things which can only be achieved through another medium. In painting I have had a continued interest in natural forms and have sought the best use of them for the enhancement of design. In photography I have strived to enhance my technical equipment for the best statement of *the immediate* facts."[39]

I emphasize the two words Kracauer omitted, possibly in order to stress *fact*. But *immediate* refers to a particularly direct, unadulterated kind of visuality which is interdependent with photographic technology and is therefore medium specific. Precisely this situation was of great interest to Kracauer, and Sheeler's development as photographer and painter is quite instructive in this context. He began to be recognized as a painter through his photography of art works, ostensibly because it helped him to make connections in New York art circles. However, photographing his clients' collections of Chinese bronzes, pre-Columbian sculpture, North and Central American Indian pots and paintings on hide, African sculpture, Duchamp, Derrain, Picasso, Braque, especially Cézanne, he found a universality of form and structure: "All the arts we revere came out of the main trunk. An underlying current goes through all the way to Renaissance, Chinese, back to cave painting."[40] The camera had proved to be an invaluable help in the process of learning to see. Transmitting this experience to his painting, Sheeler frequently used photo images, his own and others', as a visually symbiotic source for and presence in his abstractionist realist paintings. He was interested, from the beginning, in a process of mutually elucidating visual metamorphoses–for instance, in the relation between his series of photographs of his farmhouse and barn in Doylestown, Bucks County, Pennsylvania, from about 1914 to 1917 and the series of Bucks County drawings between 1915 and 1917 (figs. 14, 15).[41]

In December 1917, Sheeler had his first one-man show in Marius de Zayas's Modern Gallery, which quickly established him as an important photographer. A press release for the exhibition reads: "Sheeler says that his object has been to prove that the principal elements in modern art are sensorial and exist in nature; that the impersonal lens has furnished proof of the fundamental truths in modern art." *Impersonal* here refers to the "objective" property of the camera only, not of the photograph. Sheeler had written to Stieglitz in November about his Doylestown house photographs included in the impending exhibition: "I decided that because of something personal which I was trying to work out in them, that they were probably more akin to drawings than to my photographs of paintings and sculptures."[42]

There was critical acclaim for the technical quality of Sheeler's "straight" photographs, the clarity of their realistic subjects, the fine printing, but above all for their revelatory properties: "The camera has registered certain effects and qualities hitherto seen only in the works of Pablo Picasso and his ablest followers."[43] Half a century later, in a 1975 interview, Paul Strand looked back on that period in his and Sheeler's work: "Sheeler and I were aware that we were beginning to experiment with abstraction. . . . It had to do with understanding a painting like a Villon or a Braque–things in which there is an enormous amount of movement and no recognizable content as a whole" (fig. 13).[44] In neither Strand's nor Sheeler's case did this experimentation lead to formalist experimentalism in photography. It prepared for more persuasively articulated visual presences of people and their environments because the photographers' interest was focused on a shared and sharable visual experience. Edward Steichen remarked that "Sheeler was objective before the rest of us were."[45] He did not refer to the deliberate objectivism of socially engaged documentary photography in the thirties. Nor did he refer to the ostensibly objective focus on human variety to be found in his own hugely successful exhibition, *The Family of Man.* (Kracauer singled this exhibition out for praise at the end of *Theory of Film* because it demonstrated so clearly the authenticating properties of the photo-image). Steichen meant, rather, images like Sheeler's 1917 "Side of White Barn" (fig. 14), "an abstract, flat study in whites," which rightly has been admired for its "strong sense of inherent design and a rendering of textures which has been unsurpassed."[46] He meant Sheeler's disciplined surrender to the visible which can integrate experimentation.

3 The connections sketched here show the complexity of the experimentation issue, to which Kracauer was to return again and again in *Theory of Film* and in certain portions of *History*. He was most probably unfamiliar with the different aspects of Sheeler's oeuvre, but he had seen Weston's photographs and read his 1943 essay, "Seeing Photographically," and referred repeatedly to it. In the introduction to *Theory*, he quotes Weston's valuing highly "the unique precision with which instantaneous photography mechanically registers fine detail and 'the unbroken sequence of infinitely subtle gradations from black to white'"–gradations that had enchanted Sheeler twenty years earlier.[47]

In fact, the Weimar debates on the "new photography" in the late twenties had been anticipated in the United States by discussions of pure or "straight" photography since the early years of the century.[48] Stieglitz, though seen as a preeminent pictorialist, had been practicing straight photography for some time (fig. 11) when in the last issues of *Camera Work*, dated 1916 and 1917, he reproduced photos by the then unknown Paul Strand which he praised as "brutally direct, pure and devoid of trickery." The most brutally direct would be the well-known "Blind Woman 1916" (fig. 12). But in its disclosure of age "Portrait–Washington Square, New York 1916" is more powerfully direct in the sense of accessible, precisely because the woman's face registers her consciousness of the camera.[49] Stieglitz's own one-man show in 1921 exhibited photo images of "startling" directness that had an "electric effect" on the public and were praised by the critics for their consummate "straightness."[50] These images affirmed Strand's photographic concept formulated in 1917:

> The photographer's problem is to see clearly the limitations and at the same time the potential qualities of his medium, for it is precisely here that honesty no less than intensity of vision is the prerequsite of a living expression. This means a real respect for the thing in front of him expressed in terms of chiaroscuro . . . through a range of almost infinite tonal values which lie beyond the

> skill of the human hand. The fullest realization of this is accomplished without tricks of process or manipulation through the use of straight photographic methods.[51]

In *Theory of Film*, Kracauer was to quote from this statement in the context of arguing the urgency of the world out there to become more fully visible. Much impressed by Strand's images that bore out his advice to the photographer to have "real respect for the thing in front of him" and "intensity of vision," Kracauer would refer to him repeatedly.[52] On the advice of Stieglitz, Strand had developed a technique of optical sharpness, the fine prints for which he became known. The photographs published in the last issues of *Camera Work* document his attempts at enhancing his vision of the world of shared objects through the visual abstraction he had found in abstract modernist art. Looking back on that learning process, he wrote to Helmut Gernsheim in 1960: "Once understanding what the aesthetic elements of a picture were, I tried to bring this knowledge to objective reality. . . . Nor have I ever returned to pure abstraction, as it had no further meaning for me in itself. On the other hand, subject matter all around me seemed inexhaustible." Colson, who quotes this statement (110), poses the question of Strand's photographic realism in terms of

> three important paradoxes that exist in the traditional concept of straight photographic style. One paradox holds that straight photography must be true to the medium, that is, significantly and observably a photograph, and yet be transparent in its power to bring the viewer to realism, to a direct sense of the subject. A solarized, grainy negative might be truly photographic, but it is not suited to traditional straight photography. For the serious straight photographer, all photographic decisions and operations culminate in the fine print, complete with elegant tone and sharpness. The high order of craftsmanship does justice both to the medium and to the subject. The fine print is obviously not the subject rendered, its reference to the real world is properly called representation, and the best straight photography produces in the viewer's mind a coexistence between a sense of the print and a sense of that which the print represents. (*How* photography represents is, of course, another philosophical question.) (116)

It is curious that Colson brackets this last observation since what he thinks the "second paradox of straight photography" goes right to the heart of it: for Strand, straight photography had to aim beyond fine craftsmanship, combining accuracy of documentation with personal vision. When he praised the "pleasure of craftsmanship" in the early twenties, he qualified: "And if you can find out something about the laws of your own growth and vision as well as those of photography you may be able to relate the two, create an object which has a life of its own, which transcends craftsmanship." Half a century later, Strand clarified that he did not "make a fine print for the sake of fineness. I do it because I want to make it as expressive as possible. My whole life takes cognizance of the problem of craft and skill, of creative use of the material to say what I have to say as forcefully as possible."[53]

The "third paradox" is in Colson's view the question of photographic realism as art, that is, the "variety that exists for personal vision within the constraints of traditional straight photography"–for photographers like Strand (fig. 12), Atget (figs. 3, 4), Edward Weston (figs. 23–27), Walker Evans (figs. 30–33). Significantly, he quotes here Strand's remarks on the differences between the prints he made from the same negatives over a period of almost fifty years: "The difference is there visually; I think very clearly. It's a curious thing that as you change in life, there are differences as you grow older, in the way you feel about things, things that reflect themselves in print quality. You may find that the prints you're making now are a little more brilliant than those you made 30 or 40 years ago, and that for some reason you want that and you work for it" (117f.). The variables of the printing process extend the potential for "personal vision," and they explicitly do not subvert the documentary thrust of the photo image. Colson's "three paradoxes" are in actuality three aspects shared by all photo images insofar as they intend representation. The seductive something that we call "art" is a product of their peculiar interaction.

Strand's images, admired as models of "straight" photography, helped Ansel Adams in the early thirties to understand what photography was about (and to give up the piano for its sake). Looking at some of Strand's negatives, he saw "full luminous shadows and strong high values in which subtle passages of tone were preserved. The compositions were extraordinary: perfect uncluttered edges and beautifully distributed shapes that he had carefully selected and interpreted as forms. . . . My understanding of photography was crystallized that afternoon as I realized the great potential of the medium as an expressive art." The camera, as he rightly saw, would shape his "destiny." Promptly, Adams abandoned his textured photographic papers and began using

> the same smooth, glossy-surfaced papers used by Paul Strand and Edward Weston to reveal every possible detail of the negative. I am unsure how much this change in paper affected my photographic "seeing," but I suddenly could achieve a greater feeling of light and range of tones in my prints. I felt liberated; I could secure a good negative born from visualization and now consistently progress to a fine print on glossy paper.[54]

This feeling is expressed in Adams's contribution to the written manifesto of Group f.64. Founded informally in 1932 in the Berkeley home of a fellow photographer, Willard Van Dyke, it was named after the designation, in the new aperture-marking system, of a small lens aperture (identical with the old U.S. 256) used by most members of the group for greater sharpness and depth. The group saw itself as representing the "renewed interest in the philosophy of straight photography: that is, photographs that looked like photographs, not imitations of other art forms." The manifesto stated the group's credo that "pure" photography as an art form "must develop along lines defined by the actualities and limitations of the photographic medium, and must always remain independent of ideological conventions of art and an aesthetics that are reminiscent of a period and culture antedating the growth of the medium itself."[55]

Adams, whose "technical prowess was legendary,"[56] defined the aesthetics of his medium from the position of the practitioner. So did other members of the group, like Imogen Cunningham or Edward Weston, on whom Kracauer would draw as a witness for the photograph's extraordinary potential for reproducing and revealing presences. Weston had organized the American contribution to the 1929 "Internationale Ausstellung des deutschen Werkbunds" (the connection to the German organizers had been made by Richard Neutra, a practitioner of the "International Style" in Los Angeles since 1926). In his text for the catalogue, "Amerika und Fotographie," Weston pleaded for honest, "straight" photography in terms that anticipated the manifesto of Group f.64 three years later. The camera's potential is for a "clear" and "powerful" penetration of the "thing itself," not for impressionist fuzziness; the emphasis is on distinct objects rather than atmosphere or mood.[57] Photography for Weston is art insofar as is it a genuinely modern form of expression, the result of a particular kind of seeing made possible by the camera (14). This kind of seeing comprises abstraction as well as realism–as Weston recorded in his Mexican *Daybooks* (1922–26): "The camera should be used for a recording of *life*, for rendering the very substance and quintessence of the *thing itself*, whether it be polished steel or palpitating flesh. . . . I shall let no chance pass to record interesting abstraction, but I feel definite in my belief that the approach to photography is through realism."[58]

In Kracauer's view, the realization of this belief was not unambiguous; he always suspected Weston's fascination with visually available abstraction. And yet, Weston as well as Moholy-Nagy was important for his argument precisely because of his interest in making visible the thing-in-itself beyond easily recognizable surfaces. Partly for that reason Kracauer tended to oversimplify the inclination toward abstraction in Weston's photography.[59] If Weston shared Moholy-Nagy's enthusiasm for modern phototechnology (fig. 28) as the "golden key opening the doors to the wonders of the external universe,"[60] he did not participate in the latter's severing, as Kracauer put it, "the umbilical cord, tenuous anyway, between realistic and experimental photography" (10). Despite his own profound, if ambivalent, reservations against photographic experimentalism, Kracauer emphasized here that modern photographers, regardless of their orientation in this respect, join in their understanding of the camera's potential for a new, modern vision of the world. This vision is informed by a mobile, changing perspective that will result in changeable, not completely accessible or knowable objects. (In *History* Kracauer would argue that it is precisely this perspective that produces historical knowledge in modernity.) Coming from what seem to be different positions, they still meet in certain important aspects of their practice, namely their dependency on a modern, developing technology.

If Kracauer shows a clear preference in *Theory of Film* for the realists among modern photographers, it is because of their literally "evident" contribution to modernity. In enlarging our vision, modern photography has adjusted it to our situation in a period of rapid technological development that has consistently undermined stable sensory and intellecutal impressions: "We find ourselves increasingly surrounded by mental configurations which we are free to interpret at will. Each is iridescent with meanings, while the great beliefs or ideas from which they issue grow paler. Similarly, photography has impressed upon us the dissolution of traditional perspectives" (9). Kracauer's assessment of the role played by realist photography in the development of art in the first decades of the twentieth century is suggestive in this context. No longer a helpmate to nineteenth-century realist painters, realist photography was involved in the process of de-composing, as it were, the visual conventions of painting; in certain ways, the two media have converged. (Here the example of Sheeler would have been of great value to Kracauer's argument.) Modern photography and abstract painting maintain the same distance from the outdated images of reality characteristic of a technically less developed period. "Hence the 'abstract' character of those records and the surface similarity to them of certain modern paintings" (9f.).

Rooted in his overriding concern for the medium-specific recording and preserving potential of the photo image, Kracauer's ambivalence toward experimental photography may have prevented him from pursuing this line of thought. The implications of a symbiosis, at a certain stage in the development of modern painting, between phototechnology and the radical revision of conventions in the new spatial perception of abstract painting are highly intriguing. But Kracauer was above all interested in a clarification of what he saw as the enduring aesthetic and epistemological conflict between the photographer's artistic, or "creative," and realistic impulses. Even where they practice "straight" photography, strongly experimental photographers like Leo Katz, Andreas Feininger, Moholy-Nagy, and Otto Steinert are in his eyes the descendants of the artistic or pictorial photographers of the nineteenth century. In their images and their self-explanations, these modern artist-photographers emphasize subjective vision, fantasy, abstraction, composition over realism, documentation, and the authority of the visible world (10f.). When in 1951 the *New York Times* published an article arguing against experimental photography and for "a straight approach to life,"[61] the lively responses were split into three camps: for, against, and despairing of a solution to the problem. Kracauer observed that it was exactly this state of affairs that had to be taken into consideration by an aesthetics of the photo image. In his usage, aesthetics is interdependent with the question of knowledge (12).[62]

4 Unlike Benjamin in his "Kleine Geschichte der Photographie," Kracauer did not see an, as it were, existential decline in the use of the new phototechnology from its beginnings. Rather, he emphasized both the enduring questions associated with the photographic medium and the growing importance of its potential to the process of modernity. Benjamin's text, published in the fall of 1931 in three installments in *Die literarische Welt* and, like his review essays in general, less "difficult," that is, less opaque, was based on materials related to the *Passagenarbeit*–as was the 1939 "On Some Motifs in Baudelaire."[63] The argument in both cases is fragmentary, erratic, and diffuse. But the contradictions can be pinned down more easily in the earlier piece, simply because they are less protected by the hermeticism that Benjamin practised in his "serious" texts. If there is no coherent argument in this sometimes suggestive essay, there is a clear message concerning the aesthetic-moral superiority of images produced in the early stages of photography: "The human face was surrounded by a silence in which the viewer's gaze came to rest. In short, all the potential of this art of portraiture was based on the fact that relations between actuality and photo had not yet been established" (372).

Written under the influence of Brecht, the essay is centered in Benjamin's empathetic reaction to early portrait photographs, a reaction that needed to be "somehow" connected to "social conditions." The repeated references to the relationship between photographic technique and photo image are general and ornamental. Benjamin establishes a link between the existential quality of the image and the camera's primitivity, which was responsible for certain lighting effects that account, up to a point, for the fact that the subjects of these portraits do not yet exhibit modern alienation and fragmentation. There still is what Benjamin describes as a protective *Aura* that, penetrating and penetrated by it, infuses their gaze with fullness and security.[64] But on a deeper, much more significant level, this *Aura*, this "*Hauchkreis*" (delicately pneumatic halo), is due to the correspondence in that early stage of photography between the subject of the photo image and photographic technique, a correspondence that later will be disrupted. For Benjamin the loss of *Aura* is inseparably linked to the decline of imperialist bourgeoisie in the 1880s, which ejected *Aura* from the photo image as well as from reality. Pictorialism, which in his scenario signifies a progress in photographic technique, revealed the impotence of that generation–photographers and non-photographers alike–when confronted with the (generally negative) advance of technology.

On the other hand, Eugène Atget's portraits of preurban spaces purged of human presence initiated, in Benjamin's view, the "liberation of the object from the *Aura*, which undoubtably is the achievement of the most recent school of photography." (The publication of the essay in several installments may have more easily accommodated such obvious conceptual "indeterminacy.") Atget's images "suck the *Aura* from reality like water from a sinking ship" (378). Benjamin sees Atget seeking out what has been lost or forgotten, an activity deeply satisfying to his own fascination with the significantly insignificant. Atget's unique vision is responsible for the demolition of *Aura* because it already exhibits that increasing (modern) sense of sameness that, by means of reproduction, includes also the unique. Thus Atget's "*surrealistische Photographie*" prepares for the "salutary estrangement" between people and their environment, clearing the field for the "politically schooled" gaze. Atget, an actor by profession, wiped off his mask, disgusted by "*Betrieb*" –a pun linking empty activity and industrial capitalist organization–and proceeded to remove the makeup from (bourgeois) reality (379, 377).

Benjamin's mistrust of the visible goes deep: all art uncovers and reveals the "true" reality underneath it; the best modern photographers, Moholy-Nagy among them, were practising artists before taking up photography. The worst tendencies in modern photography were developed in "creative" photography under the influence of advertising. Renger-Patzsch's images praising the beauty of the world are a prime example. *Die Welt ist schön* is nothing but a lie for Benjamin, since it is based on that simple reproduction of reality which, according to Brecht, does not reveal the real. (Modern) reality can only be found in the artificiality of "constructive" photography developed under the influence of surrealism and in Russian film, which, with its experimental and didactic impulses, has focused the conflict between "creative" and "constructive" photography (382–84). This argument, of course, does not consider the influence of progressive photo techniques in the advertisements of the 1920s on the technical and artistic development of many "serious" photographers, among them Sander, whom Benjamin admired.[65]

Benjamin was most concerned in this essay to reconcile his newly found

Brechtian-Marxist didacticism with his old neo-Romantic sensibilities which are at the root of his conceptual (rather than visual) appreciation of surrealistic constructs.[66] Thus he was unwilling to acknowledge that the conflicts and ambiguities of modernity could be solved by neither the constructivism of dialectics nor the transcending deconstructivism of his rupturing gaze (which Adorno turned into his negative dialectics). He was unwilling, then, to consider the implications of the fact that photography was a cultural novelty that posed new, unforeseen questions. Moreover, these questions would continue to hold surprises because they concerned a technologically developing medium in a technologically developing culture. At the end of the twentieth century, the problem of photography's art status as art has, if anything, become more entangled. Consider the arguments made during the controversy surrounding the exhibition (and public support) of the explicitly homosexual photo images produced by Robert Mapplethorpe, namely that the protective art status of the exhibit would have been less permeable if it had involved paintings. There is an expectation that photography deals with, is responsible to and for, a shared social reality, the actual actors and events. But photographs have also become "aesthetic objects" that are powerfully attractive to collectors on the basis not just of rarity and quality but also of currently fashionable cultural politics that enlarge and simplify, by aestheticized moralizing, what is different or unfamiliar. Mapplethorpe's pleasing images of young gay males have become part of multiculturally correct interior design of the nineties.[67] In this respect the cultural politics of Weimar seem curiously protected, innocently single-minded sixty years later—as, most probably, will ours in 2050.

The novelty of photography remained a challenge for Kracauer a century after its inception. Moreover, the challenge grew as his experience expanded in time. It was as if the sense of seeing was becoming ever more important in his efforts to orient himself in the new worlds of exile; as if the activities of leaving, moving, navigating, finding, leaving again had directed and redirected, shaped and reshaped, his vision as he went on. His film reviews of the Weimar period had provided a certain amount of training for this flexible, mobile position, which was reflected to a point even in those essays that dealt with film in ways not so remote from Benjamin's desire to draw an authoritative map of contemporary culture and singlehandedly authorize the position of the new medium. For instance "Kult der Zerstreuung Über die Berliner Lichtspielhäuser" (1926; "Cult of Distraction: On Berlin's Picture Palaces"), would provoke resonances in Benjamin's and Adorno's writings on film.[68]

The German term *Zerstreuung* signifies distraction connoting dispersion, diffusion, dissipation, but also amusement as entertainment to fill leisure time. This symbiotically layered meaning, impossible to render in English, is the focus of the essay and indeed a new phenomenon after World War I. Amusement had become a serious matter, and central to it was the new medium of film. There is the fastidious intellectual's irony in the description of the palatial Berlin movie theaters designed for mass audiences. But there is also a serious attempt to understand the significance of a new cultural development. "Palaces of distraction," their hallmark is "surface splendor" (91): "The community of worshippers, numbering in the thousands, can be content, for its gathering places are a worthy abode." If a "glittering, revue-like creature, *the total artwork of effects*," has crawled out of the movies, this reflects the fact that films have raised distraction "to the level of culture; they are aimed at the *masses*" (92). The culture of film is that of the masses.

But is the culture of the masses that of film? Here Kracauer's argument shifts to an intriguing if somewhat opaque discussion of the dynamics of modern mass society. In need of constructing two opposites to get a grip on the elusive phenomenon of "the masses," he juxtaposes their addiction to movie-going with bourgeois contempt for them and their amusement (93). But only in the provinces, not, it seems, in the metropolis, Berlin, with its 4 million inhabitants and plenitude of movie palaces. Kracauer sees life on the street transformed by a rapidly growing population, giving "rise to configurations which invade even domestic space"–mergings of public and private spheres–and bringing about some kind of dialectic revulsion. With rising self-consciousness, there "will also develop productive powers in the cultural and spiritual domain which are worth financing. The masses are no longer left to their own devices; rather, they prevail in their very abandonment." And then the sublation: the educated classes will be absorbed into the masses in a grand coming together to form the "*homogeneous cosmopolitan audience* in which everyone has the same responses, from the bank director to the sales clerk, from the diva to the stenographer." It would be an anachronism for the bourgeoisie to complain about "mass taste" because the socio-economic reality within which such tastes develop has changed. To accuse *Berliners* of being "addicted to distraction" is wrong because their "form of entertainment necessarily corresponds to that of commerical enterprise [*Betrieb*]" (93).

If Kracauer is less condescending and judgmental with respect to mass culture than Horkheimer and Adorno, and less creatively "constructive" in his attempts to describe it than Benjamin, his argument is still notably ambivalent. It becomes less so when he tries to understand the surfaces of modern mass culture, emphasizing the sincerity of a modern skepticism regarding lofty ideals and high culture: "Here [in the movies], in pure externality, the audience encounters itself; its own reality is revealed in the fragmented sequence of splendid sense impressions. Were this reality to remain hidden from the audience, they could neither attack nor change it; its disclosure in distraction is therefore of *moral* significance" (94). The "*disorder* of society" is reflected in the films of the period exhibiting the tension that precedes the "inevitable and radical change." If, walking in the streets of Berlin, one is "not seldom struck by the momentary insight that one day all this will suddenly burst apart," this same insight is triggered by contemporary film. For this reason, movie theaters ought not "flirt with the theater." Film "must aim radically towards a kind of distraction which exposes disintegration instead of masking it" (95).

Ideally, then, distraction (*Zerstreuung*) achieved by film signifies a literal dissipation of what masks social disintegration; it makes visible the reality of daily life. The rather forced play on the term suggests, with the leftist intellectual's formulaic insistence on an inherently radical self-knowledge of the masses, the modern relevance of the medium, film. If Kracauer seems seduced here by the avant-garde ritual of rotating "bourgeois" values into their opposite and constructing a curiously continuous significant rupture, he also seems to argue for the potential of film to produce social knowledge. He does that, however, much more concretely and coherently in his film reviews of the time. Nevertheless, there are insights in this in many ways troubled and dated piece which will come to fruition in *From Caligari to Hitler* but also, and more importantly, in *Theory of Film. Distraction* appears here transformed into the open-ended, indeterminate, fragmented, provisional, modern kind of knowledge associated with photography and historiography.

Theory of Film explores the cultural significance of photo images by asking explicitly how they engage the viewer, including the photographer, in a process of knowledge shaped by the contingencies of place and time. Kracauer realized that the enterprise was more difficult for better-informed observers, but he wanted to be as comprehensive as possible.[69] When his friend Lowenthal demurred at the term *theory* in the title and suggested reversing title and subtitle, Kracauer responded that this suggestion had been made before but that the press had rejected it. Besides, the term *theory* was fine with him: "The book presents a theory and it can only reach readers who want theory. I have a feeling that today more than ever there is an unknown audience who desires a certain rigor. The subtitle alone is fancy enough."[70]

He may have been right about the general interest in a rigorously systematic study of film, but he had not delivered it. As it turned out, the combined claims made in the title and subtitle provoked and misled many readers, and in quite instructive ways. Rudolf Arnheim began his review essay "Melancholy Unshaped," with a decidedly ambivalent statement: "When a specialized subject is treated intelligently, its particular essence is described by means of general categories. Caught, as it were, in the focus of a battery of floodlights, the illuminated theme points back, in turn, by reflection to the remote sources that make it visible. In this sense, Siegfried Kracauer's book *Theory of Film* is probably the most intellligent book ever written on the subject of film."[71] Kracauer, too intelligent for his own good (so the implication), has arrested, desiccated his subject in the abstracting circularity of his general categories. Arnheim, an experienced, sensitive viewer, clearly reacts to the "ought" with which Kracauer infuses both the "aesthetic" and "philosophical" (epistemic) questions posed by the filmic medium (181). At the same time he singles out for praise Kracauer's illustrating in detail "the medium's affinitiy with the flow of life."[72] He disagrees with some of Kracauer's judgments regarding the cinematic qualities of certain films, especially those dealing explicitly with the fantastic, arguing that the "criteria of the 'cinematic' and the 'realistic' overlap but do not coincide" (184–86).

However, Kracauer's argument in chapter 5, "History and Phantasy," concerns the equation of cinematic quality not with "realism" but with "camera realism" (84, 90f.). Arnheim does not help his critique by quoting Kracauer against himself in this context: "In fact, there is a passage in Kracauer's book where he admits that 'what accounts for the cinematic quality of films . . . is not so much their truth to our experience of reality or even to reality in a general sense as their absorption in camera-reality–visible physical existence.' Precisely."[73] But Kracauer does not "admit" in this one instance the importance of "camera-reality" to cinematic quality; it is the explicit center of his argument. Moreover, the quoted statement occurs in the context of a discussion of language in film in which Kracauer is at pains to emphasize the importance for film of the visible and the visual, the image (116–24).

Arnheim thinks "valid and important" the core of Kracauer's "thesis," which he sums up: "The photographic medium has made its most significant contribution by depicting the world, more extremely than has ever been done before, as an unbound, loosely knit continuum." This culmination of a tendency toward lifelikeness, which began in the arts and sciences of the Renaissance, signifies, for Arnheim, the contemporaneity of photography. Kracauer shares this view, as far as it concerns the modern attributes of the temporary and transient. But his deeper interest, the real focus of his study, is the medium's capacity to enable and support a shared experience over time of the concrete visible world. It is clear that Arnheim does not understand Kracauer's intentions when he invokes, once more, the age-old intellectual grievance against the visible that is not yet impregnated with personal significances, against surfaces that obscure a reality beneath, above, beyond. He quotes one of Kracauer's many attempts at describing the (ideal) photographer's peculiar immersion in the details of the visible world, even at the risk of getting lost in the "jungle of material phenomena,"[74] and comments:

> After all, it is the surface of reality we explore when we touch it only with our fingertips. Do we find that modern man, surfeited with photographs that crowd out the words in his reading matter and are the staple of his leisure time edification, is being led back to the highways? He is immensely better informed about the epidermis of the world at large, the appearance of what goes on; but we have good reasons to call him less wise than his counterpart of the prephotographic era. The addicts of photography seem highly distracted. They

> think less well. Their ever stimulated curiosity makes them lose themselves in the capillaries of the particular rather than move on the mainstream of life. Photographic information, potentially a magnificent source of knowledge, seems to serve as a powerful distraction from insight. The mere exposure to the visible surface of the world will not arouse ideas unless the spectacle is approached with ideas ready to be stirred up. (187)

I quote this passage in full because it reflects so clearly the suspicion of modernity which Arnheim shares with so many intellectuals across the cultural and political spectrum, if not with Kracauer. Speaking for *all* viewers of photographs and *exclusively* in terms of impoverishment, Arnheim thinks their vision arrested at the level of mechanical recording.[75] In *Art and Visual Perception,* he asserted that the "formation of representational concepts, more than anything else, distinguishes the artist from the non-artist": "The artist's privilege is the capacity to apprehend the nature and meaning of an experience in terms of a given medium and thus make it tangible. The non-artist is left 'speech-less' by the fruits of his sensitive wisdom. He cannot congeal them in adequate form. He can express *himself,* more or less articulately, but not his experience" (163).

Kracauer's interest, however, is not in separating the artist from the non-artist, and even less in a problematic distinction between self and experience. He wishes to explore how photo images with their peculiar openness to the visible world can present representational concepts in ways that enable a plurality of viewers to appreciate, with the freshness of these concepts, also new, surprising aspects of a world that had seemed familiar, and to respond to them in many different ways. Kracauer's emphasis, then, is on what viewers can *do.* He focuses on the enabling potential of photo images, still or moving, which is available also to the "taker" of these images, the photographer, who is also a viewer. Significantly, Arnheim reads into Kracauer's text a passive viewer (including the photographer), forcefully contradicting the core argument of the book. He links a "later refinement of fatigued cultures" to an interest in the "irrationality of minutely scanned surfaces; it takes the passive sensitivity of the unengaged spectator. Here we are greatly helped by a remark of Kracauer's on the possible role of melancholy in photographic vision: 'Now melancholy as an inner disposition not only makes elegiac objects seem attractive but carries still another, more important implication:

it favors self-estrangement, which on its part entails identification with all kinds of objects. The dejected individual is likely to lose himself in the incidental configurations of his environment, absorbing them with a disinterested intensity no longer determined by his previous preferences.' This observation, valid for individuals, also applies to phases of civilization."[76]

Kracauer's text does not authorize such extension. It simply says that melancholy and the attendant self-estrangement in being lost among images and unable to focus or shape perception can be found among certain photographers and viewers.[77] Moreover, these are aspects that detract from what, in Kracauer's view, is the photographic (cinematic) potential, its medium-specific contribution to modernity.[78] Arnheim uses this quote to assert that melancholy and the attendant "tendency toward the dissolution of form" are a "prevalent disposition of our time." The realistic tendency in Western art, he argues, has "produced a gradual decrease in visibility, complementary to an increasing surrender of the formative capacity of the human mind to the raw material of experience." His examples include the late impressionism of Monet as well as the photographic media and non-representational painting. Everywhere he finds this "abandonment of pictorial organization," which, "with the concomitant loss of visibility, is nothing else but the yearning for the unshaped, a return to the raw material of reality."[79]

Arnheim professes to be frightened by this yearning: the "realistic tendency" signifies to him an intolerable relinquishing of the

> active grasp of meaning that characterizes man's relationship to reality when he is in full possession of his mental powers. . . . The painter cultivates his pastes and fluids as a gardener cultivates his soil. . . . He no longer produces images but matter. And the matter he is creating with the refined chemicals of a late civilization is the world before the Creation, the attractive infinity and variety of chaos. It is the escape from the duty of man–the final refuge and the final refreshment. . . . Perhaps in this confrontation with primordial matter we resemble the underworld shadows of the Odyssey, eager to drink from the sacrificial blood so that the scenes of life might come back once more. (190f.)

Nothing could have been further removed from Kracauer's intentions–and fully accessible arguments–in *Theory of Film* than such anguish over the sacrifice of reason and form in contemporary art and the photographic media–and such willingness to participate in the sacrifice in order to be, perhaps, reborn. Arnheim anticipates here certain late twentieth-century, neoromantic "postmodern" arguments, which are also close to Benjamin's and Adorno's thought on the photographic media but quite alien to Kracauer's informed and searching explorations of modernity. The latter's steadfast modernism is located in the central and controlling argument concerning the interdependency of photo images and "camera-reality."

The camera lens anchors expectations of objectivity, even where it clearly allows its shaping in a variety of ways. Such anchoring is of the greatest importance to Kracauer, since on it he based his claim that photo images enable "redemption," "*Einlösung*." He meant by this a clarifying reclamation, a calling back into presence, of an intertwined natural-cultural environment within and into which develop human thoughts and deeds.[80] Kracauer knew very well that no theory in the strict sense would accommodate this enlarged vision of a "life-world" so that it could appear as its own evidence.[81] This could be done only by exploring how photo images remain burdened with the camera's vision no matter how much the photographer may have wished to abstract from it and how it is precisely this situation that illuminates, in stunningly literal terms, the obscurities of the unpredictable natural-cultural life-world with its modern plurality of meanings. Importantly for Kracauer, such illumination requires the activity of viewers, who have to look to their own experience to solve the puzzles presented in the photo image, which, as an image, is neither complete nor perfect. The photographic quality of this image is synonymous with its keeping present the "raw material" of the visible world–Arnheim took this expression from *Theory of Film*, where it occurs repeatedly[82]–despite and because of the photographer's shaping activities.

It might be useful to look at some of Kracauer's (verbal) cultural criticism during the Weimar period in terms of photographic illumination: the observer as photographer–the observer as viewer of photographs. There were his sketches,[83] precise and imaginative, of life in the modern city, which he collected many decades later in *Strassen in Berlin und anderswo* (1964). There was also the 1929 series of articles on the new, politically important "class" of the *Angestellten*, white-collar workers.[84] In both cases the detailed descriptions of surfaces, many of them seemingly insignificant and selected at random from the confusing visual wealth of modern urban life, served to elucidate the shapes of its contemporary reality and also of its historicity: unstable and in flux, it was as it continued to become.

5

In the first stage of exile, in Paris, Kracauer began to extend his cultural critique to past actuality; he became a historian. It is significant that this shift in perspective happened precisely at that time, suggesting the exile's intensified appreciation for the historically developed meanings of a culture with which he needed to become more familiar. Significantly, too, the focus of his inquiry was the immense popularity, that is, the high cultural effectiveness of an artist. *Jacques Offenbach und das Paris seiner Zeit* (1937; *Orpheus in Paris: Offenbach and the Paris of his Time*, 1938) was not conceived as a biography or social and cultural history but as a societal biography, "*Gesellschaftsbiographie*," of the Second Empire. Kracauer made this distinction in the foreword to the German edition, which unfortunately is not included in the American edition. By "*Gesellschaftsbiographie*" he meant the reconstruction of the artistic life of Offenbach within the society "which he moved and mobilized and by which he was moved and mobilized."[85] Like Cole Porter, whom he resembles in some important ways, Offenbach literally made society move with his seemingly effortless, instinctively "right" balancing acts between musical entertainment and art. Like Cole Porter, too, he responded to this society in his creations. Kracauer, who does not seem to have taken notice of Offenbach's American counterpart, was interested in precisely this vital interdependency, and he focused his biography of a period on it. Thus he warned his readers that they would not find "innermusikalische Analysen und Interpretationen." The theme of the study was, rather, Offenbach's "social function." And the motto, a Baudelaire quote, alerted his readers to the peculiarities of the biographer's perspective: "Que le lecteur ne se scandalise pas de cette gravité dans le frivole."

With its monarchies and dictatorships, its world fairs and revolutions, Offenbach's life-world, the Second Empire, was the immediate predecessor of twentieth-century European society, not only because it gave birth to an international economy and bourgeois republics but also because it gave birth to developments constituting twentieth-century cultural modernity. The scene of important and highly visible social, political, and artistic events, Paris of the nineteenth century was the only city whose history is European history. For this reason, too, Kracauer wrote a "*Stadtbiographie*," the biography of a city. At roughly the same time Benjamin worked on his study of Paris arcades, *Passagen*, from which the essay, "On Some Motifs in Baudelaire," was published in *Zeitschrift für Sozialforschung* (1939). Adorno had rejected the first version, "The Paris of the Second Empire in Baudelaire" (1938), because he thought it lacked a theoretical interpretation of the objects collected in Benjamin's descriptions. Imbued with magic under the viewer's gaze which ruptured the surfaces of daily life, they remained isolated, unmediated.[86] Adorno also wrote an aggressively negative review of *Jacques Offenbach*, accusing Kracauer of having failed to give a critical analysis of Offenbach's work in his society and of constructing, instead, "a preestablished harmony between society and author."[87] Adorno's critique was based on his static concept of (high) art and his a priori construct of the (in every sense) absolute negativity of art. He thus simply turned Kracauer's intentions against him, and Kracauer would eventually point out to him the formulaic rigidity of such arrested dialectic.[88]

Kracauer's critical interest was focused precisely on the meanings of the "harmony," the peculiarly easy fit, between the artist's work and society, which existed only during certain periods of Offenbach's creative life. He had begun thinking about the study in the summer of 1934 while finishing his novel, *Georg*, which, like *Ginster* (1928), was an autobiographical and autofictional essay in cultural critique.[89] In July he told Bloch that he would have to start working "like mad" on a new project involving much collection of material, which for financial reasons he wanted to complete as quickly as possible.[90] To Lowenthal he wrote in November that his new project might have some chance for success internationally and would be finished in about six to eight months: "That will be a tour de force! Fortunately almost all the material is in Paris."[91] He did not expect to make money with the novel, but thought that there was an audience for biographies. There was, but not for this kind of biography. It took Kracauer much longer to complete the project because he characteristically could not resist immersion in the wealth of material that he found in Paris. Another exile, Ernst Erich Noth, who also had left Frankfurt for Paris, described Kracauer working away contentedly:

> Du reste, il n'est pas très aisé de rencontrer cet auteur. . . . Kracauer a une préférence pour la demi-obscurité des tables anonymes de tel bistro inconnu, presque introuvable dans une rue calme et où il est sûr d'être le seul ou tout au

> moins l'un des rares clients. Il a d'ailleurs une étrange divination pour trouver ces coins paisible. C'est là qu'on peut le voir, tranquillement assis devant son verre de café, la pipe à la bouche et devant lui une serviette gonflée de papiers, de manuscrits, de notes qu'il vient de colliger pendant de longues et fructueuses fouilles dans les bibliothèques. C'est un travailleur indefatigable, consciencieux sans pédantisme; il est de la race de créateurs qui luttent inlassablement avec la matière vivante.[92]

This description documents well the sensual quality of Kracauer's intellectual curiosity. He could not help being delighted by the amount and wealth of the material, even if it slowed him down more than he could afford. Bringing to it his capacious interest, he did not wish to impress on the material his authority but rather to "master" it by subjecting himself to it. Only after he had absorbed and been absorbed by the evidence did he feel competent to interpret and judge that "harmony" between the composer and his audiences which he had found in certain periods of nineteenth-century French culture. In his foreword to *Jacques Offenbach*, he justified the centrality of the artist to a detailed "*Gesellschaftsbiographie*" of the Second Empire by pointing out the coincidence of Offenbach's "extraordinary sensitivity to the structure of the society in which he thrives. His ascent begins at that moment when all the preconditions for the popularity of operetta are in place. It will become clear that this popularity is tied to dictatorship, to the rule of high finance, to the success of the international economy, to the Boulevard and the fashionable Bohème who is at home here" (10).

Centering his argument on a composer of operettas, Kracauer thought he was able to avoid some of the major methodological pitfalls of sociological analyses of art. He explored the phenomenon of extravagant societal nurture for both the genre of operetta and Offenbach's artistic talents. Since he focused on clearly recognizable interdependencies, he did not have to interpret "out" of the art work social conditions reconstructed from contextual materials. This fallacy is very common in sociological readings of art, as Kracauer, referring to his *Offenbach*, pointed out almost twenty years later in the context of discussing Lowenthal's work in this area. Popular art does indeed reflect dominant social trends rather accurately, precisely because, unlike high art, it does not raise the issue of artistic individuality. Since Offenbach's Paris was comparatively short-lived and "well-defined," it had seemed possible to Kracauer to "be equally thorough in the representation of society and of Offenbach's works which enabled me to explain the decline of operetta after the fall of the Second Empire through social change." However, such reciprocal effects between the artistic product and its social context, though ideal for the sociologically interested interpreter, do not apply in the case of great literature, which was Lowenthal's subject and the source of his difficulties. Kracauer suggested stating the methodological dilemma in an introductory chapter and focusing on a "sociological anatomy of the individual himself" rather than on the mutual interdependency between the individual artist and society.[93]

Though Kracauer did not see it that way, such "anatomy" was also the real focus of his "*Gesellschaftsbiographie*" of Offenbach. In the foreword he gave yet another and, I think, the most important reason for Offenbach's centrality. He points out the composer's specific talent for mocking society: "Inflated dignity, empty authority, arrogated power–they have nothing to laugh about when, laughing, he demystifies them." The composer as "*Spottvogel*" (mocking bird) does not engage in demystification for its own sake. Offenbach's music evokes laughter and light, images of the good life float by; melodies of paradisaical serenity and gaiety join with the gentle, tentative skepticism of Ludovic Halévy's libretti. But this enchanting vision of the "*Spottvogel*" perspective turns upside down the familiar world and reverses cultural values. Kracauer intended to be congenial to the spirit of "genuine" operetta (11), namely the radical implications of its utopian impulses. But was that the spirit of operetta in general or of *this* composer's operetta in particular?

Immersing himself in the materials from which he constructed Jacques Offenbach's popularity, its meanings became clearer and less clear to Kracauer. The details of daily living reflected in popular art provide access to the social-psychological energies of a period, but the kind of access depends on the particularities of that period and the nature of the artistic response to it. If the meanings of this interaction have often eluded the contemporary intellectual observer, they have posed even more difficulties for the historian. Focusing his "*Gesellschaftsbiographie*" on an individual artist whose works pleased large audiences but who for Kracauer was also clearly a "great" artist, he took more liberties regarding selection and arrangement of his materials than a social historian of the period might have done. In some cases it may be precisely such liberties that facilitate access to the past, but this depends on the nature of that past which is inseparable from its significance for the present. For our context it is important to see that the claims Kracauer made for his study in his foreword were contradictory. He wrote *Jacques Offenbach* in very dark times. If he attempted a lightness of tone to suit Offenbach's music, it was not so much to help the book's commercial success as to reassert a degree of continuity with a past that seemed, under the circumstances, more and more irretrievable. Kracauer knew it to be a shared European past, but he also knew that access to it was, for the time being, peculiarly difficult.

It is as seductive as it is questionable to suggest subtexts, but I will be seduced for a moment. There is a sense in which Orpheus, Offenbach, and Kracauer merge in their response to the temporality and therefore elusiveness of their worlds. The effort to connect the past with the present found its most poignant articulation in Orpheus's failure to bring back the dead, to reverse the irreversible, and to make the past become the present. Looking at nineteenth-century Paris culture through the life of one particularly gifted individual, Kracauer in Paris did not deliver the proposed mutual elucidation of artistic production and social energies. From his position of exile in the late thirties, he was unable to do so. The rich evidence collected with a patient generosity he could not afford brought past lives into a present that, contrary to his intentions, could not fully accommodate them. Perhaps he had looked back too anxiously. Decades later, more rather than less at home in America, he would write in the introduction to *History* that in epistemological terms historiography, like photography, was still "largely a *terra incognita*" but that he had made it the "center of his preoccupations" because it would "at least enable us to look at the contemporary scene from a distance. History resembles photography in that it is, among other things, a means of alienation."[94] Such distance and alienation, as he knew then, were not to be seen as fixed or absolute concepts but as negotiable, indeed to be redefined from case to case.

6

When, after the completion of *Offenbach*, Kracauer decided to turn to a systematic study of film, he determined the direction of his work for the next two decades, though at the time he was motivated largely by practical considerations. When Kracauer briefly visited Paris in the fall of 1936, Adorno had suggested to him that he submit a longer piece of research for the *Zeitschrift für Sozialforschung* and, meaning to help him, had immediately written to Horkheimer about the matter. Kracauer, under great pressure from loss of status and economic security and deeply anxious about the difficult situation of family members in Frankfurt, was at that time particularly sensitive and protested Adorno's unauthorized intercession. Because he had been rejected by the Institute for Social Research on several occasions, he did not want to submit any work not officially invited by Horkheimer.[95] The relationship between Horkheimer and Kracauer had always been somewhat tense,[96] but it was Adorno who from now on would criticize, censor, and, in Kracauer's view, seriously interfere with the work of his former mentor. In January 1937, Horkheimer wrote to Kracauer that the Institute was going to support for several months the planned research project, "Masse und Propoganda," and in March Kracauer gave it the exclusive rights to it.[97]

In May 1937 Kracauer received from the institute two communications that would be of great importance for his professional future. Horkheimer alerted him to the extensive film library of the Museum of Modern Art in New York, which included a nearly complete documentation of German film from its beginnings. There was interest in exploring this material in terms of a connection between German social developments and film, and Horkheimer had suggested Kracauer as the most qualified person. Following Horkheimer's advice, Kracauer established contact with the film library. Two years later the offer of a position as special research assistant to finish his historical and sociological study of German film[98] facilitated his emigration to the United States in 1941.

In May 1937, Adorno delivered, in a long letter to Kracauer, a radical critique of his *Offenbach*, a more aggressively negative version of the review he published in *Zeitschrift für Sozialforschung*.[99] Such criticism coming from the most forceful member of the institute must have made Kracauer apprehensive about the fate of the "Masse und Propaganda" project because he discussed it repeatedly with other members. Horkheimer, who had extended the support for the project, received the completed essay in December 1937 and liked it, promising its publication in the next year. In the meantime Kracauer had been thinking about a "Film-Buch" and, with the help of Walter Landauer, who had been responsible for the German publication of *Jacques Offenbach* and was intrigued by the idea of a book on film,[100] decided to concentrate on that project rather than the planned study of *fin de siècle*. The ideas Kracauer had developed in the research on mass propaganda had also become important for his perspective on the social psychological role of Weimar film.

In the meantime, too, Adorno had been at work on Kracauer's essay, now titled "Totalitäre Propaganda." The letter Kracauer wrote him in August 1938 protesting the changes in his manuscript documents dramatically the difference between Kracauer's and Adorno's approaches to fascism in particular and to social phenomena in general. It also shows very clearly–and this is an intimately related issue–Adorno's attitude toward the insights and the conceptual strategies of other writers.

Adorno, Kracauer found, had censored and rewritten the piece, changing it beyond recognition. It is not the fact of Adorno's notorious ideological interference with contributions to the journal which is of interest here but rather the ways in which he imposed himself on another author's work.[101] Kracauer had tried to help his readers understand the ascent of fascism as a process and for this reason had also accommodated seemingly contradictory or inconclusive evidence. Thus he had emphasized the importance of an overriding will to power, shared by a large and socially diverse majority, for the apparently irresistible rise of fascism. Adorno, in his rewriting of Kracauer's text, had forced on a complex processual phenomenon the preconstructed formula, "capitalist" and "petty bourgeois," which explained everything about fascism, summarily and once and for all.

Kracauer was careful to admit that such abbreviations need not be entirely wrong and that in certain cases they had their uses. But in this case Adorno's "summary" procedure, in clear opposition to Kracauer's efforts to develop a conceptual grid for processual political phenomena by a processual evaluation of the evidence, was harmful and also contrary to Kracauer's intentions. Adorno had simply rewritten the essay from a Marxian-Freudian position, which increasingly equated the regressivity of fascism with capitalist (U.S.) mass culture–a position articulated most aggressively in *Dialectic of Enlightenment* (1944).[102]

Adorno had also cut the piece to a fifth of its original length.[103] On the basis of Adorno's letter of May 3, 1938, Kracauer had hoped that cutting would result in a presentation of important passages which clearly indicated a greatly abridged argument, but Adorno's version suggested that the text was complete. Kracauer could no longer recognize the argument as his because essential elements were deleted or altered. He wrote that he had approached fascism with great caution. Since he was dealing with an "*Aktualität*," with ongoing processes of a contemporary social-political reality, he had refrained from imposing on them categories that would arrest them prematurely. From a position of "middle distance" he had succeeded, he hoped, in making understandable "the ascent of fascism" by presenting its "complex relation to capitalism" and by reconstructing the development of totalitarian propaganda. From a position of much greater distance, Adorno had caught the phenomenon of fascism in a net of categories that eliminated Kracauer's insights, which had been gained from patient, close observation: "In your version fascism is a completed affair that can be easily classified. You identify it a priori with the counterrevolution, you see its interests diametrically opposed to those of the majority, and you eliminate the ambiguities in its relation to capitalism."[104]

In rewriting the essay, Adorno had missed and thereby destroyed precisely the dimension that Kracauer thought characteristic of his "*sachlich*" approach. His conceptual organization gradually established itself within, or emerged out of, the subject matter. For Adorno, everything was subsumed, and from the beginning, in a set of categories that could be applied, arbitrarily and dogmatically, to a multitude of different phenomena. Kracauer concluded that Adorno's "arrangement" was "in part purely ornamental" (2). He saw himself forced to withdraw the piece.

Adorno's stylistic arrogation was also important. Kracauer, for good reasons, had avoided verbal analyses of the allegedly singular addressee of totalitarian propaganda, the petty bourgeoisie. He deeply resented Adorno's aggressive and condescending verbal cartoons of lower-middle-class "types," which were characteristic of his boomerang style of cultural critism. Most importantly, they did not help to explain the phenomenon of this group's particular–not, as Adorno would have it, singular–vulnerability to the temptations of Hitlerism (an explanation that Kracauer had hoped to give in *Die Angestellten*). Adorno had imposed, with his prefabricated categories, his own idiosyncratic language on another writer's work: he had not edited but rewritten Kracauer's text so that it had become his own. Never, Kracauer wrote, had he experienced anything resembling this irresponsible treatment in his long editorial experience.[105]

Kracauer's insistence on his "*Sachlichkeit*," a position of inquiry developed within the subject matter, shaped many of his texts of the Weimar period. But his work in exile after the *Offenbach* was, most of the time, explicitly focused on the study of the filmic medium, to which "*Sachlichkeit*" was, so to speak, natural. Photo images, still or moving, were uniquely responsible to the "*Sache*" as the natural cultural world into which we enter as a given and to which, in making it our own for a time, we contribute. It is instructive to trace the continuities and discontinuities in Kracauer's concept of "*Sachlichkeit*" from his Weimar film reviews to *Theory of Film*–and, by extension, to *History*–during the course of several decades. Among his papers are several exposés of a film book dating from the late thirties and early forties. The earliest one, from 1938, "Ideenskizze zu meinem Buch über den Film," states his intention to use the same approach here as in *Offenbach*: to show the interdependency of social environment and artistic production. Films seek to adapt themselves to the taste of their audiences, who, in turn, model themselves after films. "My book has to have a passage on Hollywood which deals with these remarkable mutual relations. Also, it will have to account for the fact that film, like no other art form, retains precisely the fleeting traits of social life (fashion in dress and gesture)." Writing a cultural history of film, a phenomenon contemporary to his generation, he would have to start with the fin de siècle. He would have to deal with processes that in terms of historiography were at the threshhold between present and past. In this exposé Kracauer showed his awareness of the questions and difficulties posed by contemporary history in general and by his mixed approach (historical, sociological, aesthetic, and epistemological) in particular.[106]

The 1940 outline of a film book, which was to become *Theory of Film*, was developed along these lines.[107] This carefully structured and richly detailed outline was written in the expressive and precise German of Kracauer's best Weimar pieces. A juxtaposition with the serviceable but somewhat wooden English of comparable passages in *Theory* underlines poignantly one of the most severe and painful restrictions of the exile's intellectual existence, the use of a never completely accessible language.[108] When composing the book in the 1950s, Kracauer would comment on his earlier remarks in the margins

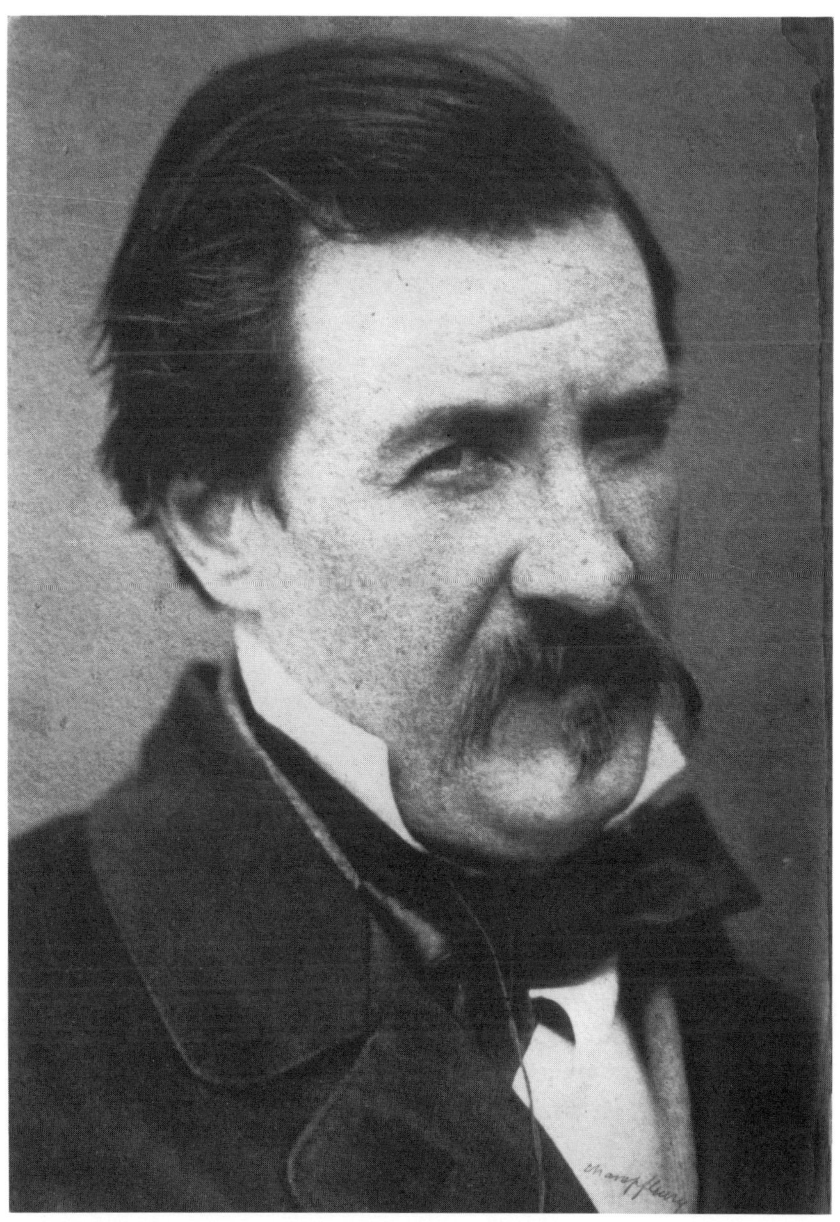

1. Nadar (Gaspard Fèlix Tournachon), *Champfleury [Jules Husson]*, 1855–59 (print, ca. 1874), salt, $13\frac{15}{16} \times 9\frac{5}{8}$ in.

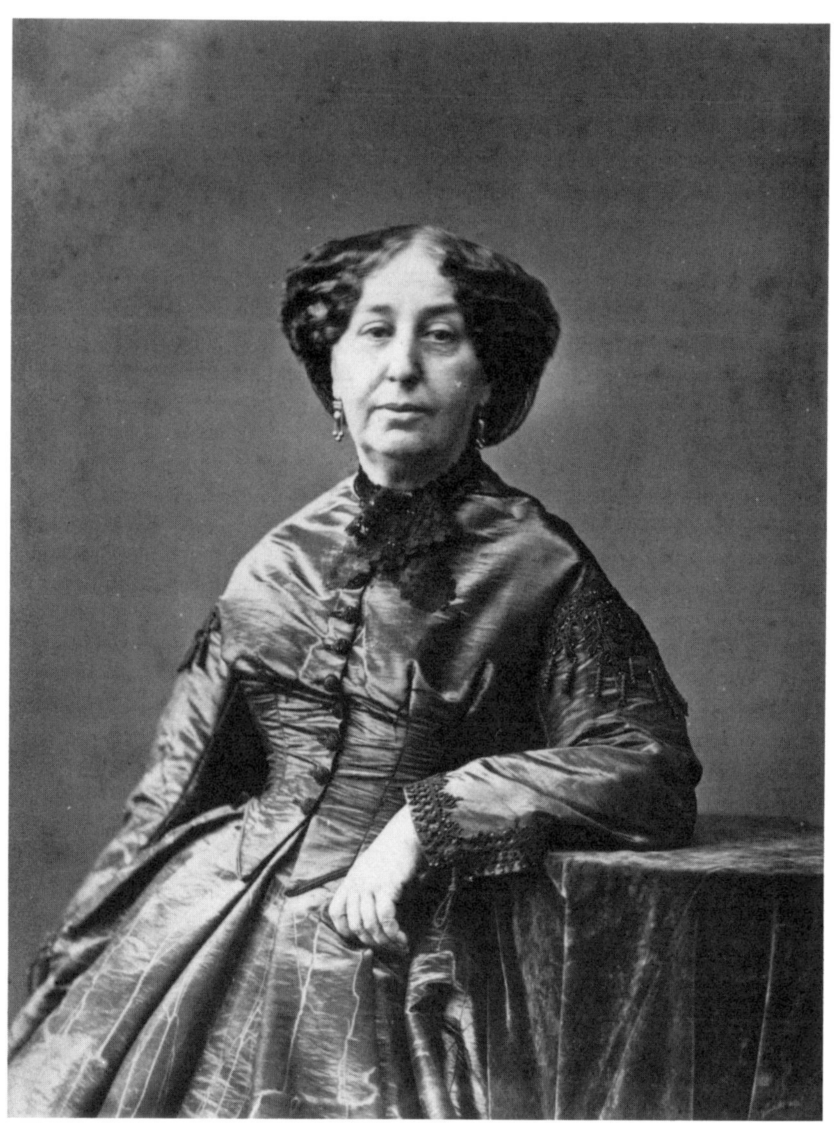

2. Nadar (Gaspard Fèlix Tournachon), *George Sand*, 1861–69, albumen, 9½ × 7⁷⁄₃₂ in.

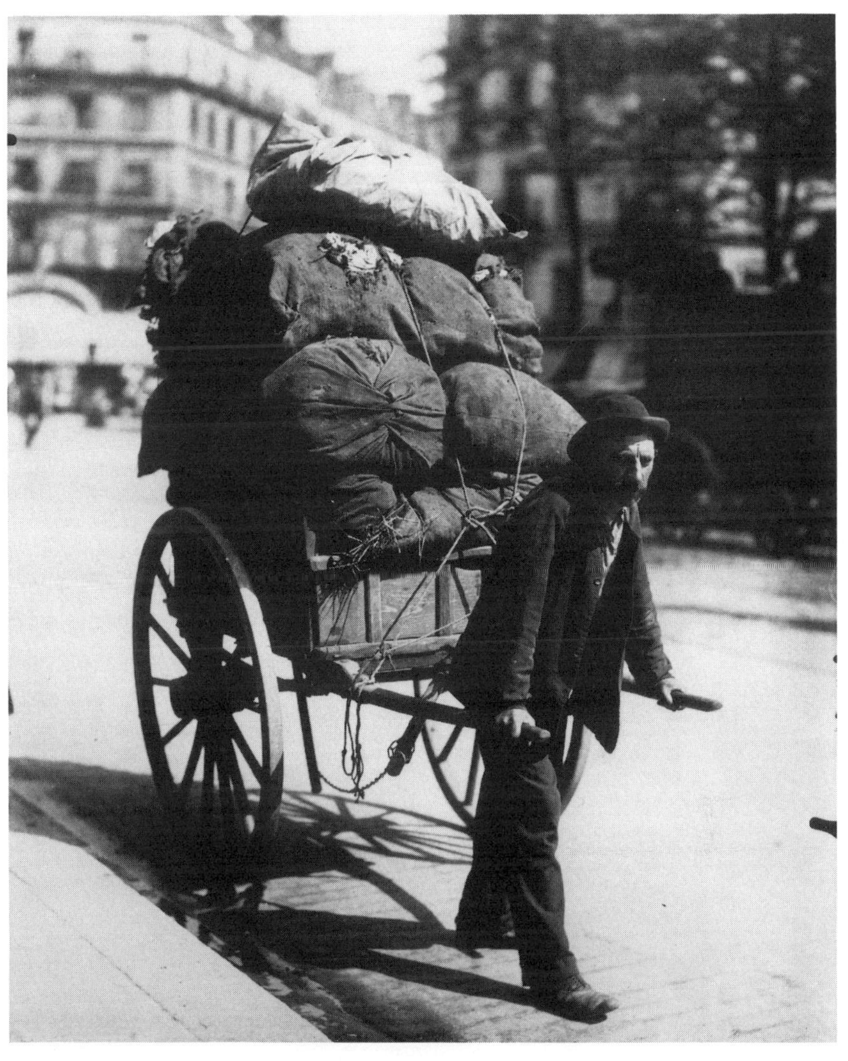

3. Eugène Atget, *Chiffonier (Rag Picker)*, 1901, albumen, 8¾ × 7$^{3}/_{16}$ in.

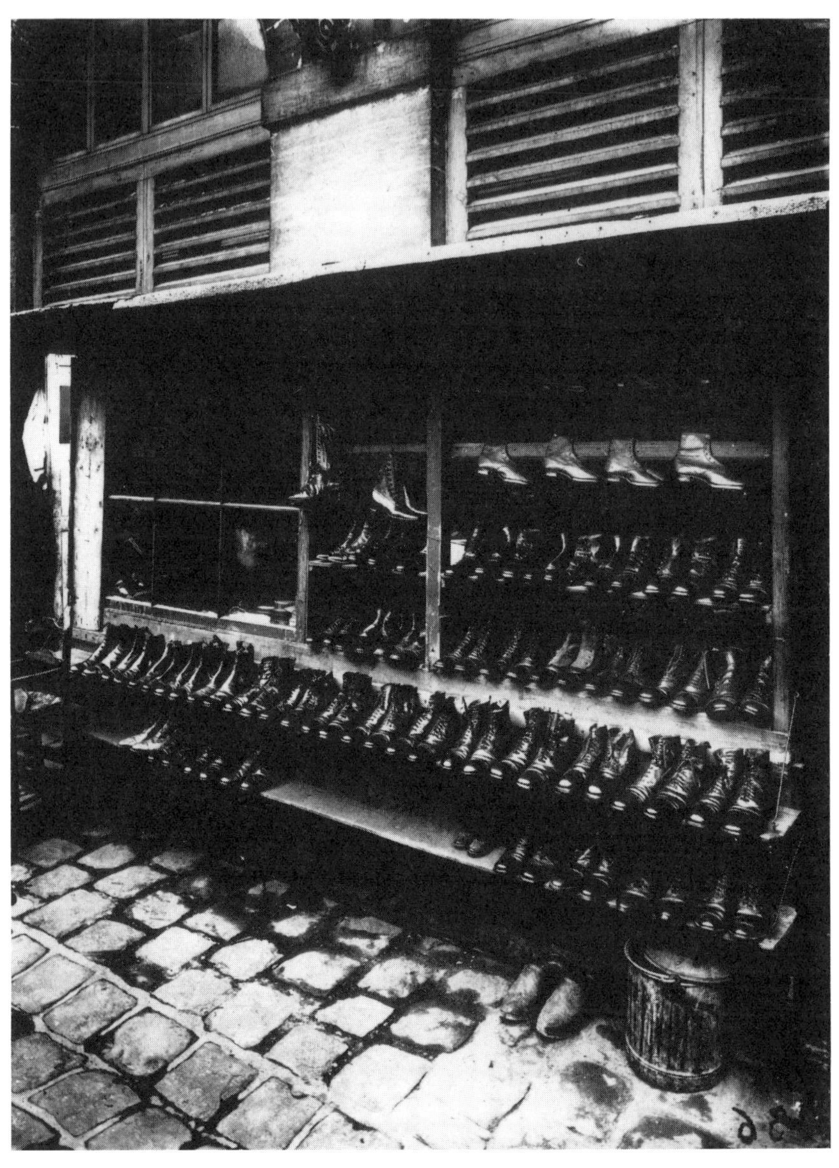

4. EUGÈNE ATGET, *Boutique de marchand de chaussures,* 1910–11 (printed by Berneice Abbott, 1927), gelatin silver, 9½ × 6¾ in.

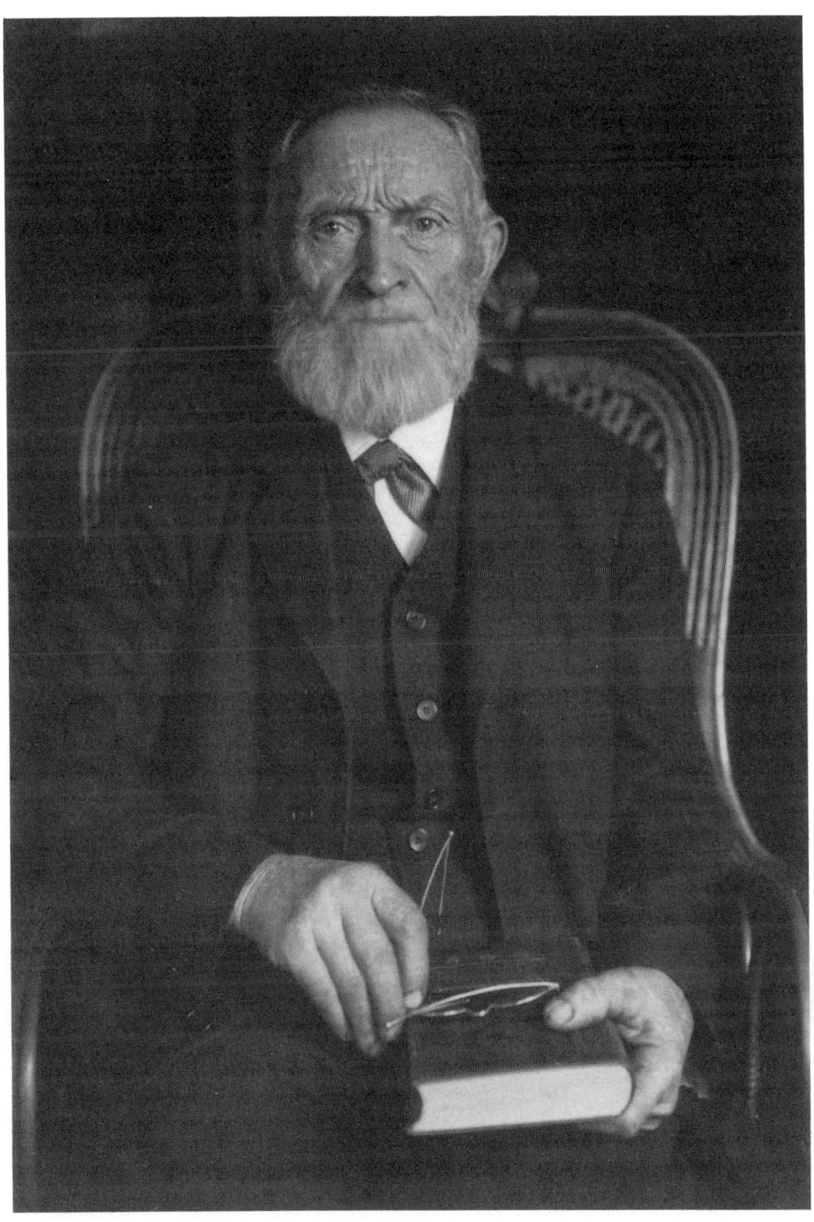

5. AUGUST SANDER, *Westerwald Farmer (Westerwalder Bauer)*, 1913, gelatin silver, $5^{15}/_{16} \times 4^{1}/_{16}$ in.

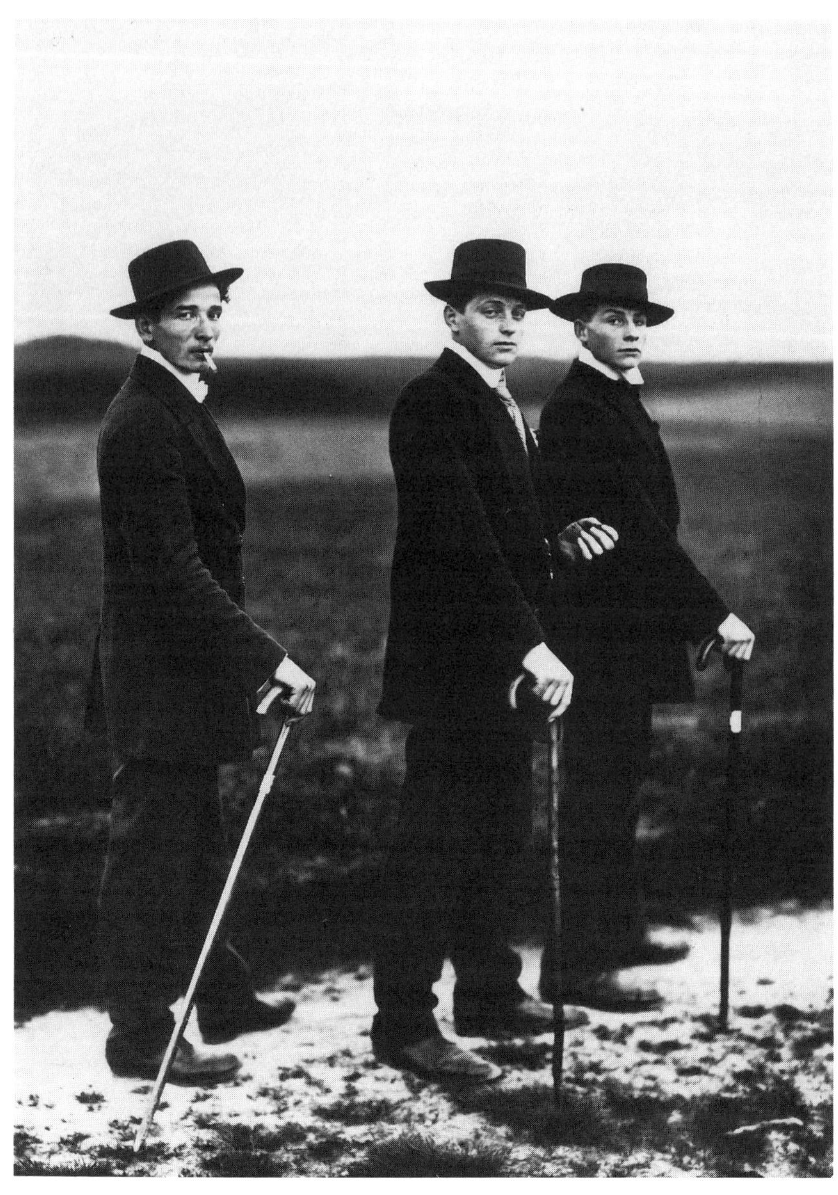

6. August Sander, *Young Farmers (Jungbauern),* 1914, gelatin silver, $9\frac{5}{16} \times 6\frac{11}{16}$ in.

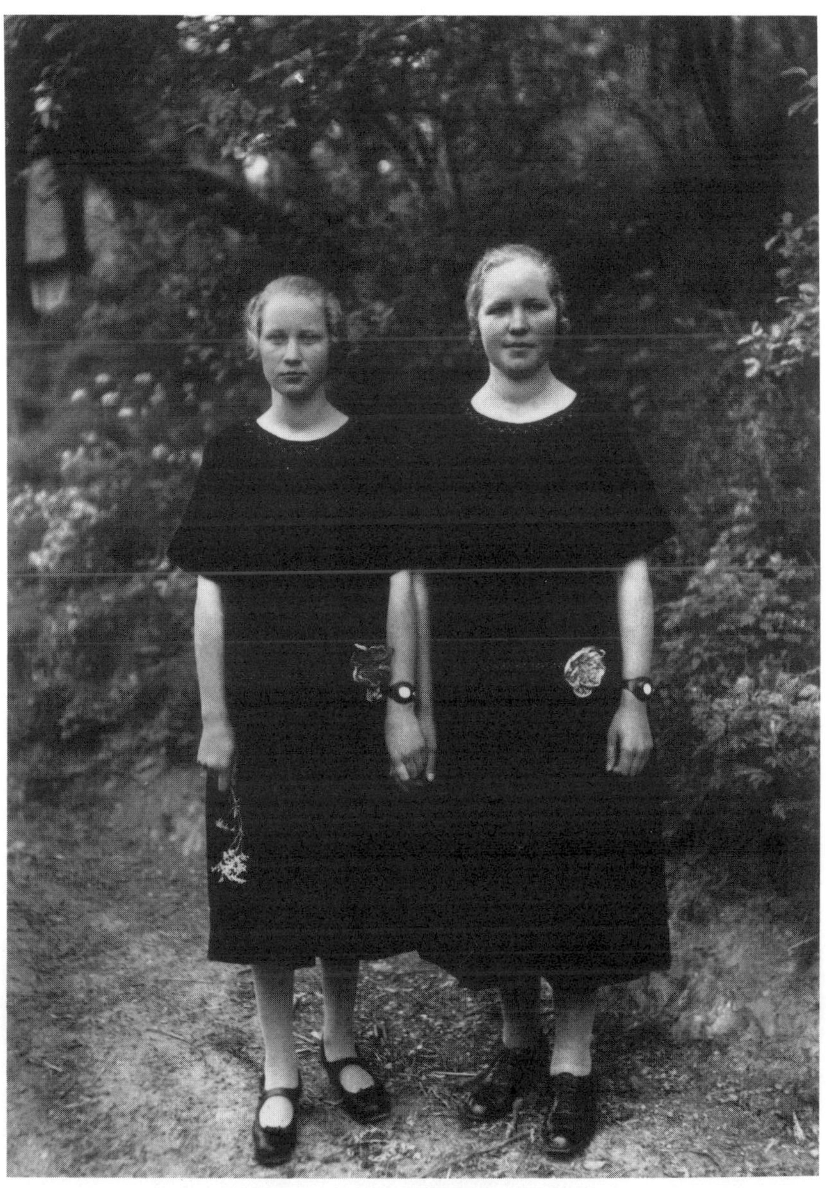

7. August Sander, *Farm Girls (Bauernmädchen),* 1928, gelatin silver, 8⅝ × 6¼ in.

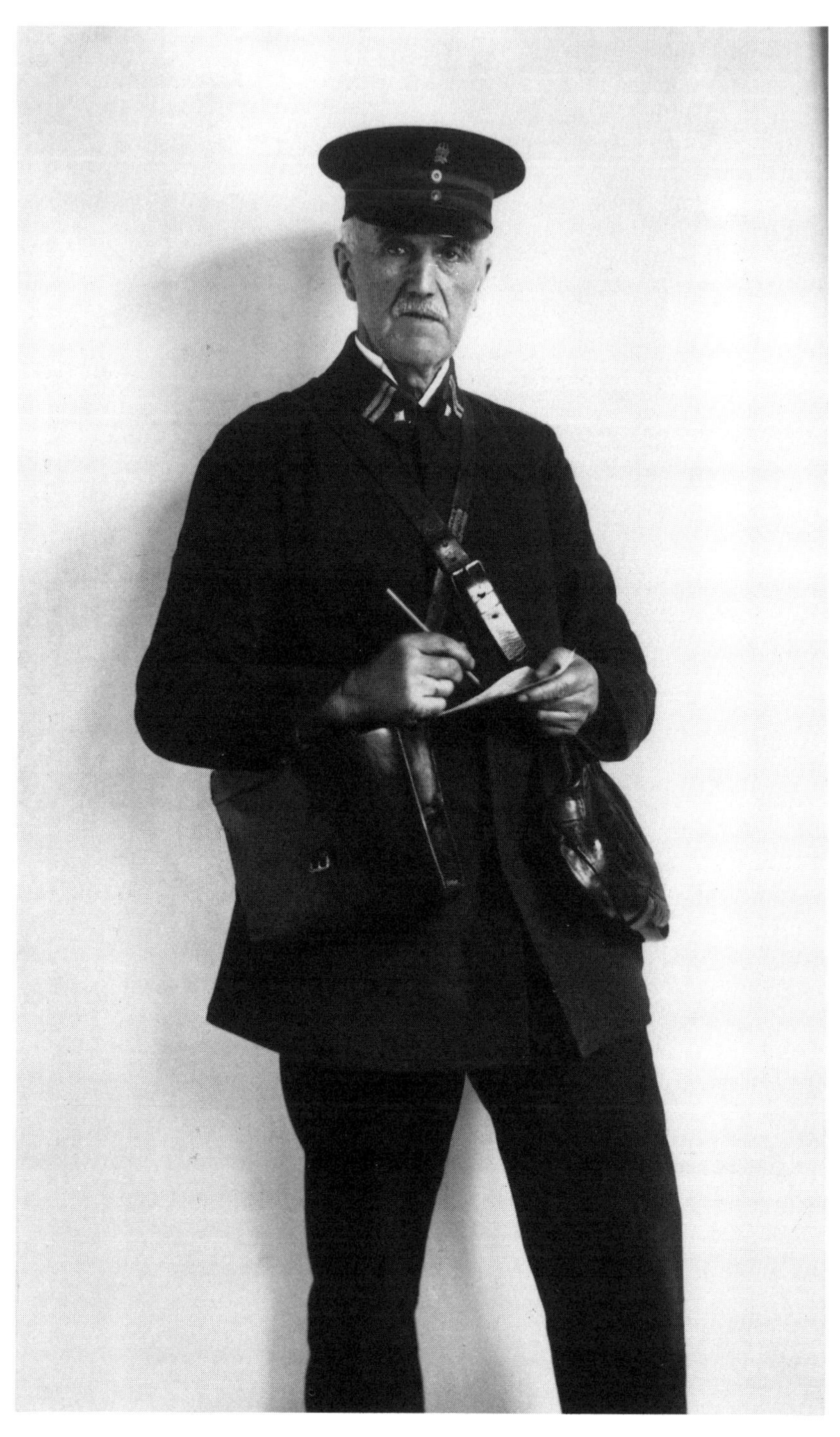

8. August Sander, *Registered Letter Postman (Geldbriefträger)*, 1928, gelatin silver, 10 × 5¹⁵⁄₁₆ in.

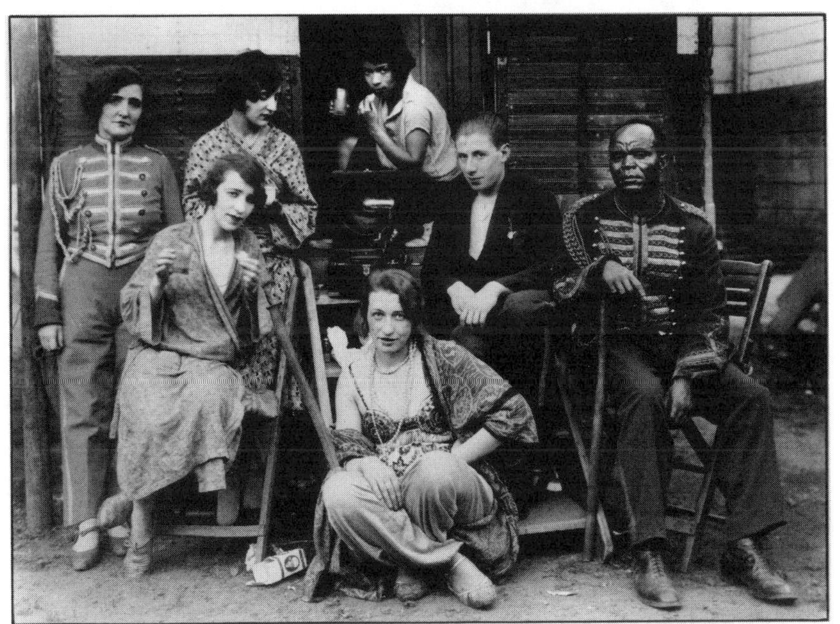

9. AUGUST SANDER, *Group of Circus People,* 1926, gelatin silver, 7 13/16 × 10 7/8 in.

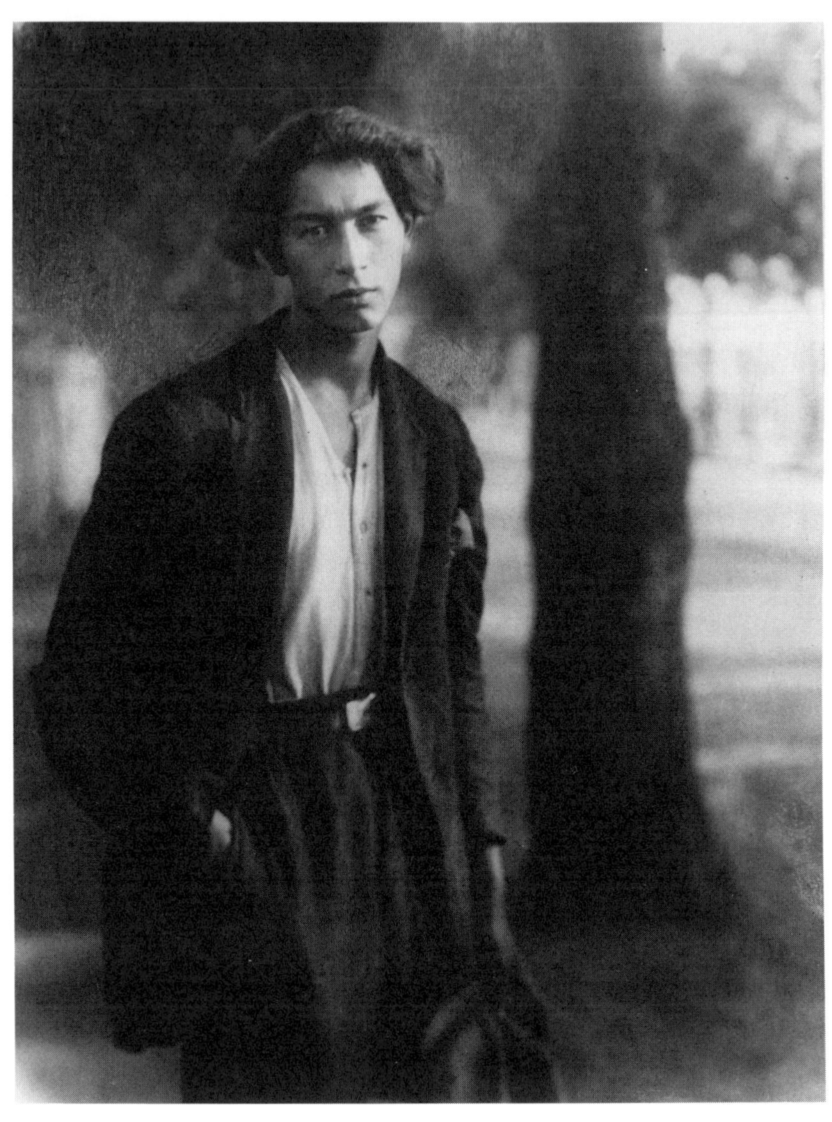

10. AUGUST SANDER, *Zigeuner (Gypsy)*, 1938 (print, ca. 1950–55), gelatin silver, 10 13/16 × 8 5/16 in.

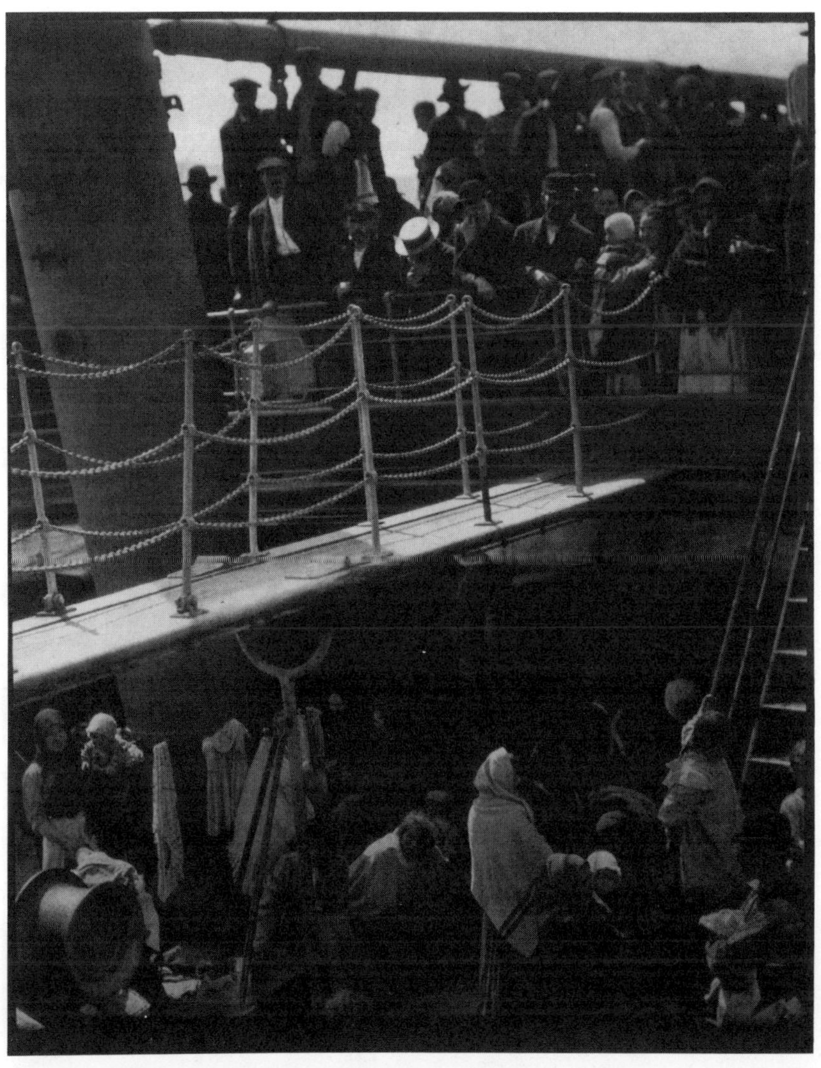

11. ALFRED STIEGLITZ, *The Steerage,* 1907, photogravure, 13³⁄₁₆ × 10⅜ in.

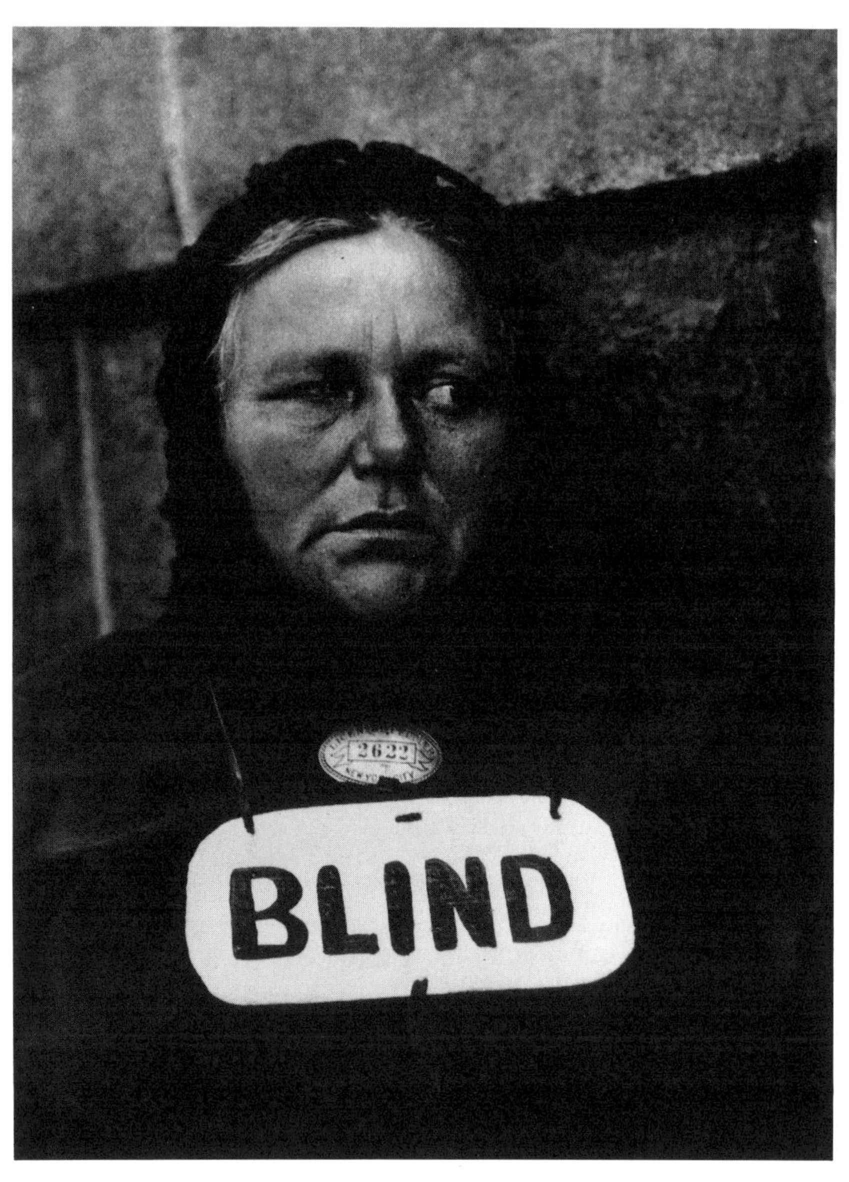

12. Paul Strand, *Blind Woman,* 1917, photogravure/halftone, 4to.

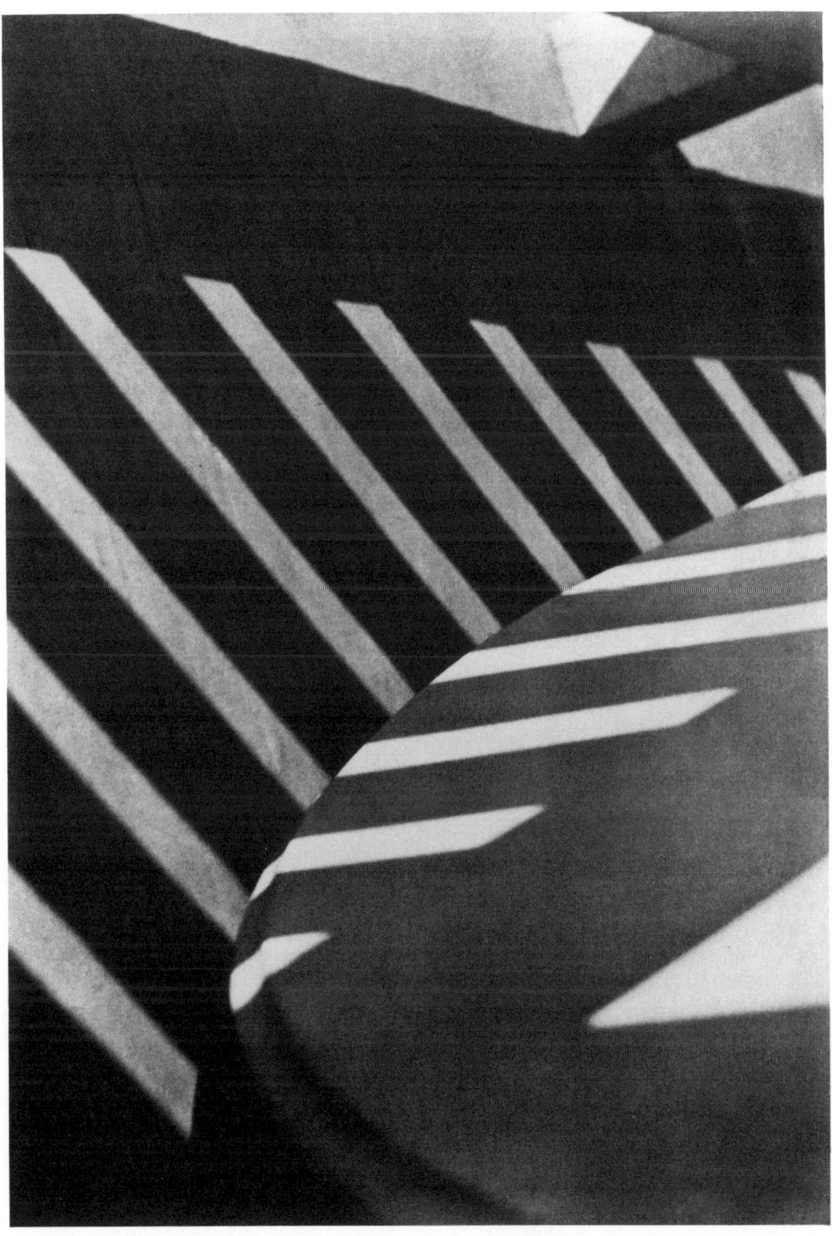

13. Paul Strand, *Porch Shadows,* 1917, photogravure/halftone, 4to.

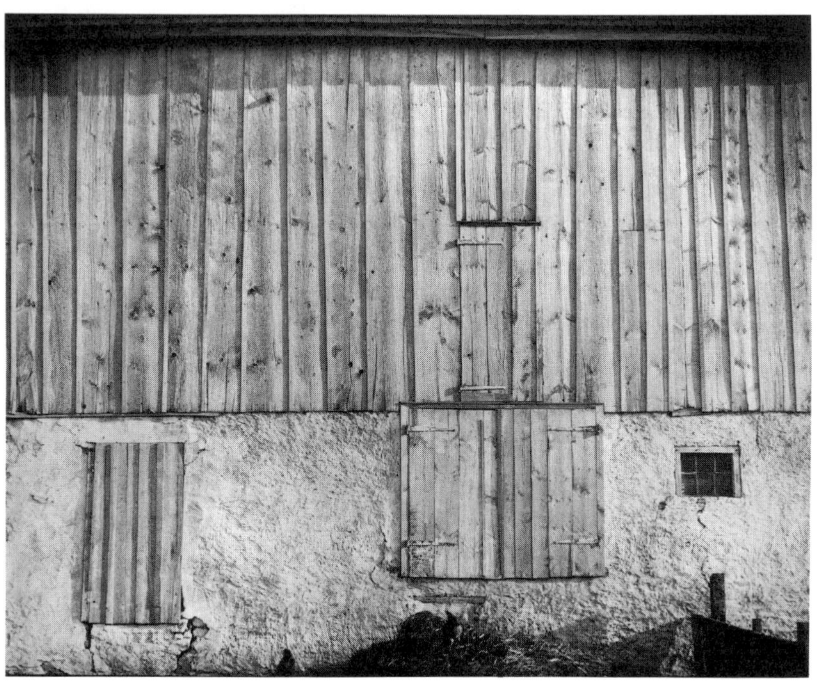

14. CHARLES SHEELER, *Side of White Barn*, 1917, gelatin silver, 7⅝ × 9⅝ in.

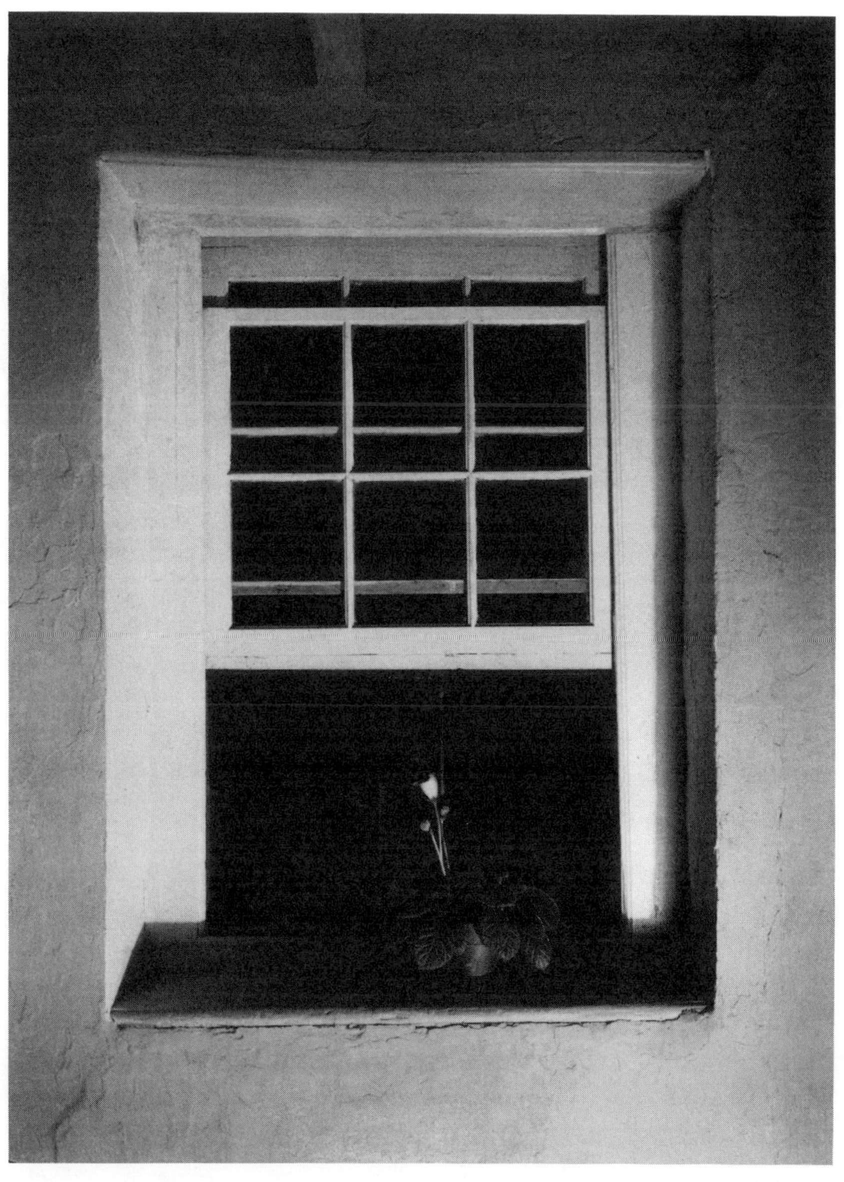

15. Charles Sheeler, *Doylestown House–Open Window,* 1917, gelatin silver, 9 11/16 × 7 1/8 in.

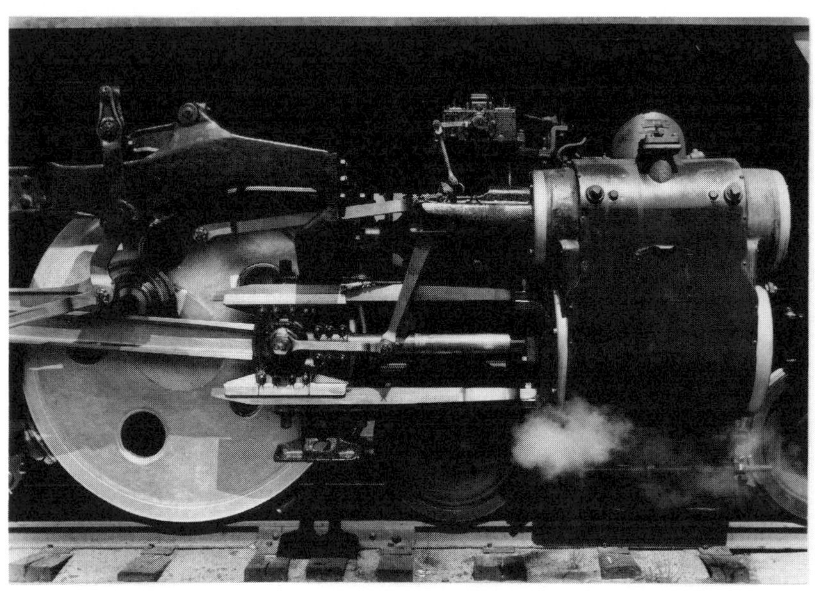

16. Charles Sheeler, *Wheels,* 1939, gelatin silver, 6⅝ × 9⅝ in.

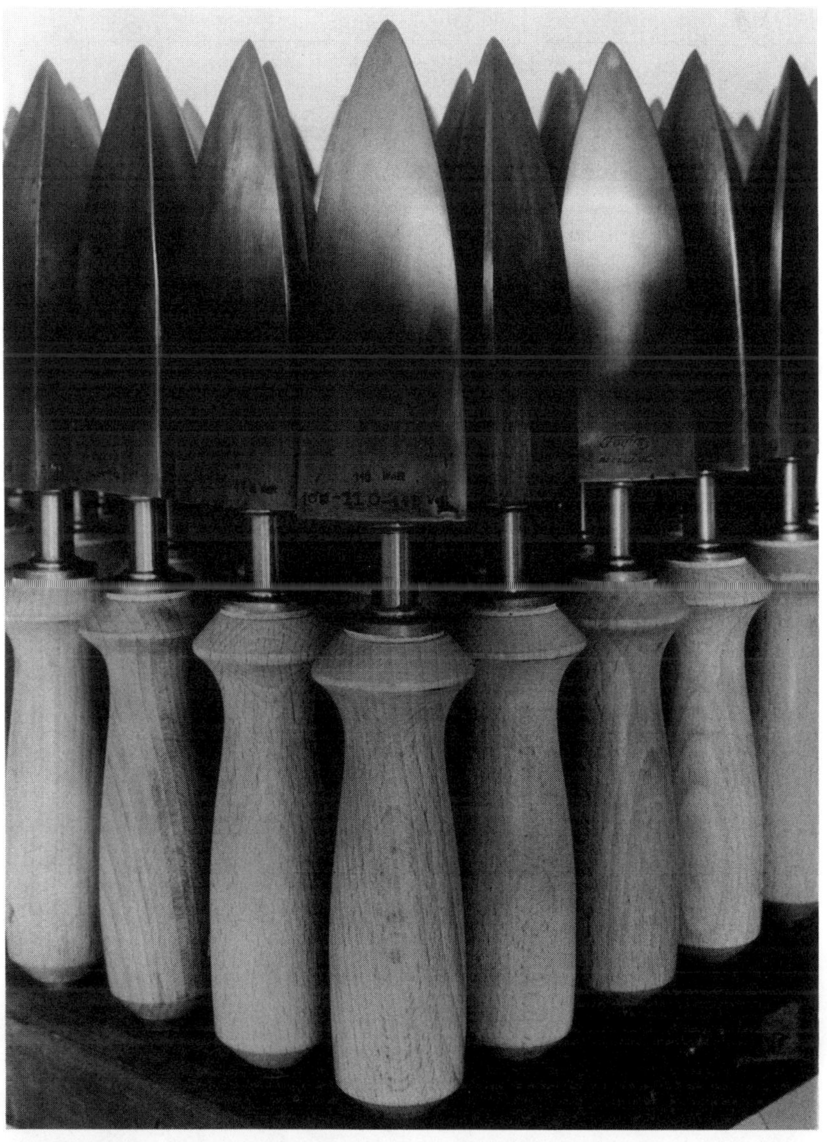

17. Albert Renger-Patzsch, *Flatirons for Shoe Manufacturer (Bugeleiser für Schuhfabrikation)*, ca. 1928, gelatin silver, $9\frac{1}{16} \times 6\frac{11}{16}$ in.

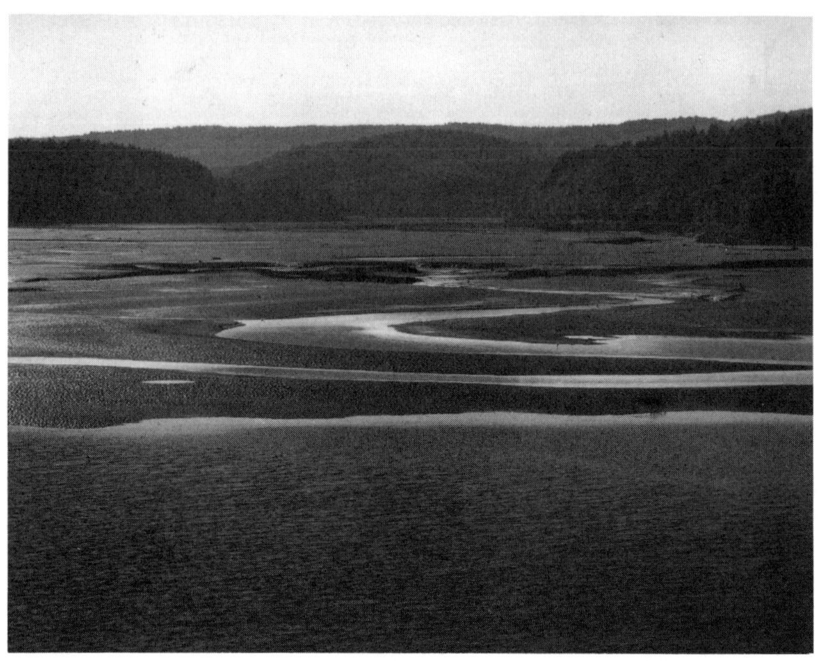

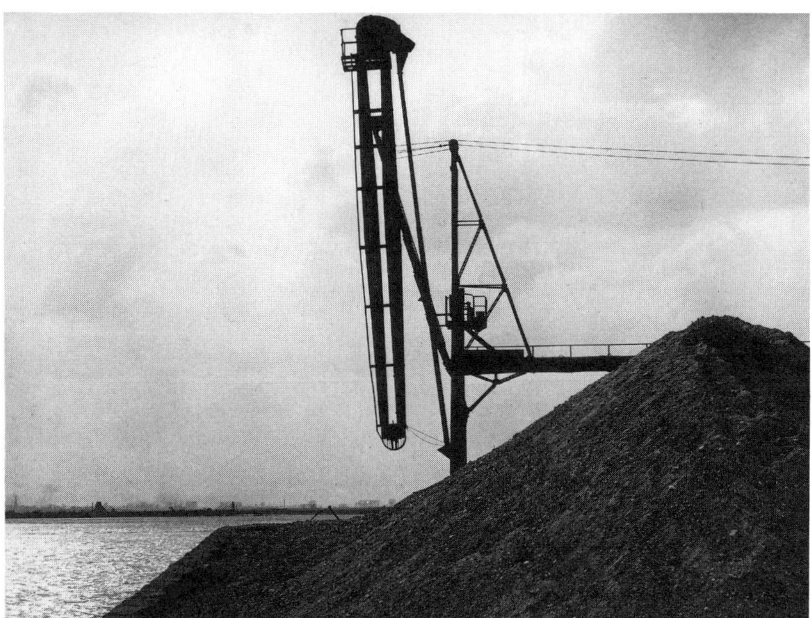

18. Albert Renger-Patzsch, *Möhne Dam Upstream on the Möhne River at Low Tide,* ca. 1950s, negative/print.

19. Albert Renger-Patzsch, *Lower Rhein at Emmerich,* ca. 1930s, negative/print.

of the outline, marking phrases he liked or thought important and underlining whole passages. Many of the complex and tentative observations that he had made as a film critic during the Weimar period are distilled here in his attempts to order a great deal of filmic material according to certain concepts that he explicitly did not wish to assume the solidity and rigidity of categories. There were many lacunae, ambiguities, suspended significances that he could keep in balance in his native German but not–or at least not so effectively–in English. Often he was after something that he could not yet see clearly, certain hunches: in German these appeared suggestive, provocatively, even usefully elusive; in English they were either opaque or prematurely, simplistically clear. This, obviously, had nothing to do with the nature of the two languages but with language use. Yet it is arguable that Kracauer, whose heroic attempts to acquire in middle age a writing competency in English had cost him a great deal of effort and precious time, also gained in that process a great many cultural insights to which he would not have had access otherwise. I will come back to this issue later; here I wish to draw attention to the difference that a particular kind of language use can make in the "mixed" area of cultural criticism, where several kinds of discourse intersect and the right, fitting choice of expression is frequently as important to the reader's understanding of the problem as is conceptual rigor.

The 1940 outline was the preliminary summary of the film book that Kracauer had conceived in 1937. During the late thirties, then, with the Film Library of the Museum of Modern Art in mind, and referring to but not yet focusing exclusively on his experience of German films, he sought to understand more systematically what film can do for the reclamation and elucidation of the "material" world of natural and cultural objects. In his application to the American Guild of June 8, 1938, the clearing house for financial help for German exiles, Kracauer proposed a book that would discuss the significance of film in terms of its social, aesthetic, cultural, and political presence since 1895. For a clarification or documentation of his own intellectual position, he referred to "my countless cultural-political essays as well as the book-length studies published before 1933, especially the study of the *Angestellten.*"[109] The title of the project, funded for March, April, and May 1939, was "Geschichte und Soziologie des Films."

The shift to German film came with Kracauer's arrival in the United States in April 1941 and a Rockefeller grant in support of his work on the "Geschichte des deutschen Films (1918–1933)" in the film library of the Museum of Modern Art. The focus of his research here was at first Nazi propaganda in feature films and news reels, which resulted in a study, "Propaganda and the Nazi War Film," completed in the summer of 1942 and buried in the State Department archives. A more broadly conceived study of German films during the Weimar period continued under the auspices of the film library and the Rockefeller and Guggenheim Foundations. It was, as Kracauer wrote to friends in early 1943, a difficult task since much of the literature on German film was unreliable and he had to check and double check a large portion of the information. "I also had to study the social and political and artistic situation in postwar [World War I] Germany."[110] In May 1943 Kracauer submitted a study, "The Conquest of Europe on the Screen The Nazi Newsreel 1939–1940," requested by the Experimental Division for the Study of War, Time Communications. Like his previous paper on Nazi war propaganda, it was labeled "confidential" and was read only by a handful of experts. It took him three more years to complete the film book, which appeared in the spring of 1947 under a title suggested by the publisher.

From Caligari to Hitler: A Psychological History of the German Film (1947) is probably Kracauer's most widely known and, on the whole, least satisfying work. Much more narrowly focused than the book suggested in the 1940 outline, it exhibits some of the more important fallacies that can trap the historian. It was the first book that Kracauer published in the "new world," from a position of considerably greater distance from his German cultural environment than had been the case in France. Analyzing the films of the Weimar era, he dealt with what he considered significant cultural aspects of his old world. These were issues he wished to make more accessible to American readers, who seemed to be separated from this world by vast expanses not only of space but also of time. In a 1943 statement for the Guggenheim Foundation, "Notes on the Planned History of the German Film," Kracauer had emphasized particularly the witnessing and documenting properties of the filmic medium itself:

> The film reflects to an extent hitherto unknown the visible world–a world including not only human beings but also objects and nature and the innumer-

> able incidents that result from their interrelationship. The whole dimension of everyday life with its infinitesimal movements and its multitude of transitory actions could be disclosed nowhere but on the screen. Not by chance do films of fact appear at the very beginning of the new art.[111] That documentaries and entertainment films alike cling so much to little things never consciously evaluated before, may be related to their descent: they originate in the sphere of popular art, and there is no doubt that the plain people are always intimate neighbors to the many objects surrounding them. This inclination is furthered by technical possibilities inherent in the film. The ubiquitous camera can detail any subject or part of a subject, show it from various angles, and thereby approach its specific nature.
>
> These few hints sufficiently evidence the unique documentary value of an art able to encompass rushing crowds, physiognomies, small gestures, occasional complexes of things and human bodies, and all the passing phenomena that constitute the surface of life. Films illuminate the realm of bagatelles, of little events. But only today is it beginning to be realized that precisely for this reason they may become a new source of knowledge.[112]

The filmic (*and photographic*) medium is uniquely capable of allowing access to processes of daily life in other places, other cultures, other times because films can record and thereby preserve also those phenomena that (tend to) escape the attention of the observer (photographer). As a cultural critic during the Weimar period, Kracauer had been interested in these literally plain, inconspicuous phenomena, and films had intrigued him precisely because they so richly reflect the surfaces of modern diversity. It is curious that this statement failed to deal with the question of the presence and role of the observer. If the camera was capable of being ubiquitous, it was still controlled, to varying degrees, by the person who used it. And that person in turn was controlled, to varying degrees, by the vision of another person who tried to realize her concept of a particular film. In his film reviews Kracauer had raised these questions of control as a matter of course and he was to raise them again in *Theory of Film*; they were also clearly present in the 1940 outline. With photo images, especially where they were linked in motion, the all-important epistemological problem of perspective posed itself with a literalness to which Kracauer, trying to sort out the cultural meanings of the new medium, was forced to respond. But in his historical study of the social psychological functions of German film during the Weimar Republic these concerns were superseded by a thesis that was too directly influenced by

Kracauer's work on Nazi film propaganda. Adhering too rigidly to this thesis caused him to approach his material too selectively and to interpret it too narrowly.

Kracauer proceeded from the assumption that German films, as he wrote in the Guggenheim statement, remain rooted in their cultural environment "more directly than films of other nations" are culturally rooted.

> That they express and mirror in so immediate a manner the world in which they grow up, is chiefly the outcome of Germany's history since the last world war. It is as if the despair after the war and the violence of the interior struggles had removed some of the opaque layers which, in more normal times, separate the course of art from that of contemporary reality. German films are particularly transparent. Their interpretation is all the more important, as it takes one behind the scenes of those events which made possible Hitler's ascent. (4)

The proposed link between the assumed "transparent" quality of German films and their yielding, in interpretation, important insights about "hidden elements of German reality" makes for a circularity of argument–an arresting of the hermeneutic circle–which clearly detracts from its usefulness. But Kracauer, intent on exposing those "hidden elements," must have thought secondary, at least in this case, the problem of reading into films (only) what one was looking for. As he stated in the preface to *Caligari*, he saw his task in terms of demonstrating how films document the "deep psychological dispositions predominant in Germany from 1918 to 1933," since they profoundly influenced political events and would have "to be reckoned with in the post-Hitler era."[113] Films, he argued in the Guggenheim statement, were particulary helpful here because, as the results of collective artistic effort, they were "never the product of an individual" and they addressed "the anonymous multitude," the constituency of a modern mass democracy; they thus allowed the most direct access to group (national) mentality: "What films reflect are not so much explicit credos as psychological dispositions–those deep layers of collective mentality which extend more or less below the dimension of consciousness" (5f.).

The emphasis is on filmic documentation of the emotional energies of the group. It was here that Kracauer located the social and political significance of the popular medium and also here that his attempts at its historical elucidation ran into some instructive obstacles. The source for his holding so single-mindedly to one line of interpretation in *Caligari*, the obstacles stand out very clearly in the Guggenheim statement. From the beginning, as Kracauer said here, German film "contained dynamite." It developed in "a period of revolutionary crisis and social insecurity."

> Under such conditions, the unhappy, homeless soul not only drove straightway toward the fantastic region of horrors, but also moved like a stranger through the world of normal reality, embracing its conventional forms with a look that had the force to change them into weird, abnormal structures. Here was an incomparable chance for a young cinema which had not yet conquered all its spheres. That free wandering soul imagined the madmen, somnabulists, vampires and murderers who were haunting the expressionistic settings of the Caligari film and its like, and, on the other hand, inspired such directors as Karl Grune, Lupu Pick and G. W. Pabst to portray in their early pictures apparently familiar objects and make them seem new. These pictures feature the city street as the place where the "Man of the Crowd" perceives the kaleidoscopic configurations of everyday life; they are full of house facades, window-dressings, strangely lit rooms and physiognomic particulars. Thus the Germans widened the dominion of the cinema in two directions: they incorporated in it the terrific visions of a mind put out of joint, and at the same time introduced a truly cinemeatic realism. This was done with a perfect insight in the language of lights and shadows, and by means of a camera that became as movable as the unfettered mind directing it. It is understood that from such technical devices important conclusions can be drawn with regard to the psychic organization in which they originate. (5f.)

This compelling and telling combination of individual-cultural dissociation and of "perfect realism" was characteristic much more of the "artistically valuable films" made by talented directors and their crews than of the "commercial films" of the second half of the Weimar period. And yet it was these mass products that Kracauer wished to give special attention to, because their "typical shape" proved "more permeable to certain traits of contemporaneous life" than the "outstanding creations" of particularly insightful individuals (6). Here he encountered, but did not deal with, precisely the methodological dilemmas that he would later point out to Lowenthal. And the fact that films are, in important ways, products of a collective effort does not, as he seemed to think, change that situation.

Kracauer was reluctant to pose these extraordinarily difficult questions. But if the political agenda of the study prevented him from addressing the art status of film and photography, it was also an obstacle to a full exploration of the film's contribution to social-political knowledge. (And these problems were in part interdependent.) In the introduction to *Theory of Film* he would restate an insight already operative in his film reviews of the Weimar period: "If film is an art, it is art with a difference. Along with photography, film is the only art which leaves its raw material more or less intact."[114] But where *Theory of Film* explicitly questions the meanings of this "difference," namely the combined "constructive"/"realist" mode of the photo image, *Caligari* brackets or defers it. In that sense the later work, written under the pressure of a recent very troubled past, is less careful about epistemological concerns than are the film reviews of the Weimar period.[115] Kracauer's emphasis on the group work of film crews in relation to "the anonymous multitude" of film audiences is a good case in point. In the introduction to *Caligari* the reader is told: "Since any film production unit embodies a mixture of heterogeneous interests and inclinations, teamwork in this field tends to exclude arbitrary handling of screen material, suppressing individual peculiarities in favor of traits common to many people" (5). Yet Kracauer's interest (like that of any thesis-oriented historian) in those "anonymous multitudes" was not so much directed to the "traits common to many people" as to a small number of specific traits or modes of behavior. In addition there is the problem of collective versus individual will. It is not the collective will expressed in "teamwork" that most effectively suppresses "individual peculiarities" but the stronger will of one of the team's members.

Kracauer's insistence on the collective as locus of the interdependency of the filmic medium and group (national) mentality raises the all-important question of perspective: who sees what from which position in the space and time of social and psychological politics? He found that films explicitly produced for mass audiences operated on "an instinctive desire to prevent the pauperized middle class from becoming aware of its plight and making common cause with the workers." These films' formulaic arrangements of emotional entanglements, then, were meant to entertain and thereby conceal the social-political crisis. "Significantly, that average film withdrew more and more into a sphere of empty neutrality–a loss of content which reflected the waning substantiality of the German Democracy" (7). But who, in making these films, had indeed perceived this emptiness as a contemporary? The directors? The cameramen? The film crews as a group? Under instructions from the directors? Had they seen it consciously? Unconsciously? Had the camera recorded it without their being aware of it and preserved it for the contemporary or future viewer, whatever the intentions of the people involved in the making of the film? Underlying the *Caligari* book is the assumption, both suggestive and assertive, that the filmic medium itself witnesses and documents.

The Guggenheim statement reflected the exile's deep interest in film's preserving properties. A once visible, now largely destroyed, world of actors in their relations to each other and to objects and events can be vividly present in film; a traumatically ruptured culture can be fully revisited. This fascination with the immediacy of recalled presence made for many intriguing insights. It also moved Kracauer largely to evade the entangled problems of historical perspective, which are especially difficult where questions of historical knowledge are posed from a position of imposed, not yet negotiated, distance. There is a poignantly illuminating passage in a letter of May 2, 1947, to Erwin Panofsky in which Kracauer, thanking Panofsky for his positive reaction to *Caligari*, describes his own ambivalent feelings about his perspective in this study: "Writing it, I felt like a physician who, doing an autopsy, also dissects a piece of his own, now completely dead past. But of course, something always lives on transformed. It is a *tightrope walking* between and above yesterday and today."[116] The past, his own and others, is never "completely dead." The historian's objectivity is larger and more diffuse than that of the dissecting physician. It was precisely the autodissection of the person he had become that had made him too strained, too single-minded an observer–indeed a tightrope walker. The fluid connections between yesterday and today resist such one-way, hemmed-in movement.

There was, of course, much interest in this streamlined approach after the social and political disaster of World War II. In an enthusiastic review, the well-known British director and film critic, Paul Rotha, wrote:

> After reading "From Caligari to Hitler," no director with half a conscience could begin work on a new film without deep pause for thought. No longer can he divorce his film from the environment, social and political, in which it is made, even if he excuses it as purely entertainment. Here, at last, is a writer who bases his whole approach to cinema on the belief that every film is a reflection of national characteristics and their adjustment to the circumstances of

> the time. The films of a nation reflect its collective mentality. Dr. Kracauer has given us a book which must at once be placed alongside the half-dozen most important works on the cinema; personally, I place it within the first three.[117]

Rotha, whose interest was the documentary, saw the filmmaker as the counterpart to the writer of contemporary (or recent) history. He welcomed Kracauer's approach, because it supplied certain kinds of information not easily found elsewhere. As Kracauer observed in the introduction, historians tend to neglect psychological energies and motivations, a neglect that accounts for the "striking gaps in our knowledge of German history from World War I to Hitler's ultimate triumph." More than four decades later this gap has not been filled substantially, because there has been too little exploration of this kind.[118] But Kracauer's analysis, though in many ways helpful and much consulted by students of German film, has its own problems. Kracauer looked closely at cultural images, and he managed to refrain from feeding them too forcefully into preestablished ideological grids so that he did come away with some helpful observations on fascism. Importantly, too, his diagnosis of the disturbing symptoms of a mass society emphasizes explanation rather than rejection. Unlike the Marxist Freudians of the Frankfurt School, he did not just accuse Hitler's future followers of total and irreversible regression, and on the whole he did not assign them a realm of—to the intellectual—inaccessible and therefore demonic stupidity. Yet the perspective established by the exile from his position in another time, in another country, *was* distorting. It made too clear and therefore too simple the connection, in the fantastic images of the films of the period, between the mass democracy of Weimar and the totalitarian rule of the Third Reich. Pressured by Kracauer's questions, film after film documented that under Hitler's rule, these fantasies

> came true in life itself. Personified daydreams of minds to whom freedom meant a fatal shock, and adolescence a permanent temptation, these figures filled the arena of Nazi Germany. Homunculus walked about in the flesh. Self-appointed Caligaris hypnotized innumerable Cesars into murder. Raving Mabuses committed fantastic crimes with impunity, and mad Ivans devised unheard-of tortures. Along with this unholy procession, many motifs known from the screen turned into actual events. In Nuremberg, the ornamental pattern of *Nibelungen* appeared on a gigantic scale: an ocean of flags and people artistically arranged. Souls were thoroughly manipulated so as to create the impression that the heart mediated between brain and hand. By day and night,

> millions of feet were marching over city streets and along highways. The blare of military bugles sounded unremittingly, and the philistines from the plush parlors felt very elated. Battles roared and victory followed victory. It all was as it had been on the screen. The dark premonitions of a final doom were also fulfilled.[119]

These films were seen by Germans, among them Kracauer, in the years following the Great War before Hitler actually "seized" power. And the study was based on, in addition to Kracauer's work on Nazi propaganda, the film reviews he had written from 1924 to 1929, mostly for *Frankfurter Zeitung.* As a contemporary observer, he had brought to these reviews his critical but not dismissive understanding of a major part of the films' audience, the white collar workers, the group that was probably most vulnerable to the seductions of Hitlerism. In the introduction to *Caligari,* Kracauer rightly referred his postwar readers to his earlier text, the 1929 *Angestellten* (11). There is indeed a significant continuity in the points of departure and the direction of the two studies with respect to Kracauer's realistically flexible perspective on class relations and his shrewd probings into the entangled social-psychological mechanisms and energies that motivated certain kinds of group behavior. But in the series of interviews that make up *Die Angestellten,* and in his ongoing film reviews during the twenties and early thirties, Kracauer's explanations had kept intact the puzzling conflicts and contradictions of daily life during the Weimar period. Now he swept them all up into the thesis of a corresponding social-psychological and artistic collectivity. In its tight control of the diverse materials, this thesis, though suggestive and in some parts convincing, prevented Kracauer from probing the relation between representation and evidence—that is, the implications of a medium-specific documentary core for the photo image, still or moving.

As reportage, the literary and photo documentary had by the end of the Weimar period become an enormously popular mode of representation. It had grown out of the experience of new social and political developments, and it was both affirmed and questioned in Kracauer's text, *Die Angestellten.* White-collar workers as a group were growing fast, politically important, and a new phenomenon whose sociological observation required a degree of spontaneity and imaginativeness. Ernst Bloch's laudatory but reductive review, "Künstliche Mitte" ("Artificial Center"), written on the occasion of rather than about *Die Angestellten*, shows very little of that. It is hard to imagine that Kracauer did not mind the inclusion of this superficial and self-centered piece in *Erbschaft dieser Zeit* (1934; *Heritage of Our Times*, 1991), Bloch's summary sentencing of the troubled modernity of Weimar.[120] In a letter to Bloch in February of 1935,[121] he stated his admiration for another of the essays collected in the volume, "Ungleichzeitigkeit und Pflicht zu ihrer Dialektik" (1932; "Noncontemporaneity and Obligation to Its Dialectic").[122] The problem of "Ungleichzeitigkeit," a contemporary noncontemporaneity as the anachronistic presence, in the middle of accelerated modernization of the work world, of old desires and modes of behavior, was indeed central to Weimar culture. Its destructive dynamics provide a powerful subtext to *Die Angestellten*, on which Bloch's essay with its "philosophical" description of an explosively concrete political issue had clearly drawn. He had seized the occasion as an opportunity to denounce the political regression of white-collar workers as typical of the petty bourgeoisie, and the denunciation had stimulated his poetic exuberance but hardly his analytical concentration.[123] Kracauer, however, had been at pains to understand the very real economic and social difficulties faced by that new group of employees. The mere "fact" that they were lower middle-class or "petty bourgeoisie," the class notoriously despised by the intellectuals, did not seem to him sufficient explanation for a complex, puzzling phenomenon.

The title that Bloch had given his review, "Künstliche Mitte," emphasized the lack of reality in the, to Bloch, inevitably dull, blunted lives of the *Angestellten*. He looked at these lives exclusively from the position of the intellectual observer, too distant to hear or see clearly but keenly interested in giving an exotic coloring to the proverbial petty bourgeois existential emptiness. Kracauer, who had based his investigative reporting on many conversations with employees and employers, had translated their experience as faithfully as possible. He had done so with respect to their ability to make themselves understood to him, with respect to his capacity to put himself in their place temporarily, and, finally, with respect to his audience's willingness to consider the evidence he presented along these lines.

In *Die Angestellten*, Kracauer attempted a cultural analysis in terms of social-economic contemporary history rather than of social-political philosophy. When, in the first chapter, "An Unknown Area," he compared the exploration of the world of the *Angestellten* with an expedition "perhaps more adventurous than a film expedition to Africa,"[124] he repeated an argument made occasionally in his film reviews of the period. He did not wish to stress the exoticism of Africa as the dark continent of fantasies and desires. Rather, he drew attention to the fact that information about Africa was easier to come by for contemporary urban readers and viewers than information about their own cultural environment, the modern metropolis. White-collar workers were an urban phenomenon; *Angestellten* culture is most pronounced, most influential, in Berlin: "Only in Berlin, where ties to people's background and roots have been undermined to the extent that the *Weekend* has entered fashion, can one grasp the reality of white-collar workers. This reality is also in good part the reality of Berlin" (215f.).

But how to gain access to it? Here Kracauer drew on his persona as film critic in order to argue against a currently sought after, but in his eyes illusionary, immediacy emphasized in the hugely popular new genre of literary and photo journalism, "reportage." Unreflected "direct" representation of social reality in "reportage" has often proved to be useless because "reality is a construction. It certainly depends on observation. However, this reality is not contained in the more or less random *reportage* sequence of observations, but solely in the mosaic formed by fitting together observations according to their content. *Reportage* photographs life; a mosaic of this kind would be its picture [*Bild*]" (216).

A randomly recording photograph is in this case less helpful than the composition achieved by a "*Bild*." Used in this context, the term *Bild* does not, however, signify a higher knowledge status in general for pictorial art. Kracauer's emphasis is not on a positive contrast between pictorial composition and mere photographic recording. Rather, he wishes to point out the limitations of "reportage" as a particulary impoverished kind of recording. The picture, *Bild*, that he proposes to construct in approaching contemporary social history through documentary analysis would give better access to the lives of the *Angestellten* than would mere transcription in verbal or photographic "reportage." He made this argument in the context of explaining *his* way of documenting the concrete social-psychological experiences of a significantly new constituency of Weimar mass democracy. And he did so precisely because he wanted to draw attention to the difficulties of recording contemporary processes of lived time, of writing contemporary history. Despite its declared intentions, most of the work going under the name of reportage showed, as he saw it, little or no awareness of these difficulties; it did not even perceive the challenge of documenting an explicitly contemporary experience.[125] A literary documentary like his *Angestellten* was different in kind[126]—as were films with intelligible documentary interests and intentions.

Kracauer generally judged the success of films in terms of their capacity to witness and document, and he understood the filmmaker's ability to use this capacity largely in terms of directive construction within the material the camera had made available: "reality is a construction." But he was also attentive, and increasingly so, to what remains outside such construction, even to what resists it. In his later work written in exile, in *Theory of Film* and in *History*, it was this "rest" that was to engage his interest most intensely: How do the photographer and the historian perceive and record it? How can it become accessible and remain so? What is its significance for the process of knowledge made possible in photography and historiography?

Chapter Four

The Shapes of Objectivity

1 "Historical reality," like "photographic reality," is a methodological issue.[1] The challenge to historians is to recognize their own temporality and historicity, which is crucially important for gaining access to and making accessible past actuality. Things past are regained from the perspectives of different lifetimes and also from different points or positions within the flow of one lifetime. Informed by the interpenetation of continuity and discontinuity, the historian's perspective is temporally composite and open-ended–thus the "uncertainty" of the light in which "fragments" of the past are gathered, and of the ends served by such gathering.[2] There is the analogous tendency of the photographic medium "to stress the endless" in its "emphasis on fortuitous complexes which represent fragments rather than wholes." Kracauer speaks here of a gravitating "toward the expanses of outer reality–an open-ended, limitless world," a "flow of random events" which clearly differs from the "finite and ordered cosmos set by tragedy."[3]

If historiography and photography require their practitioners to be tolerant of openendedness and to attend to the flow of random events as the context of human agency, this does not mean the imposition of an ideal of exhaustive recording: the reconstruction of historical events as mirror images of what actually was. In defining their perspectives, the photographer and the historian are of course selective. But in their acts of judging and choosing they are directed by "empathy" with a shared world of daily living rather than by "disengaged spontaneity." The photographer, as Kracauer argues in *Theory of Film*, does not impose himself on the visual world with independently "creative" authority; he

> resembles perhaps most of all the imaginative reader intent on studying and deciphering an elusive text.[4] Like a reader, the photographer is steeped in the book of nature. His "intensity of vision," claims Paul Strand, should be rooted in a "real respect for the thing in front of him." Or in Weston's words, the camera "provides the photographer with a means of looking deeply into the nature

> of things, and presenting his subjects in terms of their basic reality." Due to the revealing power of the camera, there is also something of an explorer about him; insatiable curiosity stirs him to roam yet unconquered expanses and capture the strange patterns in them. (16)

When Ansel Adams, his friend and admirer, expressed reservations about Edward Weston's photographic studies of vegetables, among them the famous "Pepper No. 30, 1930," he countered with the suggestion that the use of the term *abstraction* needed to be rethought. He was very well aware, he wrote, that many viewers whose judgment he respected had thought his representations of vegetables too close to sculpture and thus too abstract. But what did these viewers mean by the term *abstract*?

> No painter or sculptor can be wholly abstract. We cannot imagine forms not already existing in nature,–we know nothing else. Take the extreme abstractions of Brancusi: they are all based upon natural forms. I have often been accused of imitating his work,–and I most assuredly admire and may have been "inspired" by it– . . . Actually, I have proved, through photography, that Nature has all the "abstract" (simplified) forms Brancusi or any other artist can imagine. With my camera I go directly to Brancusi's *source*.[5] I find *ready to use*–select and isolate–what he has to "create." One might as well say that Brancusi imitates nature as to accuse me of imitating Brancusi . . . just because I found these forms first hand.[6]

For Weston, photography is "'seeing' plus"–the "plus" being the "basis of all arguments on 'what is art.'" That "plus" signifies deviations from the norms of seeing. In contrast to the human eye, the camera captures and fixes the particularity of the moment. Lenses are used to exaggerate what is seen by the naked eye, and the techniques of printing enable further variations: "This, we must agree, is all legitimate procedure–but it is not 'seeing' literally, it is done with a reason, with creative imagination."[7]

Kracauer's reference to Weston in the passage quoted above overemphasizes his role as witness for the "realism" of photography as the "only art which leaves its raw material more or less intact."[8] However, one needs to keep in mind here that Kracauer proceeds from the assumption that construction is an inevitable component of representation. At issue is the *manner* rather than the fact of the photographer's controlling, constructing, interpretive activity. The intactness of the visible is explicitly linked to the photographer's or "film artist's" "insatiable curiosity," interest in exploration, or (resorting to metaphor) imaginative readerly activities.[9] All these attributes suggest an active rather than passive role of the photographer, the "seeing 'plus'." To come back briefly once more to Weston's famous pepper, "I have on occasion used the expression, 'to make a pepper more than a pepper.' I now realize that it is a carelessly worded phrase. I did not mean 'different' than a pepper, but a pepper *plus*,—seeing it more definitely than does the casual observer, presenting it so that the importance of form and texture is intensified."[10]

The emphasis here is on the photographer's challenge to intensify (natural) forms so that they can be seen more clearly. His responsibility is not, in Weston's view, to isolate a significant 'pepperness' of the pepper. It is to share an existent particular object with his viewers by visually elucidating its particularity.[11] Weston's point is clarified by a photo image like Jan Groover's "Untitled 1979," part of her "Table Top Still Life" project. Her photograph of peppers arranged with kitchen utensils "quotes" Weston's peppers and "transforms" them, by sophisticated photographic technology, into seemingly painted peppers that are visually interesting solely because of their spatial arrangement, not because of their shape or texture. The effect is visually pleasing pictorialism—an abstraction from photographic potential that Weston wished to overcome.[12]

Here Kracauer and Weston do indeed meet; here, too, is the crucial link between the photographer and the historian. When in the notes for *History* the "genuine historian" appeared as an "insatiable reader and curious explorer" (10), it was to stress her responsibility to reclaim a once visible world of daily life, even to shed light on what had been obscure about it to its contemporaries.[13] And the reference made, in the introduction to *History*, to the relation established already in 1927 between photography and historiography,[14] served to emphasize, as a challenge, the accessibility of human worlds past and present because they are and were shared in experience.

In the introduction to *Theory of Film*, Kracauer remembered that the first film he saw as a young boy had impressed him so much that he wanted to write about it. He never forgot the title he had made up for this, his first, literary project on the way home from the movie theater: "Film as the Discoverer of the Marvels of Everyday Life."

> And I remember, as if it were today, the marvels themselves. What thrilled me so deeply was an ordinary suburban street, filled with lights and shadows which transfigured it. Several trees stood about, and there was in the fore-

> ground a puddle reflecting invisible house facades and a piece of sky. Then a breeze moved the shadows, and the facades with the sky below began to waver. The trembling upper world in the dirty puddle–this image has never left me. (xi)

It was not, then, the film as story *about* acts and events which had left an indelible impression on the boy. It was the film as complexly composite, infinitely and marvelously suggestive image, as representation of visible forms. In *Theory of Film* Kracauer was to argue that film as reclamation of physical reality does not (or should not) follow the structure of a story in the literary sense. He was looking, rather, for "cinematic story forms which assert themselves independently of the established literary genres." They were the "found stories," that is, found in the physical environment by the careful observer: "When you have watched for long enough the surface of a river or a lake you will detect certain patterns in the water which may have been produced by a breeze or some eddy. Found stories are in the nature of such patterns."[15]

Found stories, then, need to be discovered rather than constructed–or, rather, constructed in and through acts of discovery. Emerging from the "raw material" of "physical reality," they inscribe the documentary impulses of photography and film which Kracauer thinks the most important potential of the medium. Thus found stories are not restrained by ideological closures because these do not exist in the world of daily life in which cinematic story forms are found and to which they refer. He acknowledged different types of found stories in film praxis, among them Robert Flaherty's "slight narratives,"[16] which testify "to his insistence on eliciting the story from the raw material of life rather than subjecting the raw material to its [the story's] pre-established demands." For those filmic stories "whose common property it is to emerge from, and again disappear in, the flow of life, as suggested by the camera," Kracauer used the term *episode*. He refers to *The Defiant Ones* as an example of what happens to the cinematic qualities of a film when an originally episodic filmic story is turned into an ideologically closed literary story. In that case the film becomes "a theatrical morality play," which is less convincingly realistic–that is, cinematic–because its composition has been influenced too directly by its socially valuable message. An episode–the escape and eventual inevitable recapture of two prisoners, a white and a black man chained to each other—is turned into the documentation of a learning process of mutual trusting. Kracauer thought that the "ideology behind the film did not grow out of the reality depicted but, conversely, assumed the role of a prime mover; the inner change of the two runaways is a foregone conclusion which predetermines the order and meaning of the successive scenes. Hence the impression that the film is a tale of human dignity, a sermon against the evil of race bias" (251f.).

Impressed by the cultural significance of such tales, Kracauer nevertheless thought the tale could have been told more convincingly had cinematic narration been allowed to assert itself. However, though it would have created more psychological credibility, such medium-specific narrative would have undermined the clarity and certainty of a sermonizing story. In his remarks on filmic composition in the 1940 outline of a systematic exploration of the issues, Kracauer had repeatedly contrasted film, which evokes the "whole world" in its randomness and openness, with theater, which is selective and intentional and tends toward representational "totality" in both moral and artistic terms. He saw a tendency in the popular medium to move closer to theater and thereby into the world of high culture. But the peculiar potentiality of film is violated in an "act of seizure" by "parasitic" theater; in fact, as Kracauer said here categorically, there is no commonality between film and theater.[17]

Theater is limited to "one single distance," "one single placement"; stage settings are unchangeable, that is, "they are pictures also insofar as they are static." Most importantly, theater, because it cannot leave totality behind, is incapable of penetrating the "material dimension," which film "in its origin" instinctively strives to present. Theater, by necessity, is anthropocentric. Originating in cult, it remains tied to it because it cannot help natural things to be present and to speak for themselves (11). The totality of theatrical representation excludes the contingencies of the life-world, which film, being open-ended, includes. Theater tends to affirm the constraints of visual and verbal perceptual conventions; film can expand perception because of the *multiple* distances, placements, and perspectives characteristic of the medium.[18] Such expansive mobility includes precisely those inconspicuous but sociologically important phenomena of the natural-cultural world that the "totality" of theater cannot accommodate. For the sake of this crucial inclusion, Kracauer emphasized here the significance of "*Kollektivarbeit*" in the making of a film. In the filmic medium, he argues, collective work supports rather than hinders artistic perfection because no individual can "calculate" the entangled interdependencies that make up everyday life.[19] In its coordination of photo images, film is indeed the medium of communication most congenial to the modern experience of an expanding world that is multidimensional and multiperspectivist and therefore relational.

In *Theory of Film*, twenty years later, Kracauer did not separate film and theater so sharply, because he was working now with a grid of classifications derived from the practice of filmmaking, a wealth of specific, diverse, and, taken together, contradictory examples.[20] But the earlier attempts at understanding "what exactly" was (the nature of) film are instructive precisely because they involved the construction of improbably clean distinctions that, on occasion, could yield strikingly clear insights. One ought not forget here the significance of the context in which Kracauer focused his thought on what was arguably new about filmic representation of the processes of daily life. He composed the outline in Marseille in 1940 in a state of political and cultural statelessness, his life in danger, despairing that the literally incredible difficulties with affidavits (in lieu of confiscated passports), transit visas for Spain and Portugal, visa extensions for the United States, and boat tickets from Lissabon would ever be sorted out. In this real and impossible situation, such "really" impossible distinguishing, defining, and ordering may have kept him sane.

2 The truly new cultural contribution of photography and film was their documentary potential: this is the point at which the troubling, and the worthwhile, questions began. In *Theory of Film*, Kracauer raised the important issue of how to communicate the experience of rapidly changing living conditions in mass democracies and mass technocracies of which film, as he rightly saw, was an enormously important part. He saw, too, that the epistemological and hermeneutic questions posed by the still relatively new concept of the documentary were baffling. As investigative reporting, "reportage," employed literary strategies, so photography and film with explicitly documentary intentions employed artistic strategies of perspective, selection, and composition. Common since the twenties, the

use of the camera lens as a metaphor for the objectivity of good journalism[21] has clearly been fallacious. Both the literary and the photo journalist impose their own personalities, their experience, on what they perceive. But this metaphor has also pointed to the most characteristic and legitimizing properties of both literary and photographic documentary and has influenced, to an extent, the expectations brought to film.[22]

Kracauer's analytical grouping of individual films and his selection of illustrations[23] shows that he was aware of the situation. From the beginning of his involvement with the new medium, he had been trying to define the specific properties of photography and film in terms of modern epistemology, namely as increasingly enabling "empirical content"–analogous to modern scientific thought. The modern cognitive mood of curiosity about new and surprising phenomena supported an open-ended process of inquiry.[24] But within the context of a modern attitude to knowledge, Kracauer was keenly aware of the different functions of different modes of knowledge. In particular, he knew very well that the documentary mode, whether literary or photographic, was not "scientific." The documentary is a "mixed" mode. Its most obvious and most instructive problems concern the role of fictionality in a situation in which an observed natural or cultural reality is *represented*, namely pictured or documented, with a stated claim to objectivity. Because this reality is at the same time also *presented* as the construct of an observer whose subjectivity is recognizable in the literary or compositional strategies that declare her responsible for that construct. Such strategies signify the observer's diminished assertiveness as witness. But they also proclaim–and, if successful, demonstrate–the observer's particular effectiveness as rhetorically (visually) self-conscious guide of readers (viewers) seeking the fullest possible access to the subject matter of the literary or photo documentary. And there is the added complication that the photographer as selecting, organizing viewer is differently involved in a natural than in a cultural reality. This is true even if we agree that for the viewer whose interests are not primarily scientific natural realities are also explicitly cultural constructs.

Theory of Film does not attempt a systematic analysis of these indeed impossibly entangled issues. There are cumulative hints, suggestions, puzzles. Thus Kracauer points out that precisely the "pull" of two conflicting interests–the impact of the combined representational and presentational modes–may have been

> responsible for the inconsistent attitudes and performances of some photographers with strong painterly inclinations. [Henry Peach] Robinson, the early artist-photographer who recommended that truth [representation as an ideally objective picture of the pictured] should be sacrificed to beauty, at the same time eulogized, as if under a compulsion, the medium's unrivaled truth to reality. Here also belongs the duality in Edward Weston's work; devoted to both abstraction and realism, he paid tribute to the latter's superiority only after having become aware of their incompatibility and of his split allegiance. (12)

For individual photographers who have particularly strong painterly talents or predilections, this split may be unavoidable. But what does the split signify for the cultural status of the medium? The dual allegiance of individual photographers has its source in the dual nature of photographic representation: the camera reveals reality, but the meaning, that is, the interpretation, of such revelation is (to varying degrees) controlled by the photographer. Kracauer's attitude toward this phenomenon–he comes back to it again and again and it is indeed crucial to his argument–is open-ended rather than ambiguous. It is for him not so much a question of finding (defining) a solution for the duality "natural" to photographic (and historiographic) representation as of evaluating its results.

In the preface to *Theory of Film* Kracauer distinguishes his study from "most writings in the field" as "a *material*" rather than "formal" aesthetics–an aesthetics concerned with "content." *Content* here means the visible world. Kracauer wishes to impress on the reader that the notion of visibility in photo images includes many phenomena doomed to remain invisible, "were it not for the picture camera's ability to catch them on the wing." Again, he is impressed by the literalness of claims that photography enables another part of the familiar world to become ours. Photo images, especially in film, are "uniquely equipped" and therefore "conceivably animated by a desire to picture transient material life, life at its most ephemeral." Street crowds are among such "fleeting impressions," as well as small, individual gestures, unconscious and profoundly revealing, and a host of inconspicuous and seemingly insignificant visual details. For an example Kracauer here tells his reader that "the contemporaries of Lumière praised his films–the first ever to be made–for showing "the ripple of the leaves stirred by the wind" (ix).

Does the credit for noticing that detail and thereby preserving it go to Lumière? Or his camera? Or the viewers of his film? Kracauer's assumption is that film cameras and (a group of) filmmakers together are responsible for the unique achievement of film which such preservation signifies. Pointing out the film-specific openness to the "endless," "indeterminate" "flow" of everyday life (60), he does not seem to give much thought to the mental activity of film viewers who do see what they are meant to see by the filmmaker and, more than that, by virtue of the recording, storing potential of the camera. Were those viewers particularly sensitive who saw those small details in Lumière's films and who praised him for putting them there with the help of the camera? Was it because of Lumière and his camera that they could not but see them now? But had not these images been suggestive to them from the beginning? Had the viewers not observed those ripples of leaves before with pleasure and therefore, remembering, appreciated their presence in the film?

An aesthetics of film built on the assumption that "films are true to the medium to the extent that they penetrate the world before our eyes" has to take seriously the implication of "our eyes": a community of observers which includes the maker and the viewer of the photo image. "The premise and axis" of Kracauer's study, such penetration means that the world is ours and is before or around us, and that in the medium of film it is and remains accessible to us.[25] This is why an aesthetics specific to photographic images has to separate film and photography from "the traditional arts": "Works of art consume the raw material from which they are drawn, whereas films as an outgrowth of camera work are bound to exhibit it. However purposefully directed, the motion picture camera would cease to be a camera if it did not record visible phenomena for their own sake. . . . If film is an art, it is art with a difference. Along with photography, film is the only art which leaves its raw material more or less intact" (x).

This situation constitutes a specific risk for the filmmaker as well as as a special opportunity. In the Epilogue, reviewing and summing up his arguments, Kracauer reiterates that film is "the only art which exhibits its raw material."

> Such art as goes into cinematic films must be traced to their creators' capacity for reading the book of nature. The film artist has traits of an imaginative reader or an explorer prodded by insatiable curiosity. To repeat a definition given in earlier contexts, he is "a man who sets out to tell a story but, in shooting it, is so overwhelmed by his innate desire to cover all of physical reality–and also by a feeling that he must cover it in order to tell the story, any story, in cinematic terms–that he ventures ever deeper into the jungle of material phenomena in which he risks becoming irretrievably lost if he does not, by virtue of great efforts, get back to the highways he left."[26]

But such self-loss, at least as one stage in the process of decisions that shape the resulting photo image, is also central to the photographic medium. A "minimum requirement" (13) for the aesthetic success of a photo image is, then, its reflecting the photographer's surrender to the experience, sharing it with others, of a natural-cultural world that is both elusive and accessible.

The surrender is not passively receptive. The attempt to elucidate this, as it were, "mixed" composite perspective of the photographer, which makes for the "mixed" mode of the medium, is central to Kracauer's "theory" of film as a "redemption of physical reality." It is also of crucial importance for his reflections on historiography. As in *History*, elucidation in *Theory of Film* assimilates the various shades and shapes the composition can take, the various shapes of objectivity. I am enlarging here and, to an extent, extrapolating from Kracauer's heavily loaded term, *reality*. "*Wirklichkeit*," which Kracauer authorized for the German translation of *Theory of Film*, supports such enlarging because, in contrast to "reality" or "*Realität*," it carries the connation of a "made" reality, "*wirken*," of which Kracauer clearly makes use here. In *Die Angestellten*, he had based his concept of the documentary on the insight that "reality is a construction"[27] and that a mere copying or mirroring kind of reproduction of a complex state of affairs does not yield sufficient information.

All the same, we must not forget that Kracauer was not at all interested in that bracketing of the concept and term, *reality*, which has characterized much of late twentieth-century cultural criticism. He was concerned, rather, about the importance for us of its presence "out there." The phrase, *physical reality*, in the subtitle of the film book immediately draws attention to that concern, especially in the German version: "*äussere [external] Wirklichkeit.*" We may find here intimations of an Einsteinian belief in "objective reality";

but in contrast to Einstein's scientific view of a natural reality essentially independent of our culturally developed inquiring approaches to it, Kracauer's "*äussere Wirklichkeit*," as it appears in the photo image, is at the same time a human construct. This is true, too, where the pictured phenomenon seems exclusively natural–for instance, those ripples of leaves. The perhaps most important implication of Kracauer's argument in *Theory of Film* is consideration of the fact that others have seen before what the photographer sees in the moment of making the photo image by "taking" the picture. More even than a "creative," artistic perspective, this shared vision prevents the photographer from becoming the "camera-eye" or an "indiscriminating mirror" (14f.). In the absence of such culturally learned discrimination, the contribution of both photography and historiography could not be sustained. For it is rooted both in the recognition of the otherness and strangeness, the marvel of the world, and in the developed interdependencies of perception within and across cultural space and time.

Arguing against the concept of the photographer as "devoid of formative impulses," Kracauer summarizes in *Theory of Film* a 1856 realist manifesto: "The artist's attitude toward reality should be so impersonal that he might reproduce the same subject ten times without any of his copies showing the slightest difference" (14). Here he draws on the same passage from *Remembrance of Things Past* that he had used more than thirty years earlier in "Die Photographie" (1927). (He would come back to this passage with yet another differently slanted reading in *History*, when puzzling over the problem of historiographical time.)[28] The passage concerns Proust's distinction between human–temporal, cumulative, qualifying, evaluative, therefore life-enhancing–perception, and photographic–atemporal, instantaneous, quantifying, value-neutral, therefore deadening–perception. Where in his earlier essay Kracauer agreed, if not unambiguously, with many of the cultural implications of this distinction, he now distances himself explicitly from Proust's (and Benjamin's) fear of the allegedly deadening, alienating properties of photography. Photo images, he points out now, do not copy and thereby arrest nature but "metamorphose" it. There are the "unavoidable transformations" emerging from different kinds of dimensionality and color and from the partly irrepressible (because unconscious) subjectivity of the photographer's perspective–which is dependent, too, on neurological conditions of perception (15). And inevitably the photographer's "formative faculties," shaped by his sensibilities, direct the selection of motif, frame, lens, filter, emulsion, and grain.

At issue is the energy of the composite perspective on which photo images thrive. The visible is unlikely "to give itself up" to the photographer "if he does not absorb it with all his senses strained and his whole being participating in the process. The formative tendency, then, does not have to conflict with the realistic tendency. Quite the contrary, it may help substantiate and fulfill it" (15f.). But such substantiation cannot be achieved unless the photographer puts whatever "formative" interests and talents he may have in the service of the documentary potential of his medium. The question is not the externalization of the photographer's vision but rather "the 'right' mixture of his realist loyalties and formative endeavors . . . in which the latter, however strongly developed, surrender their independence to the former" (16).

Theory of Film is focused on the meanings of that surrender because Kracauer experienced so vividly the manmade magic ability of photo images to halt the flux of time. Recording lived lives, they preserve and make present the elusive complexity of what in relation to the representational image is always already the past. He never ceased to be amazed by the promised fullness of such regaining, a fullness that has its source in the particular openness of the photo image. Thus he drew attention to photography's "outspoken affinity for unstaged reality" and its "emphasis on fortuitous complexes which represent fragments rather than wholes," suggesting "endlessness" (16) and indeterminacy. Presentational *and* representational, shaped by her historicity, the photographer's perspective is composite. She cannot but construct what she sees through the camera lens; at the same time, if she is true to her medium, she cannot repress the presence of unseen things. There is the clear connotation in Kracauer's argument of an "ought." This prescriptiveness got him into trouble with critics who aimed to protect the freedom of the photographic "idiom." Kracauer wanted, however, to protect the capacity of the medium to preserve what was overlooked by the photographer as composer or constructor but might be visible to other viewers, in the present or the future. Proust, as Kracauer sees it now, exaggerates "the indeterminacy of photographs as grossly as he does their depersonalizing quality." Yet it is true that photo images exhibit a degree of distancing, even alienation, that coexists with indeterminacy and asserts itself against the photographer's selective and formative impulses. Photographs show a "tendency towards the unorganized and diffuse" that is essential to their effectiveness as records. Inevitably, photo images are "surrounded with a fringe of indistinct multiple meanings" that are differently accessible to different viewers.

The distinction that Kracauer makes here between the photo image and the painterly image is cautiously bracketed, though it is potentially of the greatest importance to his argument.

> (To be sure, the traditional work of art carries many meanings also. But due to its rise from interpretable human intentions and circumstances, the meanings inherent in it can virtually be ascertained, whereas those of the photograph are necessarily indeterminate because the latter is bound to convey unshaped nature itself, nature in its inscrutability. As compared with a photograph, any painting has a relatively definite significance). (20)

Impressed by the medium's recording properties, Kracauer was particularly interested in the openness of photo images, which can and do show what the photographer did not see. He was not interested in the fact that they also can and do *not* show what the photographer saw–or thinks she saw–when she sees the image that seems not to have captured her vision. (This, of course, is also true for the painter in his relation to the painterly image, though the photographer poses differently the question of responsibility regarding the failure relative to the vision of the produced image.) There is also the significant fact that photographers differ greatly in the ways in which they decide on the validity of an image. On one end of the spectrum is the person who takes as many photos of a subject as possible and then selects what seems the best in terms of spatial arrangement, lighting, expression, statement. On the other end is the photographer who patiently waits for that moment when, looking through the lens, he sees the magically right image offering itself. These attitudes are determined by the photographer's temperament and by the nature of the subject matter. Where photographers of natural objects, like Adams (figs. 35, 37) and Weston (figs. 24, 26), would carefully control light (time) and perspective, a socially engaged photographer like Dorothea Lange, looking for images that made relevant statements (fig. 34), would take a great number of photos, precisely because, unlike the much more popular Margaret Bourke-White, she did not wish to "stage" people. In this she, and not the photographer of nature, would come particularly close to Kracauer's sense of the openness of the photo image (though, ironically, Lange's most enduring and most informative images were also her most self-consciously composed). The documentary style of *Life* photographer Alfred Eisenstaedt is a curiously effective symbiosis of compositional imagination and accidental event. His famous V-Day photograph, which, in its much acclaimed visual spontaneity, has captured for millions of viewers the exuberant sense of relief at war's end, would not have been taken had it not been for the visual contrast between the soldier's dark and the nurse's white uniform. And his stylish image of an elegant woman with her poodles, part of a photographic essay on the essence of Fifth Avenue, would not have materialized if the woman had not accidentally appeared where Eisenstaedt was waiting for her to create this enchanting subversion of a fashion photo.[29]

Kracauer's argument for an openness specific to the photo image emphasizes its capacity for exhibiting several shapes of objectivity which are accessible to viewers simultaneously and over time. The shapes of painting reflect more distinctly–and in that sense more exclusively–the painter's position in cultural space and time. More capacious, the photo image diffuses its spatiotemporal position by including what may be seen only later, in another place or time, but which existed. Implicit, here, is again the argument for recognition of both the otherness and strangeness of the world and the acculturated nature of seeing. In contrast to a photo image that is true to its medium, the painterly image is more restricted by this acculturation. Kracauer locates in this comparison his insight into the uniquely modern status of photography. To a modern culture that is conscious of the flux of time and therefore anchored, if precariously, in historicity, photo images can contribute an enlarged historical experience precisely because they inadvertently retain traces of what has existed. It may or may not have been seen before the photographer "took" the picture; it may or may not have been seen by the photographer; it may or may not be seen later. Potentially, like the natural world but in terms of historical time, it has always been there to be experienced, and its presence is recovered and preserved in the photo image.

3 When Kracauer was sorting out the meanings of photographic objectivity in *Theory of Film*, he had not so much left behind as transformed his earlier positions in his Weimar film criticism and in *From Caligari to Hitler*. The transformation concerned importantly the historicity of the viewer, and it was was more radical in relation to the later (postwar) than to the earlier (prewar) position. In both cases the viewer was engaged in evaluating the status of social-political knowledge of filmic representation. However, there are instructive differences between the judgments made by Kracauer in his role as film critic writing a weekly review in the twenties and early thirties and as historian who, drawing on those contemporary reviews, looked back at the meanings of filmic images for Weimar culture. Both roles share the hermeneutic difficulties inherent in the "mixed" mode of photographic (and historiographic) representation. Rooted in the viewer's composite position—at this particular point in time and space—they concern above all his responses to the image maker's composite vision. This vision may be equal to the viewer's in its degree of complexity; it may even share the viewer's cultural "there and then." Yet, differently interested in social-political issues, differently tolerant of conflicts and ambiguities, it is different with respect to the kind of complexity.

When the exile Kracauer tried to argue, from a position of hindsight, a foreshadowing of future political developments in Weimar films, the issue of a combined "material" indeterminacy and formal determinacy in the making of films proved to be a major problem. The modernity of Weimar had been a dynamic, exhilarating, and troubling urban experience to which the new medium of film was particularly responsive and to which it contributed the powerful presence of photo images. Abundant discussions concerning filmic rendering of the fast flow of urban daily life brought to the surface profoundly contradictory concepts of the meaning and the cultural status of photographic images and of their social value.

Emphasizing the documentary imagination, Kracauer argued that Walter Ruttmann's cross-section editing in the classic *Berlin: Die Symphonie einer Grosstadt* (1927) had produced a "surface approach" inimical to the intentions of both the project's author, Carl Mayer, and the cameraman, Karl Freund. Mayer, who was tired of "fictional invention" and wanted his stories to "grow from reality," had conceived the idea of a city symphony one day in

1925 while standing on a busy corner in Berlin with the traffic whirling around him. Freund had set out "to shoot Berlin scenes with the voracious appetite of a man starved for reality," knowing full well that he had to come up with all sorts of contrivances that would allow him to do candid camera work, "the only type of photography that is really art. Why? Because with it one is able to portray *life* . . . A very fast lens. Shooting life. Realism. Ah, that is photography in its purest form. . . ."[30] But Ruttmann, who was known for his abstract films and in *Berlin* collaborated with the young composer Edmund Meisel of *Potemkin* fame, was mainly interested in the purity of the *form* of filmic realism. His editorial emphasis on "pure patterns of movement" caused Mayer to withdraw from the project. Kracauer had taken Mayer's and Freund's position as a contemporary reviewer of the film, and he took it again as a historian:

> Machine parts in motion are shot and cut in such a manner that they turn into dynamic displays of an almost abstract character. These may symbolize what has been called the "tempo" of Berlin; but they are no longer related to machines and their functions. The editing also resorts to striking analogies between movements or forms. Human legs walking on the pavement are followed by legs of cows; a sleeping man on a bench is associated with a sleeping elephant. In those cases in which Ruttmann furthers the pictorial development through specific content, he inclines to feature social contrast. One picture unit connects a cavalcade in the Tiergarten with a group of women beating carpets; another juxtaposes hungry children in the street and opulent dishes in some restaurant. Yet these contrasts are not so much social protests as formal expedients. Like visual analogies, they serve to build up the cross section, and their structural function overshadows whatever significance they may convey.[31]

Ruttmann, recording with indifference the prevailing political-moral indifference of modern urban populations, was fascinated exclusively by the formal quality of the "tempo" of Berlin. When Mayer called *Berlin* a "surface approach," he did not object to formal editing as such but condemned,rather, Ruttmann's "formal attitude toward a reality that cried out for criticism, for interpretation." Mayer, in Kracauer's view, would never have "misused social contrasts as pictorial transitions, or recorded increasing mechanization without objectifying his horror of it" (187). Instructively, in his contemporary review of the film in *Frankfurter Zeitung* (1927), Kracauer had focused on Ruttmann's lack of attention to the *visual* reality of Berlin–a focus that produced an even more severe but also more effective critique because it helped to clarify the meanings of *formal.* He had listed here the many aspects of Berlin not captured in the film: its different centers, woods, lakes, districts; its different populations, such as blue-collar workers, white-collar workers, shopkeepers, haute bourgeoisie; its different looks at different times of the day. But most importantly, Kracauer had blamed the filmmaker's failure on the fact that he had set out to compose a "symphony" of Berlin before he had really *looked* at it. Ruttman had started with an intellectual-ideological concept, *Berlin,* rather than with an informed vision. His images were distorted by his superimposing, without attention to what *could* be seen, abstracting formal impulses on an urban reality that in social-political terms had an overwhelming visual presence. Precisely his lack of attention to that presence had made him vulnerable to ideological preconceptions.[32]

In *Caligari,* Kracauer left open the question whether the candid camera work of Freund, without focused editing, would have achieved "objectification" of the meanings of accelerated mechanization. On the whole, he did not like the cross-section or "montage" films that came into a vogue after *Berlin.* "They could be produced at low cost; and they offered a gratifying opportunity of showing much and revealing nothing" (188). A qualified exception was the silent movie, *Menschen am Sonntag* (1929), made by a collective including Robert Siodmak and Billy Wilder. Kracauer attributed its partial success to it characters, lower-middle-class white-collar workers who at the end of the Weimar Republic were wooed by the Nazis as well as the Social Democrats. The "whole domestic situation," Kracauer pointed out here, "depended on whether they would cling to their middle-class prejudices or acknowledge their common interests with the working class" (189).

Kracauer had written his investigative series on the *Angestellten* that same year, and his findings not only documented but also explained their vulnerability to Nazi propaganda. His postwar comments on the film emphasized rightly the politically pivotal role played by this group but dwelt too much on their psychological deformation through lack of identitiy. Thus he approved of the ways in which the film showed them spending their Sundays at one of Berlin's many lakes, cooking out, bathing, and making "futile contact." A beach photographer taking snapshots, which appear within the film itself, freezes the characters in motion. As if by black magic, average individuals are transformed into "ludicrous products of mere chance"; and these snapshots "seem designed to demonstrate how little substance is left to lower middle-class people. Along with shots of deserted Berlin streets and houses, they corroborate . . . the spiritual vacuum in which the mass of employees actually lived" (189).

Nevertheless, Kracauer found this film, too, essentially flawed. The issue of "truth," namely the right kind of evidence, was clearly a subtext here, though it never fully surfaced. Neither Ruttmann nor the filmmakers who contributed to *Menschen am Sonntag* had sufficiently contemplated the social reality that they photographed with so much attention to detail. But why had they not? Quoting himself, Kracauer enlisted the contemporary film critic's help to enlarge the historian's observational perspective, but in fact he just repeated an earlier attack on Ruttmann (187f.). He still agreed with his earlier judgment that a lack of balance between "form" and "content" produced that lack of "true understanding" so clearly reflected in the filmic images. But as a historian of Weimar film, Kracauer was not much interested in analyzing how the filmmakers' cinematic decisions were indeed connected with flawed social-psychological judgments. He simply presupposed such interdependencies. Films he had admired then and still admired now, for instance Hans Richter's "film essays," inevitably managed to show the "truth" of a particular social situation. But then Richter was "one of the few truly incorruptible film artists of the left." Contrasting the cinematic approach of Ruttmann with that of Richter, who also came from abstract painting, Kracauer pointed out that Richter rejected Ruttmann's "formal transitions in favor of cutting procedures designed to bring about a true understanding of what inflation really meant" (193f.). Or, commenting on a group of films strongly influenced by Soviet cinema, he had special praise for *Mutter Krausens Fahrt ins Glück*, based on a script by Heinrich Zille, because of the "veracity of its North Berlin milieu." He was impressed by the "truthful" documentation of the "abominable housing conditions" characteristic of that milieu. But how was such veracity achieved? Kracauer explained that the filmmaker was a former cameraman and that, in contrast to earlier Zille films with their "studio-built proletarian surroundings" he had used documentary shots (197). The circularity of the argument here goes back behind the position stated in *Die Angestellten*. "Somehow" the documentary mode, whether in verbal or photo representation, now *eo ipso* achieves a vision that reveals the truth of reality. A documentary shot is equated with untainted evidence, regardless of the position from which it was made or from which it was or is viewed.[33]

In the notes to *History*, written in the sixties, Kracauer explicitly connected the "found story" of film with the discourse of historiography:[34] the photographer's and the historian's business is to reclaim both the entangled (natural) randomness and (cultural) constructedness of daily life. A few years after the war, writing the history of a recent and very troubled past as he saw it reflected in the films of the period, Kracauer disregarded many of the questions that arise from this entanglement. They concern the precise nature of the authority of the perspective on which are based the photographer's (and the historian's) photographic or cinematic (narrational) judgments. This authority controls the crucial interrelation between presentation and representation, construction and discovery, story and evidence. Later, in his reflections on the reading and writing of history, Kracauer would be sharply aware of the intimate connection between the historian's point of observation and the kind of information gathered and presented, which would lead him to question the authority of the historian's narrational position and strategies. Arguably, the link established in *History* between photography and historiography would be important to him because it affirmed a shared responsibility to the actuality of others' lives which would keep such authority in check.

Yet when he emphasized in *History* analogies between verbal and visual representation in knowledge production, Kracauer did not open his argument to the host of problems stirred up by that connection. To what extent does the photographic medium "really" share, share in kind, the age-old hermeneutic difficulties of verbal representation? Writing about historiography, Kracauer was very much aware of the difficulties faced by all historians in gaining access to past reality—not to speak of their sharing that access with readers in a future relative to that past which would, in time, include their present. He used the analogies to photography in order to state and clarify these difficulties; he did not submit the implications of the analogies themselves to analysis.

But writing the history of Weimar film, Kracauer did not consider a different epistemological status of different representational modes. Moreover, he glossed over questions of access which touch on the much more obvious differences of observational position. There were different interpretations of social reality in his verbal and the filmmakers' visual reconstructions—a reality at which the latter looked from a (roughly) contemporary position but he from a position of *remembered* contemporaneity and, more powerfully, of hindsight. Their observational position was in the present relative to the events; his was in both that present and its future and was therefore more comprehensive and mobile—or so he thought. Since he did not explore the implications of his double perspective but simply expected from it privileged access to knowing a particularly difficult and demanding past, it in fact tended to arrest his critical vision. The problems he found with Weimar films were too exclusively associated with individual filmmakers who just did not have the right (ideal) documentary competence and imagination. In *Theory of Film*, able to distance himself from this past, he would describe (rather than demand) this desirable talent and attitude in terms of an ideal to be approached rather than fully realized: the photographer's "intensity of vision," "insatiable curiosity," and involvement in the process of searching for a balance between "formative aspirations" and the "desire to render reality," the "balance between empathy and spontaneity" (12, 16f.).

Consequently, when looking at Weimar films from the postwar position of a cultural historian of the period, Kracauer did not contemplate the fact that the economic, social, and psychological reality of Weimar to be "redeemed" in photography and film was a multifaceted and rapidly shifting cultural construct. After the cultural rupture caused by the war, it could not be the same for him and for prewar observers who did not share his cultural "there and then." Yet he imposed such sameness in his hindsight evaluations of Weimar filmmakers' "desire to render reality"—a reality, moreover, that in this case included the cultural reactions to and influences on the making of photo images. Rigorous consideration of positional historicity can of course be paralyzing for the historian, especially where knowledge of the past concerns the complex perceptual interdependencies of a modern culture. Kracauer's thesis concerns a politically harmful symbiotic connection between filmic images and the troubled national psyche from which they originate and to which they return, thereby exacerbating a group's explosive anxieties and desires. One might argue that in this case the historian has to be able to bracket, up to a point and for the sake of the thesis, the more subtle epistemological entanglements. But historical judgment in *Caligari* appears too rigidly preshaped by an ideological message that has obscured the awareness, central to historical inquiry, of the positionality of knowledge.

4 In the 1940 outline, and more clearly in *Theory of Film*, Kracauer realized the significant capacity of photo images to preserve, beyond the representational-presentational image construct, the hidden "inscrutable" repose or traces of daily life. This capacity signified that a medium-specific uncertainty of knowledge was an important aspect of photography's unique contribution to modernity.[35] An instant in the process of Kracauer's intellectual transformation, that realization took him beyond the observational awareness of his Weimar texts. But they had prepared him for it, especially his film criticism and *Die Angestellten*. Impressed by the constructed nature of social reality, Kracauer had elicited from white-collar workers their own stories. He had deassembled and reassembled them to show more clearly the confusing diversity of private and political motivations that had gone into their making. At the same time he had tried to sustain their authorship as much as possible in his narration, since he had noticed and found instructive the stories' resistance to it where it fit too closely his own observational position. Retelling their stories, he needed to be tolerant of lacunae and contradictions.

Much of Kracauer's ongoing film criticism during the Weimar period had shown sensitivity to that problem. But his concerns in *Caligari* would prevent him from acknowledging any uncertainty vis-à-vis the complex social-political reality of Weimar culture. Having looked at many quite different films, he forcefully unified in his thesis observed multiple practices of filmmaking without reflecting on the position from which he did so. He used this approach despite deep-rooted intellectual reservations regarding the usefulness of generalizations in this field of inquiry. (It is true that images with their suggestive promise of greater immediacy and therefore accessibility may have made it easier to suspend such reservations in the interest of the message. Kurt Tucholsky, one of the most intelligent, shrewdest, and funniest of Weimar literary journalists, used to say that an image says more than a thousand words.[36] Obviously, it depends on the image and the words, both of them exploitable and corruptible. Then there is the argument that the multiplicity and diversity of photo images and language Kracauer encountered in the United States were the source for the much greater hermeneutic openness and epistemological caution of *Theory of Film*, not to speak of *History*).

In *Caligari*, it was precisely the observer's temporally combined perspective that elicited such generalization because, unquestioned, it gave even more credence to the notion that the observer from hindsight can determine a particular truth, social or political, to which the filmmaker in the past had to be responsible. Kracauer had been more open to the uncertainty of knowledge and more content with approximation in his regular film reviews for *Frankfurter Zeitung* and for other journals from 1924 to 1939. Here he wrote as a practising journalist contemporary with the acts, actors, and events represented in films about the function and meaning of a new genre of communication that was rapidly becoming an important medium of cultural self-expression. When he was working on *Caligari* and going back to his own earlier views on these films, Kracauer described to Hermann Hesse his intentions in the postwar, postholocaust study: "I am analysing German films from 1918 to 1933 in ways which will allow me to make precise statements on the psychological disposition predominant among Germans at that time. It is an attempt to get a grip on the decisive psychic processes which at that time occurred in Germany deep underneath the surface of diverging ideologies."[37]

From the historian's position in the future–the present tense of writing the *Caligari* book and the letter to Hesse–Kracauer knew that events seen through the filmmaker's contemporary perspective would profoundly, traumatically rupture his personal life and his cultural environment. Since he based his interpretation of Weimar culture so exclusively on what he saw as "decisive" aspects of the collective national psyche, Kracauer closed this past, which was Weimar, to its future enlargement by different readings supported by different kinds of evidence. Looking back to this past in the forties, he thought that film after film documented, over a period of almost a decade, that it could not have happened otherwise.

As a historian, Kracauer was involved here in the past in ways that caused him to transfer it too directly into its future. There were no surprises in his material, the films of the past, because there could be no future for that past other than the present of the historian's position as a German intellectual, exiled in America, who had lost his culture to Hitlerism. In this perspective, his postwar present was indeed a "future past."[38] Though the historian's temporality may support the tendency to project in this way, it can also be called on to check it. As a historian of Weimar film and "knowing" the outcome, Kracauer was more certain in the selection of his evidence than he ought to have been. When he was viewing and reviewing films as a contemporary over a period of time, he shared with them a present becoming a past rich in social and political conflict and technological development. He did not write the history of these films from a perspective that was informed by a future unknowable to the people who made them. As a contemporary observer he combined, for his readers in this future, a much more instructive perspective of openness to the filmmakers' potential development and informed opinion regarding their cultural responsibility.

Reading these reviews in the sequence in which they were written, one gains a multifaceted and contradictory sense of the Weimar cultural climate. For the reviewer Kracauer, film was preeminently the medium for representing a contemporary reality as cultural construct in whose making he and his readers participated[39]–otherwise it would be no more than a medium for escape. The actitivity of the critic who reviews his experience of a work is based on such contemporaneous cultural sharing. In all his reviews Kracauer measured the successes of films against a contemporary "reality (*Wirklichkeit*)," the actuality of life in the twenties and thirties, defining its representation by its visual accessibility. In terms of its cultural contribution, the magic of film, quite literally, was located for Kracauer in its power to record and thereby to preserve the traces of lived time, to extend lifetime. Reviewing Joe May's *Asphalt* (1929; he criticized the film because of its inept handling of the street milieu),[40] Kracauer marveled at the presence in the movie of an actor who had died recently: the dead man's continued life on the screen seemed "almost incomprehensible."[41] The miracle of film, then, is the time-defeating preservation of an (always already past) reality, and thus it is connected to the cultural enterprise of historiography.

The important question, "Whose reality?" which is not dealt with in *Caligari*, explicitly informs *History* in its extended version, "Whose history?" Remarkably, it is posed already in the film reviews. There is an instructive logic to this, as it were, subterranean connection. As a genre, reviews of artefacts stress the presence of others: they, too, will see the work under discussion and, examining their own experience, will agree or disagree with the critic. Given a thoughtful, informed critic, critique, even if it is forceful, can serve as an experimental guide to experience. In contradistinction to high-cultural, academic interpretation of art works or to rigorously interpretive historiography (like *Caligari*), it preserves a spontaneity and immediacy of insight that keep it open-ended, subject to discussion. When Kracauer praised a circus film for its "hundreds of correct obervations," he agreed that "this is the way a manager eats his supper, the way riding masters look, circus artists behave toward their director." Asserting that these detailed observations added up to a "film which at least convincingly reflects reality,"[42] he based his judgment both on his own view, his access to such reality, and on his assumption that it was shared by other viewers. Instructively, he contrasted this film's "decent work" with Murnau's first Hollywood film, *Sunrise*, which had used an idiosyncratic mixture of fictitious East Prussian villages (made of boards) and fantasized American towns. Here the filmic work was sloppy because it disregarded the conventions of reality. Whether his judgment was–would be proved–right or not, it was based on his assumption that a recognizably "true" reality in the film has to fit the shared experience of many viewers. Central to Kracauer's critical position was the recognition of film as a public, a mass medium, a condition that did not diminish but rather enhanced its cultural importance and potential value.

The question of access or evidence was not answered with these observations, because Kracauer had posed it only indirectly. Three decades later, in *History*, he would pose it directly in broadly conceived epistemological terms, but even then he would not proceed systematically. As a reviewer, he circled around the question of knowledge in his critique of filmic constructs or presentations of the modern world, but he was openly prescriptive with regard to the poetics of film. Cinematic presentation of daily life as its (partial) "redemption" from misrepresentation and forgetting in time was the measure of the contribution of film to a modern culture defined by temporality. Such presentation, then, had to be judged rigorously in terms of an achieved representation, the relation of the pictured to the picture. In arguing the importance of this relation, Kracauer did not, of course, avoid the hermeneutic circle that is central to all examination of artefacts, verbal or pictorial. The question, again, is one of degree: he was less in danger here than he would be in *Caligari* of arresting that circle. The varied, reflected descriptions of films guided his tentative definitions of what was and what was not adequate cinematic response to the challenges of a difficult contemporary reality. Most important, he continuously enlarged his repertoire of descriptive (rather than analytical) definitions from the *poiesis* of the films under consideration.

5 As reviewer, Kracauer excelled in intelligently concise paraphrases of the cultural messages, intentions, and assumptions of movies. He used them to direct the reader to the film-specific issues connected with the filmmakers' choice and treatment of subject matter in terms of both larger conceptual structures and their use of images and sound. The representational, preserving potential of film was for Kracauer preeminently visual. One could say that his judgment here was logically based on the properties of the medium. But (from hindsight) it seems that he was overly critical, in view of its obvious infancy, of the early examples of the "talking film (*Tonfilm*)." It was hard for any *Tonfilm* to measure up to good silent movies, which, being centered in the image, met more readily the challenge of representing and preserving reality. *Tonfilm* failed not only in the cinematically meaningful coordination of sound and image. It (therefore) also succumbed too easily to uncritical borrowing, against its own inner logic, from the novel, the drama, the operetta. It is true, of course, that verbal signification can (and does) distract from or distort or limit the understanding of iconic signification, but Kracauer's position in this respect was rather extreme.[43] Somehow the increasing technical sophistication of the medium seemed to provoke anxieties concerning the cultural role of technology. This was an anxiety common among Weimar intellectuals, and it was clearly present in Benjamin's deep ambiguity and Adorno's outright hostility toward film.[44] Kracauer usually had better informed and more sensible opinions in that matter, for instance in an unpublished essay "Zur Frage der Internationalität des Tonfilms" (1930), where he argued that the film's message was the filmic medium, that is, the internationally and interculturally mediating, connecting potential of visual images. The usurpation and domination of film by speech undermined precisely the international

character of silent films, causing the all-embracing language of images to regress into Babylonion verbal chaos. Intent on showing the culturally superior potential of silent film in a period of increasing political polarization and isolation,[45] Kracauer's argument here did not—as it would in *Theory of Film*—consider the acculturated nature of seeing.

In the important review "Tonbildfilm" (1928),[46] Kracauer first emphasized, with its marvelous technological advances, the cultural potential and responsibility of the brand new talking film. He praised Walter Ruttmann's *Tonbildfilm des Systems Tri-Ergon* as an interesting experiment but complained about the "meaningless way" in which Ruttmann had dealt with the challenge to reproduce as many sounds as possible, subjecting them to an uncinematic "literary idea" (409f.). Yet these reservations did not diminish his fascination: "People speak while their lips move, machines creak, sea lions snort and hiss. Life repeats itself in image and sound, what is past comes up again and again." More directly and more powerfully, talking film can reclaim and preserve human experience centered in the awareness of time passing because its reflection ("*Abbildung*") of human reality is potentially more complete than that achieved by the silent film.[47]

Kracauer also thought uniquely promising the capacity of the new technology to "redeem" the "spontaneous sounds of the street." *Redeeming* here meant uncovering, rediscovering these collective, anonymous universal sounds that surround us everywhere, so much so that we are no longer aware of them.[48] Reclaimed as an audible presence, they would actively change the audience's perception of a shared world over and beyond what the silent film had already contributed in making "accessible to our consciousness the life of lights and shadows."[49] The "real meaning" of *Tonfilm* lay in making accessible what so far had been so familiar as to be unfamiliar: "the sounds and noises around us which have never before been communicated in filmic images and thus always escaped sensory perception" (411).

However, in a long concluding passage prefaced by the phrase "in parentheses" and indeed sharply separated from the preceding generally optimistic argument, Kracauer delivered a both ambiguous and emphatic warning of the dehumanizing potential of film technology—a warning that clearly privileged the significance of the image. He began with what seems an exuberant celebration of the time-defeating potential of the most technologically advanced film:

> Up to now the talking film [*Tonbildfilm*] is the last link in the series of those magnificent inventions that, with blind certainty and as if guided by a hidden will, press toward the complete representation of human reality. It would make it possible, in principle, to snatch away life in its totality from transitoriness, yielding it up to the eternity of the image.

But the rest of the argument is taken over by the darker subtext of this passage, hinted at in the reference to hidden powers beyond human control whose inhumanly irrational nature suggests itself in their blindness:

> Not, of course, life in general, but only that aspect of life which presents itself in space. It is coordinated with measurable, chronological time, which Bergson separates from nonmeasurable, nonrepresentational time, which houses, in general terms, our lived experiences. It is only their substance that Proust wishes to conjure up when embarking on his search for lost time. The human reality preserved in the talking film has so little to do with that of Proust's search that they are mutually exclusive rather than complementary. Nothing that occurs in the time of lived experience (*Erlebniszeit*) can be filmed, and no film could fit into the order of that inner time. It almost seems as if intensive inner life, which cannot be represented, is diminished proportionate to our increasing capacity to capture and halt extensive spatial life. If that is the case, then technology will have defeated us and three-dimensional humans will have assimilated completely to [one-dimensional] humans on the screen. We will be able to control technology only if we keep ourselves open to that life which does not appear in the lens of the camera but only in remembrance. (411)

This passage clearly echoes the troubled, Proust-influenced argument of "Die Photographie" (1927), a resonance quite uncharacteristic of the body of Kracauer's film criticism and, significantly, in a piece concerned with the talking movie. In *Theory of Film* and *History* such dichotomies would be carefully negotiated or rejected. Kracauer would then use Proust to work out the complex of distinctions and connections between the reclaiming and alienating properties of photography, between the images of photography and memory, between lived and chronological time. The sharp and isolating distinction he makes here is puzzling and contradictory in terms of his stated desire to emphazise the cultural potential of the new medium, *Tonfilm*. Essentially cinematic, the image is juxtaposed with nonspatial experience of inner time which, curiously, is not connected with the new reproducibility and thereby fuller experience of sound. The forceful reference to remembrance at the end of this position paper on the cultural meanings of *Tonfilm* seems to emphasize the danger of misuse over the promise of potential. This is due not so much to the intellectual's general skepticism regarding mass culture as to Kracauer's groping attempts at descriptive definitions of a new medium.[50] He saw it centered in the production and transmission of sequences of images with their repeatable repeating on the screen of acts and events of a past present whose reclaimed actuality was grounded in the representation of spatial and temporal experience.

The distinction between "intensive inner life" and "extensive spatial life," encouraged by the Proustian thought-image of remembrance, was not limited to this review; Kracauer used it several times in the late twenties. But the concept of reality with which he worked in his reviews of films was clearly oriented to a social, rather than private, spatial and temporal experience–in clear contrast to the Proustian remembrance as mapping of inner time. It seems curious that Kracauer found such a concept of remembrance suggestive when discussing filmic compositions of images in terms of their (more rather than less) truthful representation of a contemporary collective reality. One would have expected him either to acknowledge the problem of the filmmaker's inevitably individual, selective perspective, or to modify explicitly the notion of remembrance. On the whole he did neither but asked instead almost every film he reviewed to be more open to the challenge of documenting "*Wirklichkeit*" in the sense of social conditions or relations. In some reviews of "music films," which are popular at the end of the Weimar period, Kracauer tries to fit the concept of remembrance more closely to the medium-specific recording potential of films. Less interested here in the obvious critique of escapism, he points out that the films were too narrowly focused on specific sounds. They neglected to record the sounds "waiting to be made accessible in *Tonfilm*," the ordinary, "natural" inconspicuous sounds of everyday life which, in contrast to the artificial, obtrusive sounds of operetta, needed to be preserved for remembrance.[51] This foreshadows the sharp distinctions drawn in *History* among different kinds of remembrance regarding the historian's time-traveling selection and transmission of verbal images. These distinctions had developed with his own increasing distance from a Proustian emphasis on the time of the "intensive inner life."

The general tenor of the film reviews was to acknowledge, wherever possible, film's contribution to an ideally direct witnessing and reclaiming of the unobtrusive, inconspicuous images and sounds of daily living. But though Kracauer judged the perception of the filmmaker as witness in terms of such directness, he was fully sensitive to the supportive role of artfulness in faithful representation. In a 1930 collective review, "Bemerkungen zu Tonfilmen," he praised a film for its successful handling of the connection between dialogue, noises, and image sequence, which had resulted in an "interpenetration of impressions" effected by clever stylistic use of "inarticulate" events.[52] He applauded the explicit absence of a witnessing pespective in the artful simulation of a random recording of reality. If film's cognitive contribution to a modern culture is the articulation of human reality as the everyday experience of social beings, then the filmmaker has to consider all its aspects, including randomness, in her presentational strategies that shape the representation of that experience.

Kracauer was particularly impressed with the documentary quality of Pabst's *Westfront 1918*, which forcefully confronted the viewer with the irrational horrors of war. He drew attention to a front-line hospital, which was set up in a church and filled with mutilated soldiers and exhausted physicians and nurses–a scene visually reminiscent of elaborately grotesque medieval torture scenes. Here the laudatory term *realistic* signified the documentation, through presentational decisions, of the inalienable strangeness, the randomness and meaninglessness of extreme physical pain. The fact that this documentation was supported by an arrangement of visual clues which called up associative sequences of images, a deliberate perspectivist ordering or staging, enhanced rather than undermined the faithfulness of representation. In addition, the thoughtful use of sound forced on the audience a "cruel proximity" to the events: here distance, which the viewer could maintain in the case of the other visual arts–painting, photography, even silent film–was negated. It was precisely this enforced "proximity," which the viewer could not escape, that made the film so important. The past reality of war had to be preserved by any means, because Germany's youth, Kracauer argued, needed to understand exactly what it had been like to be a soldier.[53]

Past reality is the past actuality of experience: through images and sounds filmic representation directs sensory perception toward a clear and firm knowledge that war is not, or should not be, in the interest of any human being. Instructively, Kracauer found wanting in this respect the American-made *Im Westen nichts Neues* (*All Quiet on the Western Front*) even though he praised its "extraordinary faithfulness to reality" in presenting the horror of trench warfare. This "faithfulness" to reality was accessible to the critic as an informed contemporary of the war experience but not, so the implication, to the younger person viewing this past experience from a position in the future. However, Kracauer's real objections concerned what he considered the film's insufficiently developed antiwar stance or concept. He complained that it did not go beyond a sentiment, a mood, and thus was inadequate to, or at odds with, the documented experience in the trenches.[54] Similarly, he criticized the much praised film, *Der blaue Engel*, for obscuring rather than revealing a contemporary experience because it placed the protagonists in a vacuum, removing them from the prevalent social conditions and contingencies.[55]

This was true, too, in Kracauer's eyes, for *Berlin Alexanderplatz*, a film based on Alfred Döblin's widely acclaimed novel about modern urban life. This successfully experimental text ought to have been an interesting provocation to filmmakers because it demonstrated with verbal means the increasing influence of cinematic conventions on the visual perception of urban dwellers.[56] Nevertheless, in its "uncinematic" focus on star actors and story line, the film failed to show the confused and troubled human collectivity in this busy part of working-class Berlin; the characters hover in an imaginary space. I agree with Kracauer's critical observations here, but not with his attributing the film's failure to the fact that "there is no social reality in Germany."[57] He might have pointed out, instead, the difficulties of properly seeing and recording ordinary people's experience of social chaos and political polarization at the end of the Weimar Republic. That profoundly troubled social reality was responsible for the novel's highly instructive conceptual and representational conflicts about the interdependencies of collectivity and individuality–conflicts the film did not deal with.[58]

Had language succeeded where the camera failed? The emphasis for Kracauer was not on a comparison with or transmission from the literary medium but on the integrity of the cinematic medium, which also signified a specific cognitive potential. In his review, "Der Mörder Dimitrij Karamasoff," he had high praise for this "first German *Tonfilm* that can compare to the good silent movies." Its successful coordination of image and sound did not, Kracauer emphasized, preclude the primacy of the visual because "the talking film, too, preeminently speaks to the eyes."[59] The scriptwriter's skillful translation into the "language of film" had made possible a cinematic composition of optic and acoustic elements sufficiently independent to allow the flux of images, rather than words, to carry the process of knowledge. And, with the help of the script, the makers of the film had mastered the "syntax of the visible components of the world."[60]

For the practicing film critic Kracauer, the medium's unique contribution to cultural modernity was the documentation of these "visible components" in compositions of images that then have the status of evidence—*evidens,* what can be seen clearly. He was not interested in a modernist aesthetics of film that sought to establish its art status by having recourse to expressionist concepts of perception.[61] Whenever he tried to assess the cultural value of a film, he posed the question of evidence: what could be learned from the film concerning a contemporary social-psychological reality? Film produces knowledge by a successful "*Durchdringung der Wirklichkeit,*" literally a "penetration" to the point of opening up to insight—a phrase that in Kracauer's critical practice assumed an almost formulaic character. In its suggestive abbreviation, the phrase can be irritating because it can easily be seen as a premature arrest of the hermeneutic circle. Yet—and this is a crucial consideration in our "soft" field of inquiry—the film critic's detailed observations, reservations, qualifications, and subtly modified repetitions demonstrated that he was intent on making himself understood, that his concern was primarily for the films under discussion and not for his own "brilliant" insights on the occasion of viewing them. In circling around the cultural status of the filmic (photographic) medium as preeminently modern, these reviews approached the issue of its particular cognitive accessibility—a kind of openness Kracauer hoped was reflected in his addressing the experience of the films' audiences, his contemporary readers.

Kracauer's insistence that the cognitive accessibility of photo images was central to their modern effectiveness was also central to his position as cultural critic. This made sense in general terms; but, depending on the kind of film under review, it could cause argumentational circularities. In the case of the *Dreigroschenoperfilm,* Kracauer pointed out that the "eccentric" style in which Brecht's text had constructed its own reality might be suited to the stage or the cabaret but was not suited to the filmic medium because it did not lend itself to the film-specific "optical penetration of reality."[62] This did not mean, he was quick to add, that he expected films to picture the visible world as it appeared to "normal eyes." Chaplin films, for instance, demonstrated that time and space could be shifted dramatically so that perceptions were reversed. However, "the transformation of reality as it occurs in film has to be based on purely filmic means. . . . On stage, the optical connection may be arbitrarily ruptured, reality may be sabotaged by reflections and lyricisms; in film reality can be preserved and redeemed [*ist aufzuheben*] only within its own medium."[63] Filmic representation can "penetrate" reality only if it uses "truly" or "purely" filmic means, which are preeminently image centered, and the authenticity of these means is judged on the basis of their successful representation of reality. The degree rather than the fact of circularity is troubling here. Kracauer posed the question of filmic "penetration" in the case of the *Dreigroschenoperfilm* in order to contrast filmic with theatrical representation. In making this distinction, he obscured the interdependencies of representation. How can one determine "true" filmic representation of that "true" contemporary reality, when the two truth statements are inescapably interlocked?

The nature of filmic representation is determined by what is represented; the picture is judged by the nature of the pictured, which is to be captured by the picture. This dilemma, alas, applies to all representation of cultural activity because it concerns intersubjective perception. But it was (and in many ways still is) particularly true for the photographic media, because of both the nature and the newness of photo images. In his role as film critic, Kracauer was very much impressed by the dilemma. Basing his critique of individual works on what was "fundamental" to filmic representation, he took seriously from the beginning the tensions and obscurities inherent in the relation between picture and pictured. The usefulness of his film reviews for the reader more than half a century later is that they both enlarge historical knowledge and are aware of its fallacies. There is, in most of his reviews, at least a passive openness to the difficulties of judging representation. On the whole, Kracauer was more helped here than hindered by the fact that he dealt with a preeminently nonverbal medium because stressing the visual permitted his references to a shared world of everyday life to be less self-conscious. He worked with a concept of "found [cinematic] stories" which distributed the validity of the evidence more broadly than did verbal (literary) stories with their denser interpretational core and therefore more entangled potential of meaning and significance. In short, as a critical viewer of films he seemed to encounter more self-evident meanings. Yet he also knew that such intelligible "self-evidence" was the result of thoughtful concentration on the image. The "found" cinematic story, that is, film as a medium of explanation, interpretation, and cognition, required acts of finding in which spontaneity and deliberation worked symbiotically to produce knowledge.

In order to become knowledge, information has to be judged. In his review of Heinrich Hauser's film on Chicago, Kracauer praised the director's "optical discoveries" but regretted his recording of impressions without asking about their meaning. In delivering to the viewer material that had not been "penetrated," he had reached the limits of, but not gone beyond, mere reporting.[64] Similarly, in the review of a film about an inner-city, low-income apartment house, Kracauer complained that there was observation but no "penetration" of the apartment house milieu. "What is lacking is the glance behind the scenery of everyday life, the glance that leads the photographic focus to show, and thereby explain, the familiar in an unfamiliar light."[65] In both cases the directors had stopped with spontaneous, as it were unmediated, impressions. On the other hand, Moholy-Nagy's abstract films, too, lacked the fruitful tension between spontaneous sensation and deliberate perception.[66] Beautiful formal experiments, of great "artistic interest," they were "workshop affairs." Without the meaning of "material" grounding, their beauty was without significance; worse, it could lead to escapism.[67]

Knowledge depends on the viewer's as well as the filmmaker's judgment. At the end of the Weimar period, Kracauer's deliberately "objective" praise for thoughtfully composed documentary objectivity was increasingly shaped by the experience of politically and socially dark times–thus his overly pedagogical concern with the escapism of films and their audiences. But his concept of film as an eminently public medium was and remained tied to his general understanding of the representational characteristics of the photo image; here, too, is the connection with history. Accessibility and communicability of evidence concerning the shared actuality of everyday life are the main components of this connection. They also protected Kracauer from ideological fallacies rampant among Weimar intellectuals (many decades later he would discuss the temptations of these fallacies for the historian, using analogies to photography). In his 1932 review of the film, *Kuhle Wampe*, made by the collective Brecht, Ottwald, Dudow, and Eisler, Kracauer expressed both amazement that this film had been banned by the board of censors and sympathy for what the filmmakers had tried to do. (Partly due to his influence, the film was later admitted but with cuts intended to neutralize its political message.) However, he was by no means uncritical of the social analysis presented here. The collective, he thought, had not made sufficiently intelligent use of the fact that it operated independently of the film industry. Kracauer called for a more thoughtful and more spontaneous approach to a situation that was politically and socially entangled and obscured. He saw the decisive mistake of the film's composition in the sharply contrasting visual presentation of the resignation of unemployed middle-aged, petty bourgeois workers and the unalloyed optimism and exuberance of unemployed proletarian youth. This juxtaposition was clearly meant to demonstrate that the old, tired social democracy would be replaced, inevitably and irresistibly, by young, vital communism. Central to the film's message, the juxtaposition lacked convincing cinematic evidence, that is, a cinematically constructed life-world of both old and young workers to which the viewers could relate empirically.

Kracauer did not distinguish explicitly between the filmmakers' social-political intentions and their filmic evidence, but he had chosen his explanatory examples along these lines. His most emphatic criticism concerned the film's condescending and ridiculing treatment of the older "petty bourgeois" workers[68] because its spiteful, snobbish attitude seemed to him counterproductive, in terms of an adequate filmic perspective on reality. Dismayed by the fact that a multifaceted political conflict was treated simplistically as a generational conflict complete with the glorification of radical youth in their athletic splendor, he rejected the empty optimism (a serious deception under the circumstances) of the concluding apotheosis.

Pointing out that all contemporary youth, leftist or rightist, were preoccupied with sport and that athletic excellence was no solution to economic chaos, Kracauer took more seriously the cultural meanings of sport in these last years of the Weimar Republic than the collective of filmmakers, who ostensibly had misinterpreted its importance (538f.). It was only in *Caligari*, from the position of the historian looking back at catastrophic events caused in part by that economic chaos, that Kracauer stated explicitly a general oscillation between Left and Right underlying the extreme political polarization at the end of Weimar:

> *Kuhle Wampe* is not free from glorifying youth as such, and to some extent its young revolutionaries resemble those youthful rebels who in numerous German films of the oppposite camp are finally ready to submit themselves or to enforce submission. This resemblance is by no means accidental. Towards the end of the pre-Hitler period many anguished young unemployed were so unbalanced that one evening they would be swayed by a communistic spokesman and the next succumb to a Nazi agitator's harangue. (247)

Yet the reviewer Kracauer, a contemporary of that period, had suggested that these ambiguities, denied by ideologues on the Left and exploited by practitioners of power on the Right, ought to have been recorded in a film made by politically concerned contemporaries. He saw these filmmakers' task in guarding and using the unique potential of their medium to create and preserve access to the increasingly difficult modern experience of rapid social change. Importantly, he was concerned about their contemporary as well as their future viewers–who would be concerned contemporaries in the future of the making of the film. The filmic potential was located in the documentary mode, which, in the modern accelerated experience of time, was rapidly assuming the status of photo historiography. Elucidating the physical presence of shared social, psychological, and political dynamics, films could show more fully the manmade nature of the contemporary world as a process of intersubjective activities. Such representation signified the possibility of knowledge that might support cultural memory as a process of nonforgetting: with the record of that contemporary world's changes over time also the challenge of its alterability.

Chapter Five

Orpheus and Ahasver: The Strangeness of Things Past

1 In the Weimar period, Kracauer's cartography of newly accessible areas of experience and inquiry had been successful. His critical analyses of the cultural function and role of photography and film, his documentary stories about new politically important groups had found appreciative readers who respected such thoughtful posing of new questions. Like Adorno, Benjamin, and Bloch, Kracauer had focused his cultural criticism on the phenomena of modernity. But his perspective on the new and explosively contradictory culture of the masses had been better informed and less predictive than theirs. Where their concept of culture and of the critic's point of observation had been ideologically selective and intellectually certain,[1] his had been anthropologically circumspect and intellectually searching. As a contemporary, he had looked with attention, negotiating the familiarity and strangeness of what he saw. Exile was to multiply his concerns and expand his curiosity. Though he wrote to Adorno in the sixties of his gratification that the "younger critics" emphasized the "kinship between you, myself, Benjamin and Bloch," and though he wanted the German translation of *Theory of Film* to be published by Suhrkamp so that the book could be in the "circle of friends gathered" in Frankfurt,[2] it was clear that for a long time now he had gone his own way.

The relationship with Adorno, intense during the early years of the Weimar period, when Kracauer was the mentor of the precociously brilliant young man, had become uneasy by the time Kracauer was working on his *Offenbach* book and detiorated notably with the disagreement over Kracauer's manuscript "Totalitäre Propaganda," which had been commissioned for the Frankfurt Institute's journal by Horkheimer and then edited in a highly authoritarian manner by Adorno. To recapitulate here briefly the letter that Kracauer wrote to Adorno on that matter during the summer of 1938: Adorno had shown himself unable to understand that the contemporary political crisis called for an intellectual position of "middle distance" that would be open to its contradictions and ambiguities. At issue was the messy actuality of events leading up to the crisis, which ought not to have happened as it did–a situation that required the historian to renounce "oughts" and "ought nots." Tracing the ascent of fascism, Kracauer had seen many signs of an ambiguous relation between fascism and capitalism rooted in a majority's overriding, and in certain ways revolutionary, will to power. Adorno had superimposed on Kracauer's text the ideological construct of a purely counter-revolutionary fascism. This summary approach was in clear opposition to Kracauer's "*sachlich*" involvement in a process of developing a conceptual grid from corroborated observation. "In part purely ornamental," Adorno's "arrangement" was not rationally accessible and therefore was also not refutable.[3] Adorno's "arrangement" was the outcome of what he would later refer to as his practice of "*emphatische Theorie*"–an intellectual rigor he thought was notoriously lacking in Kracauer's practice of critical realism.[4] The concept of authority underlying this position was indeed alien to critical discourse in Kracauer's sense, since it demanded complete, unquestioning acceptance.

Kracauer's complaint was curiously provident. Adorno's work was to shape the consciousness and aspirations of more than one generation of postwar German intellectuals, and the most important text in this regard would prove to be *Dialectic of Enlightenment*, written with Horkheimer and published in a private printing in 1944. In contrast to the exquisite, custom-made cultural pessimism of *Minima Moralia* (1951), which appealed to intellectual individualism, *Dialectic* claimed the intellectuals' loyalty as a group. For years an underground classic, passed around in pirated editions, it signified a program to be followed–not, to be sure, in any reproducible shape of argumentation, but in the intellectual *gestalt* Adorno that was inseparable from his precious and didactic language use. When Habermas reread *Dialectic of Enlightenment* in the early eighties, he noted rightly that this "blackest, most nihilistic" of Frankfurt School texts had had its greatest impact during the first two decades after its publication.[5] But the attractions of the Frankfurt core position, presented here for the first time in full aggressive rhetorical splendor, have been remarkably resilient. Habermas himself, the most enduringly representative figure in West German intellectual politics, is the best witness.

It is true that Habermas has been increasingly unambiguous in affirming the cultural value of rational modern scientific thought. Yet, ostensibly critical of a "postmodern" condition of knowledge, he still shares with Adorno and Horkheimer an abstract and narrow attitude toward modern mass culture and technology. He shares their eschatologically pure juxtaposition of "a truly human condition" and "a new kind of barbarism," of critical and instrumental reason.[6] The impact of *Dialectic of Enlightenment* did depend partly on its pervasive mood of cultural despair, which struck a deeply resonant chord after the war and the holocaust. But its two central theses, that "myth is already enlightenment" and that "enlightenment reverts to mythology,"[7] reflected more generally the troubled experience, in the West, of modernity as technocracy and mass culture, which in West Germany was confusingly compounded by the specter of an uncompleted past. The attractions of an intellectual position that would radically relieve this burden with ready-made explanations and a solidarity of meaning–echoing Lowenthal's "we were different, and we knew the world better"[8]–must indeed have seemed considerable.

Dialectic of Enlightenment is a collection of three long essays that, together with two excursuses, circle around the central thesis of a paradoxical symbiosis, or "dialectic," of reason and power in the service of the status quo. It was the second essay, "The Culture Industry: Enlightenment as Mass Deception," informed by the exiles' dystopian perspective on a country and a culture about which they knew very little,[9] which found the greatest resonance. The best and the brightest among West German intellectuals were irresistibly drawn to the assertion of a "regression of enlightenment to ideology which finds its typical expression in cinema and radio. Here enlightenment consists above all in the calculation of effectiveness and of the techniques of production and distribution; in accordance with its content, ideology expends itself in the idolization of given existence and of the power which controls technology" (xvi).

Arguably, this critical vision had its roots not so much in the culture industry of late U.S. capitalism as in Adorno's thesis, developed in the late 1930s, about fascist proganda. As Kracauer had seen clearly, this thesis was too rigidly ideological to accommodate the contemporaneous and historical meanings of a phenomenon like fascism. Yet it became the core of Adorno's critique of Enlightenment alias fascism alias culture industry, which was to have a profound influence on the postwar, postfascism intellectual scene. In the 1969 preface to the slightly revised edition of *Dialectic of Enlightenment*, from the hindsight of twenty-five years, Horkheimer and Adorno reminded their readers that the book had been written "when the end of the Nazi terror was within sight." They stressed, then, not so much the near total cultural rupture characteristic of the situation at the end of a total war. Rather, they pointed to the implications of an assumed continuity of Western mass democracies after the end of the war. They admitted that "in not a few places [in the 1944 texts] the reality of our times is formulated in a way no longer appropriate to contemporary experience." But they also asserted that "our assessment of the transition to the world of the administered life [in Western democracies] was not too simplistic" (ix).

Differences between Adorno and Kracauer multiplied and intensified after the end of the war when Kracauer began, in late middle age, a new professional life in the United States and Adorno went back to West Germany, where he became a cult figure. They surfaced powerfully in Adorno's 1964 essay, "The Odd Realist" ("Der wunderliche Realist"), published in *Neue Deutsche Hefte* on the occasion of Kracauer's seventy-fifth birthday, and in Kracauer's reactions to it. By then enormously influential in West German cultural politics, Adorno had helped to arrange for new editions of his old friend's earlier work. The most successful of these publications, and indeed the one that eventually started the Kracauer "renaissance" in Germany, was the essay collection, *Das Ornament der Masse.*[10] Adorno was responsible for the choice of the title essay, and Kracauer dedicated the book to him. The selection and grouping of essays suggest a Kracauer closer to the "circle of friends" and more separated from the American Kracauer of *Theory of Film* and *History*. He must have been aware of this situation as well as of mutually ambivalent feelings. Yet he seems to have been completely unprepared for the hostile thrust of an essay ostensibly meant to make his work more visible in postwar Germany. In a sense his reaction was naïve, since his intellectual distance from Adorno had grown immeasurably in exile. Kracauer's "*sachlich*" position was predicated on participation in cultural transformation; Adorno's "emphatische Theorie," refined into an increasingly hermetic poetry of thought, resisted such participation.

When Adorno sought to sum up Kracauer's work in 1964, he was unable to appreciate Kracauer's writings on film and therefore stressed his prewar rather than his postwar texts. Important aspects of pre- and postwar cultural developments were outside Adorno's understanding. The most signficant result of this impoverished vision was its enduring sameness over many decades of rapid and dramatic social and political change. During all these years, he had not modified his simply rejecting attitude to all mass media, including film, which he had stated in 1936 in one of his essay-length letters to Benjamin.[11] Reacting sharply to the presence of Brecht in Benjamin's "The Work of Art in the Age of Mechanical Reproduction," Adorno emphasized his own interest in the liquidation of bourgeois high culture and the demolition of the *Aura* associated with its art. However, in his scenario such demolition was dependent not on mechanical reproducibility but on autonomous formal laws in art that signified the "technicity" of avant-garde art. What he resented most was that Benjamin had assigned the loss of *Aura* through reproducibility to the, in Adorno's view, socially autonomous avant-garde art work, which then would be reduced to the sorry counterrevolutionary status of bourgeois art. Darkly, he warned Benjamin not to politicize art in a (Brechtian) way that would destroy its truly progressive, because dialectically transcending, potential. Benjamin's privileging of film was very dangerous, he wrote, because the alleged progressive components of film were mere illusion.[12]

Thirty years later, in the short impressionistic essay "Filmtransparente" (1966), the memory of Brecht's influence on Benjamin in the matter of reproducibility still rankles, and the familiar Freudian-Marxian perspective on fascism and the culture industry is still in place.[13] Benjamin, Adorno writes,

> did not elaborate on how deeply some of the categories he postulated for film–exhibition, test–are imbricated with the commodity character which his theory opposes. The reactionary nature of any realist aesthetic today is inseparable from this commodity character. Tending to reinforce, affirmatively, the phenomenal surface of society, realism dismisses any attempts to penetrate that surface as a romantic endeavor. Every meaning–including critical meaning–which the camera eye imparts to the film would already invalidate the law of the camera and thus violate Benjamin's taboo, conceived as it was with the explicit purpose of outdoing the provocative Brecht and thereby–this may have been its secret purpose–gaining freedom from him. Film is faced with the dilemma of finding a procedure which neither lapses into arts-and-crafts nor

> slips into a mere documentary mode. The obvious answer today, as forty years ago, is that of a montage which does not interfere with things but rather arranges them in a constellation akin to that of writing.[14]

It was impossible, from this position, to understand, much less value, Kracauer's attempts over several decades to explore the meanings of the photo image for twentieth-century culture. When he responded to Adorno's "provisional commentaries" on *Theory of Film* concerning the cultural status of film, he pointed out that his attempt to show what was specific to film had required a working definition of the notoriously fuzzy term, *art*. Important in view of Adorno's radical denial of such specificity in the 1966 essay is Kracauer's insistence on the implications of the historical plural and diverse reality of film: "Throughout its history, the specific possibilities of the medium have been realized, again and again–despite all economic and social obstacles. I did not invent these possibilities–though there was, of course, some construction–but I have found them within the existing material. . . . You are not right, then, when you maintain that film has never realized its immanent potential. It has done so in the past and is occasionally doing it now."[15]

Kracauer was probably most angered by Adorno's explicit emphasis in the birthday essay on the "potential" rather than the realized achievements of his "*geistige Existenz*" (388). Arguably, the situation was exacerbated by the fact that Kracauer had been a respected influential participant in the diverse, lively business of Weimar culture when the young, ambitious Adorno was trying to make his mark. He kept the copy sent him by Adorno after he had underlined it, annotated it in the margins, and extensively commented on it. Among his papers are also three long letters to Adorno in October and November of 1964 which contain lists of objections to what he thought were serious misrepresentations of his intellectual position and his character. In contrast to Adorno, Kracauer had to earn a living, and much of his time was taken up by his work for various American foundations and research institutes. But quite apart from that, his work rhythm reflected his patient and unprejudiced involvement with the subject of his inquiry. Energized by "*emphatische Theorie*," unfettered by gathering information, notoriously incurious about evidence to the contrary, Adorno produced an abundance that never ceased to amaze and trouble the ambivalently admiring Kracauer.[16]

Significantly, his critique focused precisely on Kracauer's "*erbittliches Nachdenken*," exorable reflection[17]–a play on "*unerbittlich*," inexorable–connoting intellectual laxness. He was unable to appreciate a thinking activity responsive to the process of experience in a life-world of contingencies and indeterminacies, and in that so different from his own "*unerbittlich*" theorizing energies. Moreover, he linked such (in his view) undesirable "*erbittliches Nachdenken*" to the fact that Kracauer was self-taught in his reflections about history and historiography. Underlining both assertions in his copy of the essay,[18] Kracauer rightly understood Adorno's statements to signify a devaluation of his nondialectical intellectual temperament and style (394), which were responsible for his slower-paced production and the circumspect, tentative development of his argumentation.

As Adorno observed, Kracauer's thought was open to–it could be swayed by–experience; it grew out of his attention to the concrete details of a natural-cultural world shared with others. Taken by itself, "*erbittlich*" would be an ingenious attribute. But Adorno associated with such attention an argumentation too loosely structured, worse, the "*Umständlichkeit*," circumstantiality, of the person who has to "rediscover everything for himself, including the familiar." Kracauer underlined these passages, too, writing an ironical "Ah" in the margins. But he accepted with an "ok" Adorno's view of his openness to instances of "incommensurability" in human existence, his "aversion to absolutes," his "persisting in the moment."[19]

Understandably, he was upset by a series of objections culminating in Adorno's definition of his position as shallow "*Empirismus*"–in the Frankfurters' usage, nineteenth-century philosophical obscurantism–and his finding "a hidden willingness to adapt, to conform."[20] Adorno thought his old mentor's work particularly unsatisfactory where it attempted to approach the "universal from the extreme of particularity;" he had failed in "the strictest mediation of the thing itself, subsequent to showing the essential in the innermost core." Kracauer's marginal "White Rabbit," the busybody incarnate in *Alice in Wonderland* who lectures everybody on everything and always on the authority of Higher Meaning, was a nicely ironical comment on the familiar mechanics of Adorno's neo-idealism. He also questioned with a marginal "but how?" Adorno's demand to resolve the antinomy of experience and theory by a "mutual penetration of the contrary elements." And he demurred (by underlining the phrase) at the accusation of epistemological autism: instead of theory, Adorno had claimed, Kracauer was "always there himself." The only statement in this portion of the essay that got an "ok" was Adorno's reference to Kracauer's "material" thought, his intellectual habit of situating ideas in a concrete context.[21]

In his first letter in response to the essay, Kracauer remarked that several of Adorno's definitions of his position had seemed "truly illuminating," helping him to gain "greater objectivity." He was moved, he wrote, by Adorno's attempt to construct a public portrait "which interweaves a perspective of the old personal closeness with a more distanced view informed by your own conceptual grid." But he also pointed out that the article seemed to him "motivated, too, by the desire to give definite shape to those feelings or dimly recognized thoughts connected with our relationship so that you could now draw objective distinctions between our intellectual temperaments. However that may be, your construction of my intellectual character—that is, of my relation to truth—clarified for me your intellectual character."[22]

2 In the last chapter of *History*, "The Anteroom," Kracauer has a few suggestions of an Adorno portrait in a passage titled "Proposition." They are based on his notes on a 1960 conversation with Adorno, in which each tried to define the other's position in relation to the "concept of utopia" and "Dialectics vs Ontology"—the two headings used in Kracauer's memorandum. Since both men were notably humorless, exhibiting the high seriousness typical of German intellectuals of their generation, the attempt at stating their differences is a deadly earnest affair. But Kracauer's agitation when writing them down in English (referring to himself in the third person) caused inadvertently comical literal translations of Adorno's notoriously aggressive phrasing, such as "The Ontology will have nothing to laugh [will be in bad shape], he says." Here is Kracauer's dismayed reaction to Adorno's well-known dialectic slipperiness:

> He rejects any ontological stipulations in favor of an infinite dialectics which penetrates all concrete things and entities, and, taking its clue from what they may reveal, works its way through them in a process which has no goal outside the movement itself and no direction that could be stated in terms other than those immanent in that movement. Krac. told Adorno that many of his articles concocted this way made him just dizzy; that he had often the feeling that other

> interpretations might be as conclusive than his, or even more so; that his whole dialectics seemed inseparable from a certain arbitrariness to him; and that, in sum, Kracauer's dizziness was presumably caused by the complete absence of content and direction in these series of material evaluations. Krac. traced thus his dizziness to the fact that Adorno seemingly deals with substances without, however, actually being attached to any substance. Hence the arbitrariness, the lack of orientation. Kracauer related this argument against Adorno's dialectics to his (Krac.'s) statement on the formality, the emptiness of Adorno's Utopian concept: indeed, if the movement, he unchains gravitated towards an Utopian goal, it still remains unoriented throughout because the term "Utopia" as used by him, is nothing but a conceptual stopgap.[23]

Kracauer thought that Adorno "was struck" by these accusations, but the reaction, recorded painstakingly, suggests otherwise. Adorno found

> that Kracauer's objections reveal that he still clings to obsolete, ontological habits of thought in requesting that something fixed must be given, postulated or desired. No sooner does one fall into this common error than the consequence is a "ready-made system" starting from the vision or postulate and passing above the concrete material of things and entities instead of *through* them. And he insisted that, contrary to ontological bias, the truth, as revealed through this immanent processing of concretions, is always "hovering" (schwebend). As for Kracauer's reproach of dizziness, arbitrariness, etc., he declares that there is after all a definite outlook in his writing which, of course, is *accessible only* to those *absorbing* his production *in its entirety*. He demands, in fact, that the student should understand each meaning from the context of what he, Adorno, had written (and will write in the future.) The *answer* to this is: since his dialectics consists of an unending sequence of concrete moments and each moment is supposed to be interpreted in depth, the sum total of these moments is unattainable. Which means that the reader familiar with all of Adorno's writings will feel exactly as insecure and dizzy as one who has read only part of Adorno's output. The emphasis lying on the movement from moment to moment, more samples of the same may increase the impression of the movement punctuated by "hovering" truths, but are extremely unlikely to endow it with the substance it deliberately negates as sheer movement.
>
> Kracauer resumed his objections from an entirely different angle. He compared Adorno's dialectics with a film made up exclusively of close-ups. Such a film is of course imaginable, he said; but the close-ups of which it consists would be completely undefined and, hence, puzzling rather than revealing, were they not every now and then interrupted by "establishing" shots relating them to the reality with which we are confronted after all and thus defining,

> however tentatively, their approximate position. Otherwise expressed, *the radical immanence of the dialectical process will not do; some ontological fixations are needed to imbue it with significance and direction.* . . . Kracauer supplemented what he was saying by the observation that a really meaningful dialectics would have to bring into play some ontological vision also. Thereupon Adorno admitted that some ontological elements might indeed be needed–but only in the form of hypostasized elements, not as eternal truths. Kracauer replied: no one has spoken of eternal truths; rather, what is required is a dialectic between the endless, purely immanent movement–Adorno's procedure–and an ontological stipulation outside it, a "Schau" [gaze] which, itself, may, or should not assume a definite character. (1f.)

The redundancies in Kracauer's awkwardly groping attempts to nail down the self-referentiality of Adorno's dialectics emphasize the seriousness, for him and for the late twentieth-century reader, of its ahistorical implications. Habermas's intention in "Rereading *Dialectic of Enlightenment*," stated at the beginning of his essay, was to sort out the confusions caused by a poststructuralist or postmodern Nietzsche as constructed by "Derrida and the recent Foucault": this construct had fostered current intellectual attitudes, "which appear as the spitting image of those of Horkheimer and Adorno in the *Dialectic of Enlightenment*" (13). In what is for Habermas a situation of beleaguered modernity, such erroneous connection needs to be rejected emphatically. Without the shadow of a doubt, he sees Adorno and Horkheimer as enduring "advocates of the Enlightenment" (23). And he does so despite their undeniable indebtedness to Nietzsche's concept of (aesthetic) modernity as reason-denying appeal to the lying terror of the beautiful, which would unmask the deceits of science and morality. Strongly rejecting this appeal, which has indeed been claimed (or constructed) for a "postmodern," "posthistoire" condition of knowledge, Habermas argues that (the French) Nietzsche sought "refuge in a theory of power." Adorno and Horkheimer, however, "took the opposite route: no longer desiring to overcome the performative contradiction [read: irrationality] of a totalizing critique of ideology, they intensified the contradiction instead and left it unresolved" (29).

Though earnest Habermas has always been suspicious of Nietzsche's capricious brilliance: where he does not have to explain away the "postmodern"–actually neo-Platonic, neo-Romantic–associations of the Frankfurters' position, his own Nietzsche construct is an intriguingly ambiguous rather than clearly negative presence. He can then also be considerably more cautious with respect to a theory of power as the single most important route for Nietzsche, allowing him to vascillate between two strategies: "On the one hand, Nietzsche sees the possibility of an artistic contemplation of the world carried out with scholarly tools but in an antimetaphysical, antiromantic, pessimistic, and skeptical attitude."[24] Engaged in such "historical science," even in the service of the will to power, Nietzsche would still be immune to the illusion of truth; and so, following him, would be Bataille, Lacan, and the earlier Foucault. But this (acceptable) Nietzsche, too, trying to validate his position, needed to assert that he could develop a critique of metaphysics without relinquishing the authority of his own philosophizing. It is that Nietzsche who in Habermas' scenario becomes the last disciple of Dionysos, the philosophizing god. The same path was taken by the late Heidegger, following Nietzsche, and by Derrida and the late Foucault, who followed Heidegger. But the cultural critic Nietzsche, accessible in the larger part of his essayistic philosophy to many readers whose agendas were less clearly preestablished than were those of Habermas, did not even seek to resolve the dilemma of authority; he posed it and left it open.[25] It was his followers who, resolving it, abandoned precisely his antimetaphysical, antiromantic, and skeptical position, the indeed modern dimension of his thought. And in this, no matter what Habermas needs to believe, Adorno and Horkheimer preceded all of them.

Against the "endless, purely immanent movement" of Adorno's dialectic, which does indeed anticipate Derridian "*différance*" with its endless play of signifiers, Kracauer set his acts of looking at the world out there ("*Schau*"). *Not* the Benjaminian significantly dissolving gaze but the curious, attentive gaze that connects the viewer and the viewed and transforms the viewer in the acts of viewing. It is important that Kracauer used in this context a reference to cinematic practice, "close-ups" and the "'establishing' shots relating them to the reality with which we are confronted after all." It is also important to keep in mind here that close-ups, if they are thus connected or grounded, are cognitively valuable precisely because of their puzzling and richly suggestive, indeterminate nature. In *History* Kracauer would introduce these filmic devices as explanatory analogies to instabilities of historical judgment and the nonhomogeneous nature of the historical universe.[26] Against the self-referential solipsism of Adorno's dialectic, which excluded and eluded him, Kracauer posed the inclusionary historical reality of his own and others' existence. Adorno was right when he pointed out Kracauer's clear rejection of "the idea of intellectual [*geistig*] splitting of the atom, of the irrevocable break with appearance," his "stubbornly taking the side of Sancho Panza." He was shockingly wrong to extrapolate from such respect for the visible world shared with others a resigned acceptance of its impenetrability and, going one nasty step further, a justification of the status quo and glorification, as socially relevant, of personal idiosyncracies.[27]

Kracauer was particularly upset by this passage, which he rightly understood to be an unequivocal attack on his intellectual integrity, marking it in the margin of his copy with a "decidedly not" and underlining "Sancho Panza." Yet a year later, sorting out old affinities and differences in a birthday letter to Bloch, he was to associate his own realism with that of Sancho Panza. (We will come back to this text.) His at first negative reaction to this association was caused by his deep anger and frustration over Adorno's persistent insinuations, throughout the essay, that he acquiesced in things as they were, the status quo of what he, more than many other intellectuals, had always seen clearly and concretely as a world in need of many changes. He therefore was most troubled by the causal connection drawn here between his alleged tendency to adapt himself to conditions rather than resist and analyze them, and his opting for happiness, "*Glücksgelöbnis*."[28] Trying to defend himself against these allegations, Kracauer had referred Adorno in an earlier letter to the success of his writing during the Weimar period–texts that could not possibly be seen in this light. He also pointed out Adorno's enormous success in postwar Germany: did that signify *his* adaptation to the status quo?

Kracauer quoted repeatedly the word *Glücksgelöbnis*, one of the Frankfurters' terms for American rationalist shallowness in contrast to German "critical" authenticity. Adorno, Kracauer complained, had confronted his constant attentiveness to the world of objects, events, and acts with his skepticism regarding a possible alterability of the *condition humaine* in a manner that "I find unacceptble because it exaggerates my skepticism. See here my film theory." Dialectics was not the answer for Kracauer because he had never ceased to be troubled about the possibility of generalizing concerning particular experiences of temporality and historicity. Adorno's accusation that he "avoided trying to extrapolate the general from the extreme particular" was mistaken, Kracauer wrote. "I believe, rather, that it has always been one of my main concerns to find out how that could be done. . . . My book on history will culminate in the attempt at an explicit solution of this problem."[29] But he also made it clear here that, like the attentive, curious gaze, this "solution" (if it could indeed be envisioned) "should not assume a definite character." And it did not, remaining instead an *attempt* at a more broadly informed, more prudent and imaginative survey of the intellectual spaces in which historical understanding could take place–spaces sufficiently capacious to accommodate the temporality and historicity that entangle alike the observer and the observed.

The description of Adorno's position in the "Anteroom" chapter of *History* contains passages that were copied almost verbatim from the notes made in 1960. But Kracauer was now interested not so much in fending off Adorno's "unfettered dialectic" as in breaking it open.[30] Juxtaposing him with Loewith, he argued for a composite perspective in historiography. He had in mind a "complementarity principle" which, concerned with the particular, still retains intimations of the timeless in temporality and of "the total nature of the universe." However, these intimations were recognized as "speculations," and their presence and function as both "unpredictable" and "vital" (200). In what he clearly considered a tricky portion of his argument, Kracauer's language is tentative and searching, even clumsy. He is dealing with the challenge to the historian to work with the principle of a "coexistence" of both aspects, though "difficult to imagine," a "'side-by-side' replacing the 'either-or'." There were other options, in his view, than choosing between Loewith's "transcendentalism with its penchant for the ontological" and Adorno's self-referential "immanentism."[31] The rejection in his *Negative Dialektik*

> of any ontological stipulation in favor of an infinite dialectics which penetrates all concrete things and entities seems inseparable from a certain arbitrariness, an absence of content and direction in these series of material evaluations. The concept of Utopia is then necessarily used by him in a purely formal way, as a borderline concept which at the end invariably emerges like a *deus ex machina.*

> But Utopian thought makes sense only if it assumes the form of a vision or intuition with a definite content of a sort. Therefore the radical immanence of the dialectical process will not do; some ontological fixations are needed to imbue it with significance and direction.[32]

Such significance and direction arise out of the experience of a life-world shared with others, an experience largely inaccessible to Adorno.[33] Kracauer's use here of the term *ontological* does not suggest a general concept of being but a general validity of the actuality and particularity of human existence. Yet his letters to Adorno, who had arrogated the role of judge in matters intellectual and psychological, intruding forcefully on what Kracauer understood to be an open-ended process of self-determination, exhibit a resigned reluctance to denounce such intrusion in general terms. Adorno had assumed a fixed distance from which he could impose a closed fiction, which Kracauer perceived to be a serious distortion of his ongoing reality. There was no way for him to reach Adorno from his own position of a "middle distance," which reflected his having moved around, away from, toward the object of observation: "You'll have to see me as you see me," Kracauer summed up their differences.[34] He realized that he was unable to fight off effectively the ideologue of a solipsistic "*emphatische Theorie.*"

Two letters that Kracauer wrote while working on *History* explicitly relate his own intellectual approach to that of the addressee and show the importance to his own position of such mediating and negotiating of similarities and differences. In his "open" letter to Ernst Bloch on the occasion of his eightieth birthday in 1965, "Zwei Deutungen in zwei Sprachen" ("Two Interpretations in Two Languages"), Kracauer first stated what separated them. He did not, for that purpose, delineate Bloch's intellectual temperament, but rather summed up for the old friend and adversary some of his own deepest hesitations, which had, in effect, troubled their relations.

> There is much that separates us, and you have known it for a long time. You know my fearful mistrust in big dreams that are not marginal annotations but allowed to interfere to the extent of making so radically transparent what is closest to us in experience that we are almost left incapable of seeing what and how it is. And you have known my tendency to soberness–"colorful soberness" you called it many years ago–that has caused me to linger in dealing with nearby things and relationships, and to refrain from promptly interpretating

> them in the light of last things. There is so much in-between and things themselves are so tenacious and of so many shapes. In short, my attitude is not unlike that of the figure identified by Kafka as Sancho Panza. Hence my conviction that one does not get to a "there" without having been truly involved in a "here." But in saying that I realize that I am also marking, more or less precisely, the place you have occupied. What connects us is located, not least, if not only, in what I am tempted to call your nonutopian side.[35]

There was that side to Bloch, and occasionally he even cultivated it. Seeking it out, Kracauer lit it up too sharply and thereby obscured Bloch's lively ideological windmill chasing. But he may have wished, on this occasion, to draw Bloch in gently; this may have seemed to him how Bloch would have liked to be seen at that point in his life. Important for our context is the tentative, searching description of an intellectual temperament that includes both the writer and the addressee of the letter. In Kracauer's nicely metaphorical account, Bloch's meandering narration merges with the narratives embarked on by the time-traveling historian: "He who tells stories lingers; lovingly he circumnavigates [*umfährt*] also what is and shall be changed" (146). The historian as narrator is the explorer who "umfährt" the space and time of the existing changing world and thus opens it up to "*Erfahrung*" (experience), makes it "*erfahrbar*" (able to be experienced, able to be transversed)–in a figurative and literal way.[36]

In the spring of 1966, Kracauer wrote to Robert Merton in an uncharacteristically unguarded manner of his admiration for and delight with his *On the Shoulders of Giants*: "Not only that it revealed much to me I didn't know about you, the things it did reveal, including a tender whimsicality, are so close to my own outlook and temper that I was almost frightened by the many parallels in a deeper layer of the mind." He declared himself "really excited" by Merton's

> profound awareness of what makes history into history. The way in which you hold talk about "influences" up to ridicule, the roundabout manner in which you approach your subjects, your insistent love of digression, the feeling you give one that the whole matter is inexhaustible, and throughout the whole book your concern with discontinuities and possibilities which never came true–all of this could not do more justice to the stuff of which history is woven–this strange "science" which numbers of scientific-minded contemporary historians tend to confuse with science proper. I am afraid I have to con-

> fess to you that your conception of history is much of a piece with the one I try to develop in the book I am preparing on the theory of history.[37]

To Merton Kracauer owed the quote from *Tristram Shandy* concerning Sterne's "technique of historiography," "a veritable gem of a find," which he promptly put at the end of his introduction to *History*. He used it to warn the reader of the tentative, discontinuous, indeed circumstantial manner of the arguments to follow (15). Tristram, he wrote to Merton, "seems to have anticipated me, alas," declaring himself to be "strongly impressed by what I dared call your whimsicality–this meandering and hanging on to scattered names, locales, and traits." Like Merton and Tristam Shandy, Kracauer traveling in the realm of historiography would be diverted by the particularities of the world, his curiosity stirred, his attention held. His progress would not be linear. He would come to know more, but not everything; he would not be able to grasp the "last things." Ideas and philosophical truths, he noted in the "Proposition" part of "The Anteroom," "come closest to puncturing the screen that separates us from what we fathom to be Truth. The *coincidentia oppositorum*, which Cusa in *De visione Dei* called 'the wall of paradise behind which dwells God,' does not materialize this side of the screen" (202). On "this side" is located the realm of historicity and temporality, which has little use for the radically self-referential, formal dialectic with which Adorno hoped to resolve the antinomy of experience and theory.

However, Kracauer did not exhibit the unquestioning "hostility against theory" of which Adorno had accused him in "Der wunderliche Realist" (400). An "inveterate anteroom dweller," he advised historians who share that habitation to employ the "side-by-side" principle, which in his eyes was central to historiography: it would be a good thing

> to acknowledge the possible significance of philosophical truths with their claim to objective validity (which precludes Heidegger and his existentialist aftercrop)[38] and at the same time to be aware of their limitations in terms of absoluteness and controlling power (which precludes any definite ontological position). Ambiguity is of the essence in this intermediary area. A constant effort is needed on the part of those inhabiting it to meet the conflicting necessities with which they are faced at every turn of the road. (216)

3 *History* clearly reflects Kracauer's mistrust of the "big dreams" of complete interpretations that mark a secure road toward a totality of meaning. As an observer he allowed himself to be drawn into the many shapes of historical events, actions, relations. His explorations in the anteroom of historiography show that he was precisely that "insatiable reader and curious explorer," the "genuine historian" who, in his careful attentiveness to what might be found, had seemed to him so much like the filmmaker.[39] The many folders of well ordered notes he left behind–he had always insisted on taking them along on even the most difficult of his journeys through different countries and cultures–richly document a life of intellectual activity. Such an attempt to make accessible the sedimentation of lived time can be read, in part, as the exile's resistance to the experienced chaos of cultural rupture. But above all, such tenaciously "*sachlich*" gathering of the self involved with the images and the thoughts of others points to Kracauer's capacity for that "exorable reflection," which Adorno thought inauthentic. In its consistently questioning openness to the contradictory historical complexity of our world, Kracauer's thinking could indeed be easily deflected from a priori assumptions by the articulated experiences of others, the stuff of history.

His momentous decision to write in English also has to be understood in the context of his capacity to be influenced–his willingness to change and be changed, which seemed unacceptable to Adorno, as to many other German exiles.[40] Kracauer wrote to Adorno in the fall of 1955:

> I know that you mean well when you warn me that essential things can be said only in German. This is certainly true for certain areas in literature–poetry, the novel, perhaps the essay, too. (I am not really attracted to the essay anymore, without having tried to formulate my current mistrust in this form.) But your Catonian dictum is certainly invalid for the expression of thought, of theory–I am referring here to *my* thoughts, *my* theory. . . . My ideal style would have language disappear in the subject of inquiry, as does the Chinese painter in the picture, though I am aware of the fact that the painter and the picture are one–up to a point."[41]

Up to a point: in another country, in another time of life, the older Kracauer in America used language as a processual incomplete means of communication which does not aspire to the depths of the essential and rigorously authentic. For this reason, too, he mistrusted the function of the essay form in Adorno's and Benjamin's terms: to preserve the transcendentally significant insignificant and to bring about an epiphany of totality in the fragment.[42] Since he was more interested in the subject of his inquiry than in the interested self, he wished to communicate this subject as clearly as possible. Yet he was well aware of the implications of the fact that neither his inquiry nor its communication could ever be free of his own involvement. Thinking in the anteroom of historical experience did indeed mean that one "is always there oneself," not, however, as Adorno had reproached him, *instead* of theory, but *before* theory. The acts of "construction in the material of history"[43] in which Kracauer was engaged came before a unifying theory and retard its premature levelings and indurations. Importantly, such retarding would not be possible without the self-conscious, self-motivated participation of the constructor in the construction and in the material, which includes her language use. Only then will she be able to reject the theoretician's demands for authentic and decisive insights based on an authority that cannot but be arrogated where the experience of others is concerned. In the anteroom of temporality and historicity, such "last" theoretical authority can all too often be shown to have supported the intellectual arbitrariness and willfulness of the person who has claimed it.

Kracauer's decision to say only what could be said in English, then, made it possible for him to say more than he would have said in German, despite the fact that his English was not always idiomatic and seldom elegant. With the language he was discovering also a larger, more varied, more differentiated cultural space in which to move, change perspective, open up to new beginnings[44]—a change that guided, too, his appreciating the provocative self-limitations of modern history. Adorno and Horkheimer remained notoriously closed to new cultural experiences, all the more fixed in their familiar position by the, to them, unalterable alienness of America. Kracauer in contrast became increasingly "extraterritorial" in terms of chronological time[45] as well as of conceptual grids and circumscribed cultural spaces and periods. As he would argue in *History*, some people are outsiders to the periods in which they live, and this position does not *eo ipso* signify lack of understanding or of efficacy. He used Vico and Burckhardt as examples of "chronological extraterritoriality": "Like great artists or thinkers, great historians are biological freaks: they father the time that has fathered them. Perhaps the same holds true for mass movements, revolutions" (69).

Traveling in history and historiography, Kracauer explicitly and as a matter of course employed such cultural and temporal extraterritoriality. He was drawn above all to those periods of (intellectual) history that most directly seemed to call for the historian's mobility. The most useful information could be obtained from the "nascent state of great ideological movements, that period when they were not yet institutionalized but still competed with other ideas for supremacy." He was interested in the disputes themselves more than their outcome because here he could still find all those "possibilities which history did not see fit to explore" (6). The history of ideas, more often than not a history of beliefs, has been a history of misunderstandings, since beliefs that make history tend to overgrow the roads taken by the time-traveling historian:

> Every idea is coarsened, flattened and distorted on its way through the world. The world which takes possession of it does so according to its own lights and needs. Once a vision becomes an institution, clouds of dust gather about it, blurring its contours and contents. . . . An idea preserves its integrity and fullness only as long as it lacks the firmness of a widely sanctioned belief. Perhaps the period of its inception is most transparent to the truths at which it aims in the midst of doubts. (7)

Such transparency did not, however, signify the availability of coherent truths that might add up to reliably cumulative historical knowledge.[46] Kracauer's deepest concern was for "a way of thinking and living, which, if we could only follow it, would permit us to burn through the causes and thus to dispose of them–a way which, for lack of a better word or a word at all, may be called humane" (8). He knew, of course, that outside the hopeful rhetoric of intellectuals such "humane" bridging and negotiating of ideational conflicts was not so easily achieved. But he was interested in its possibility "at every juncture of the controversy which threads the historical process"–more so than in its realization. This possibility is a diffuse utopian energy, perhaps a broadly perceived direction. It is not a clearly visible goal but rather an opportunity that, unpredictably, might present itself: "There are always holes in the wall for us to evade and the improbable to slip in" (8).

Right at the start, in the introduction to *History*, Kracauer suggested the improbable possibility of reconstructing an alternative complementary history by seeking out its traces in certain historical periods, events, acts, actors–for instance the character and the position of Erasmus. Self-consciously a contemporary of the intellectual conflicts of his era, for instance, the battles between Luther and Münzer,[47] Erasmus was not part of them. More, it was precisely his thoughtful extraterritoriality to these battles of intellect and will that made it possible for his person and his activities to have "a bearing on the humane." When in their unshakable, inexorable piety both Catholics and Protestants attacked his undecisiveness and fickleness, his all too "exorable" attentiveness to matters of the world, they really attacked his intelligent navigating toward peace. "Utopian visionaries condemn those who stick to the middle of the road on the ground that they callously betray mankind by trying to perpetuate a state of imperfection. In the case of Erasmus the middle way was the direct way to Utopia–the way of the humane. It is not by accident that he was the friend of Thomas More" (14).

Kracauer did not so much identify with Erasmus–such appropriation was not in his nature. But he he was happily stirred by Erasmus's past presence. Moreover, recalling it so fully in the introduction, he advised that it be read as an improbable possible instance of reconstructing an alternate history that was located precisely in Erasmus's elusiveness. This elusiveness, an often noted unwillingness to take sides, was not an attempt to escape the messiness of the world:

> His satires on monasticism and the corruption of the clergy were no less public property than his demands for Church reform in the spirit of Christian humanism. Nor did he easily miss an opportunity to publicize his ideas about the pitiable conditions of the poor, the greed of the princes, and other secular affairs; his tracts and letters teem with references to topical issues, conveying views whose often far-sighted modernism owed much to the de-dogmatized Christian outlook. (9)

Erasmus seemed such a good example of the possibility of the humane because of his intense involvement with the world despite rejecting all the positions offered him by popes and kings (9). His thought developed within, not above or outside of, human affairs. This connectedness made it impossible for him not to see the other person's (or party's) side; it also made it impossible for him to accept the other side as the true reality, the real truth. Like Kracauer, Erasmus was not the outsider for whom, as Adorno had it, remoteness was the medium of knowledge. Adorno's juxtaposition, "humaneness not through identification but through its absence,"[48] was profoundly mistaken—not just in the case of Kracauer. It was not a question of either "inexorable" oneness or irreversible separateness, the poles between which was stretched Adorno's attempt to distinguish once and for all, and with absolute certainty, his from Kracauer's position. In their pure form, identification and its absence are possible only in the fictions of one's own and the other's clear and distinct enduring identity, which obscure the reality of transformation. On the testimony not of "*emphatische Theorie*" but of historical experience, such identification has divided rather than related, commanded rather than listened, appropriated rather than set free. Erasmus's famous ability to negotiate "concord" had its source in his willingness to "rather forsake part of the truth than trouble the peace" (13). It sprang neither from withholding himself from a position or person nor from identifying with them but from approaching them, case by case, with "tact." In the "Anteroom" chapter, in a passage titled "Co-existence," Kracauer reflected on the "kind of relation that actually obtains between the general and the particular"—but in the context of history rather than philosophy. The historian's thoughts in this respect "may not at all converge toward a philosophy. And if they converge, this philosophy may not be the fountainhead of his particular insights. The general truth and a pertinent concrete conception may exist side by side, without their relation being reducible to the fact that logically the abstraction implies the concretion. 'Tact' is required to define this relation in each particular case" (206).

Tact is the ability to mediate, to act sociably, to observe the provisional, temporary nature of human relations, and to accept changes in oneself as well as others. It means putting oneself in the place of the other and anticipating what might hurt—that is, diminish the other's presence—or what might please—that is, enhance it. Tact means not presuming the other's innermost truth and thereby defining, fixating her but letting her be present in relation to others. Erasmus, Kracauer argued, "was possessed with the fear of all that is definitely fixed. To state the same in terms involving his spiritual self, he was essentially motivated by the conviction that the truth ceases to be true as soon as it becomes a dogma, thus forfeiting the ambiguity which marks it as truth" (10). It was this fear and this conviction, rather than remoteness, which caused him to be perceived as elusive. If he was not a person with whom to identify, he also did not arrest other people in such fictitious identities. For Kracauer, Erasmus's elusiveness was central to his humaneness because it enabled him to find "a way of living free from ideological constraints" (9).

This construct of Erasmus's intellectul *gestalt* clearly contained some aspects of Kracauer's own temperament; it was also clearly set against Adorno's. When he reminded his readers that Thomas More was the friend of Erasmus, he also referred them by implication to the elaborate games of identity played in *Utopia*.[49] More presented his *Utopia* not in absolute but in relational terms. Book 1, which explains the connections between Utopian discourse and Utopian traveling, was as important to him as book 2, the fiction of the perhaps better place. For him, if not for most Utopians after him, Utopia was the projected anteroom of the counterthinker Hythloday. Traveling, like the historian, in the elsewhere and elsewhen, observing the unfamiliar from the position of extraterritoriality or "middle distance," this tactful visitor of many different places looks and listens more attentively, asks more pertinent questions, and tells his stories with fewer illusions about their provisional character.

Modern historiography is all about telling the "whole story," which retains the fragmented, conflicted, contradictory nature of evidence and which may or may not become a part of the multiple-story complex that is history. The "whole story," then–the story that tells everything that can be told in any given situation, at any given moment–is the story that acknowledges its own incompleteness. In telling this kind of story, the historian is not in pursuit of a clear ideal of objectivity but of the obscure reality of historical justice.[50] One of the most exciting "adventures on which history can embark," as Kracauer remarked in *History*, has been the "impossible quest" for the hidden thirty-six just men who, according to Jewish legend, uphold the world in each generation (15). Nobody, they themselves included, knows who they are. Their effectiveness in remaining both hidden and sought in the world reaffirms the importance of abstaining from last truths. The historian's impossible and, for a modern culture, crucially important intention to do justice to history with her incomplete story is supported by her willingness to go on looking for more and better evidence.[51] Whether it affirms or negates her story, it most probably will never be fully conclusive.

4 The discourse of historiography mediates provisional insights into the texture of historical action in which freedom and necessity are interwoven in disturbingly unclear patterns. The search for regularities in history, the realm of contingencies and therefore new beginnings, is of limited use. But downright harmful, in Kracauer's view, is the "theological" proposition that a good, that is, sanctioned purpose justifies all and any means.[52] There is in human affairs a kind of relative freedom to will and to act–the German "*Freizügigkeit*" nicely points to the player's liberties within the rules of the game that restrict, or enable, her draws. Where it concerns making use of the potentiality of new beginnings, this liberty calls for granting to historical sequences of events and actions a dimension of incommensurability that is most effectively accommodated in the medium of the story. In the first chapter of *History*, "Nature," Kracauer suggests supplementing "the negative characterization of history as a nonscience, or a science with a difference, by a first positive, if still incomplete definition: the historian must tell a story" (32). His concept of *story* is explicitly broad, including exploratory, explanatory, interpretative discourse. Most importantly, it acknowledges, with the story's capaciousness, the open beginnings and endings that enable it to be linked to other stories. Importantly, too, the emphasis is not so much on the construct of the story as on the historian's telling of it, that is, the historian's acts of constructing. These acts have to be responsive to his experience of "invariably" coming across "irreducible entities–units which, besides resulting from the junction of otherwise unrelated series of happenings, mark the emergence of something new, something beyond the jurisdiction of nature. . . . In our dealings with these events, ideas or situations, determinism no longer serves as a reliable guide. . . . In telling a story the historian conforms to a necessity founded on a peculiar quality of historical reality" (32).

The historian is charged with doing justice to all of history by recognizing and accommodating the inevitable fragmentedness of historical experience in stories whose shapes reflect perspectivist degrees of approaching multiple possible truths rather than guidance by one "true" truth. There is little profit for Kracauer's historian in the dogmatically divided or dialectically accelerated story. His own approach, as he warns his readers in the introduction to *History*, is slow, non-linear, circling around, doubling back.

As an author he is like Sterne, who deliberately keeps his protagonist from being born and setting out, with determination, on his life's journey. So is the historian's journey in time held up by a host of retarding observations that guide and change his view of historical evidence and thereby cause his story to have gaps, even indeterminacies. "Much closer to the practically endless, fortuitous, and indeterminate *Lebenswelt*," Kracauer remarks in "The Anteroom," historiography as a "distinctly empirical science" differs dramatically from philosophy with its general statements of value concerning the cultural meaning, or meaninglessness, of history.[53] In "exactly the same manner as the photographic media render and penetrate the physical world about us," historiography "explores and interprets given historical reality." Viewed "from the lofty regions of philosophy, the historian devotes himself to the last things before the last, settling in an area which has the character of an anteroom. (Yet it is this 'anteroom' in which we breathe, move and live)" (194f.).

The complex, obscure, and urgent biological self-evidence of the "anteroom" for the cultural critic became increasingly important to Kracauer over time. Supporting it with detailed analogies between historiography and photography, he used it here to confront the often seductive philosophical solutions of the burdensome dilemma of historicity. The price paid by historians trying to reconcile the inquiry-specific "relativity of knowledge" with "the quest of reason for significant truths of general validity" has been too high. "Transcendental" solutions attempted by many of the great historians–Ranke, Droysen, Scheler, Rickert, Troeltsch, Meinecke, Loewith–present an "aftermath, or indeed the backwash, of secularized theological concepts and traditional metaphysics, with the idea of evolution thrown into the bargain." Trying to swim "in the stream of time" and to land on shores that bring them "face to face with eternity," "somewhere en route they inevitably perform what to all intents and purposes resembles the famous Indian rope trick" (196f., 201). This is true, too, for the followers of Dilthey's "immanentist solution"–Croce, Collingwood, Heidegger, Gadamer, Adorno–since they radicalize, absolutize, or, in Adorno's case, totalize history to the point where the desired "objective" arises as if magically out of "History itself."

> Building from, and exploiting Dilthey, the Heidegger of *Sein und Zeit* goes farthest in this direction; he postulates a historicity of being itself, thus radically

> uprooting the subject-object relation, and the venerable notions of substance and essence in its wake. (But radicalism is not necessarily a virtue; and of the subject-object relation Hans Jonas judiciously says that it "is not a lapse but the privilege, burden and duty of man.") (197f.)

Kracauer had a habit of putting between parentheses issues that were to him of the greatest personal importance: the palpable reality of our living, breathing, moving in the anteroom space and time of our historicity; the historian's pity for the plea of the dead to be included in the future.[54] The statement he quotes here from Jonas's essay "Heidegger and Theology,"[55] is part of an argument that confronts "the terrible anonymity" of Heidegger's being with the distinct plurality and diversity of human beings who call and respond to each other. They do so less through thinking than through acting, though, as Jonas hastens to add, acting involves thinking. The action may be "one of love, responsibility, pity; also of wrath, indignation, hate, even fight to the death: it is him or me. . . . In this sense indeed also Hitler was a call. *Such calls are drowned in the voice of being to which one cannot say No*; as is also, we are told, the separation of subject from object." But precisely this separation marks the condition of human beings in the world to which, as the non-identical, they respond and for which they are therefore responsible. For Jonas, the "subject-object *relation*, which presupposes, holds open, and stands through the duality" (258), is emphatically not a postlapsarian deficiency. It is, rather, the measure of the not unlimited but considerable potential of human beings for understanding and including the mutually external–the *world outside* to be approached concretely.

Like Jonas, Kracauer situated the subject-object *relation* in the context of modern historicity. As his abbreviating quote indicated, he was considerably more reticient about the meanings for his own work of twentieth-century mass destruction–experiences crucially important to the formation of his critical realism. Hitler, who appears once in *History* and then in the subjunctive mode (31f.), was for the later Kracauer a complex historical phenomenon not (yet) fully understood. Unlike Adorno, Kracauer did not, from a position of absolute (moral-political) righteousness, attack Heidegger's fascism.[56] He attacked, from the historian's position of middle distance, Heidegger's philosophical radicalism. His critique has been borne out beautifully by Karl Loewith's recently published experiences in the twenties and thirties with his teacher's intellectual seductiveness and "dark magic." Loewith attributed the powerful fascination of Heidegger's intellectual personality to his "impenetrability": nobody knew him; he remained the essential stranger, and the controversies, so helpful to his philosophical stardom, circled around his remoteness. Like Fichte, half scholar, half preacher and provocateur, he was driven by his discontent with himself and the times. The young people who shared this discontent were easily addicted to Heidegger's radically regressive "*Destruktion*" in his single-minded search for the one (and only) that is needed and to the appellative intensity of his philosophical will centered on (nothing but) himself.[57] Kracauer, Jonas, and Loewith pointed out this solipsism, in action as much as in thought, as the archphilosopher's primary flaw.

Many of the reflections collected in "The Anteroom" were still in the stage of notes that Kracauer wrote to himself, not yet fully articulated. This is also true of the passages on the "transcendental" and "immanentist" "solutions" in historiography. But they clearly and usefully call attention to the huge and yet mostly unacknowledged contradictions and leaps of faith encouraged by philosophical attitudes toward historical experience. Kracauer's historian travels in the realm of the nonabsolute, noncomplete, nontotal, nonradical–the anteroom of the relational with its risks and surprises. He is suspicious of Heidegger's mollusklike being, of Adorno's "unfettered dialectics"[58] feeding on itself, and of Gadamer's sanctification of the tradition for its own sake. Because these concepts, especially where they explicitly deal with historical phenomena, are abstract and exclusionary. With the outside world, they will shut out not only "the lost causes, the unrealized possibilities,"[59] but also the new beginnings, the unforeseen perspectives, the fragile intimations of alternate histories. It is for their sake that the historian protects the incompleteness of the stories she tells.

However, Kracauer was curiously unperceptive regarding Droysen's exploration of historical narration pursued over three decades (1858 to 1883) of lecturing on the methdodology of history. Droysen's critique both of the three key concepts of Ranke's "*Quellenkritik*"–objective fact, autopsy, and completeness–and of Ranke's artistic completeness of representational narrative in the service of an (impossible) ideal of objectivity ought to have been of deep interest to Kracauer. Droysen is concerned about the historian who expects from "*Quellenkritik*" the clarification of a diffuse historical event so that it can be perceived as a coherent processual complex of cause and effect, purpose and enactment, a "pure" historical fact. He has to understand, Droysen argues, that an allegedly "pure" historical fact is itself a temporary phenomenon, its distinctness being lost again (and again) for later observers, who will have new facts and a differently organized consciousness. Moreover, the sources themselves are resonant with the temporality of observation, that is, its positionality, cotemporal or subsequent. Droysen is impressed by the infinite hermeneutic regress that is responsible for the overwhelming and therefore confusing richness of sources. This situation is of crucial importance to historical narration charged with representing historical developments, past *becoming* rather than *being*.[60] Historical narrative does not intend to give a "picture, a photograph of what once was" but rather a *mimesis* of becoming–in contrast to the completion intended in artistic representation.[61] In his preface to the first edition of his *Grundriss der Historik* (1858), Droysen explicitly linked the midnineteenth-century belief in "'critique of the sources,' the establishing of the 'pure fact'," to a pervasive admiration for "the 'historical artwork'" as the "essential task of our science," which makes "the person [Ranke] whose narrative was closest to Walter Scott's novel" "the probably greatest historian of our time" (322). Droysen does not approve, since the past must not be closed prematurely in the complete story of the "historical artwork" fed by "pure facts." Historiographical representation, then, is distinctly and genuinely different from fictional representation in that it holds open concretely, with the relation between the subject and the object, that between different points in time, thereby preventing completion.

This is indeed very close to Kracauer's position. One is reminded here of his observation in a letter to Lowenthal during the work on *History*: he finds more instructive "the occasional reflections by practising historians on their field of inquiry . . . than most philosophies of history, including Hegel, Collingwood, Croce etc. I adore the diffuseness of the historians' ideas; it is entirely fitting that they have not been completed."[62] His main concern in *History* is with the historian's mobility in time, which enables her to consider the inevitable fuzziness of "pure" historical facts and the incompleteness of her story. Like Orpheus, she moves from a point in her own present back into the past. Unlike Orpheus, she is aware of the temporary, changing nature of that point. Were her conception of the past nothing but an expression of present interest or present thought, pertinent only to her point of departure, her assertiveness–like Orpheus's–would cause the past to withdraw from her. And yet, such assertiveness and loss are crucial to the historian's experience.

> Like Orpheus, the historian must descend into the nether world to bring the dead back to life. How far will they follow his allurements and evocations? They are lost to him when, re-emerging in the sunlight of the present, he turns for fear of losing them. But does he not for the first time take possession of them at this very moment–the moment when they forever depart, vanishing in a history of his own making? And what happens to the Pied-Piper himself on his way down and up? Consider that his journey is not simply a return trip. (79)

Kracauer does not explain in this concluding passage in chapter 2, "Present Interest," whether–and if so, how?–the "history of his own making" is related to the historian's changing in time. As this history *has* to be partly of his own making–the story *he*, and *she*, tells unlike anybody else–it must be related to the storyteller's going and coming in time, and therefore changing. The child "of at least two times–his own and the time he is investigating . . . his mind is in a measure unlocalizable; it perambulates without a fixed abode" (93). The past to which Kracauer's historian travels develops her willingness, even desire, to be uprooted, to be a stranger who, focusing differently, sees certain things more clearly and others dimly or not at all. History, we are told in the introduction, "resembles photography in that it is, among other things, a means of alienation" (5). But, seeing more clearly and more exclusively, the historian-as-stranger also appropriates. The dilemma for her, and yet an important guide for the story that she will tell, is her profound attraction, like Orpheus's, to the presence of the past, and her desire, in looking back, both to acknowledge its fragility and to deny it. Orpheus loves Eurydice, and he wants her back as she was. Going back into a past present no longer hers, and his only in imagination, he goes into another place, where he is the ultimate stranger. Into his story he may lure and evoke the past, but he cannot look back at it so that it might return his gaze and reassure him of its full and familiar presence. When he does, it vanishes.[63]

The issue here is not the fact that the historian's story is interpretive but the manner of the interpretation. Moving in the epistemological anteroom of historical and photographical reality, Kracauer's historian is asked to develop a mode of understanding that can accommodate the peculiarly interdependent character of historical phenomena. "Products of necessity as well as chance and freedom," they are "immensely concrete and virtually inexhaustible," making up a historical universe that "has many traits in common with the *Lebenswelt.* They stand out in it sphinx-like, as do their counterparts in the world we live in." We perceive their impenetrability and yet we deal with it very much in the way in which we "proceed in everyday life when we assess, often seemingly on the spur of the moment, a person's character, argue about a political decision, ponder the possible outcome of an individual or social crisis, etc." This is the way in which we "orient ourselves in the jungle through which we are passing"–whether we are going toward the future or toward the past. "The patterns of the historian's story reflect those of his accumulated life experience, nourished, as it were, by what the past confides to him. In a way his story *is* his interpretation" (95–97). The historian's interpretation–impure, uncertain, and incomplete–arises out of a shared temporal life-world. Moving Hades to remove temporality, the poet Orpheus does not question and thus does not interpret the past. His full recreation of it is an act of pure imagination.

Kracauer knew very well that acts of imagination influence the writing of history in ways both profound and imponderable. But historical knowledge is formed in the temporal, multi-layered world of everyday life, which is simultaneously self-evident and opaque. The historian has to rely on value judgments, approximations, hunches, ad-hoc hypotheses, instinctive decisions that do not fully fit into causal connections or systemic localizations but that also resist the completeness and purity of fictions. For Orpheus, desiring to undo the ravages of time and to bring back, have back fully, there is the one enchanted instant of regaining and losing. Knowing that time cannot be reversed but only traced, and often dimly, and yet driven by the impossible desire to understand fully, the historian is engaged in the process of many partial regainings and losses.

5 In his critical reflections on various historiographical positions, Kracauer was not so much concerned with embracing or rejecting them as with keeping open their possible meanings. This attitude was the source of the literally essayistic, tentative, searching discursive presentation of the argument in *History*. It also informed the arrangement of the eight chapters–a spiral sequence that emphasizes, as if graphically, the entanglement of the different historiographical problems. The argument of chapter 2, "The Historical Approach," is resumed in chapter 5, "The Structure of the Historical Universe," having been enriched en route by the questions of the historian's perspective posed in chapter 3, "The Present Interest," and mobility in chapter 4, "The Historian's Journey." The same is true for the connection between chapter 4 and chapter 6, "Ahasuerus, or the Riddle of Time" which, mediated by the argument concerning micro and macro histories in chapter 5, underlines the bewildering puzzles of time travel. The reflections on historical knowledge versus natural laws in chapter 1, "Nature," are echoed in chapter 7, "General History and the Aesthetic Approach," which explores the role of science and art in the narrative strategies of historiography. Finally, chapter 8, "The Anteroom," a summary and interpretation of the preceding arguments, picks up all these connections and links them explicitly to the question, raised in chapter 3, of the historian's contemporaneity in her own culture as the point of departure for the past.

Moving from the general problem of understanding the relation of nature and history to its different reflections in various historiographical positions, to the role of the historian's experience and self-knowledge in his understanding of history, to the experience of time in art and historiography, Kracauer was concerned mainly with a complex of mutual dependencies. The place that he created in *History* for the thoughts of others was spacious enough so that they could be balanced, tactfully judged in terms of their relative usefulness, and above all related. Positions that seemed diametrically opposed emerge changed by such mediation. When Kracauer counseled to link, rather than choose between, Ranke's and Dilthey's historiographical positions (although to make his point he first separates them more than is necessary), he echoed the advice given in *Theory of Film* that photographic perspective should combine "formative" and "realistic" tendencies. Ranke pleads for the historian's near-total "self-extinction" in approaching his material; Dilthey urges him to seize the past with his "whole being." But obliged to construct from already extant conceptual structures, the historian does not normally extend his subjectivity unless he first contracts it:

> And why should it be impossible for him to check the thrust of subjective influences? Actually his self is much more flexible and manipulable than Dilthey seems to realize. The historian, that is, may go far in putting it in brackets or indeed effacing it–in any case far enough to respond to many signals which would otherwise be lost on him. In the intermediary dimension of history, differences in degree and approximations are anything but negligible. Ranke's yearnings point in the right direction. (81f.)

It is precisely by acknowledging her historicity that the historian is less tempted to overlook, and thereby exclude, some parts of the past. Kracauer did not take Ranke's position. He thought more useful his desire to keep at a minimum the historian's intrusion into the past–provided this desire was recognized as a direction rather than a concrete goal. At issue was the historian's mobile perspective, which, combining different points of observation, hovers at a "middle distance." Instructively, at this tricky stage of his argument, Kracauer explicitly calls up the experience of photography and of exile. Once more–and again from a a different angle–he comes back to Proust's description of the irrevocably distancing and alienating properties of the photo image. When Marcel sees his beloved grandmother after a long interval, he finds himself looking at her, a dejected old woman sitting on a sofa, not as himself but as "only the witness, the observer with a hat and traveling coat, the stranger who does not belong to the house, the photographer who has called to take a photograph of places which one will never see again. The process that mechanically occurred in my eyes when I caught sight of my grandmother was indeed a photograph" (quoted in *History*, 82).

The viewer's mind, Kracauer explains, had become a "palimpsest with the stranger's observations being superimposed upon the lover's temporarily effaced inscription" (83). Such a palimpsest is also formed in the mind of the exile in the experience of cultural rupture. In some ways like Marcel, the exile is confronted, through the disruption of "his life history," not only with a fragmentation of the self but also with a dislocation of its different parts. His "natural" self of already formed loyalties, expectations, and failed hopes for a future continuous with the past is "relegated to the background of his mind," where it is only subliminally alive.

Describing the "exile's true mode of existence" as "that of a stranger," Kracauer was clearly influenced by Alfred Schutz's essay "The Stranger" (1944).[64] The exile Schutz analyzed the difficulties experienced by the stranger when trying to obtain knowledge concerning his daily life and finding that the ways in which he had proceeded (before the rupture of exile) as a member of the "in group" no longer yielded the desired results. A system of knowledge acquired in the context of everyday life is "incoherent, inconsistent, and only partially clear," but for the members of the in group it takes on "the appearance of a *sufficient* coherence, clarity and consistency to give anybody a reasonable chance of understanding and of being understood." For anybody in this group, but not for the stranger, the

> knowledge correlated to the cultural pattern carries its evidence in itself–or, rather, it is taken for granted in the absence of evidence to the contrary. It is a knowledge of trustworthy *recipes* for handling things and men in order to obtain the best results in every situation with a minimum of effort by avoiding undesirable consequences. . . . Thus it is the function of the cultural pattern to eliminate troublesome inquiries by offering ready-made direction for use, to replace truth hard to obtain by comfortable truisms, and to substitute the self-explanatory for the questionable (95).

This cultural pattern is not easily available to the stranger who approaches the in group–the exile who tries to find his way in American society. In the absence of the self-evident, no longer able to resort to "thinking as usual," or to make "of course" assumptions, he will have to look for evidence, that is, he will have to "place in question nearly everything that seems to be unquestionable to the members of the approached group." In relation to this group the stranger is "a newcomer in the true meaning of the term," a person without history. Such newness signifies with the losses also the possibilities of new beginnings: in the effort to penetrate the cultural pattern of the approached group, the stranger undergoes a process of transformation from an "unconcerned onlooker" into a "would-be member of the approached group" (95–97).

The sociologist Schutz was interested in the stranger as the person whose strangeness diminishes in the acts of approaching, which are meant to enable him eventually to enter the group as an actor rather than observer. The stranger is the one who, moving toward what is strange to him, undergoes transformation. The process, the motion of change is not linear since it involves a going back and forth, acts of mediating, indeed translating, between the cultural patterns of his home group and the in group he wishes to join. And, like any translator, he will for the longest time be uncertain about the adequacy and fittingness of his translation–an uncertainty that involves a going back and forth between passive and active language (98–100).

Kracauer pointed out that the exile's "inevitable efforts to meet the challenges of an alien environment" would indeed change him and that the change would not result in a stable new identity but rather in an identity in flux: "the self he was continues to smolder beneath the person he is about to become." Neither will he ever think of himself as fully belonging to the community he joined, nor will he be thought to belong fully by its members. The exile has, in fact, ceased to "belong," living now in the "near-vacuum of extraterritoriality," the realm of estrangement, "the very no-man's land which Marcel entered when he first caught sight of his grandmother" (83).

But the usefulness of the analogy to Marcel's experience stops right here, and the limitations of the analogy to Schutz's stranger become clearly visible. Because in time, the stranger, the exile, becomes the person who feels (temporarily) at home–as indeed Schutz and Kracauer felt at home in New York. After all, the very patterns of American culture have been profoundly shaped by that moving in time from strangeness to familiarity. Schutz concludes his essay with the sentence: "But then the stranger is no stranger anymore, and his specific problems have been solved." For Kracauer the thought-image of the exile as stranger is useful precisely when he is at that stage in between strangeness and familiarity, hovering at the point of "middle distance." And in contrast to Marcel (who shares more the problems of Schutz's "homecomer"[65]), the experience of strangeness is illuminating and enabling in its own right. Released from unquestioned loyalty to his own past, the exile, like the historian, is now free to step outside the time and space of his own culture and enter another, new one. She can now be the curious, attentive visitor who comes and goes, approaches and draws back. This visitor is highly aware of the difficulties of gaining access (historical knowledge) and exhibits what Schutz described as the two most important properties associated with the stranger's position: (relative) "objectivity" as the result of continued questioning, and "doubtful loyalty."[66] For the stranger, the cultural patterns of the group to be approached are not, as they are for the insider, a help in solving the puzzle, but are themselves the problem and thus the cause for her critical attitude, which undermines expectations of solidarity. As Kracauer describes it in *History*, "It is only in this state of self-effacement, or homelessness, that the historian can commune with the material of his concern. . . . A stranger to the world evoked by the sources, he is faced with the task–the exile's task–of penetrating its outward appearances, so that he may learn to understand that world from within" (84).

The historian traveling, simultaneously, in several spaces of time develops "a sort of active passivity" regarding her material. If she immerses herself in it, coming close, being familiar, her insights into a temporal entity now irreversibly passed by the present are still shaped by her *post festum* perspective. Here Kracauer might have found suggestive Schutz' analysis of the difficulties faced by the homecomer, because in important ways they are shared by the historian, who changes while traveling in time, including her own lifetime. She has better access to the complex meanings of the *post festum* perspective if she understands that when she goes back to the spaces of her own past, both they and she will be different in unexpected ways because the futures of that past have been different. Even if sought and desired, the recurrent cannot be the same: "what belongs to the past can never be reinstated in another present exactly as it was."[67]

A poignant example of an experience of irreversible pastness related here by Kracauer emphasized precisely that aspect of the historian's learning process. Trying to answer a young historian's questions about the intellectual life of the Weimar period, the older historian, the exile, knew that all the information gathered by the young man was indeed factually correct. Yet as Kracauer remembered it, nothing had actually happened that way. For the past contemporary of that period, the incommensurability of the relation between the later construct and the remembered reality in flux was disturbing because it drew him into the extraterritorial state of the historian. Here he found himself deprived of his memory, the seemingly unmediated presence of things past. But having been removed from this imagined present tense in the confrontation with the *post festum* perspective, Kracauer also realized that he now saw differently, that is, different things. New aspects of the past opened up to him precisely because it was no longer his but was shared with others, and in unforeseeable ways.[68] From the future of the past that once was his present but that is his no more, the time-traveling historian, exile, stranger, and homecomer can now question his own witnessing and thus appreciate the unpredictable surprising extension into the future of past events. Literally, he can appreciate, with the meanings of pastness, the fact that the historian's inquiry is both constructed and open-ended. It is not that history is part memory and part imagination but that memory is a product of the imagination, changing with it in time.

For reasons of historical knowledge, the historian is advised to travel light as far as notions of a fixed, enduring identity are concerned. Engaged in "acts of self-emptying" and assuming a "state of passiveness," she is able to immerse herself in the details of past lives and open herself up to the "influx" of information.[69] In contrast, the writers of grand historical narratives, carrying the weight of creative authorship and authority, let their "formative urges get the better of [their] curiosity about the real course of events" (89f.). But what counts for Kracauer is precisely this curiosity. To clarify the enterprise of historiography with a "realistic tendency," Kracauer pointed to the documentary film as counterpart in its search for "(unattainable) objective truth." His examples concern deliberately nonartistic, unadorned documentation of social problems resulting in films that "picture appalling living conditions with a matter-of-fact soberness."

> Highly skilled craftsmen, the directors of these films proceed from the conviction that pictorial beauty and suggestive editing would interfere with their intention to let things be as they are. They practice self-restraint as artists to produce the effect of impersonal authenticity. Now the salient point is that their conduct is based on moral considerations. Joris Ivens relates that during the shooting of *Borinage*, a 1934 documentary about the miners in this Belgian coal district, he and his co-director Henri Storck realized that their very subject matter required of them photographic "simplicity." "We felt it would be insulting to people in such extreme hardship to use any style of photography that would prevent the direct honest communication of their pain to every spectator." Human suffering, it appears, is conducive to detached reporting; the artist's conscience shows in artless photography. Since history is full of human suffering, similar attitudes and reflections may be at the bottom of many a fact-oriented historical account, deepening the significance of its pale objectivity. (90f.)

Kracauer is obviously sympathetic to this significance, though he is aware of its complex implications. The "pale objectivity" of the observer's socially (morally) responsible perspective cannot of course be equated with objective truth. For the "fact-oriented" perspective, too, truth has the status of a goal. But even if it seems clear that this goal cannot be (fully) realized, it needs to play a part in the shaping of historiographical or photographical representation. The observer's determination to submit to this shaping concerns knowledge as well as morality, morality as part of knowledge. This determination, then, rather than commendable moral intentions, supports the goal of the "right" balance between formative and realistic tendencies in photography and historiography. (Significantly, Kracauer came back here once more to Butterfield's argument in "Moral Judgments," which has the "technical" historian "assist the cause of morality by describing, in concrete detail and in an objective manner, a wholesale massacre, the consequences of religious persecution, or the goings-on in a concentration camp.")[70]

The issue has become more difficult and more important in the twenty-five years since Kracauer's death, which saw an explosive growth of communication through images and, with the growing power of different (multicultural) perspectives, a host of documentary problems. In a recent review, "Good Intentions," of Sebastiao Salgado's photography exhibitions, "An Uncertain Grace" and "Kuwait Epilogue," Ingrid Sischy perceptively points out some of these problems. She argues that Salgado's "finding the 'grace' and 'beauty' in the twisted forms of his anguished subjects"–for instance the starving people from the Sahel region in Africa–makes for a "beautification of tragedy" that does little to help the viewer gain access to the depicted experience.[71] The focus of these technically self-conscious photo images is more on *Salgado's* experience, filtered through his aestheticizing sentimentalism, of the extremely difficult lives of others, than on those lives themselves. These photographs, Sischy writes in conclusion, are "less than their subjects deserve. We can be sure that if truly appropriate images should ever surface they will not be so 'beautiful' that they could work as packaged caring."

Her point is well taken–though the judgment "truly appropriate" has always been wide open to discussion. Sischy's title is a reference to a statement made by W. Eugene Smith, a famous photojournalist for *Life* who was admired for both his technical skill and his integrity, and who clearly influenced Salgado. In a "moment of clarity about his work," Sischy writes, Smith described his photographic tools as "the fragile weapons of my good intentions." This insight is repressed, she thinks, in another, more characteristic statement about the meanings of his work: "I frequently have sought out those who are in the least position to speak for themselves. By accident of birth, by accident of place–whoever, whatever, wherever–I am of their family. I can comment for them, if I believe in their cause, with a voice they do not possess." Such presumption, Sischy comments, is "at the core of what is self-aggrandizing about Salgado's photography."[72] It is a presumption that, with the best of intentions, prescribes a completeness of access to the "truth" of the subject of the photo image, which in fact obscures it. Instead it illuminates the maker of the image, who then is frozen in the persona of the artist who cares, speaking in his own voice for all those voiceless whose experiences he appropriates. John Szarkowski, too, thought problematic Smith's belief that "the photojournalist was responsible to a standard that went beyond factual accuracy and pictorial effectiveness" to a representation of the "psychological and moral truth of the subject."[73] He reproduced images from Smith's 1948 *Life* series, "Country Doctor" (226f.), which are among his best and remarkably successful in their visual focus on the physician's intense and resigned concentration on his young patient (fig. 38). Their undeniable emotional power arguably derives from Smith's identification with the total, selfless dedication of the physician. Still, this "stern and demanding" standard, Szarkowski pointed out rightly, is difficult to evaluate: "To be simultaneously a socially responsible photojournalist and an ambitious artist is difficult enough; to serve also as the designated conscience for one's guild is perhaps too heavy a burden. As Smith's ambitions became grander and more beatific it became harder for him to resist the temptation to make every moment momentous" (228).

Kracauer's historian is explicitly wary of such creative appropriation of others' experience because it would suppress his being changed by it. In Leo Strauss's words, quoted with approval by Kracauer: "He embarks on a journey whose end is hidden from him. He is not likely to return to the shores of his time as exactly the same man who departed from them."[74] He is Schutz's homecomer who, changed himself, finds things changed. Observing past lives in the flux of his own lifetime, getting older, he has had new experiences that change his understanding of previous experiences. In the continous flow of thought, of new interpretive insights, his state of mind cannot remain the same. Even if the place of his departure had remained the same–an unlikely event–it would not appear so to him. "All these basic features of our mental life bar a recurrence of the same. Being recurrent, the recurrent is not the same anymore."[75]

Time-traveling in many directions, going back and forth between the states of the stranger and the homecomer, the historian cannot afford a return ticket. Her mobility, as Kracauer described it in *History*, makes for uncertainties that profoundly shape her inquiry:

> The change of identity he undergoes must be traced to his stay in the past. To be precise, it is an aftermath of the discoveries which the historian is making in the state of self-effacement–that phase in which he opens himself up to the suggestions of the sources. Need I repeat that his findings may obstruct his original research designs and therefore determine him to alter the course of his investigations? At any rate, they are apt to tell him something that he did not, and could not, know before. This points to the direction of the change. It is inevitable that the yield of the historian's active passivity should ferment in his mind and thus eventually effect a broadening of its scope. Self-effacement begets self-expansion. . . . In consequence, Dilthey's belief that historical understanding calls for the total mobilization of our being turns out to be not sufficiently specific. What is required of the historian is not merely his "*whole* inner man" as he happens to be but a self which has expanded in the wake of its near-extinction. (91f.)

It is precisely in her "active passivity" toward the past that the historian can be linked to the photographer.[76] Having clarified his disagreements with Dilthey's concept of historical understanding, Kracauer now qualifies the parallel he just drew between Proust's Marcel and the historian. Both pass through the "same phase of estrangement" from their former selves, but it is only the protagonist in the novel who comes out unchanged: "While the reinstated complete Marcel falls back upon the ideas which he entertained of his grandmother prior to her transformation into a photograph, the historian assimilates to himself the very reality which was concealed from him by his ideas of it" (92f.). Where Marcel–like Orpheus–recovers his grandmother, Kracauer's historian lets go of his (preconceived ideas of) history. A traveler, a stranger, a homecomer who will not really feel at home, she is forever curious to learn about the different routes she might take and where they might take her.

6 Whose history is the past? This is the question central to Kracauer's enterprise and the one most difficult to ask intelligibly. At the end of his reflections on the many different routes taken by the historian, Kracauer admits that the two greatest obstacles to such travel–the heterogeneous structures that make up the historical universe and the discontinuities of lived time–remain largely unexplored: "Did history not exist, one might almost say that it is an improbable undertaking" (103).

But emphatically it does exist in the accumulated stories told over time by many well-intentioned, hard-working historians. Yet these stories, which collectively have made history, cannot but reflect the many different viewpoints, interests, and associations of their authors. Themselves the stuff of history, these interests also compromise historical knowledge by guiding the historian dependent on the stories constructed under their influence for her own construct–which itself is not free of such interests. It is a difficult enough task to sort out such interdependencies from case to case. More complicated, indeed an (almost) improbable undertaking is to look at whole chains of stories for an understanding of the time of history. Traveling in several spaces of time, the historian, consciously or unconsciously, brings to the story she tells the experiences she had at different times in different times. These experiences of change and of the changeability of all things in time are mediated by her own person, namely the experience of an identity that has not been stable at any time, the experience of the selective synchronic processes of memory.

It is true, these experiences can be of direct help to the historian in the sense of making it easier to perceive the non-simultaneity ("*Ungleichzeitigkeit*")[77] of chronologically co-temporal phenomena and to reject the concept of homogeneous linear time as the time of history. Subjected to such a perspective, a clearly definable space of time breaks down into the conflicts of different coexisting tendencies whose specific dynamics affect the historical process by dissolving one circumscribed period and establishing another. Noting that many practising historians have pointed to evidence that would contradict a distinctness of historical periods in their chronological sequence, notwithstanding surface coherences or "physiognomies," Kracauer expects them ready to "jump from one period to another" (152, 155). On the other hand, there is a strong experiential basis for the perception of coherent long-term developments in an, as it were, linear chronological flow corresponding to the culturally important "true" (complete) stories of personal identity.[78] Here the challenge to the historian to refrain from full authentication—not to allow her story to be too certain, too complete—will be greater. Kracauer suggests shrewdly that the honesty of probability is more difficult to maintain in the case of assumed coherence than in observed discontinuity.

Out of the experience of her own temporality, the historian describes the temporality of the past, and in doing so she inevitably alters the latter as well as the former. The richer her experience, the more complex is what Kracauer refers to as a "web of interpretations" (93), the text of these alterations. Here, where the historical analysis of historiography may become lightheaded with intimations of the infinite and incommensurable, Kracauer resorts to one of his suggestive thought-images, which, for the moment, can brilliantly focus the reader's attention—for the sake of the problem. The riddle of time, which makes time travel and its documentation such a complicated affair for even the most thoughtful historian, appears most strikingly impenetrable in the legendary figure of Ahasver:

> He indeed would know firsthand about the developments and transitions, for he alone in all history has had the unsought opportunity to experience the process of becoming and decaying itself. How unspeakably terrible he must look! To be sure, his face cannot have suffered from aging, but I imagine it to be many faces, each reflecting one of the periods which he traversed and all of them combining into ever new patterns, as he restlessly, and vainly, tries on his wanderings to reconstruct out of the times that shaped him the one time he is doomed to incarnate. (157)

The profound desire to articulate a continuity that could resist the rush of time and mitigate the inequities of human temporality has driven the cultural construction of history since its beginnings. But modern historiography has been challenged to acknowledge the terrifying confusions of this "eternally" shifting face whose reality the historian then cannot escape. In *Theory of Film*, Kracauer gives an account of the "fascinating experiment" made by the German photographer Helmar Lerski in the thirties in Palestine, of which he told Kracauer when both were in exile in Paris. He took a hundred close-ups of a young man's as yet unformed face, screening the light differently each time, with the amazing result that none of the images produced showed any similarity to the others or to the model (fig. 39).

> Out of the original face there arose, evoked by the varying lights, a hundred different faces, among them those of a hero, a prophet, a peasant, a dying soldier, an old woman, a monk. Did these portraits, if portraits they were, anticipate the metamorphoses which the young man would undergo in the future? Or were they just plays of light whimsically projecting on his face dreams and experiences forever alien to him? Proust would have delighted in Lerski's experiment with its unfathomable implications.[79]

They are the implications of the riddle of time as the riddle of identity. When Kracauer comes back, again and again, to Proust's comparison between the distancing photo image and the centering memory image, he is sharply aware that it is part of a fictional, not a historical, narrative. It is the novelist Proust who can halt the flux of time because he constructs his fictional worlds in no-where and no-when. Marcel, who then merges with Proust, knows in the end that it was the meaning of his traveling through time to prepare him for artistic activity. When he begins writing the novel which he has written, he begins to construct the continuity of the discontinuous worlds of his past. In the work of art—in that sense it is indeed timeless—his past has been delivered from the curse of time, and this deliverance is inviolable. But such reconciliation of a substantially chronological with a discontinuous experience of time[80] is possible only a posteriori—in the backward glance from the end of Marcel's story—and in the realm of fiction. In contradistinction to stories as artefacts, the stories of history just end, without having an ending. Historical ambiguities and conflicts cannot be represented fully; to do so would require an aesthetic solution. For the historian, the contradictions inherent in the experience of time are unsolvable. It is only at the "unthinkable" end of time, when dissolution is imminent, that Ahasver can first look back on his extraterritorial migrations through time (162f.). What he will see at that imaginary moment has to remain hidden to the historian because this literally decomposing backward glance destroys, by transcending it, the possibility of historical knowledge. But the historian is responsible for precisely this possibility, no more, no less. She will have to bear with the temporal complexity of her stories feeding on other stories dependent on yet other stories—all of them attempting to relate to and account for the unstable life-worlds of times past.

7 Who, then, is the author of these stories? To whose authority do they defer? Telling her incomplete, open-ended stories out of the stories of others, Kracauer's historian seems remarkably undisturbed by these questions. She defers to the authority of what has been lived in that past, that is, *outside* her inquiring (*historein*) mind–a relative authority mediated in her imagination. As she shares this imagination with many other historians, her authorship, too, is a relative, partial affair. In that the time-traveler as exile, stranger, and homecomer differs notably from many of Kracauer's co-exiles who showed little tolerance for such "ungrounded" intellectual mobility. Attempting to rethink a cultural tradition profoundly ruptured in the *Zivilisationsbruch* caused by the Third Reich, they were preoccupied with questions of value and meaning in history that need to be grounded in an authority of origin. This preoccupation can be found in the works of intellectual exiles with widely diverging political sympathies and affiliations, who often differed greatly in their readings of the past in its relation to the present. They were connected in their search for enduring cultural value, and in their attempts to explain the significance of cultural continuity in the face of cultural and political chaos. Here they shared an overriding interest in establishing the meaning of history, which leaves behind the meanings of historical inquiry. Their reaction to (Western) culture in crisis has been both a highly selective and a broadly inclusive concept of historiography that disregards most of the troubling and intriguing questions of that enterprise–questions of position, selection, and perspective, of cultural memory, reality, and fictionality.

The intellectuals' mental state of exile preceded–as I argued above[81]–the experience of political exile, but it was arguably intensified by that experience, most directly and problematically in the case of the Frankfurt School. In contradistinction to immigrants to whom most strange things become familiar in time, intellectual exiles or emigrants tended to see themselves as Utopian travelers in America, the self-proclaimed *novus ordo saeclorum*. Their interest in their new environment rarely went beyond noting and recording the enduring strangeness of people in relation to their cultural spaces and objects. More importantly, they used this strangeness to reflect on the significance of their own dissociation from the familiar places of their past. Max Weber's cultural pluralism and conditional functional value neutrality, and Karl Mannheim's restatement of it in the politically polarized situation at the end of the Weimar Republic,[82] might have prepared them for the experience of exile as temporary and of strangeness as changing. But this position had not been acceptable to intellectuals with explicitly political-philosophical concerns who worked in the material of history, such as Adorno and Horkheimer in *Dialectic of Enlightenment*, or on the other side of the political spectrum[83] Eric Voegelin in *Order and History*, one of the more interesting if problematic metahistories of this century. I am not speaking here of reactions to the actuality of day-to-day life in America, which were simply rejecting in Adorno's case and thoughtfully curious in Voegelin's. My concern is the exiles' shared enduring intellectual experience of large-scale cultural dissociation.

Voegelin's monumental *Order and History*[84] presents an instructively clear (because extreme) version of the hermeneutical dilemma that confronts the twentieth-century historian searching for meaningful order in history. Both the troubling and the usefully provocative aspects of his political-philosophical history are located in his focus on history as an expanding, increasingly "differentiating" consciousness, that is, a developing (collective) human insight into the "order of being" as a history of order. There is the important fact that, in contrast to Adorno and Horkheimer's charting of the predestined course of rigid and limiting bourgeois rationality since antiquity, Voegelin gathered an enormous amount of historical information in his attempt to record the expansion of human consciousness. The first three volumes–*Israel and Revelation* (1956), *The World of the Polis* (1957), and *Plato and Aristotle* (1957)–have been admired by experts in their fields of inquiry even where they explicitly did not agree with Voegelin's "agenda." Voegelin had begun to develop his concept of order in history in the midforties, exiled in America and waiting for the war to end and the Hitler regime to collapse. Working on a "History of Political Ideas" that eventually became *Order and History*, he was certain that this kind of intellectual historiography, carried out systematically on the basis of sufficient material, would inevitably lead to a philosophy of history that would show the order of history emerging from the history of order.

During this period Voegelin exchanged a number of essay-length critical letters with his friend Alfred Schutz to sort out their differences about

Husserl's transcendental phenomenology—his philosophical description of "*Lebenswelt*"—which instructively complement Kracauer's position.[85] Schutz, Husserl's student, had become increasingly critical of many aspects of his teacher's work, as he wrote to Voegelin on December 7, 1940 (though he made it clear that, given the political situation, this was a private, not a public acknowledgment). In the late summer of 1943, Schutz, who was then working on the knowledge problems that confront the stranger, read a chapter of Voegelin's "History of Political Ideas" manuscript and stated certain important reservations.[86] In response Voegelin wrote what amounted to a critical essay on Husserl's last work, *Krisis der europäischen Wissenschaften* (1936), for which Schutz, who like Kracauer had a busy extra-academic professional life, thanked him on September 30, 1943, with the promise of a detailed answer. Like Voegelin's, it would be a long and rigorously argued essay on which he worked for the better part of two months.

Though Schutz had reassured Voegelin in the first short letter that his objections to the major tenets of Husserl's philosophy were in some ways as serious as Voegelin's, they were quite different in kind. Rejecting Voegelin's categorical refusal to grant Husserl's phenemonological epistemology the status of a well-founded philosophical enterprise, he pointed out the personal dimension of such judgment. But asserting his own belief that some of Husserl's discoveries did indeed touch on the fundamental questions of philosophy, he also conceded that most of Husserl's published work was "phänomenologische Psychologie" rather than philosophy.[87] Husserl, then, had failed in his claim to have "begründet" (founded and grounded) "a genuine and final system of a universal philosophy."

These, however, were clearly not issues of great importance to the philosophical sociologist Schutz, who was interested in the acculturated nature of perception. The most disturbing element of Husserl's work, in his view, was phenomenology's inability to overcome its inherent "*transcendentalen Solipsismus*," which had caused Husserl to propose a philosophical constitution of the experiential world in the consciousness of the one (then godlike) "*transcendentales Ego.*" For Schutz, as well as for Kracauer, this experiential world, Husserl's "*Lebenswelt*," signifies the presence of many others.[88] Voegelin's Husserl critique, in contrast, focused on the absence of the metaphysical dimension in Husserl's thought—the absence of "ground" without which there is no philosophical thought. From the position of his "History of Political Ideas," Voegelin criticized Husserl, as Schutz noted, for not having written an intellectual history of mankind aiming at objective knowledge. He also blamed him for not having posed questions concerning the relation between "world soul" and individual soul that belong to the realm of a metaphysics of history. Rightly Schutz did not see Husserl as a philosopher of history or as a historian. Thus it did not make sense to him to accuse Husserl of having both rejected empirical-historical arguments and neglected to deal with the historical-philosophical testimonies of the great thinkers of the past.

The important difference between the two exiles was indeed Voegelin's desire to go back to the origins. As Schutz explained, Husserl (and by implication Schutz) saw himself in a long tradition of philosophical interpretation of the world that has motivated our thought and guided the posing of our own questions. Our own possibilities and tasks, then, are contained in the "typical forms of the problems and the typical possibilities of their solutions." Within a generational chain, philosophers are the founders of new traditions, handing down their inheritance, which they have altered and sometimes enriched, and concerned with the problem of a both original and concluding foundation ("*Urstiftung*" and "*Endstiftung*") of the tradition.[89]

The tradition is not self-evident but literally questionable, "*fragwürdig.*" Schutz characterized Husserl's position as that of the philosopher who puts questions to the tradition concerning its origin and the history of its interpretations. However, this is not the position of an "objectifying onlooker who wants to know what it had actually been like" ("wie es denn eigentlich gewesen ist") but of a passionately involved participator wishing to explicate the contents of the tradition only insofar as they pertain to his own self-knowledge. This position, Schutz argued, is typical for thinkers in the periods of great intellectual-spiritual (*geistig*) crises, which call up problems of foundation in philosophy–thus the title of Husserl's "comprehensive analysis" projected in his last work, *The Crisis of the European Sciences and Transcendental Phenomenology.*

Schutz's attempts to define Husserl's position to Voegelin, whose thought was indeed "grounded" in the search for metaphysical rather than scientific truths, were clearly informed by his own experience of the crisis of a ruptured tradition. If Husserl was isolated, exiled in Freiburg in the late thirties, the cosmopolitan international banker Schutz was the thinker in exile. He was the stranger for whom it was necessary to select certain elements of the tradition and to interpret them. Yet he found himself unable to approach them within the constructs of significance ("*Sinnstrukturen*") in which they had been embedded for the thinkers who had authored them. He had to seek them out within constructs that made sense to *him* in his specific situation.[90]

Schutz, who was learning to negotiate the strangeness of America, pointed out the useful or positive aspects of the philosopher-as-stranger's activities on uncertain territory. They concern a critical understanding of the historicity of philosophical knowledge, which develops in time. This historicity, the relation between the (historical) thinker and the thought, makes for the incompleteness, indeed the questionableness at any given moment, of philosophical problems and their solutions. If anything was intellectually useful in historicism, Schutz adds here, it was its contribution to this insight. (Voegelin put a question mark to this sentence.)[91] Husserl saw these connections even if he did not articulate them clearly: tracing his own philosophical concerns, he arrived at the original foundation of philosophy by the Greeks and the original foundation of mathematics-based sciences by Galileo. This, Schutz thought, should make it possible for Voegelin to see the analogies to his own enterprise: an autobiographical anamnesis of those parts of the philosophical tradition that have had a motivating influence on his own thought. The philosopher's mobile position is located within the tradition. Looking back at it from his present, he will, in his future, have become a part of that tradition to be looked back at, interpreted by those who come after him. It is here that Schutz's account switches to the first person. He has learned from Husserl that he shares with those coming after him the problem of the concluding foundation of the tradition, which in each case is infinitely remote relative to the respective presents. He also has learned to see that his present activities will be part of the sediments contained in the future's inheritance. The philosopher-as-stranger will approach the tradition, be changed by it, learn to find his way in it, and in doing so contribute to it, that is, change it in certain ways. His stay will be temporary, but through his (cultural) activities he will have left traces–for a time.

Voegelin, of course, was not impressed by this secular understanding of culture reflected, if not in Husserl's, then certainly in Schutz's philosophical position. He was quick to point out, in his equally lengthy answer of December 28, 1943, the indeed serious hermeneutical problems posed by such philosophical historicizing of a linguistically complex tradition. (Ingeniously, Derrida's indebtedness to Husserl comes in the shape of the infinite remoteness not of significances but of signification itself). Husserl's concept of tradition, Voegelin noted rightly, neglected to deal with the immense plurality and variety of philosophical positions–which tradition, then, did he mean when he wrote about the crisis of philosophy?

For Voegelin this crisis was the collapse of the ordinates of our concepts of the world and of man founded on a common Christian belief. The "terrible burden" for anyone engaged in philosophizing was now to build up again such a system of ordinates. Clearly, he did not think that the "responsible philosopher" could contribute anything significant toward understanding that crisis by simply inserting himself into a largely unquestioned complex of traditions. Going back to Schutz's remark about the "objectifying onlooker" trying to find out "wie es denn eigentlich gewesen ist," Voegelin explained that Ranke had formulated this statement in answer to "Niebuhr's 'wie es denn *wirklich* gewesen ist.' . . . Ranke is of the opinion, that the historian's role is *not* to give critical-objective accounts of the facts. . . . His substitution of '*eigentlich*' for '*wirklich*' is meant to indicate that history is '*eigentlich*' [actually] concerned with facts in the light of interpretative maxims." History of ideas, then, does not mean to Voegelin a general overview of a sort of eternal trove of philosophical problems. A historically oriented position in philosophizing means, rather, the "integration (*Einbeziehung*) of the dead into the community of philosophizing."

Voegelin posits such "*Einbeziehung*" against both Husserl's selective use of the tradition and his, in Voegelin's view, vacuous concept of this tradition moving on, as it were, automatically into an indefinite future. In contradistinction to what he sees as Husserl's philosophically empty historicism, he emphasizes the interrelated problem of the actual stupendous difficulties of interpretation in historiography and of the philosopher's "concrete" historicity. By that he means the responsibility of the philosophically grounded historian also to the "reality of the direct, not historically mediated, philosophical experiences," which for Voegelin are eminently the "*Transzendenzerlebnisse*" of aging and death.

Kracauer's historian would agree, though importantly she would contain these experiences within the human condition, which in modernity has been defined by temporality and historicity, that is, the absence of any "ground" other than the changing value of cultural activities. Schutz's explanatory (partial) defense of Husserl's concept of tradition came from a position that acknowledges this absence. Yet precisely such acknowledgment seemed difficult to many intellectual exiles who had no tolerance for the stranger's negotiable attitude toward knowledge that Kracauer called "middle distance." There is an instructive example of emphatic resistance to this attitude in the response to Schutz's essay, "The Stranger," by one of his closest friends, Aron Gurwitsch. Thanking Schutz for the offprint, Gurwitsch protested that Schutz had given an unconscionably shallow account of the philosophical (intellectual) crisis that was inevitably and inexorably shared by all exiles. The exile, Gurwitsch argued, is an involuntary immigrant, a stranger against his will who

> not only *in fact* comes from a specific historical world, but is very much aware of the historical constellation to which he belongs, and of his place in this constellation. In addition: We have not, after all, broken with this world of ours; on the contrary, it has been shattered. If we have brought anything with us, then it is precisely the historical forces which have made us what we are. We did not want to break with our past, we didn't want to leave the world in which we grew up. The forces which drove us out were the enemies of Europe. When it was no longer possible to live in Europe as a European, at precisely that moment, we had to leave in order to save our bare lives. We had to leave Europe precisely because we were Europeans. And it is just this that makes us exiles,–a title which was very respected in earlier times.
>
> And so we find ourselves in new surroundings, and we soon discover that we are on another planet. We thought–I appeal to the philosopher Schutz–that man must be responsible for the world. That is what we learned from our master Husserl and read in Plato.[92]

The crisis of the exiled intellectual cannot be understood in terms of Schutz's categories of adaptation–"pattern of behavior," "scheme of orientation," "recipe"–but only in its etymological meaning, "decision." Decision, in Gurwitsch's scenario, leads the philosopher to the things themselves, that is, away from what they seem to others or "*what they say*," away from "the *consensus communis* and 'public opinion.'"[93] The philosopher's genealogy, going back to the "fool and martyr" Socrates, emphasizes for Gurwitsch the responsibility of inquiring into the existential rather than the social-political problems facing the human being. What he perceives to be Schutz's focus on (mere) "*adjustment*" and "*average opinion*"–echoing Adorno's complaints about Kracauer in America–suggests to Gurwitsch a concept of man as (nothing but) the "human animal." More, this apparent lack of interest in the nobility of man made in the image of God is synonymous with surrender to the final rupture of that philosophical tradition in which the claims to such nobility were grounded. It is synonymous, then, with the inability to face the crisis of European culture.[94] We don't have Schutz's answer; he would have sympathized, one suspects, with the friend's mourning the irreversible pastness of things past, made more dramatic by the enforced separation from a familiar culture. But like Kracauer, he had found exile to signify losses as well as new beginnings. Engaged in the process of familiarization, the exiled intellectual as stranger would gradually see more clearly the meanings of what was in the past and begin to recall and to reconstruct what was becoming accessible.

For Kracauer's historian, such reconstruction was focused on the past experiences of daily life which do not submit to a hierarchy of value, namely a distinct and then normative order. Voegelin, in contrast, reconstructed the order of history by ranking the truth of the order he found in history, rewriting the history of that order as a process of increasingly "differentiated" insight into the "order of being." However, this "order of being" is God's construct, in which man can participate–and thereby develop consciousness–only by accepting the responsibility of its truth. The substance of history, Voegelin asserted in the introduction to the first volume of *Order and History*, is the fight for the truth of order, which creates historical consciousness. Looking back on the particularities of this battle spanning thousands of years, Voegelin curiously limited his twentieth-century vantage point of a highly expanded, "differentiated" historical consciousness. He insisted on a comprehensive, absolute, nonrelational concept of truth that caused him simply to transcend his own temporality. This limitation affected the development of both his historical and his political thought.

The history of political ideas, which he discussed with Schutz in the forties, would eventually be concentrated in *The New Science of Politics*

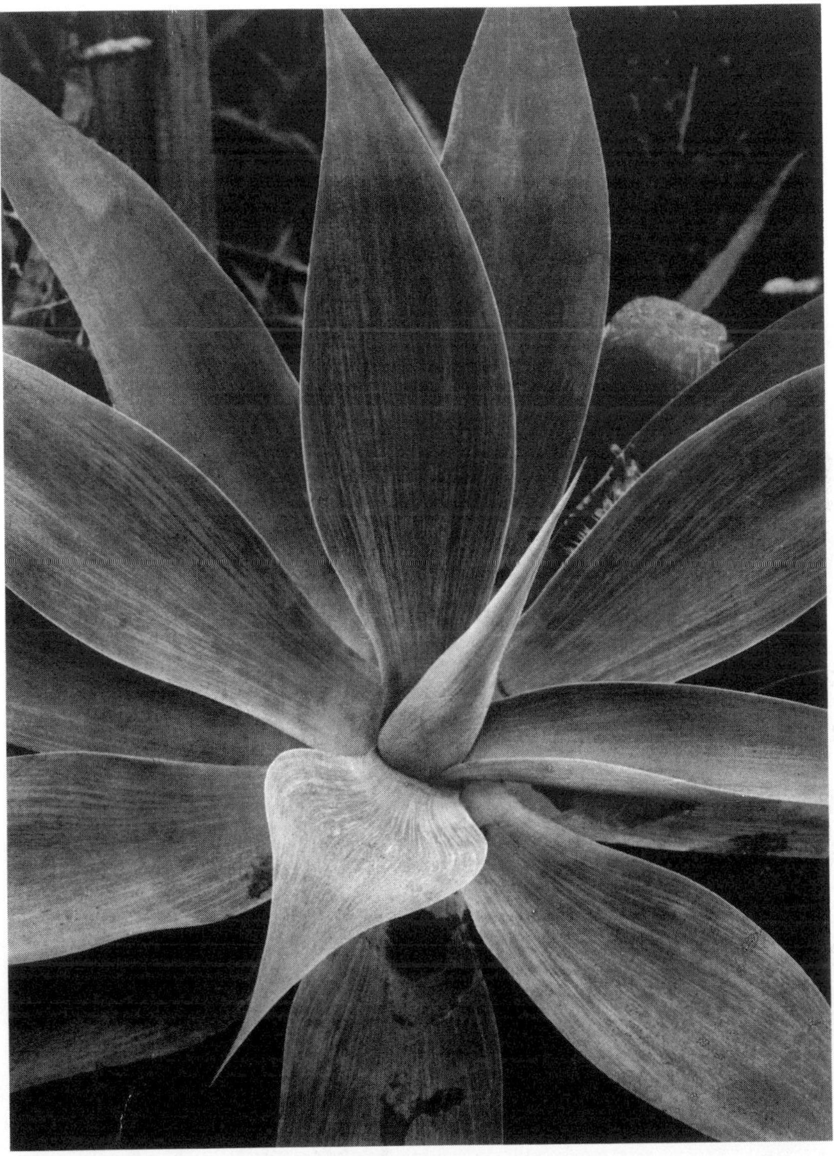

20. Albert Renger-Patzsch, *Agave,* 1928, negative/print.

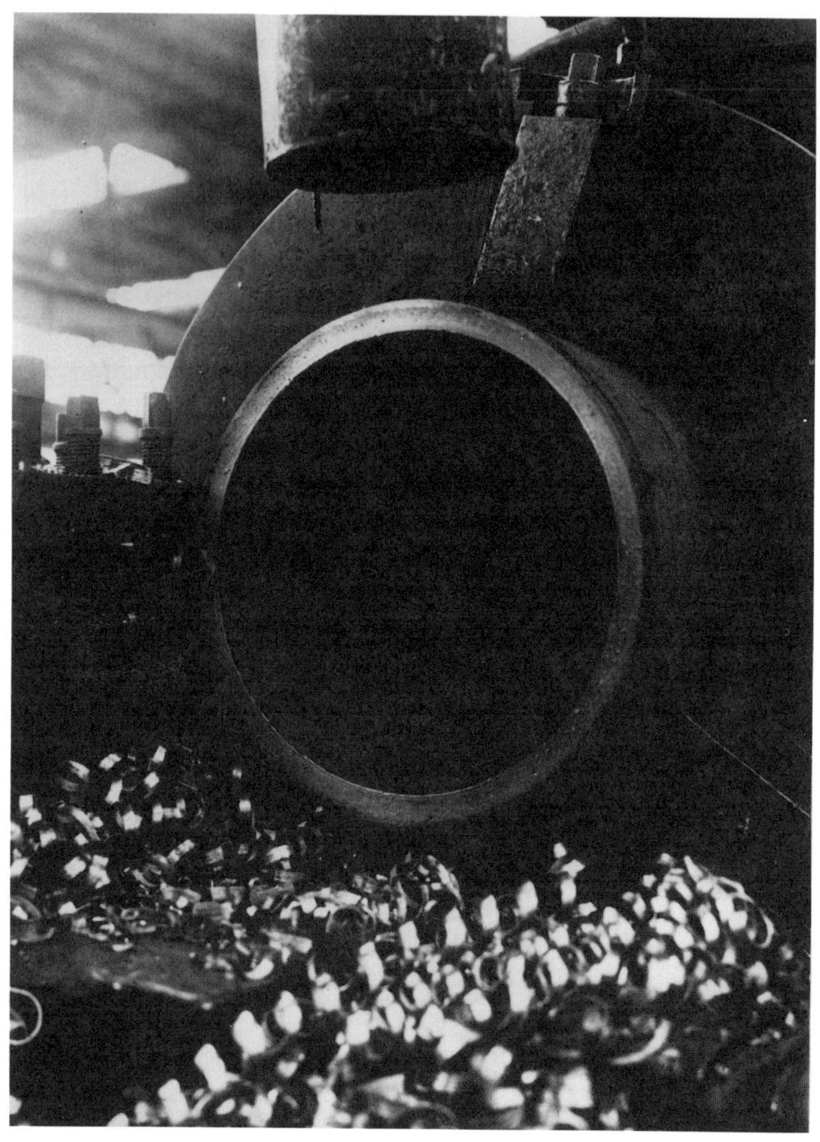

21. Albert Renger-Patzsch, *Untitled (Machine Composition)*, ca. 1930, gelatin silver, 9⅛ × 6[11]/16 in.

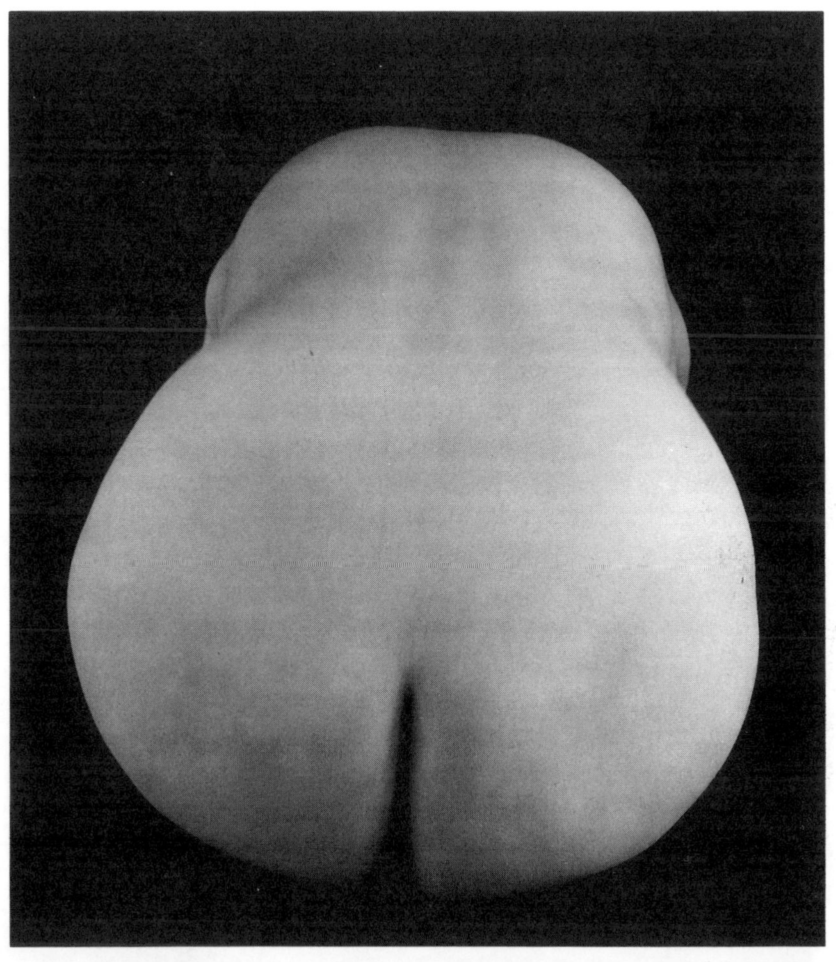

22. EDWARD WESTON, *Anita, Nude I,* 1925–39, gelatin silver, square 4to.

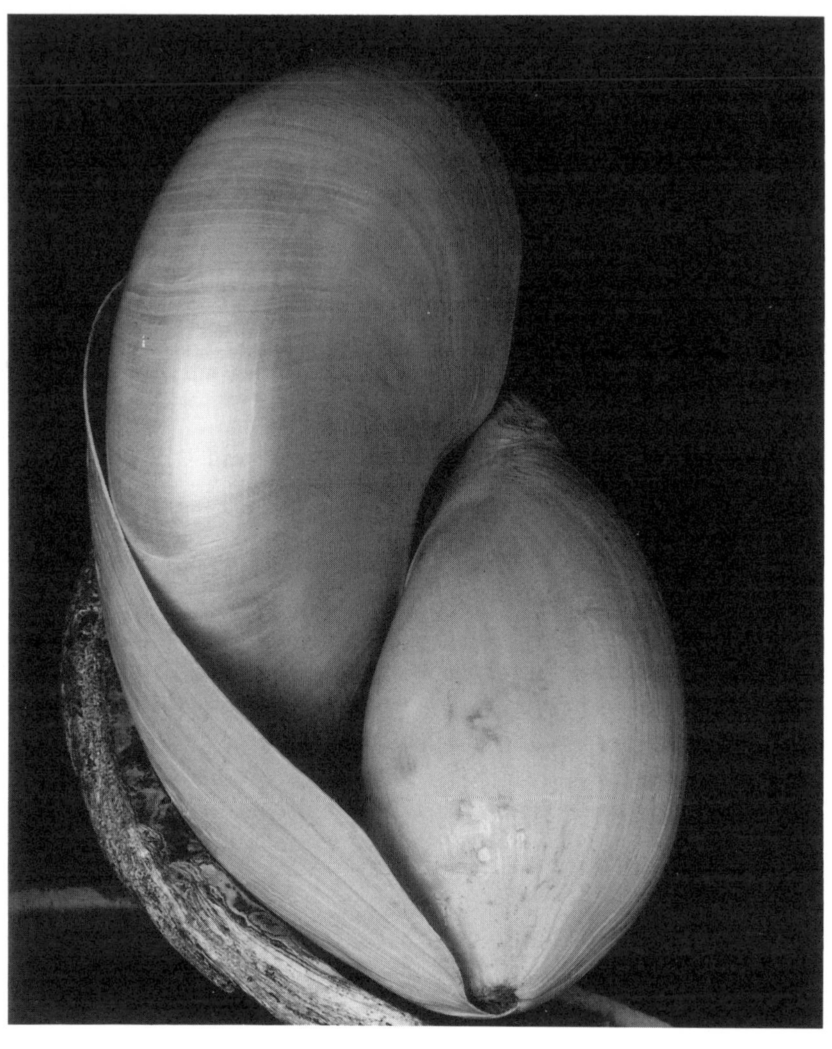

24. Edward Weston, *Shells,* 1925–39, gelatin silver, square 4to.

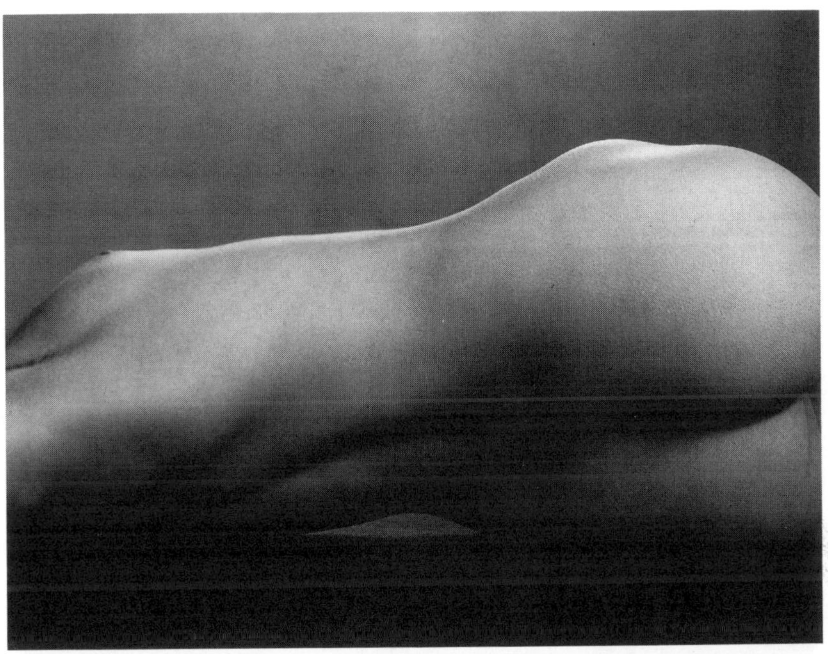

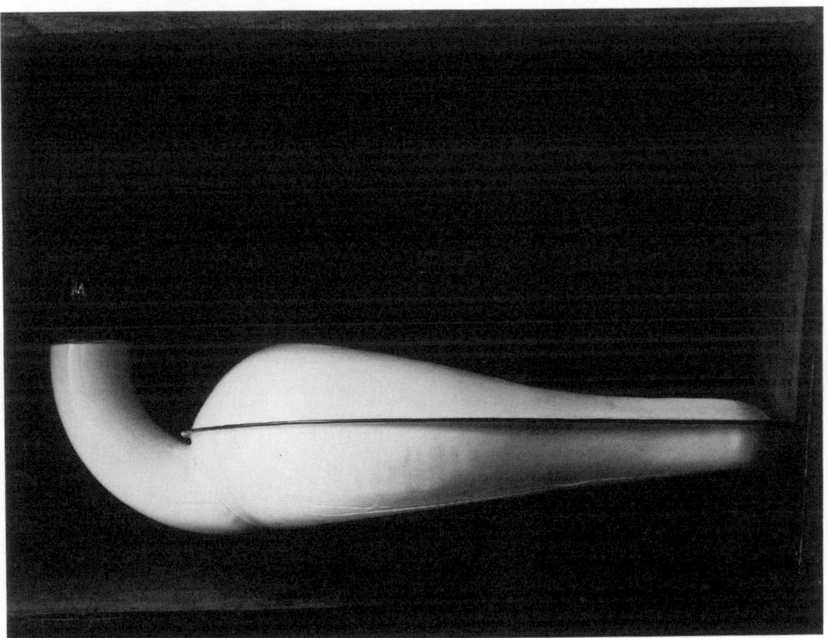

23. Edward Weston, *Miriam Lerner: Buttocks and Back,* 1925–39, gelatin silver, square 4to.

25. Edward Weston, *Bed Pan,* 1930, gelatin silver, 9⁷⁄₁₆ × 7⅛ in.

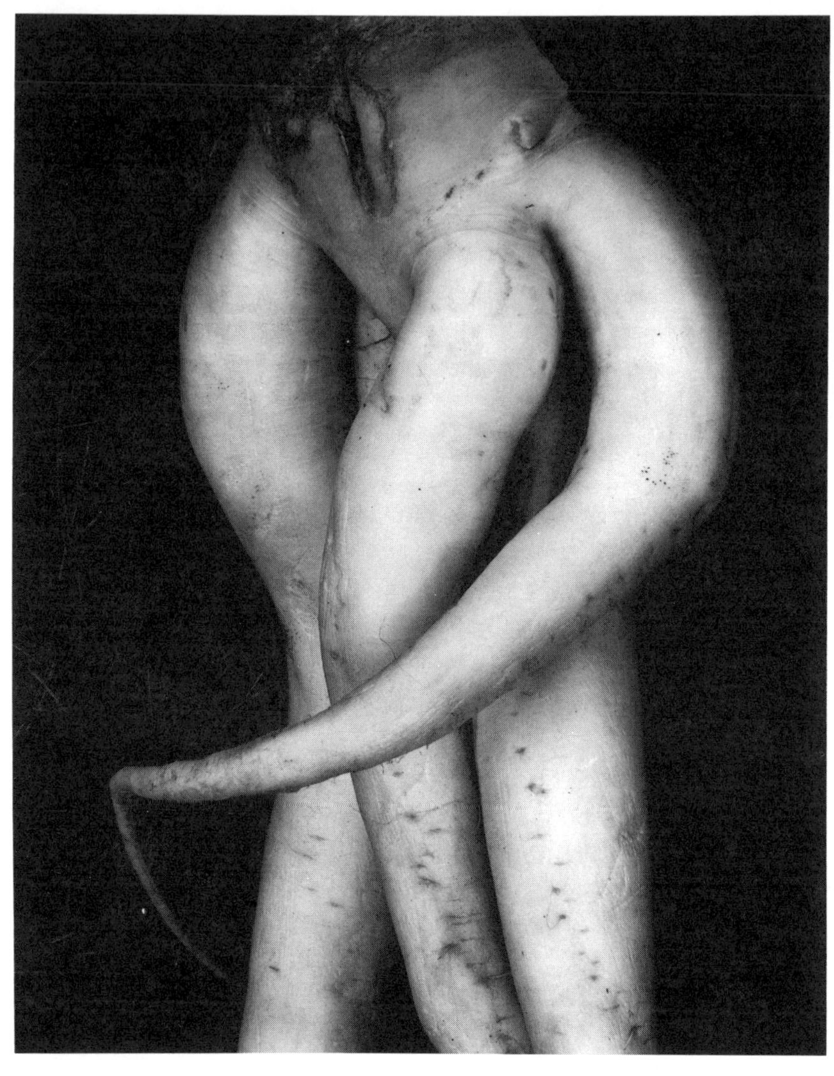

26. EDWARD WESTON, *White Radish,* 1933, gelatin silver, 9½ × 7⅝ in.

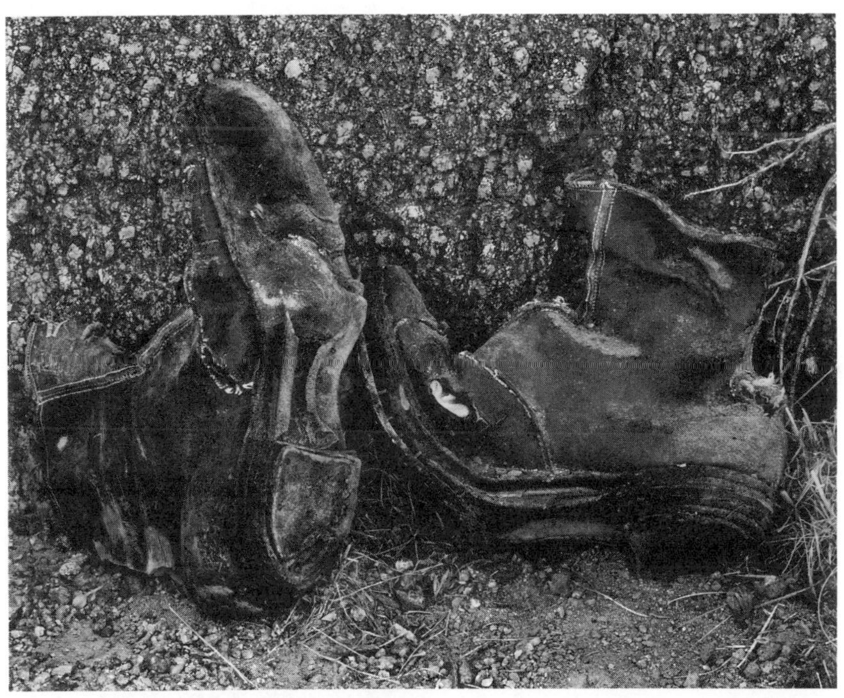

27. EDWARD WESTON, *Old Shoes, from abandoned Soda Works, Owen Valley,* 1937, gelatin silver, 7½ × 9½ in.

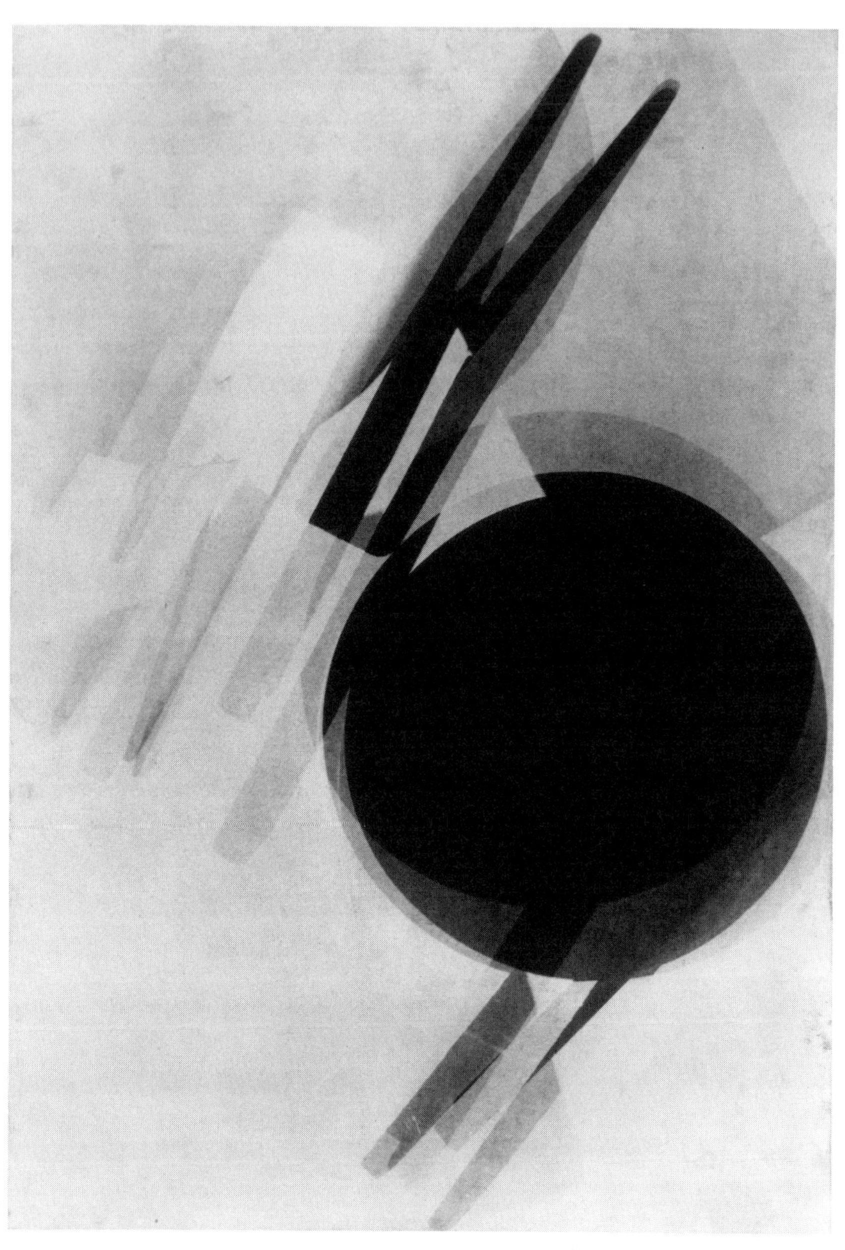

28. László Moholy-Nagy, *Photogram No. 1–The Mirror (Fotogramm No. 1–Der Spiegel),* 1922–23 (print, ca. 1928), gelatin silver, 25⅛ × 36¼ in.

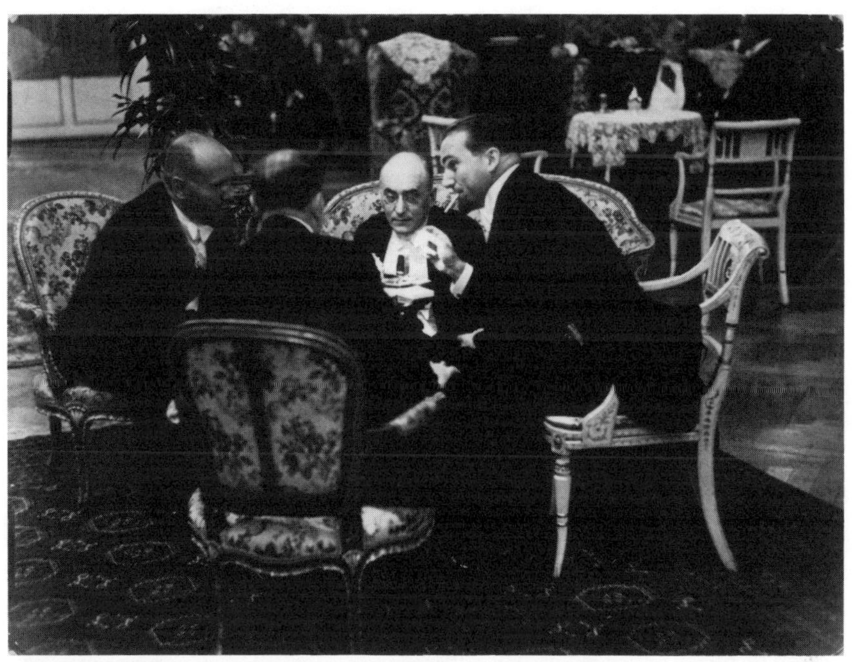

29. Erich Salomon, *German Statesmen in Rome,* negative/print.

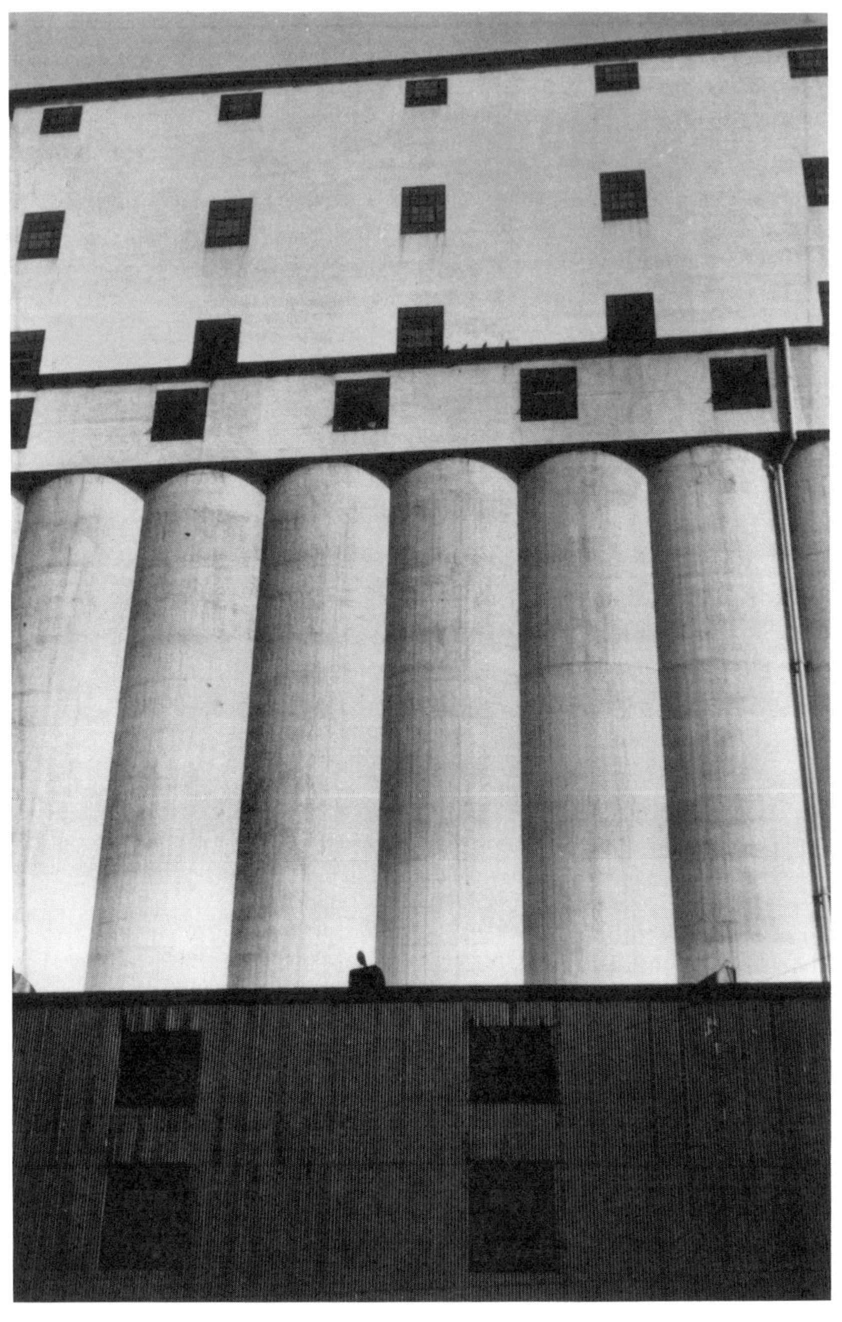

30. Walker Evans, *Grain Elevator,* ca. 1930, gelatin silver, 8¾ × 5^11^⁄16 in.

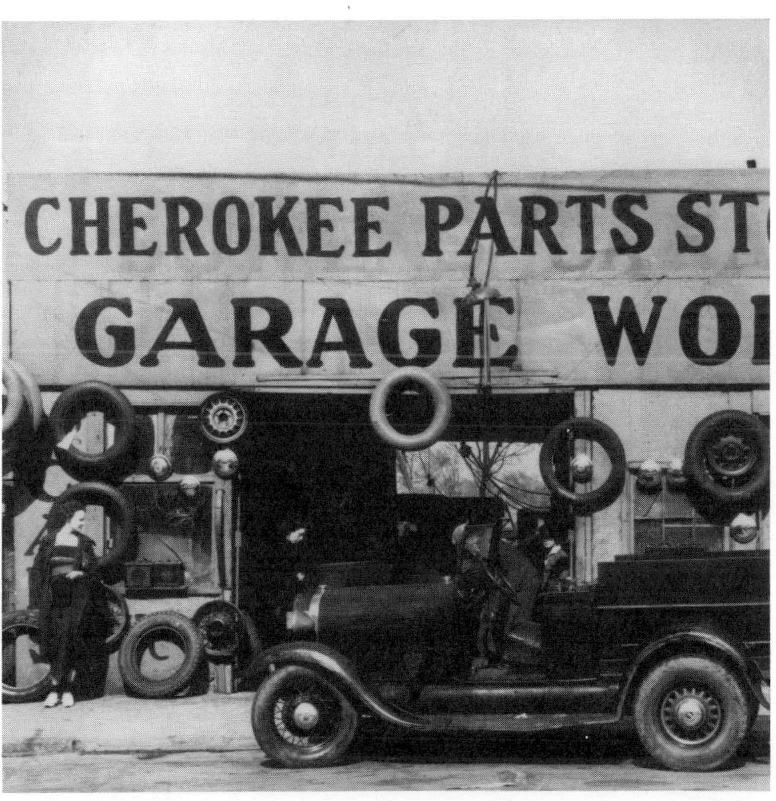

31. Walker Evans, *Garage, Atlanta, Georgia,* 1936, gelatin silver, $6^{27/32} \times 6^{15/16}$ in.

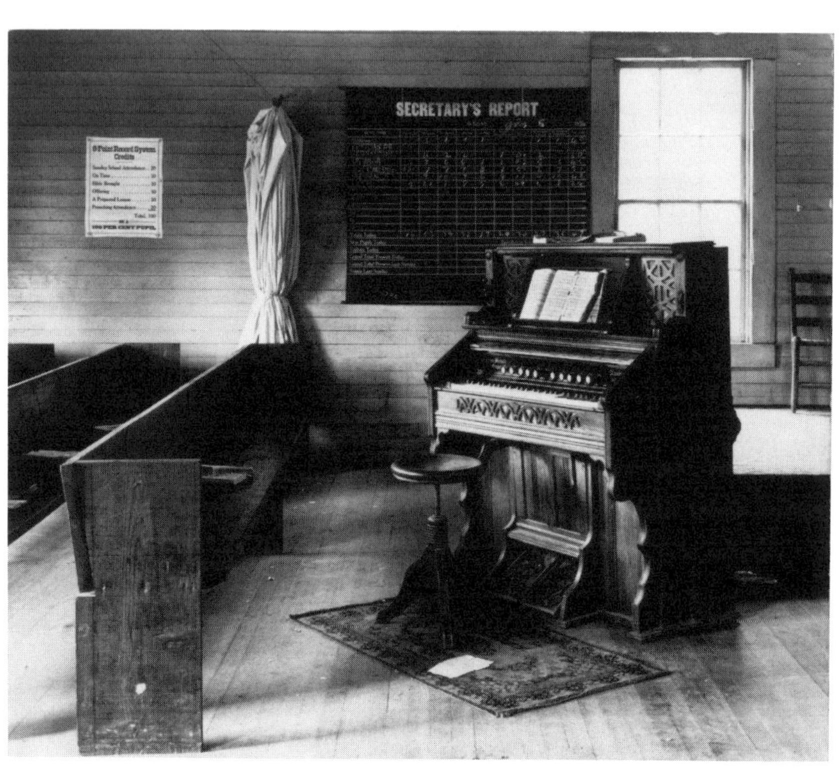

32. Walker Evans, *Church Organ and Pews/The Church Organ, Rural Alabama,* 1936, gelatin silver, $7\frac{1}{2} \times 8\frac{5}{8}$ in.

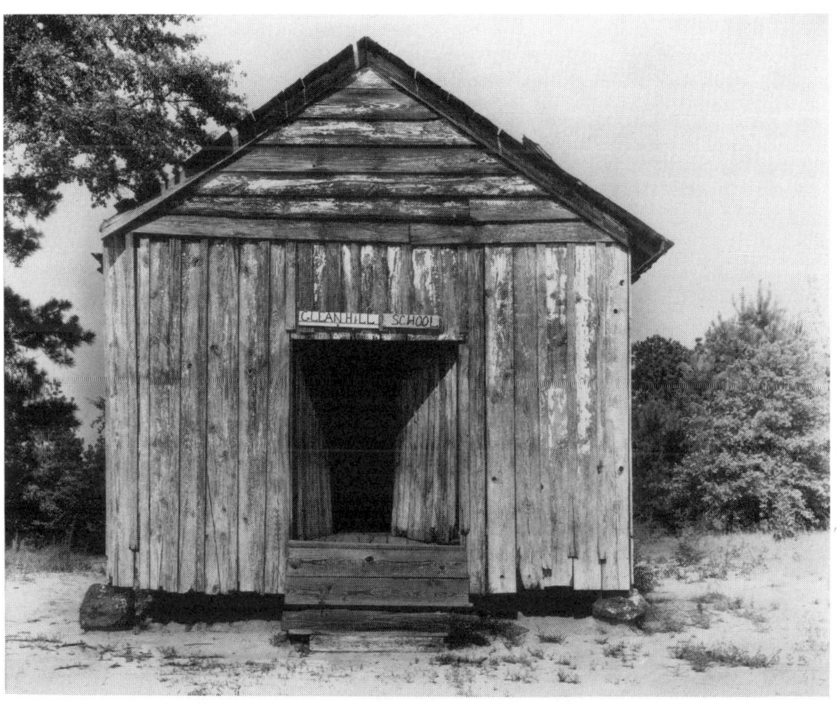

33. Walker Evans, *Gleanhill Schoolhouse, Hale County, Alabama,* 1936, gelatin silver, $7\frac{9}{16} \times 9\frac{17}{32}$ in.

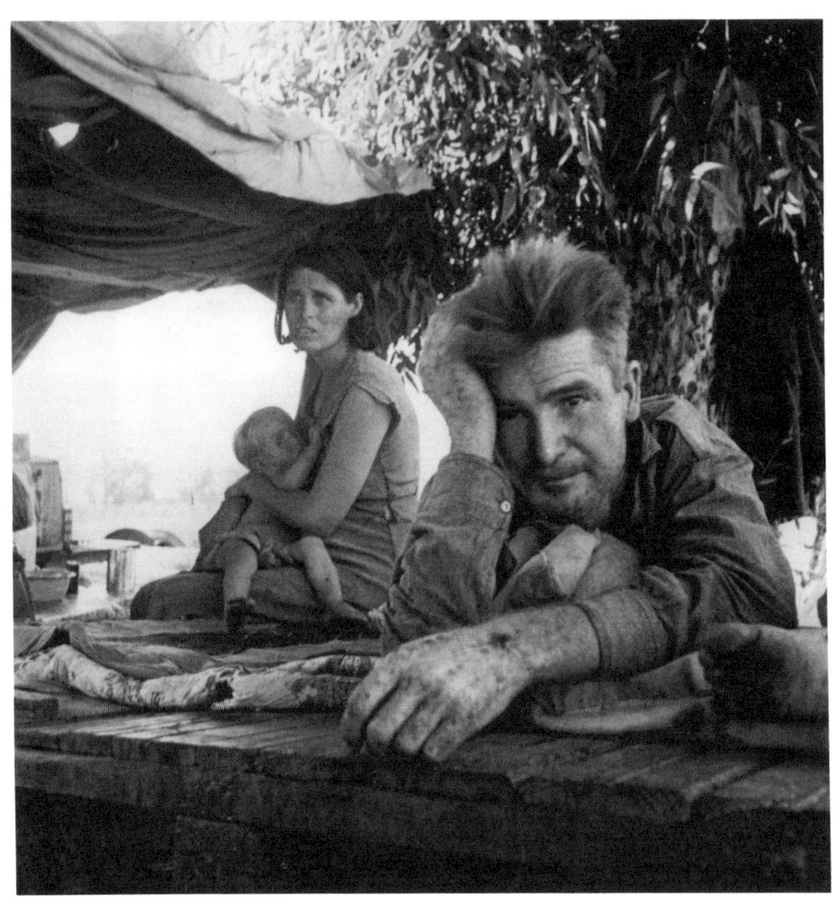

34. Dorothea Lange, *Drought Refugees from Oklahoma–Blythe, Calif.*, negative/print.

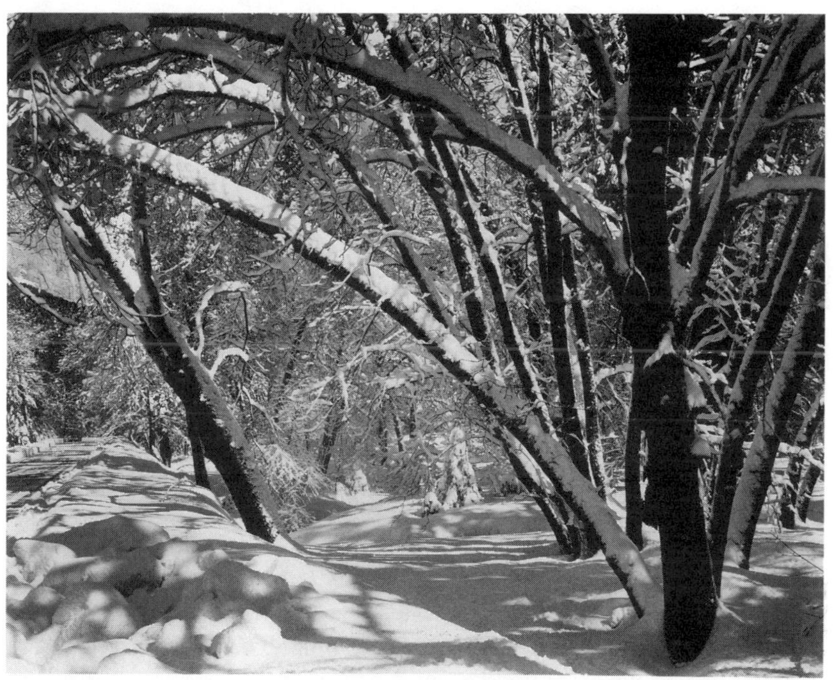

35. ANSEL ADAMS, *Shrubs in Snow, Yosemite Valley*, 1936, gelatin silver, 7⁵⁄₁₆ × 9¼ in.

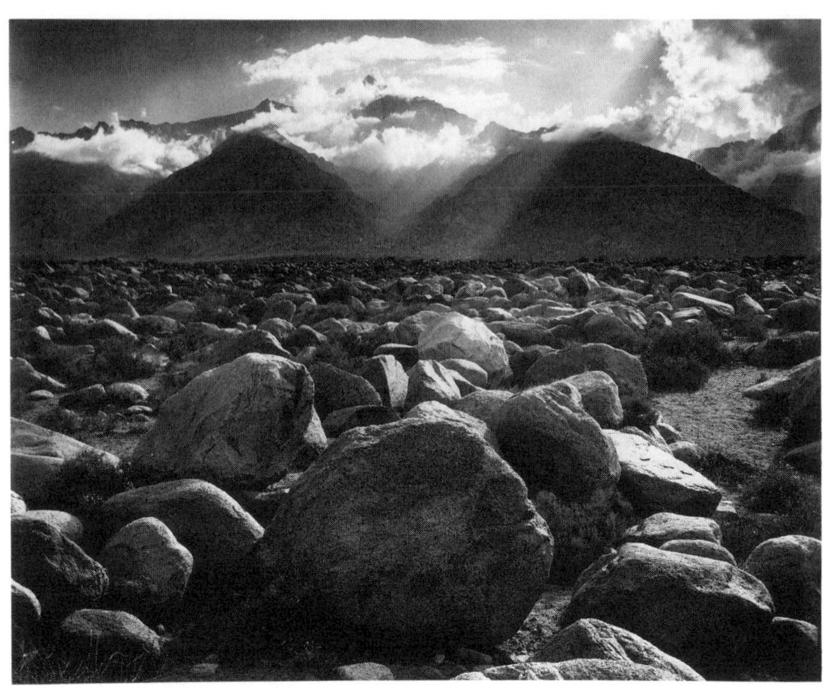

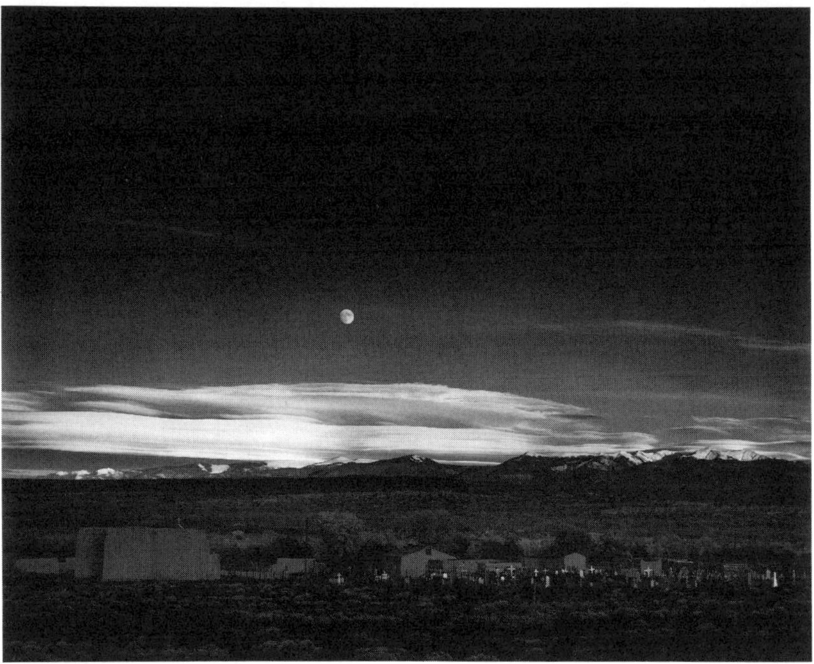

36. Ansel Adams, *Mt. Williamson from Manzanar, California,* 1944, gelatin silver, 7½ × 9⅜ in.

37. Ansel Adams, *Moonrise, Hernandez, New Mexico,* 1941 (print, 1948), gelatin silver, 13¾ × 17$^{15}/_{16}$ in.

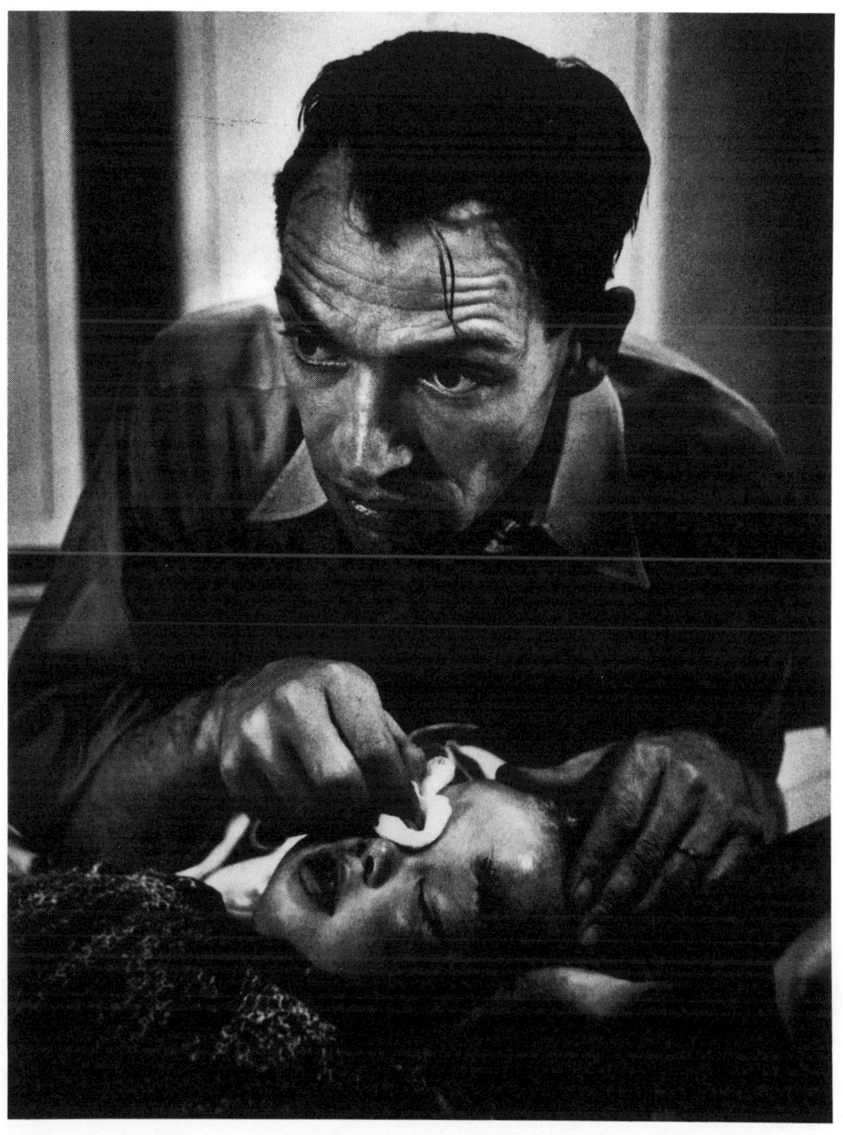

38. W. EUGENE SMITH, *Country Doctor,* 1948, gelatin silver, 7¾ × 5¹³⁄₁₆ in.

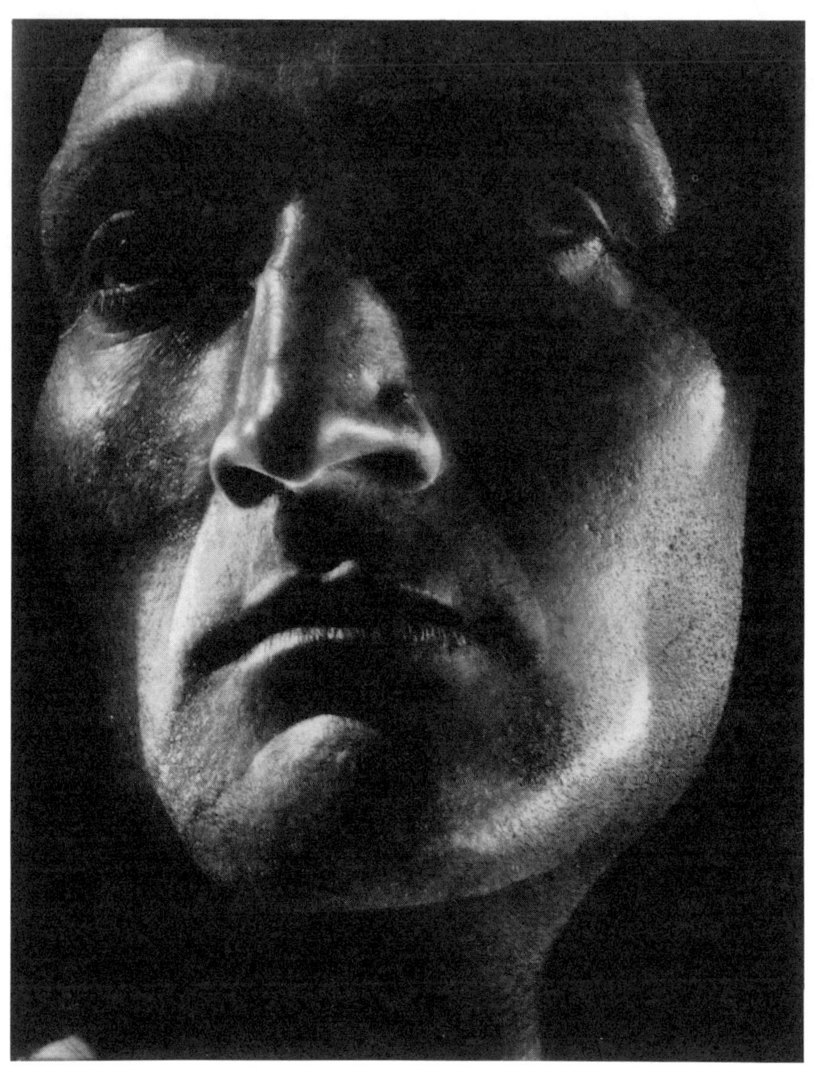

39. HELMAR LERSKI, *Metamorphose*, 1936, gelatin silver, 29 × 23 cm.

(1952) and expanded into *Order and History*.[95] The fifteen-year pause between volumes 3 and 4 was caused by a "breakdown" of the project, namely the need to rethink, within a wealth of historical material, the emergence of order from a history perceived as a "course."[96] In the texts that mark the transition–for instance, the essay "What is Political Reality?" (1965)–the connection between the order of history and meaningful political order was made by calling for an opposition of political thought (political science) to concepts of order valid within any given society. The point of reference and of authority for such oppositions would be the knowledge of order based on an expanded, "differentiated," more progressive consciousness not *eo ipso* connected with linear progress. In Voegelin's scenario, the historian as political philosopher can navigate the flux of time without restrictions and establish connections to (and between) different periods, above all to classical antiquity. The important and highly problematic point is that a higher degree of insight into order becomes itself a higher, more valid normative order against which any existing political order needs to be measured.

This assertion is not made less problematic by the fact that Voegelin did indeed immerse himself in masses of historical material. His concept of "historiogenesis," developed in an essay of 1960, which was to become the first chapter of volume 4, corrected the conventional distinction made in the first three volumes between the symbolism of linear time signifying historical consciousness, and that of cyclical time signifying prehistorical consciousness.[97] Reexamining the sources of the old empires of the Near East, Voegelin found symbolic forms of linearity that caused him to rethink the cultural connection of social with divine order. He located this "historiogenesis" in historical situations of disturbed and reestablished order–in the old cyclical cosmological empires, in Israel, Hellas, and in modern historiological speculations. As a symbolization constant, it is *the* most important historical phenomenon, since it is here that eternal being is realized in time and that history becomes transparent as the field of force between the two poles of being. Historiography, then, is in crucial need of a historical-philosophical perspective based on a philosophy of consciousness, which, for Voegelin, is a philosophy of order. He used this perspective to support a synchronic ranking of levels of consciousness–preference given to Greek antiquity, Plato and Socrates, and to their prescriptive authority as models.

His movitation for posing questions of meaning and value in this way was the desire to reestablish order and meaningful continuity in a contemporary (Western) culture that appeared profoundly dissociated and confused.

The clearest exposé of Voegelin's concept of order is found in the essay, "Reason: The Classic Experience," which was published the same year as volume 4 of *Order and History*.[98] Voegelin introduces his argument here with the statement that he will not deal "with the 'idea' or nominalist 'definition' of Reason, but with the process in reality in which concrete human beings, the 'lovers of wisdom,' the philosophers as they styled themselves, were engaged in an act of resistance against the personal and social disorder of their age." But the reader realizes quickly that Voegelin's account of this engagement is a complete–that is, closed–story. "From this act there emerged the Nous as the cognitively luminous force that inspired the philosophers to resist and, at the same time, enabled them to recognize the phenomena of disorder in the light of a humanity ordered by the Nous. Thus, Reason in the noetic sense was discovered as both the force and the criterion of order."[99]

Voegelin does not trace a process of emerging conceptual order in concrete historical thinkers; rather, he transposes it directly into the needy twentieth-century. In his narration the ordering process is not one of shared human trial and error in time but one of revealed, privileged insight. Capitalized throughout the text, *Reason*, with its neo-Platonic and Hegelian connotations, is distinctly reminiscent of the Frankfurters' *Critical Reason*. The issue in both cases is a "truly" human consciousness that constitutes meaning in history, the one and only meaning of history, outside of which is barbarism.[100] Once this stage has been reached, there is no going back "to less differentiated modes of experience and symbolization"–or to a view of the modern world other than that of the Frankfurt position. For Voegelin, the "central symbol" in Greek culture, and the healing model for twentieth-century Western cultural disorder, is "the 'philosopher' in whose psyche humanity had become luminous for its noetic order." It is not, as it is for Hannah Arendt, that culture's interactive self-presentation in the *polis*.[101]

Reason in Voegelin's usage means an anti-"gnostic," anti-ideological position that "does not put an apokalyptic end to history either now or in a progressivist future. It rather pervades the history which it constitutes with a new luminosity of existential order in resistance to disordering passion"

(266). For the exile Voegelin, who had to flee Hitler's fascism and who loathes Soviet communism, there is no history outside that revealed order, and historiography can make significant contributions only by recognizing its authority. He sees twentieth-century philosophers "engaged in the same type of resistance against the disorder of the age" as their counterparts in the fourth century B.C., in need of "Reason as the ordering force in existence" (267). This forceful connection denies the multiplicity and globality of twentieth-century cultural problems, for which classical antiquity cannot be a useful model. From a profoundly ahistorical position, Voegelin superimposes a past of his own making on the present and thereby simplifies both beyond recognition; in that, too, he is not unlike Adorno and Horkheimer.

Survivors of the German catastrophe, they shared the desire to transcend the temporality and historicity of the human condition in the twentieth-century. In Voegelin's case this desire was openly and honestly the force that motivated his writing, perhaps most intelligibly in his voluminous epistolary dialogues with exiled friends, where he tried sincerely to clarify and defend his position. Intensely curious, with a peculiar ability to be amazed by the amazing thoughts recorded in the histories of cultures, he was a generously responsive dialogue partner. A good example is the exchange of letters with Karl Loewith in the winter of 1944–45 about Nietzsche's importance for the midtwentieth-century philosophical historian facing a cultural catastrophe of unforeseen dimensions.[102] Despite their plan to co-author a book on the subject, they differed greatly in their understanding of Nietzsche's pivotal role. Loewith was interested in the meanings of Nietzsche's social-political-psychological *gestalt* for a Western culture in crisis. Voegelin, remarking on the "historian's reservation" in Loewith's argument, showed a curiously intimate fascination with the "demonic" forces of Nietzsche's personality, which had enabled him to immerse himself in the "wild adventure of initiating a new 'civilisation' (on the level of Christianity)." Profoundly impressed by these forces precisely because they made possible the disruptive confrontation with the true dimensions of the cultural collapse, he thought them the source of Nietzsche's centrality to modernity.

But this confrontation was also a "megalomaniacal failure" in Voegelin's view, especially Nietzsche's doctrine of eternal recurrence, since he did not deal with the "antinomies of the infinite," which are rooted in "transcendence, . . . in the sense of the Augustinian *intentio animi* towards God." Loewith in his answer of January 7, 1945, conceded the antinomies, suggesting, however, that Nietzsche did not retain too little but rather too much of the Christian heritage. Lacking the naiveté of antiquity, Nietzsche could not trust himself to pure inspiration but had to determine and thereby limit inspiration by an act of will. Hence the passionate exaggerations of his anti-Christian position. Reminding Voegelin that Augustine had been a powerful bishop as well as a Christian martyr, Loewith emphasized that the "theoretical ideal of a *comprehensive* method of historical interpretation presupposes an interest in all of intellectual history." And precisely that ideal seemed to him "irreconcilable with any kind of Christian transcendence." Voegelin's answer of February 8, 1945, praised Loewith's "rational-scientific world orientation" for its dialogical openness, declaring, however, quite categorically the end of history without an interpretative method based on a meaningful historical order ("*Sinnordnung*"). Clearly worried about the eclectically but powerfully Christian dimension of Voegelin's approach to history, Loewith wrote on March 31, 1945, that European superiority over the East had become a fairy tale. He had lived briefly in Japan before coming to the United States, much impressed by its "living, genuine paganism," something that he had known before only from books about Greek and Roman culture. "It is true that Christian Europe has opened up to us and brought into universal history all other parts of the world, but this is precisely the reason why the classical grid of East and West, which was still valid for Hegel, is outdated."

Voegelin was to expand the "*Sinnordnung*" of history to include not only Judaic and Greek culture but also the more ancient cultures of the Near East. But the central focus of his work on the "movements of the divine-human encounter"–ascending from the bottom of the cave up toward the light (consciousness) or down from consciousness–retained the concept of duality in the existential terms characteristic of Christianity.[103] Reason for Voegelin is not a faculty that develops in the symbiotic relation of self and world but a means of salvation, insofar as it is bound to existence "in openness toward the ground"–an openness whose loss in modernity has caused the "breakdown of philosophy." His examples for the modern phenomena of "disorientation" and "deculturation" are remarkably "undifferentiated": Hobbes as well as Hegel and Marx, Freud as well as Heidegger, Sartre, and Lévi-Strauss (274–78).

The conceptual structures associated with these names (Hobbes excepted) are indeed flawed, but because of their unrelatedness to the temporary historical *Lebenswelt* in Kracauer's and Schutz's sense rather than to "the ground" in Voegelin's sense. His answer to the sickness of the time was the Platonian *metaxy* developed in the *Symposium* and *Philebos*: the space "between God and man" is the "realm of the spiritual," "the reality of 'man's converse with the gods.'" The *metaxy* "symbolizes the experience of the noetic quest as a transition of the psyche from mortality to immortality" (279).

In his readings of the *Symposium* and of *Philebos*, Voegelin emphasized the formative, structuring force of the divine ground, the legitimate order that creates and supports, authors and authorizes Truth and Reason. The source of his fascination with the allegorically concrete Platonic motion between order and disorder, and with Reason as "grounded" in the *metaxy* of the human and the divine, was his deep-seated fear for the philosopher's authority and authorship. It was a fear he shared with many exiles who had experienced the extremes of social-political disorder and the collapse of a powerful and complex culture. In the spring of 1949 Voegelin was reading Thomas Mann's *Doctor Faustus*, which seemed to him "a highly respectable historical-philosophical discussion of the collapse of Germany." He wished, he wrote to Loewith, that "some 'professional' historians and sociologists had shown that much understanding of the dynamics of spiritual-intellectual [*geistig*] decline." Loewith, as he wrote back immediately, had read the novel the previous summer, "with much anger and discontent, I have to admit."[104] He did not give any details, but the historian Loewith could only have reacted negatively to Mann's profoundly ahistorical, self-absorbed fiction, both prettifying and demonizing, of a truly good Germany gone irreversibly bad. Historical "truth" would be less orderly and less complete. In a quite literal sense, it would be less authoritative.

In the first chapter, "The Beginning of the Beginning," of the concluding volume of *Order and History*, *In Search of Order*, Voegelin deals explicitly with the concept of authorship. The context is the multiplication of philosophical languages as soon as they concern "the historical materials." He explicitly accepts "this manifold of languages . . . as a structure in the history of the quest for truth."[105] But there is also the need to ground such multiplicity and to order it–to author and authorize it in the construct of the story, which mediates the presences of the human and the divine:

> One of the profoundest connoisseurs and practitioners of story-telling in the twentieth century, Thomas Mann has symbolized the divine-human metalepsis of the story in the concluding sentence of his Joseph novel: "And thus end the beautiful story and God-invention of Joseph and his brothers." Telling a story in this metaleptic sense of the term is not a matter of choice. The story is the symbolic form the questioner has to adopt necessarily when he gives an account of his quest as the event of wresting, by the response of his human search to a divine movement, the truth of reality from a reality pregnant with truth yet unrevealed. Moreover, the story remains the constant symbolism of the quest even when the tension between divine and human story is reduced to the zero of identity as in the dialectical story told by the self-identical *logos* of the Hegelian system. (24)

Voegelin is not so much interested here in Thomas Mann's overriding preoccupation with the higher authority of the artist as author, that is, (second) creator of the world. It is the phenomenon of the story itself: Genesis 1, which he reads as the story of the beginning of language and consciousness, is not told by "a revelatory God or by an intelligently imaginative human being. It is both, because it is neither the one nor the other. . . . The participatory structure of the event and the account given in the referential structure of the narrative are inseparably one in the paradoxical structure of the story" (26f.). "The story," always the story of the quest for truth, originates in the "in-between" of the human and the divine, the "plurality of Middles" (28f.), which signifies for Voegelin the location of all stories in the tradition as the process of increasing consciousness of that interaction. In intellectual and psychological terms, this "in-between" is light years away from Kracauer's "anteroom" of provisional, fragmented, troubled historical understanding. "The story" of the quest for truth in history will inevitably make that quest "reflectively intelligible for its own structure," thus confirming, as Voegelin emphasized, "the statement by which this study *Order and History* opened, the statement: 'The order of history emerges from the history of order'" (32). It is authored and authorized by the philosophical historian who is privy to a higher order which reveals itself in "the story" he tells of the quest for it.

Loewith, of course, put his finger on that central motivation of Voegelin's historiography when he doubted that such authoritative transcendence in its unifying thrust could do justice to all of history. In the introduction to *Meaning in History* (1949), he distinguished between Greek, Christian, and modern historiography:

> The Greek historians wrote pragmatic history centered around a great political event; the Church Fathers developed from Hebrew prophecy and Christian eschatology a theology of history focused on the supra-historical events of creation, incarnation, and consummation; the moderns elaborate a philosophy of history by secularizing the theological principles and applying them to an ever increasing number of empirical facts. It seems as if the two great conceptions of antiquity and Christianity, cyclic motion and eschatological direction, have exhausted the basic approaches to the understanding of history. Even the most recent attempts at an interpretation of histoy are nothing else but variations of these two principles or a mixture of both of them.[106]

Proposing to start his explorations with an analysis of Jacob Burckhardt's *Force and Freedom: Reflections on History* and to work his way back to Judeo-Christian eschatology, Loewith looked at the issue of meaning in history from his own historical position: the war won by the Allies, the Hitler regime collapsed, the strangeness of America negotiated. In the early sixties, back in Germany, a culture economically successful and profoundly disturbed by the implications of the Eichmann trial, he saw the question of meaning differently, indeed more as Voegelin saw it. His 1963 lectures on the philosophy of history, published only in 1968 under the title *Permanence and Change*, exhibit a profound skepticism regarding "the modern faith in history," in Croce's words "the ultimate religion of intellectuals":

> for who today could really still believe in history after the backbone of this faith, the belief in progress, is broken to bits in Europe. The faith in history is the result of our alienation from the natural theology of Christianity, both of which gave history a context and both of which provided a non-historical frame of reference and understanding. Only the loss of this understanding of history and of its placement into a larger setting, as it was believed in classical cosmology and Christian theology, has raised modern history to that absolute relevance which we now accept as something self-evident, although it is the most questionable of all things.[107]

The argument of the lectures focuses on the need to recognize the essentially unchanging nature of man, the Promethean hubris of modern science, and the "possibility of an eternal time." The third and last lecture, on the idea of progress, ends with the plea: "Only if there is something like an everlasting universal time in which new things are continuously born and old things passing away, progress would loose its disproportionate gravity that it has for us nowadays because we do not know of anything that lasts forever" (81).

Removing the Greek from the future-oriented "Western" view of history, Loewith argues against the subordination of philosophy, the inquiry into the permanent aspects of the human condition, to history, the immersion in the change of all things. He traces the "surrender to historical thinking" from Vico via Hegel and Marx to Dilthey and Heidegger, pleading that we learn from the upheavals and confusions of history rather than take history as a guide to thinking and living: "To want to orient oneself on history, while tossed around in the midst of it, would be like wanting to hold on to the waves in time of shipwreck."[108]

When Loewith surveys the futile efforts of modern philosopher-historians to establish a meaningful historical linearity and coherence, he uses the image of the shipwrecked tossed about by huge waves to evoke the disruptive turbulences of historical time. Dealing with the "general historians'" similarly precarious search for ordering principles, Kracauer predicts that they will be "caught in a cataract of times."[109] But the analogy ends here. The escape from the chaos of shipwreck or cataract is judged completely differently by the two exiles. Kracauer looks critically at the role played in the search for ordering principles in history by ideological decisiveness and rhetorical skills. Only by telling complete authoritative stories can the general historian pull himself out of that cataract and guide the reader so that she will not resist the teleological suggestions:

> In the case of general history the nonessential [i.e., for historiography] function of art becomes an essential one; aesthetic arrangements turn from an external embellishment into an internal requirement. In conjunction with the pressures put on story content, these arrangements are contrived to yield patterns which connect the unconnected, establish illusory contexts, and, all in all, solidify the unity of temporal sequence. So the willing readers are safely guided through Time.

Like caravans of tourists on preplanned, prescribed routes that hide from view the astonishing and disturbing life-worlds of other cultures in other times and places.[110]

If, at the end of the twentieth-century, readers are no longer easily seduced by the high rhetorical sheen of nineteenth-century general histories, there remains the seductive power of the ordering story itself, which connects beginning and end and achieves the aesthetic reconciliation of historical conflicts. This is especially true for the intellectual to whom the experience of exile, existential or political, does not signify the possibility to change and to perceive change–in himself and others. Like Schutz, Kracauer used the state of exile to gather certain kinds of knowledge and, in the process, changed from the state of strangeness into that of relative familiarity. From this perspective he did not think useful to historiography the closures of order and completeness, though he was fully aware of their enduringly powerful attraction. Historiography (as well as photography) must do without such comforting closures because they misguide the historian's vision. She needs to think "through things, not above them" (192) so that the strange disorderly realms of things past may escape oblivion.

In this context Kracauer stated explicitly what had already been suggested by the reports of his journeys through the interwoven time spaces, the time texts of historiography: We will be disappointed in attempts to "extrapolate the general from the extreme particular"–attempts Adorno had found lacking in Kracauer's work, and which he himself had hoped to bring to fruition in *History*. In their high generality, theoretical statements, like philosophical "truths," do not adequately address or accommodate the past actuality of everyday life. The challenge to the historian is not to "extrapolate" the general from the "extreme" particular, but to ask, "How can particularity first be grasped? What are the terms of such grasping? How are they connected with the general? How do we grasp the general?" Grappling with the knowledge status of the general and the particular in their interconnectedness and interdependency requires what Kracauer referred to as the historian's "tact."

Tact signifies a social–that is, a mediating–attitude: the definition made with tact is expected to be communicable, supportable, or falsifiable by the experience of others. Tact is located in the mediating, coordinating "anteroom-thinking and conduct" (206f.) of historiography. Kracauer agreed with Burckhardt's characterization of the philosophy of history as "a centaur, a contradiction in terms; for history is coordinating and hence non-philosophy, philosophy subordinating and hence non-history."[111] He did not, however, agree with Burckhardt's concession to Hegel: "All the same, we are deeply indebted to the centaur, and it is a pleasure to come across him now and then on the fringe of the forest of historical study."[112]

The experience of a catastrophic cultural rupture had made Kracauer insist, more unambiguously than did Burckhardt, on the cultural independence of historiography as an "intermediary area" (16). Its margins, too, were to be protected from the claims made by last truths. This attitude does not preclude the historian's interest, admixed with intellectual pleasure and apprehension, in the ingenuity of ahistorical theoretical constructs. But for the sake of not forgetting life-worlds that have been, the historian, like other inhabitants of the epistemological anteroom, will have to treat them with caution. Aware of the role of contingency in human affairs, she cannot afford to be sure about their meanings. In a very literal sense, the risk of shipwreck, the unforeseeable real dangers of being cast away from the known and the nurturing, has seemed necessary to develop tolerance for the alterity of past time and space. Without such tolerance there is no sharing with the past, from the vantage point of the present, the always desired future of the past, and thus no tolerance for its alterity. The historian's challenge is also, and perhaps most importantly, to break open projections of the future as nothing but future pasts.[113] If she succeeds at all, her stories of bygone lives, because of their acknowledged incompleteness, will retain the disruptive surprises offered by these pasts as the upredictable futures of other, more distant pasts. At the end of his journey, Kracauer therefore said of historiography that it points "to a Utopia of the in-between—a *terra incognita* in the hollows between the lands we know."

This is the last sentence of the last, incomplete chapter of an unfinished book. But this fact ought not be seen as in some higher sense necessary, therefore meaningful. Nor ought the historian's enterprise of navigating and negotiating the strangeness of the past be seen as particularly heroic in its (partial) successes or failures. History is a culturally important and difficult challenge that Kracauer surveyed with fascinated and skeptical admiration. He died over this, his last and most beloved, book. But then, one's last book is usually one's most beloved, because it signifies the best that one is capable of at that particular point in one's lifetime. Traveling in the large temporal spaces of historiography, the exile's most poignant contribution was his insistence on the importance of that capability within the temporal, historical constraints of the human condition. For Kracauer, modernity did not signify the disenchantment of existential exile but rather the marvels of greater access to other lives. His imagination tempered by sobriety, his sobriety lightened by imagination, he saw everywhere the changes wrought by the time of history. Yielding to its guidance, the cultural activities of those who lived before him, he came upon the unfamiliar spaces of that Utopia of the in-between. If *History* has taught its reader anything, this intermediary area of inquiry is not a no-place to be freely appropriated and constructed. Terra incognita, it may exist and may become known–unpredictably and surprising.

CHAPTER SIX

Image, Imagination, and Historical Evidence

1 The entanglement of both observer and observed in the experience of historicity and temporality signifies the historian's experience of time shifts both without and within her lifetime. Kracauer was an old man when he reflected on the significance of this entanglement for the reading and writing of history. His particular concern about human temporality–a sensitivity that had always been an aspect of his temperament though it naturally increased with age[1]–led him to focus on the implications of the historian's temporally and culturally mobile self and changing identity. There will be, during the historian's lifetime, several selves through which the past is entered, and shaping her perspective on the past, they may be effective both sequentially and simultaneously. Historiographic perspective is the product of such shaping: composite and unstable, it subverts the notion of an ideally homogenous, consistent, enduring objectivity. Exploring the implications of such subversion, Kracauer kept intact its particularity and concreteness because he wished to clarify the independent status of history as an "intermediary area" or "anteroom"[2] of inquiry, an area of provisional, partial truths.

This exploration goes back to the Weimar period, when Kracauer had been concerned, as a critical commentator, with the complex temporal actuality of a modern culture in flux, when he had, in fact, been engaged in the writing of "contemporary history." Reviewing films for *Frankfurter Zeitung* in the twenties and thirties, he was struck by their potential to enlarge the viewers' visual capabilities in relation to a rapidly expanding natural-cultural world. The cultural contribution of photo images, still or moving, was to show new phenomena and, suspending an assumed familiarity of the world, extend and preserve its visibility. If they are true to the medium, photo images show what they picture because it is real. Visible things–events, acts, actors, objects–are real in that their presence can be shared. Reality is the presence of others in their sharable cultural activities–for instance, as I argued in chapters 3 and 4, multiple acts of viewing. The analogy between photography and historiography that Kracauer established in *History* is based on the recognized importance of that presence.

The "redemption of physical reality" to be achieved by photography and film signifies a clarifying reclamation of ideally all the phenomena of the modern life-world. But such reclamation does not deny the tension, inherent in any artificial image, between the picture and the pictured. The visually composite perspective of the photographer, like the temporally composite perspective of the historian, is interpretive and produces many different shapes of objectivity. But like historiography, too, photography is "art with a difference."[3] In both cases we look for corroboration; that is, we have come to expect, from photographical and historiographical practice, shared and sharable acts of seeing and of reading. The problems of this practice, but also the fascination, the satisfaction, are located in understanding the particularities of these acts shaped by different degrees of temporal distance and of acculturation in perception.

When Kracauer stated the connection between historiography and photography in the introduction to *History*, he quite fittingly started by giving the time and cultural place from which he did so. His authority in this case was the ancient historians who, prefacing their histories with autobiographical statements, informed their readers immediately of that "Archimedan point from which they would subsequently set out to roam the past" (3). That Archimedan point was for him the realization of a continuing effort to work out problems that had preoccupied him since the twenties, when he began to think about the cultural status of the photographic media. Looking back, from the vantage point of his reflections on the reading and writing of history, he now saw *Theory of Film*, which had occupied many of his years in exile, "in its true light," namely

> as another attempt of mine to bring out the significance of areas whose claim to be acknowledged in their own right has not yet been recognized. I say "another attempt" because this was what I had tried to do throughout my life–in *Die Angestellten*, perhaps in *Ginster*, and certainly in the *Offenbach*. So at long last all my main efforts, so incoherent on the surface, fall into line–they all have served, and continue to serve, a single purpose: the rehabilitation of objectives and modes of being which still lack a name and hence are overlooked or misjudged. Perhaps this is less true of history than of photography; yet histo-

> ry too marks a bent of the mind and defines a region of reality which despite all that has been written about them are still largely *terra incognita.* (4)

For the observer of his development, Kracauer's attempts at reclamation through documentation appear "coherent on the surface" precisely in their accommodation of changes. In all his works, not only in those he mentioned here, he had tried to account for certain culturally important but also at the time still "unclassifiable" phenomena: *Die Angestellten* (1930; "white-collar workers") examined a new social group (class) both elusive and crucially important for an understanding of Weimar politics. *Ginster* (1928), an autobiographical novel, showed the Weimar intellectual defined and obscured by modernity. *Offenbach* (1937), the biography of a society, reconstructed the professional life of a composer whose music had moved, in more than one sense, the popular culture of Paris, the center of Europe. These recountings of the modern experience, from different angles and at different points in his lifetime, prepared him for the task to formulate "an aesthetics of the photographic media, not less and not more" (4). An aesthetics that had its source in the perceived need to clarify the recording and preserving power at the core of photo images.

Kracauer gave serious consideration to the fact that photographic recording also stores phenomena that were not seen by the photographer in the act of "taking" the picture. These literally overlooked phenomena may of course have been seen by other viewers in the past. More importantly in terms of the specifically modern contribution of the photo image: they may be seen by other viewers in the future. Kracauer's emphasis was on the enabling power of the photo image to retain, for *all* to see, what had been there all along in the visible world but was not seen before. I cannot find in the film reviews of the Weimar period that self-conscious perspective of "*Abseits*" (off the beaten track), that cult of the ephemeral, insignificant, inconspicuous, which then is elevated to enduring significance. Unlike Benjamin's "magic gaze," still strangely seductive to intellectuals at the end of this troubled century, Kracauer's curious and attentive gaze did not elicit such significance.[4] It is true that Kracauer was a social moralist when it came to what films could (ought to) and did not do, but he had developed a good sense of the reality of others, also other viewers. Depending, then, on the relation between the pictured, the picture, and the viewer (including the photographer), photographic reproduction enlarges and enriches the perception of what can be seen; moreover, it does so collectively and cumulatively. In that it is different in kind from artistic (painterly) representation, which may be diversely suggestive to a number of viewers, simultaneously or sequentially. But they are nevertheless controlled to a high degree by the artist's vision, which, by the nature of the medium, is more exclusive than the photographer's. (Modern art, which can play on and with that control, has done so in response to photography.)

For Kracauer, the open-endedness of modern experience presents itself literally in the dimension of the photo image, for that image allows the unexpected, the unforseen, to emerge in moments that are in the future of its own taking. Although the whole point is that this open-endedness should not be controlled by the photographer's perspective, she is nevertheless aware of it, and it is an important part of the peculiar visual compositeness of her perspective. This compositeness links the modern maker of photo images to the modern historian who is aware of time shifts, within and beyond his lifetime, as they give shape to the writing of history.

The profound impact of time passing on historiographical objectivity is Kracauer's central concern in *History* and arguably the book's most illuminating aspect. Kracauer was fascinated by the implications of the historian as traveler in time–a mobility that called up deep resonances in his own experience of temporality. He had never ceased to marvel at the possibility inherent in the photographic media for a continuing visual cotemporality of observer and observed. But as he came to see in *History*, the navigation of historical time confronts the historian with extraordinarily difficult obstacles. Not only does she travel simultaneously without and within her lifetime, she also has to be aware of the multiple time shifts experienced by other (earlier) historians on whom she relies for information. Both the historian's time travel and the photographer's (filmmaker's) instantaneous "taking" of images, in their retaining temporal flux, pose for their readers and their viewers the difficult but important question of perspective and selection. At issue is the quality of *their* historical and *their* camera reality. By whose authority is it made present?

Kracauer might have agreed cautiously with John Clive's assessment that "unlike poetry . . . , the art of history is cumulative–that is to say its most recent practitioners tend to know more about events and problems of the past than their predecessors, however exalted."[5] He might have expressed reservations about an, as it were, irresistible progress of historiography suggested in Clive's commonsensical account, but the contrast with poetry might have made sense to him. As a novelist, as a literary essayist, in interaction with writers like Adorno, Bloch, and Benjamin, he had himself experienced the ambivalences and ambiguities, the peculiar anxieties, of intertextuality in poetic language use. A literary tradition presents an entanglement of influences, that is, responses in acceptance and rejection. But it does not, as does modern historiography, invoke a critical community of inquiry. At the end of his life, an insatiable reader preparing for the writing of *History*, Kracauer found great intellectual pleasure in participating in this community–well aware of the fact that it suggested a goal rather than a reality. There was, he thought, an increase of historical knowledge precisely because it was increasingly questioned. In agreeing and disagreeing with other historians, the exile was reassured by the unforeseeable and unpredictable capaciousness of cultural memory, which seemed to accommodate changes in time. As "art with a difference," historiography has indeed preserved many acts of reading–despite the inevitable errors, distortions, and misunderstandings. And it has done so because, on the whole, it has managed both to avoid fully self-authorizing decisions and to circumvent paralyzing claims to pure objectivity. Kracauer wished to protect its rich and diverse practice by searching out and reflecting on its troubles.

Professional readers and writers of history have been in agreement that good historiography can also be good literature. However, as a historian has put it (and, interestingly, he refered to the authority of a well-known novelist here): "unlike the novelist and the poet, the historian can never be the absolute ruler of an imaginary kingdom. For, however skillful he may be, he cannot invent his facts."[6] It does not seem–it *is*–as simple as that; and everything else follows from it.[7] The historian's imagination is not equipped to bracket reality because, by temperament and training, she is so literally responsible for its reconstruction, its re-presentation. This does not mean that facts cannot be gotten wrong or distorted or finally gotten more than less right, and all for a host of different reasons. Facts are of course "made" in the mind, the products of interpretation. But the processes of perception which guide such construction involve the mind's coming upon (*invenire*) the world *outside* it. The difference between historical and fictional narration concerns the invention of facts–not the *fact* of such invention but its *locus*. That *locus*, the past or present actuality of other lives (experiences), is essentially the same for the historian and the documentarist but not for the novelist, whatever the setting of her fictions.[8]

Such acts of approaching, coming upon, and meeting have of course been shaped by historians' interdependent acculturated belief systems and individual intellectual temperaments and talents. The achievement of cultural modernity has been to ask of the world not what or how it *is*, but how it is *perceived* in experience, by myself and a multitude of others–that is, to recognize and acknowledge its being simultaneously separate and mediated.[9] The difficulties for modern historians–but also the cultural value of modern historiography–have been located in the challenge to make *is perceived* transparent for *has been perceived*.[10] Traveling in time, their acts of coming-upon have been multiple and greatly varied because of the diversity of their subjects' and their own experience. In that they have depended to a high degree on verbal communication: historiography has essentially concerned the reading and writing of history. There have been, over time and in many places, its individual and very different practitioners who nevertheless have managed to learn from one another.[11] There have been different traditions; and in the modern period there have been different schools, movements, positions. But there also has been, and from the beginning, the authority of what was lived in that world *outside* the inquiring (*historein*) mind–a relative authority, to be sure, if one looks at the history of historiography. Still, an authority questioned so that it could be protected.

This was exactly what Kracauer had asked of photography and film and what made the analogy to historiography so important to him. In establishing the connection, he chose to stress its helpful rather than its more troublesome aspects, notably the different conceptual strategies involved in the composition of verbal and visual representation. For instance, he did not bring to bear on this issue the arguments he had made in his film reviews for the filmic superiority of the silent film, which reflected his awareness of the strained and ambiguous relation between words (stories) and photo images. But there are also the staggering perspectivist difficulties encountered in the traversing of temporal distances. Yet the analogy between photography and historiography, a composite of fragmented, tentative, illustrative, suggestive relations rather than a sustained, coherent argument, does show in a different light some of the most entrenched conundrums of historical representation. Kracauer's cumulative attempts at description, his circlings, over so many years, around a definition of the cultural contribution of the documentary, verbal or pictorial, are useful here pecisely because they are shaped so single-mindedly by the authority of what could, and therefore should, be seen. Whenever he used the analogy to photography to support his argumentation in *History*, he referred to this authority. This did not make the problems of historiography any easier; it made them more directly, more urgently puzzling.

One curiously inconclusive and illuminating example: In the first chapter of *History*, "Nature," Kracauer illustrated (rather than argued) the impossibility of constructing coherent chains of cause and effect in historiographic representation by referring his reader to an instance of filmic representation. For an intended screen adaption of Dreiser's *An American Tragedy*, Eisenstein had planned a montage sequence that was to accommodate in a plural simultaneous presence–rather than relate individually and sequentially–the jumble of thoughts and emotions coming together in the decision to kill and in the subsequent act of killing. The film never materialized, but Eisenstein's "montage lists" survived: scattered words before a black screen, which together with silent images and "polyphonic" sounds, were to show the protagonist in the battle of calculation, fear, desire. Eisenstein's use of these visual means was aimed at opening the audience's awareness to the 'infinitely' intricate complex of mental processes which became the protagonist's decision and act. Eisenstein's "aesthetically presenting" such infinity seemed effective precisely because it impressed on the viewer the impossibility here of discursive representation. Kracauer used the example not to argue that film could do something that historiography could not do but to show why historiography should not be asked to do it. In human affairs, and therefore in historiography, a rigorous linking of causes and effects is an uneasy fit.

> There are actions and emerging situations which so stubbornly resist a breakdown into repeatable elements or a satisfactory explanation from preceding or

> simultaneous circumstances that they had better be treated as irreducible entities. My hunch is that even a Laplacean Demon [a demon being able to look at the smallest parts and sharing Laplace's constructional optimism] would be hard put to incorporate them into the chain of causes and effects. Human affairs, that is, transcend the dimension of natural forces and causally determined patterns. In consequence, any approach to history which claims to be scientific in a stricter sense of the word will sooner or later come across unsurmountable obstacles. If history is a science it is a science with a difference. (29f.)

Is this an insight we need to be alerted to at the end of the twentieth century? Clive, in his argument for rereading the "Great Nineteenth-Century Historians," assumed that the "old battle against those who wished to make history a science has been fought and won."[12] But the current heated debate of the "objectivity question" among historians may suggest otherwise.[13] Even more so, perhaps, the "new battle" that Clive himself perceived "against those who wish to make it into pure literature" (35). A conscientious and effective reader and writer of history, Clive did not see that the (pure) science and (pure) literature issues are related and that the second battle owes its aggressive vitality to the fact that the first battle has neither been well fought nor clearly won. Kracauer's concern was the first battle. Had he lived to see the second one, he would have deplored its absolutism, that is, its lack of historical imagination and its ungenerous concept of cultural memory. I think the photography-historiography analogy useful precisely because it explores the much traveled and unclaimed areas of "art with a difference" and "science with a difference."

2

A late twentieth-century reader may easily become irritated by Kracauer's use of the phrase "physical reality" when trying to give a coherently focused description of the matter-of-fact magic of photography and film. It is no accident, Wright Morris wrote in "The Camera Eye" (1981), "that the present renaissance of interest in photographs and photography follows a period given over to the 'abstract' and our perplexity as to what, if anything, is real."[14] This, however, is an accultured perplexity, both superficial and forceful, and it was not Kracauer's. His fascination with photo images was for *their* sake and *his* sake, very much in that order, because visible things were real, that is, sharable. Captured in the arrested flow of time, they had the power to penetrate the viewer's self-absorption to the point of reshaping the spaces of memory. It was, in a sense, the photograph's rather than the photographer's magic,[15] and its use, indeed its instrumentality, was left open to the viewer.

Up to a point–and here the differences are as instructive as the similarities–Kracauer as documentarist and film critic shared the beliefs of the American documentarists of the Great Depression. They were to inform his analogy between photography and historiography–though, ironically, it was probably his concern for this analogy which kept him from exploring what was to them the most important aspect of their work: the power of photo images to both "make history" and substantially supplement, even substitute for historiography.

For the men and women working for the photography unit of the Farm Security Administration program, it was the photographer's responsibility to literally focus on what was there to be seen but had been overlooked and to keep it in focus. Descendants of Heinrich Zille, and, more remotely, of Eugène Atget (fig. 3),[16] they produced their sharp-focus, "straight" photo images in order to send important social messages. Zille, in Freund's account,

> was the first "concerned" photographer for whom the message his subject matter conveyed was of most importance. He was the first in a line of incorruptible photojournalists who surfaced later, in the 1930s, and who followed in his footsteps without knowing of his existence. For all these photojournalists, the camera was thought to be more important than the photographer; the camera was the sensitive tool that would allow a situation or a personality to reveal itself.[17]

Some of the FSA photographers believed in the challenge of such self-revelation more than others, and it is impossible to say how many "really" believed that it was possible. The two most talented among them, Dorothea Lange and Walker Evans, had different opinions in this respect. Evans later described himself as "interested, selfishly, in the opportunity it gave me to go around and use the camera. I did anything I pleased and *ignored* what I was expected to do." He was not trying to be a photojournalist on the famous *Let Us Now Praise Famous Men* project: "No, I was trying to be myself. I certainly didn't want to be what anybody else wanted me to be." Intent here on presenting himself as an artist rather than documentarist, he may have emphasized his self-centeredness.[18] But his photographic ideas were to a large degree formed–more so than Lange's–when he joined the FSA. Lange firmly believed in the social usefulness of her work; Evans was more ambivalent in this respect. Having become seriously interested in photography in 1928, Evans looked through the whole run of Stieglitz's *Camera Work* and among some five hundred photographs reproduced over a span of fifteen years found only one he really liked, Paul Strand's "Blind Woman 1916" (fig. 12). Szarkowski thinks it "the most frontal, bluntly composed, least artful of Strand's street portraits of the preceding decade."[19] But arguably–and importantly, given the nature of Evans's images (figs. 30, 31, 33)–the appellative effectiveness of Strand's photograph is the result of his choice of subject which includes considerable compositional self-consciousness.

From experience even the most dedicated FSA photographer knew in some part of her mind that the camera's "sensitivity" was symbiotically linked with the photographer's, and that the subject's "self-revelation" needed to be complemented by a sympathetic viewer. Inevitably, Freund's description draws on metaphors, and she has in mind degrees of emphasis: *more* attention given to subject matter; *more* focus on a particular message, *more* interest in the control of the viewer. But for Roy Stryker, the head of the FSA photography unit, witnessing meant that the photo image could literally serve as, in the sense of replace, the viewer's eye. (In that, he echoed John Spivak's claims, in his famous "*Reportagen*" of the thirties, to see *for* his readers, that is, include them in his acts of seeing.)[20] A good documentary, Stryker asserted, "should tell not only what a place or a thing or a person *looks* like, but it must also tell the audience what it would feel like to be an actual witness to the scene."[21]

The socially engaged documentary, then, was intended to emphasize the appellative force of the medium.[22] Addressing the viewers, it was meant to draw them in and to make them co-witnesses, thereby bracketing the knowledge problems associated with witnessing. An investigative reporter during the Weimar period, Kracauer had become increasingly aware of these problems and allowed his concept of the documentary to be influenced by such awareness. Concern with the fallacies of perception in general, and the interpretive role of the documentarist in particular, led him to draw attention in *Die Angestellten* to the constructedness of the documentarist's vision.[23] Moreover, he showed how, given the spatial and temporal particularity of the observed and the observer, it could not be otherwise. The life stories elicited by the observer from the observed were themselves constructs carrying their own energies, which, attracting or repelling him, inevitably guided his shaping the larger construct of documenting these lives. The achievement of *Die Angestellten* was precisely Kracauer's self-conscious manipulation of perspective, which both documented and questioned his fairness as observer. He was interested not so much in denying the possibility of objectivity as in showing its modalities.

As a verbal documentarist, then, Kracauer went further than Erik Barnouw did in his judicious comment on the objectivity question in documentary film:

> The interpretive role has kept the documentarist under fire. In contentious times especially, he has been under frequent attack. To be sure, some documentarists deny any interpretive element in their work, and claim to be 'objective.' This may be strategic, but is surely meaningless. The documentarist makes endless choices. He selects topics, people, vistas, angles, lenses, juxtapositions, sounds, words. Each selection is an expression of his point of view, whether he is aware of it or not, whether he acknowledges it or not. The documentarist who lays claim to objectvitiy is merely asserting his conviction that his choices have a special validity and deserve everyone's acceptance.[24]

This was true for the documentarists of the Great Depression. The documentarist Kracauer did not join them in that claim to objectivity, but he did share with them the justification of the choice of subject matter. This choice was based on making visible and thereby real to the viewer what, in the documentarist's opinion, had so far been invisible. There were the poor, who were completely overlooked or, in Roosevelt's translation, "forgotten," in America. There were the lower middle-class *Angestellten*, who were more exotic to the Weimar intellectual critic than the remotest band of Stone Age people. But when the American documentarists of the Great Depression claimed that photo images meant a direct, unmediated transfer of visible reality to the viewer, they were in danger of freezing their medium into a doctrine.

The results of this doctrinal directness are curiously contradictory. It produced images that clearly reflect the photographer's attempt to record, without any interference, what could be seen—which does not mean that they succeeded or that the images were successful photographically. But it also provoked images of great poignancy whose (desired) appellative power lay precisely in their reductiveness, which was the photographer's–not the photograph's–responsibility. A highly gifted FSA photographer like Dorothea Lange chose to "take" and show her subjects, individuals or groups, in ways that she thought particularly expressive of their present life situation and that, for the duration of the documentation, told the "whole" story. But in its rhetorical selectiveness and emphasis, this story directed the viewer to appropriate its meanings in a manner that might abstract from the subjects' individuality where it explicitly concerned intersubjective relations. These true-to-reality images were focused so much on controlling the viewer that the visibility of the subject could be peculiarly reduced. This is literally true in Lange's "Migratory Cotton Picker," taken in Arizona in 1940.[25] Yet this photograph, one of her most haunting, most successful images precisely because it is most self-consciously composed and visually engaging, is also complexly and ambiguously suggestive. Holding his arm in front of his face, the young man shields himself from the sun–and, according to the expected message, from a hostile, rejecting world. His handsome face is partly obscured by his beautiful, toughened, and delicate palm, which, turned to the viewer and enlarged by the focus of the perspective, draws her in irresistibly. If his individuality is reduced to this hand, which shows his youth, beauty, vulnerability, and exploitation, does this not hold–for the viewer, if not for the young man–an "infinite" poignancy?

Both Evans and Lange had their own visual agenda and were, in the eyes of the FSA, excessively independent. (When the budget was cut in 1937, Evans was let go after twenty months of work. Lange was fired several times but always succeeded in getting reinstated.) Documentary photographs acceptable to the FSA had to be images of people which would reliably draw the viewer into the presence of human suffering. But, as a critic remarked shrewdly, "a remarkably high percentage" of the people photographed as victims by Lange were "handsome, even if troubled and worn. We see them–and were meant to see them–as people of exceptional value, proud and independent and competent, who are unlikely to ask for help, but who clearly deserve it."[26] Importantly, in Lange's photos the victims of social injustice are not difficult to look at; they are literally attractive, they attract the viewer's gaze. Photographed, they are not the lost and forgotten people Roy Stryker was looking for.

He also did not think acceptable images without human subjects. "Where were the people?" Roy Stryker asked when Morris offered a sampling of photographs of old barns and houses in which the presence of their equally worn-down inhabitants was implied rather than openly shown. "In his concerned and troubled eyes I saw that he meant to say, where were the suffering, the hurting, the humiliated People of the Great American Depression? In the absence of such people he saw me as an impostor. Why would anyone take pictures of time-tired, life-worn structures, and not include the wasted, exhausted, brutalized people, with their rag-clad, fly-bitten, half-starved children?"[27]

Because this "anyone," a particular photographer, had more affinity for the ambiguities created by the photograph's openness to the visible than the FSA documentarist thought affordable under circumstances that called for the photographer's responsibility to focus on certain overlooked phenomena more than others. The implication in Morris's passage is that FSA photography claimed universal relevance–to reveal things as they are–for a particular vision. Dorothea Lange, whose work found its focus in the documentary of the Depression, declared herself firmly guided by a quote from Francis Bacon that she had posted on her darkroom door in the thirties: "The contemplation of things as they are, without substitution or imposture, without error and confusion, is in itself a nobler thing than a whole harvest of invention."[28] But the results of such ideal contemplation, Lange's photographs of the time both show "invention" in the sense of composition and suggest "confusion" with regard to the "true" meaning of the situation: meaning for whom? from which position? through what kind of perspective? A terse statement on her concept of the documentary precedes the Bacon passage:

> For me documentary photography is less a matter of *subject* and more a matter of *approach*. The important thing is not what's photographed but *how*. . . . My own approach is based upon three considerations. First–hands off! Whatever I photograph, I do not molest or tamper with or arrange. Second–a sense of place. Whatever I photograph, I try to picture as part of its surroundings, as having roots. Third–a sense of time. Whatever I photograph, I try to show as having its position in the past or in the present. But beyond these three things, the only thing I keep in mind is that–there it is, that quotation pinned on my darkroom door. (47)

(In the Aperture monograph this quote is aptly placed next to her famous "The General Strike, San Francisco 1934" with its abundance of contradictory visual clues.)

Unlike Margaret Bourke-White, who was notorious for arranging her human subjects like objects, indeed, pushing them into position physically, Lange respected the people she photographed.[29] There is a curiously independent, world-absorbed quality in all of them, even when they are not involved in some activity but seem to be looking directly into the camera. They never are, really, since there is always the shadowy presence of something that engages their interest or needs their attention, and it is not the photographer in the act of taking their picture. The encounter experienced by the viewer is not so much with a person as with a person within the surroundings of lived space and time. Lange, the photographer, is responsible for this presence, and yet it is precisely her openness to it which creates ambiguities, multiple meanings–a complexity that has made her images enduring.

A documentary photograph, Lange said in an interview in the early sixties,

> is not a factual photograph per se. [The documentary photograph] carries with it another thing, a quality [in the subject] that the artist responds to. It is a photograph which carries the full meaning of the episode or the circumstance or the situation that can only be revealed–because you can't really recapture it–by this other quality. There is no real warfare between the artist and the documentary photographer. He has to be both. . . . The documentary photographer is trying to speak to you in terms of everyone's experience.

In *Photographs of a Lifetime* (108), this text is placed next to "Homeless Family, Oklahoma, 1938," the image of a family walking briskly on a rural road, seen from the back. The desolation is not so much in the landscape or the people themselves as in their grouping, which focuses, in an indirect and very effective way, on the smallness of the cart carrying their possessions. In one sense Lange means: the "world outside" is concrete because it is shared and thus resists improper appropriation. But she also suggests that the documentary photographer has a special, a privileged access to the universal experience of Everyman. And perhaps this double meaning, whether intended or not, underlines once more the conflict to be assuaged and smoothed out, but also temporarily sharpened, between the authority of the observing (perceiving) self and that of the observed (perceived) other–who in many cases is herself an observer of the act of being observed. This is a conflict that cannot be resolved in general epistemological terms but can at best revise its own boundaries in its acknowledged confinement to the time and place of one perceiving person's act of observation. Such an acknowledgment ideally ought to include also the meanings of this act for the observed.

The documentary for Lange was circumscribed by political-social questions: in her view of them, the time and place of most of the people she photographed was defined by their being oppressed. Lange's friend Ansel Adams sincerely admired her "extraordinary qualities as a photographer," her "devotion to the art and the severe discipline and effort." He may have responded to that searching, open quality in Lange's images which allows the life of the observed to go on beyond the moment when its picture is taken and independently of it. Technically much more sophisticated, he would occasionally do her printing for her–certainly a labor of love for her images. In his autobiography he quotes from a letter he wrote her in 1962 that sums up their disagreements over the thirties-style documentary, which had proved so influential: "Photography, when it tells the truth, is magnificent, but it can be twisted, deformed, restricted and compromised more than any other art. Because what is before the lens always has the illusion of reality; but what is selected and put before the lens can be as false as any totalitarian lie." He resented the connotations of much documentary photography because of their rigidity, and it is true that subject matter was extremely important for Lange. Adams did not want the photographer to be imprisoned in these terms:

> I resent being told that certain things have significance; that is for me, as spectator, to discover. I resent being manipulated into a politico-social formula of thought and existence. I resent the implications that unless photography has a politico-social function it is not of value to people at large. I resent the very obvious dislike of elements of beauty; our friend Steichen has shocked me time and again by a self-conscious fear of the beautiful. Does he feel that way about a painting, about sculpture, architecture, literature and just plain nature? He does not. I am not afraid of beauty, of poetry, of sentiment. I think it is just as important to bring to people the evidence of the beauty of the world of nature and of man as it is to give them a document of ugliness, squalor and despair.[30]

Adams, expectedly, was more tolerant of the beauty of Bourke-White's depression photographs (265). In Steichen's case he did not address differences between the photographer's social-political agenda articulated verbally and the vision reflected in his images. Many of Steichen's urban images are technically brilliant and of great visual beauty–in some cases quite close to what Adams tried to achieve: see for instance the extraordinary architectural photograph, "The Maypole," 1932.[31]

The real issue here is the subject–a beautiful, wild landscape–and the integrity of its beauty. Where this integrity was threatened by either denial of the validity of the subject or (what he saw as) self-consciously artistic photography with abstracting formal tendencies, Adams protested–hence his disagreements with Weston. His sensibility was very much documentary in terms of the recording and preserving properties of the photo image in relation to the integrity of the outside world. The important difference was his interest in precisely that aspect which was not his social responsibility–or, rather, which called up a different dimension of such responsibility. The beauty of his images is in their curiously intimate timelessness and familiar grandeur. Their appeal to a great variety of viewers is rooted in a delicately detailed modern version of the sublime, a magnificence both accessible and self-sufficient (fig. 36). When Adams photographed relocated Japanese in Manzanar in 1943, he saw beauty here, too, and in explicitly cultural terms. In a vast, barren landscape, amid taut, starkly present natural objects, he showed the retreating shacks, and within them the admirably ordered human spaces–as he recalls in the *Autobiography*, most of them "softened with flowers and the inimitable taste of the Japanese for simple decoration":

> I was profoundly affected by Manzanar. As my work progressed, I began to grasp the problems of the relocation and the remarkable adjustment these people had made. It was obvious to me that the project could not be one of heavy reportage with repeated description of the obviously oppressive situation. With admirable strength of spirit, the Nisei rose above despondency and made a life for themselves, a unique macro-civilization under difficult conditions. This was the mood and the character I determined to apply to the project. (259f.)

Before this civilization had been achieved, in the first stages of relocation, "the great documentary photographer Dorothea Lange," Adams noted, had "made some moving photographs that reveal the despair, bewilderment and misery of the thousands of American citizens as they were apprehended and isolated almost as prisoners of war" (258). This was not the stage that Adams wanted to record. He remembers his shyness and fear of intrusion and the graciousness of the people he photographed. What he showed was what *they wished* to show: their sense of control in what was a very difficult, in many ways chaotic, situation. He presented them to the viewer as they wanted to appear. There is that well-known image from *Born Free and Equal*, "A Young Lawyer and His Family," of a husband, wife, and son sitting in an extremely simple but very orderly, kitchenlike room. Looking at the camera, they are composed, almost smiling, neither relaxed nor stiff, revealing only that moment of allowing themselves to be looked at and looking back.[32] I am not emphasizing here that Adams, mainly a photographer of nature, did not treat these three people as objects. I would not have expected him to anyway since the literal and easily accessible magic of his nature images seems to me rooted in their coaxing the viewer into a curiously mixed private and universal correspondence that defies appropriation and objectification. My point is that he kept a distance that allowed them to be active in looking back at the camera and the photographer behind it; he even allowed them how to *control* the act of looking back. They are clearly there and their own; the recording of the particularity of their presence extends its moment immeasurably because it is *their* measure–a measure both accepted and granted with gracious and serious attentiveness by the person who "took" their photograph.

Is it such seemingly effortless, "naturally" negotiable distance, then, that makes for the ideal documentarist of other lives? It seems to be so in the case of the subjects of Adams's images. But the important point here is that it took the coming together of both the particular photographer, Adams, and the particular Japanese-Americans in that particular situation to produce the images suggesting that ideal. Robert Flaherty, who in the early twenties established the genre of the documentary film with his extraordinary *Nanook of the North*, differed dramatically from Adams not only in temperament but also in his relation to the subjects of his film. And yet in certain ways he shared with Adams the sensitivity to his subjects' desired self-presentation as an important source of knowledge. He saw a people with admirable qualities who were diminished by a modern present to which he, as a filmmaker, inescapably belonged. Profoundly influenced by his conflicted vision of them, his filmic strategies in *Nanook of the North* raise intriguing questions about the complex interdependencies between the documentor, the documented, and the documentary image.

The most notorious example is the intense and creative involvement of Nanook, a celebrated Eskimo hunter, in the acting of himself. Flaherty encouraged Nanook's physically demanding, even dangerous, elaborate self-presentation, which was literally driven by the self-enhancing feedback from the camera–the Eskimos were shown every sequence immediately after the shooting. He did so because he realized that this active cooperation between the maker of the documentary and the subjects of the film produced images of absorbing human interest and great beauty. There is the famous sequence of the obsolete walrus hunt that was revived solely for the sake of the filmic images, which would endure beyond the short-lived drama and the acute danger of the men's pursuit of the animal. In this situation, the probable compromising of the kill was unimportant to the chief hunter, though it was crucially important to the real-life survival of his group. "Suppose we go," Flaherty said to him. "Do you know that you and your men may have to give up making a kill, if it interferes with my film? Will you remember that it is the picture of you hunting the ivuik that I want, and not their meat?" "Yes, yes," Nanook assured him. "The aggie [film] will come first."[33]

But for Flaherty the sequence was so important because it would document most persuasively the extraordinary courage, ingenuity, and endurance of this isolated small Eskimo tribe "left behind" by modern progress. Did these "romanticized" images show the "truth" about their life in the present? As far as we can judge, they were true to Nanook's nostalgically heroic self-perception. Flaherty of course understood very well the exhilarating, intoxicating effect on Nanook of the "aggie's" recording power: the fantastic visibility in other places and other times of his and his people's feats of skill and courage. Flaherty's romanticizing perspective fed on Nanook's–as Nanook's fed on his. Curiously, this "archdocumentary" film also made visible with stunning clarity the hermeneutic entanglement of observer and observed, an entanglement of temperaments and sensibilities that were developed in and shaped by experience.

For all her documentary fervor, Dorothea Lange was by disposition more intrusive than Adams. But her different professional experience, too, is crucially important; she had "found herself" as a photographer through her work for the FSA. She would, then, as Adams pointed out, look for and record the characteristic "despair, bewilderment and misery" of newly arrived camp inmates rather than that group's equally characteristic attempts to cope with a difficult situation. Yet she was also aware of the problem of the documentarist's intrusiveness, an attitude exacerbated by a photographic perspective that exclusively stressed its subjects' victim status. On the whole, particularly in her later photos, she controlled this problem effectively.

These are different temperaments and different achievements. Even though he did not take many photographs of people, Adams's interest in their "thereness" was much stronger than Morris's. For Morris, the absence of people from their used and abused, frail and confining habitats signified "somehow" their fuller presence. In these absences, which he recorded in his photo images, he explained, he would search for "the *persona* behind the social abuses, one that would prove to be the same with or without them" (40). Stryker and his group had set out to demolish in their documentary constructions precisely the assumption or postulation of such sameness. Adams, too, subverted it in the Manzanar photographs, if with a different emphasis. Documenting the observed's surrender to the reality of the observed, he protected the observer's attempts to remain themselves. The title leaf of *Born Free and Equal*, "Young Man, Manzanar Relocation Center, California 1943," shows a young Japanese in profile, sitting in the right foreground of a solitary but not desolate landscape. The composition moves the viewer's eye on a diagonal line from left bottom to right top, holding in a curiously gentle balance the human figure and the natural world. The pose suggests a calmness not only in resignation but also in adjustment, which guides the (this) viewer's feeling that the young man is shown as he wished to appear: not only, not mainly, a victim. But–as is clear from the group of Manzanar images if not, perhaps, from the individual image–that calmness shows as much a cultural as an individual quality. It is *not* the young man's inviolable *persona* behind or beyond social abuses; it is his particular acculturated response to them, in which the landscape plays a part.

The first paragraph of Adams's "Foreword" to *Born Free and Equal* reads:

> Moved by the human story unfolding in the encirclement of desert and mountains, and by the wish to identify my photography in some creative way with the tragic momentum of the times, I came to Manzanar with my cameras in the

> fall of 1943. For many years I have photographed the Sierra Nevada, striving to reveal by the clear statement of the lens those qualities of the natural scene which claim the emotional and spiritual response of the people. In these years of strain and sorrow, the grandeur, beauty, and quietness of the mountains are more important to us than ever before. I have tried to record the influence of the tremendous landscape of Inyo on the life and spirit of thousands of people living by force of circumstance in the Relocation Center of Manzanar. Hence, while the people and their activities are my chief concern, there is much emphasis on the land throughout this book.[34]

3 Morris, too, was not interested in an elusive, "essential" human *persona* behind or beyond the realm of the social. He was drawn to the camera's ability to render sharply and precisely what he saw in those time-worn structures, the "endless gradations from black to white in stone, shingle, clapboard, painted or peeling"–for him a life-enhancing visual pleasure that has its own justification and authority.[35] Kracauer, too, was sensitive to such pleasures but with an important difference: he articulated them in the intimate, impressionistic *verbal* sketches of urban scenes during the Weimar period later collected in *Strassen in Berlin und anderswo.* Their charm lies not so much in the viewer's surrender to the lines, shapes, spaces of city streets as in their surrender to him. It lies in his attempts at coaxing significance out of acts of viewing–not unlike Benjamin's approach in some of his *Städtebilder.*[36] Under the observer's intent gaze the observed is transformed into something that is more alluring, more exclusively his–also, particularly in its retreat, its elusiveness. In his film criticism, he subjected the pleasures of the visible to questions of social and political meaning, that is, to a different concept of sharing. When he emphasized the filmmaker's responsibility to be true to the medium-specific documentary core of film (including fiction film), he meant the reflection in the photo image of the observer's full absorption in the conflicts and ambiguities of real-life situations. His concern was for the observed rather than the observer. This important distinction informed his interest in the openness of the photo image to the fullness of the visible world. Guiding much of Kracauer's argument in *Theory of Film,* this interest did not lead him to deny the shaping of objectivity but to continue to question the ermerging shapes.

Erik Barnouw's remarks on this issue, which I quoted above, suggest an almost impatient "of course, there is no objectivity"–a position articulated by many documentarists who openly admit, even stress, that the documentary reflects *their* view and that it could not be otherwise. This, however, is not the end but the beginning of the objectivity question. At issue is the active participation of the observer in the "truth" of or about the observed, that is, in the experience *and* construction, the experience *as* construction, of that truth. Kracauer made his most emphatic statement on the importance of such construction for knowledge–the documentarist's and the audience's–in the context of verbal rather than photo representation, asserting that mere recording of subjects "as they are" would be seriously reductive. His remark that "reality is a construction" is meant to distinguish a largely random reporting of observations from the documentary as "a mosaic which is formed by fitting together observations according to their content. *Reportage* photographs life; a mosaic of this kind would yield its picture."[37]

It is true, that this distinction seems to echo some passages in the essay on photography published two years earlier (1927) that juxtapose photography with the work of art. But at issue is not, I think, an evaluative comparison between merely recording photography and significant pictorial composition but rather a questioning of the shapes of recording. The "*Bild*" in whose construction the observer, Kracauer, has self-consciously involved himself would give better access to the lives he seeks to describe than would mere verbal or photographic transcription. Mimicking rather than questioning the phenomena of automatism and randomness characteristic of modern technology, such transcription was much used in the mass media of the twenties.[38] As a documentary *Die Angestellten*, too, was written for the day.[39] But, composing their image so that it would reflect in its organisation the novelty and the symptomatic nature of that group in Weimar mass technocracy, the text was also meant to reflect the difficulties faced by, and the achievements of, the writer of contemporary history.

The Depression documentarists approached the visible guided by a belief in documentary immediacy which was informed by a remarkably absolutist version of "as they are." In a sense, the visible/invisible drama was for them the most important truth to be recorded by the camera, quite independent of what their photos had actually captured. Moreover, acting out that drama demanded the fiction of artlessness in writing the contemporary history, as objective recording, of the troubling and exotic culture of poverty–an objectivity that surely would turn out itself to be a fiction. And yet, the illusion of objectivity was also a powerful motivation for the documentarists to explore to the fullest the recording potential of their medium. If the culture of poverty was a recent discovery, so was its photographic documentation, and certain questions—though given more or less instinctive consideration by particularly talented individual photographers—could not yet be asked in a coherently probing manner.

The documentary as the questionable and necessary symbiosis of truth and fictionality, of real-life situations, and of artfully arranged sequences is brilliantly argued in Errol Morris's *The Thin Blue Line*, a tour-de-force interrogation of the execution of justice and the meanings of the documentary. The "thin blue line," the proverbial reference to the police lined up in their blue uniforms to uphold the law, separates truth and nontruth, order and anarchy—but not as rigidly as some documentarists or, in this case, the law assumes. In order to disentangle one "convicted" murderer's extraordinary[40] yet real experience of the Texas judicial system—a man accused of having shot a police officer—Morris used a highly self conscious composition of image sequences that suggest shifting concepts of reality in which the photography participates.

Errol Morris said in an interview with Bill Moyers that his position in making this film, dubbed by some viewers the "first nonfiction film noir," had not been one of despairing of truth: "We have access to the world out there. I wanted to make a movie about the fact that truth is difficult to know, not that it is impossible to know."[41] If we understand truth as trust in (true to, loyal to) evidence, that is, trust in *seeing*, if not with full clarity and certainty, the actual nature (*veritas*) of a situation, then Morris's film aspires to the truth of the documentary film. But *is* it a documentary in the accepted terms of the concept? Morris himself points out the expensive camera, the sophisticated camerawork, the artful lighting, the reenactments in the mood of film noir, which flaunt the fictional mode, having been done at a time and in places other than that of the real event action (many years later, in Boston instead of Dallas), and the music by Philip Glass which underlies and comments on the action. In parts of a documentary film, then, he used "purely" visual means or visual fictions to clarify a conceptually intricate complex of questions with respect to perceptions of reality that are inescapably rooted in the experience of power and violence.[42] These visual fictions enable the viewer to use a composite perspective through which she can trace experientially (here sequentially) the composite nature of reality as a cultural (political) construct. Visual fictions have become part of a learning process that turns out to have yielded–and this is the fascination of the film for many viewers–a kind of evidence or knowledge sufficiently concrete to change the course of events for real-life protagonists.

Moyers, who described himself in this interview as coming from the documentary tradition, seemed particularly impressed by these "formal" variations on the documentary because they signify an as it were fudged line between the presence and the absence of the fictional. In the interest of *showing the deception*, of tracing visually the difficulties of knowing the truth, Morris has even left out details that supported the innocence of Randall Dale Adams, the man wrongly convicted of murder and in imminent danger of being executed because the film, though intended to help Adams, is focused on the theme of the thin blue line between truth and deception, between the willingness to seek out and trust the evidence and the willingness to make up and surrender to fictions. It was for the sake of this focus that the maker of the film himself used fictions created by the camerawork and the selective interpretation of evidence.

The title, *The Thin Blue Line*, plays ingeniously on the judge's explanation for his decision to pass the death sentence. His mind was made up, he told Morris, by a phrase used in the prosecution's concluding statement that "gave me the shivers": the district attorney had invoked the "thin blue line" between anarchy and order–for which Adams would have to die. The judge was not himself a "hanging judge," but weak and impressionable. And the documentarist's photo recording of the man physically shrinking, bending away from all uncomfortable facts, underlines these qualities most effectively. His face appears to be dissolving, almost grotesquely distorted with anxiety. This is not a random but a controlled significant distortion, and it will help the viewer understand the ambiguities and contradictions inherent in that notion of a "thin blue line." They here concern a judge who does not, as he is charged to do, make choices and decisions but allows the "hanging" district attorney to compose, "cook" the evidence that will be put before the jury with the help of "Dr. Death," a notoriously bloodthirsty psychiatrist called by the state in the murder cases tried in Dallas. (Errol Morris had originally planned a documentary about "Dr. Death" and came upon Adams's case in the course of interviewing inmates on death row. That unmade film, presumably, would have been about the nature of psychiatric evidence and objectivity in extreme situations.)

The "thin blue line" between chaos and order proved to be the line between truth and deception. Order was carefully composed, a coherent deceiving fiction; chaos was not without elements of fiction, but its composition was incoherent, incomplete, contradictory, like the difficult processes of knowing the truth. Chaos, then, would be truth, difficult to know; and order, deception. The judge, almost always photographed frontally, appeared several times, and his face and gestures underscored the frightening silliness of his fictive and fictitious stern impartiality. Rigidly self-composed, he did not allow himself to be partial to the better evidence. There were only a few images of the hanging district attorney but repeated images of his literally keeping score. We see the beautifully composed orderly lists on which he records his successes in getting high sentences for the accused: how many years, how many life sentences, how many multiple life sentences, how many death sentences. These lists document most effectively what one of the attorneys for the defense, speaking about the DA, describes as the maxim of this man's professional pride: anyone can convict the guilty; it takes a good DA to convict the innocent. It takes the ability to surrender totally to coherent fictions in the face of evidence to the contrary.

The film puts the documentary on trial by showing the perversion of order and fiction in the practice of the law: it is this perversion that *can* indeed be documented in the court scenes. The main attorney for the defense, an intelligent, experienced trial lawyer who is sympathetically photographed, says that he has given up trial law for the duration; he could not bear to deal with another jury after the Adams jury accepted and enacted the perversion. Truth in its partial absence or precarious presence is more difficult to document. The viewer is shown what the different actors in the drama wished and needed to see. In the case of the crucial scene of the shooting we are shown repeated and changing constellations of the car allegedly driven by Adams, the officer walking toward it, the driver opening the window, the officer hit by the bullets. These reenactments, done long after the event, are not meant to reconstruct the crime in order to obtain evidence. They are intended to show the viewer the different actors' different versions of what happened, namely fictive samples of (perhaps) true and of fictitious evidence. Importantly, these reenactments, which introduce clearly fictional components into a film meant to demonstrate the true innocence of a man falsely accused and convicted of murder, do not undermine but rather support Morris's assertion that "there is a world out there; it is not just in our minds."

The film is probably more engaging intellectually than visually–an impression supported (perhaps unfairly) by the engrossing interview. But the intellectual interest of this film essay on the elusive and yet culturally essential nature of truth as seeking out and trusting evidence is considerable. (There is, of course, the added appeal that the sophisticated distinctions made in this "philosophical film" were derived from a real life-and-death situation.) The proof that Adams was not the killer is not *shown but heard*: we see only the cassettte recorder sitting on the table and listen to the cat-and-mouse interview between Morris and David Harris, the young man whom he suspects to be the true killer, now on Death Row for another murder and soon to be executed. By this time the viewer has seen many (sequences of) images of him: an obviously intelligent, articulate, diffident, and gentle, but also brutal, compulsive liar. Lies to him are stories that might or might not be believed, and the reasons for their success or failure remain mysterious because they are ineluctibly tied to his being outside the human condition. Harris never says, "I did it" or, "He did not do it." He says, "I am the one to know that he did not do it"–this is as far as he is willing to go but also as far as, under the circumstances, he has to go. It is a statement that affirms his existential mistrust of the possibility of knowing the truth–and here the camera shows him as a curiously appealing, villainous victim, androgynous, elusive. For Morris, who has carefully composed the circumstances of that final interview–and for his viewer, who has been able to follow the making of this composition–it affirms the evidence that truth can be known, if with difficulties, and precariously.

This scene, showing the instrument transmitting the complex message it has recorded, is a splendid conclusion to Morris's tracing the "thin blue line" between truth and deception. Evidently he did not have to make it up–if the viewer trusts his evidence. This evidence was enough for the state of Texas to let Adams go—after the movie was shown commercially—but not to rehabilitate him. They were afraid to give him another trial, in which he might have been proved innocent beyond reasonable doubt, because the process of establishing the jury's trust in the evidence, the truth of his innocence, would have exposed the fictions of their previous lies of his guilt.

The truth of Adams's innocence, though most probably knowable, is dependent on good judgment and consensus. With the same judge and prosecution, another jury *might* have cleared him, depending on their and the court's attitude toward evidence. In the interview with Moyers, Morris said that he was against the death sentence because he had observed its dangerous availability to the prosecution as a principle controlling an ideological, absolutist position of revenge—a principle that radically diminishes the capacity to seek out and trust evidence. To extrapolate from this statement: in the trial situation, such surrender to the desire for perfect order, which would exclude anything that might disturb it, the desire for perfect fiction, becomes the desire for the ultimate exclusion, death. Taking the meanings of deception and truth to their very limits in cultural, if not in epistemological, terms, Morris's film-noir documentary is a highly effective statement about the difficulties of making a documentary.

These difficulties have to do with the nature of the documentary mode, including historiography, and they concern general questions of objectivity and evidence. Morris may show Adams frontally photographed, an open, clear face, direct, calm, amazingly rational after what he had lived through, saying matter of factly: "It happened and there is nothing you can do about it." This is the Adams constructed by Morris, who seeks out and constructs the evidence that will set Adams free. Why do we trust this to be the real Adams? Because he fits his innocence, which fits the evidence. Why do we trust the evidence? Because we have been admitted to the difficulties of its construction; we have been shown the processual nature of knowing the truth. But who has shown us? The same person who has controlled this process. Why do we trust him? Because he makes sense. But why and how does he make sense? Because he has enabled us to participate, if passively, in the making of the construct. He has made it possible for us to reconstruct, to our satisfaction, what must have happened, what happened. That is, we have been put in the situation of a person capable of reproducing a difficult, if well-made, argument. But there is no getting around the fact that the viewer's acts of re-production depend on the acts of production–which are Morris' acts.

Trust in evidence is subject to hermeneutic circularity, whether it concerns the viewer (reader) of a documentary or its maker. Determining, selecting, and composing the facts of the case–activities that cannot be clearly separated–Morris was first motivated by his trust in the availability of evidence. This trust was based on the nature of both the case and the man, Adams. But was not the case Adams's case? A thorough analysis of the composite nature of this trust is impossible, because it would mean attempts to clarify a host of intensely entangled and complicated psychological reactions, that is, an "infinite" deferral of even the beginning of the process of knowing the truth. Instructively, for his documentary film on the documentary Morris chose a case that was overwhelmingly the case of the state of Texas, a case in which Adams had played an uncommonly passive role. This situation presented itself in ways that led to Morris's trust in the availability of evidence. Many of the prisoners on death row claimed to be innocent; Morris chose Adams because of the nature of his case. Epistemological questions are, of course, cultural questions shaped by psychological, social, political experience, and thus concepts (models, standards) of objectivity and evidence vary from case to case. In Morris's case the evidence was sufficient: *against* the state of Texas–in the persons of police officers, the prosecuting attorney, the judge, and the jury–and *for* the effectiveness of the documentary. If, using components of fictionality, he documented the difficulties of knowing the truth, he did so in order to be able to show that it could be known, at least partially. Such documentation is of crucial importance to a modern culture. But it is equally important to know that truth, even a part of if, cannot be gotten at artlessly.[43]

4 Kracauer thought the presence of the observer's "formative" energies in the photo image not only inevitable but also desirable and importantly linked to the cultural contribution of that image. As a film critic during the Weimar period, he had proceeded from the assumption that the photographer needed to be a contemporary of the problems of modernity: social conflict, the urban experience, the growing importance of popular culture, and political polarization. There was a symbiotic "ought" in

which the "formative" and the "material" components of photography were to fuse.

In *Theory of Film*, the authority of the visible was considerably expanded because Kracauer's "theoretical" perspective inspired "measurement," that is, looking at a great many different films in order to see how their makers discovered, uncovered, and reclaimed the *realia* of the physical (as) visible world. But by temperament, training, and professional experience Kracauer had been aware early, and to an unusual degree, of the photograph's power to present visual impressions that seem to challenge language beyond its capabilities. To use the description of this challenge given by a late-twentieth-century photographer and writer: "the ineluctably visible, eye- and mind-boggling world. This image is there before words, even as words strain to create a new image."[44]

Images call up the reality of the "world out there," which is difficult to know but knowable. I have argued that Kracauer's sensitivity to the cultural importance of (photo) images had made him wary of the intellectual's inclination toward elaborate linguistic solipsism that tended toward hermetic complete fictions. This wariness also shaped the argumentation in his reflections on the difficulties of writing history. The analogy between photography and historiography clarified difficulties; it enlarged rather than solved them. The complexly suggestive connection between the two activities needed to be traced within that "eye- and mind-boggling world" that encompasses past and present and is often too much for words—hence also the aphoristic style and open-ended discourse of *History*. Reviewing films, writing the social-political history of Weimar film, attempting to establish a poetics of still and moving photo images, Kracauer was not at all reluctant to describe the cultural contribution of particular films, even to generalize, if by extension and cautiously, on meaning in film. But he explicitly refrained from questioning history in these terms; he even argued against the usefulness of this approach. Reading *History* at the end of the twentieth century, it is important to be aware of the more general implications of this unideologically skeptical, "exorable" position,[45] rare among Kracauer's intellectual contemporaries of the Weimar period and later in exile.

It is unfortunate that one of the first attempts to introduce Kracauer to an educated American audience not primarily interested in cinema obscured rather than illuminated this position. Martin Jay's relatively early interest in Kracauer would have been useful had he not presented him as striving for but never quite making membership in the Frankfurt School. Looking at his work exclusively through the perspective of the much more successful Adorno, "who was helping Kracauer to achieve a modest degree of immortality,"[46] he was not sympathetic to his attempts to define his own position and discourse. An assumed Benjaminian presence in *History* allowed Jay to read into Kracauer's argument a redemptive reconciliation in historiography on the level of Proust's esthetic reconciliation–a solution explicitly rejected by Kracauer–and to impute to his work a religious dimension that was profoundly alien to his intellectual temperament: "Here the redemption Kracauer sought in so many secular ways was finally allowed an explicitly religious moment."[47] The key witness for this reading was a passage in *History* that Jay thought was "taken almost directly from Benjamin":

> So the question as to the meaningfulness of "technical history" would seem unanswerable. There is only one single argument in its support which I believe to be conclusive. It is a theological argument, though. According to it, the "complete assemblage of the smallest facts" is required for the reason that nothing should go lost. It is as if the fact-oriented accounts breathed pity with the dead. This vindicates the figure of the collector.[48]

Below I reconstruct the context in which the passage occurs, the argument in chapter 5, "The Structure of the Historical Universe," which is most closely linked to the discussion of the "Historical Approach" in chapter 2. In these two chapters Kracauer raised some of the most enduringly difficult questions that have confronted historiography and, dealing with puzzling and perhaps unsolvable problems, he made frequent use of analogies with photography. It seems to me that his probing, circumspect, multilayered argument here sharply contradicts Jay's reading.

In chapter 5 Kracauer weighs the reasons given by historians for their decision to use small-scale or large-scale historical investigation–decisions based on either historiographical principle or recognition of historical particularity. The epigraph for this chapter is a quote from Raymond Aron's *Dimensions de la conscience historique* (1961): "Nothing would further the progress of both the logic of science and the philosophy of history more than a rigorous analysis of the different ensemble types from the top to the bottom of the ladder" (104). Adorno had claimed that in *History* Kracauer had returned to what had always preoccupied him: the philosophy of history.[49] But Kracauer's reservations regarding a coherent philosophy of history, developed in the twenties and thirties in the discussions with Adorno, Benjamin, and Bloch, had, if anything, increased in exile. That "rigorous analysis" might further the progress of the philosophy of history–but was it possible? Was it even desirable? The notorious absence of such analysis in *History* indicated precisely the "anteroom" status of historical investigation–very much so in questions concerning the "structure of the historical universe." Kracauer had found no critical consensus here, not even false consensus in need of changing. But without even that, how was the historian to know, that is, be (relatively) certain of his knowledge? Historical knowledge, though in some ways cumulative, does not "add up" in the way in which scientific work is perceived to add up.[50] It remains peculiarly incomplete because it cannot be separated from the implications of the historian's place and time but carries with it the impurities of positionality. (Scientists do of course share this positionality, but its influence on method has been different since the scientific revolution of the seventeenth century because method in the sciences has been based on a different concept of a community of inquiry.)

In the beginning stage of the work on *History*, fascinated with the immensity and complexity of the "*Geschichtsthema*," Kracauer liked to share with his friends the fact of his immersion in the voluminous literature: "I have already filled more than four hundred file cards with my own thoughts and excerpts," he wrote to Leo Lowenthal in March of 1961. About a year later he told him: "I am of course constantly studying history and whatever I can find of theories of history. Philosophically the occasional reflections by practising historians on their field of inquiry are more instructive than most philosophies of history, including Hegel, Collingwood, Croce, etc. I adore the diffuseness of the historians' ideas; it is entirely fitting that they are incomplete [*nicht zu Ende gedacht*]." Thinking around them, there was still much more to read, because it was necessary to articulate "thoughts in the material."[51] Something like Aron's "different ensemble types," Kracauer thought, would have to be analyzed within the historical material rather than imposed on it from the frequently remote vantage points of the various philosophies of history. But the evidence offered in support of one or the other "type" was highly contradictory.

To the reader who considers the different opinions regarding the structure of the historical universe, history appears composed of different histories. The fact of such compositeness, its implications of instability and provisionality seemed obvious to Kracauer. He was intrigued by the complex of relations between the stories that make up history: with their great differences regarding scale and composition, they can be arranged in many different ways. If the individual histories or stories are shaped by differences in scope or degree of generality which mark differences in the observer's distance to the observed historical events, actions, and actors, so are the different versions or concepts of history. The fact that the observer's distance increases with the chronological remoteness of the observed, no matter what scope is used, inevitably influences the story's composition and, complicating matters, is reflected in its contribution to the composition of history. In the beginning of chapter 5 Kracauer uses a spatial image to suggest the coexistence (with fluid boundaries) of what he calles micro and macro histories[52]–an image that nicely balances a delicate and complicated symbiotic gradation: "The whole set calls to mind the Chinese gadget of the hollow ivory sphere which contains different spheres of diminishing size, each freely circling in the womb of the next larger one" (104).

How, then, *do* they relate and interact? How can their contribution to history be judged, evaluated? Surely, historians have not withheld judgments that were based on very different shapes of historiographical objectivity. Discussing them, Kracauer's judgment is conditional and provisional, restrained, as it were, by its being reflected off the many historiographical and photographic or filmic practices. Especially where he deals explicitly with the compositional nature of both histories and history, in chapters 5 and 2, his argument relies a great deal on the mutual elucidation of these practices.

Examining the "Historical Approach" in chapter 2, Kracauer treats the most basic (and most important) compositional question of a (desirable) "equilibrium" beween philosophically expanding and scientifically narrowing perspectives in historiography, on which are based the different ideas concerning the structure of the historical universe:

> Modern historiography would seem to come into its own if it manages to elude not only the Scylla of philosophical speculations with their wholesale meanings but also the Charybdis of the sciences with their nature laws and regularities. What then enters the historian's field of vision is a conglomerate of

> "particular events, developments, and situations of the human past"–successive and/or coexistent phenomena which altogether make up historical reality. In the light of mundane reasoning this universe shows the following (minimum) characteristics: It is full of intrinsic contingencies which obstruct its calculabiity, its subsumption under the deterministic principle. . . . In addition, historical reality is virtually endless, issuing from a dark past which is increasingly receding and extending into an open-ended future. And finally, it is indetermiminate as to meaning. Its characteristics conform to the materials of which it is woven (45).

The historian deals with the world of everday life, "the very world which Husserl was the first to endow with philosophical dignity." Kracauer was not aware here of the core problem of Husserl's philosophical phenomenology, that is, the ideal type character and hence the solipsism of his concept of what he called "*Lebenswelt*" (life-world).[53] He used the term loosely–as it has been used in intellectual discourse ever since Husserl introduced it. However, the important aspect of his argument for our context is that he qualifies the usefulness for historiography of Husserl's notion of the relation between the sciences and "*Lebenswelt*":

> The sciences, says he, idealize the experiences we make in that common intersubjective world; they "hover, as if in empty space, above the *Lebenswelt*."[54] But actually history differs from the natural sciences in that it hovers there in a much lower altitude than they, for it directly deals with the kind of life which falls into the orbit of everyday experience. To think of this life as a continuous process would be rather venturesome.

There are discernible "patterns, strands and sequences." But they "thread a material which is for long stretches inchoate, heterogeneous, obscure. Much of it is an opaque mass of facts." The historian's challenge is to "chart a course through these expanses," to plan and map her journey in time and space, both guided by an idea and willing to have her hunches contradicted by the evidence so that her "spontaneity" can be "constantly alternating with receptivity." And then the description of the historian's composite perspective, which clearly echoed the photographer's: "One might also say that the historian follows two tendencies–the realistic tendency which prompts him to get hold of all data of interest, and the formative tendency which requires him to explain the material in hand. He is both passive and active, a recorder and creator" (46f.).

Admitting certain similarities between the scientist's and the historian's attitudes, Kracauer insisted on qualitative differences concerning their fields of inquiry:

> Remember that, unlike the scientist's nature world, historical reality, this mixture of natural events and relatively free decisions resists a breakdown into repeatable elements which relate to one another in definitely fixable ways. Nor is the whole of it amenable to (longitudinal) laws. This constitution of the historical universe–which has more in common with the *Lebenswelt* than with the reduced nature of the scientist's making–poses problems not found outside it. (48)

They are the problems of differently shaped objectivities.

The beginnings of modern historiography, which Kracauer explicitly linked with the birth of photography, do not signify scientism. The "significant analogies between history and the two media which portray the world around us with the aid of the camera" were meant to support the "realistic tendency" in historiography which was gradually asserting itself against histories centered in philosophical, political, and moral schematizations rather than recorded (available) facts. Kracauer professed to be intrigued by the chronological vicinity of Ranke's "famous statement that he himself only wants to show *wie es eigentlich gewesen*" and the invention of photography. Because this interest in how things had actually been, what had actually happened, pointed to the empiricist, antisystemic tendencies of modern historiography: "In the dimension of the representative arts, Daguerre's invention raised issues and demands similar to those which played so large a role in contemporary historiography" (49). The issue here was not the possible methodological naïveté of Ranke's statement but rather the great historian's modern eagerness to look at the historical world around us. Probing their sources, he tried to gather historical facts insofar as they were still accessible. The emphasis is on the historian's responsibility to the actuality of what had been, *wie es gewesen*, regardless of the difficulties she encounters in her attempts to meet it.

Ranke's notorious *eigentlich* can be translated by either *actually* or *really*; instructively, Kracauer chose *actually*. In *The Shapes of Time*, Peter Munz argues the importance of a distinct separation between the two meanings of *eigentlich* for attempts to distinguish between explanation and interpretation, an undertaking riddled with difficulties. His ingenious but troubled reasoning here does not so much separate modes of knowledge as provide a useful comment on their inevitable entanglement in historical understanding. If, for instance, we take note of the fact that medieval people believed in a causal connection ("law") between relics and the rise of dynasties, and if we then "stretch our imagination far enough to understand why and how they could have persuaded themselves of something so improbable, we have found out what *actually* happened." Munz relates this kind of knowledge to Collingwood's concept of "reenactment" and equates it with explanation.[55] If, however, we want to find out what *really* happened, we must come up with connections between events governed by laws that *we* believe in. In this case we would have to find "supplements to," or "substitutes for," the medieval belief in the power of relics to ensure the rise of dynasties, for instance the connection between the power of (any) belief and political action.

Munz locates the "real problem of hermeneutics" not in the area of *actually* but rather in that of *really*; for him, the hermeneutic problem concerns the question "which substitutions are licit, desirable, and helpful and which are not. . . . The need for hermeneutics, therefore, comes from the differences in standards of the truth of general laws, not from difficulties in comprehension."[56] The historian's difficulties are indeed caused by different acculturation–hence her need to be mobile in a variety of directions and dimensions. But contrary to Munz's assumption, this difference or distance has proved to be a considerable obstacle also in the area of *actually*: how to gain and articulate any kind of critically sharable access to other people's laws when these laws do not make (much) sense to the differently acculturated observer. Arguably, it is the realm of *actually* rather than *really* that signifies the cultural achievement of modern history as an open-ended, ongoing, self-correcting process, and it is very much a hermeneutic problem. If, in her confrontation with past cultures, the time-traveling historian becomes more aware of her own acculturation and of the need to negotiate it, she also becomes aware of the temporality and relativity of the general laws characteristic of her culture. In actuality, there is no *really* for the historian; the realm of *actually* is thorny enough.

5

When Kracauer enlisted Heinrich Heine's help to bring into clear focus the midnineteenth-century ideal of *wie es eigentlich gewesen*, he had chosen a good ally. Most scrupulous in his concern with the intellectual's contemporaneity, Heine was highly adept at pinning down the ever-elusive *Zeitgeist*. Kracauer aptly quoted from Heine's dedication of his

Lutezia (1854) to Prince Pückler-Muskau, in which he described the purpose of his critical journalism directed at politics as well as the sciences, the arts, popular culture, and politics. It was, he wrote, an attempt

> to give the genuine picture of the time itself in its smallest nuances. An honest daguerreotype must render faithfully a fly as much as the proudest horse, and this is what my reports are: a daguerreotypic history book in which each day entered its own picture and the artist's ordering mind, by assembling such pictures, produced a work in which that which is depicted documents its faithfulness authentically. But in any case, my book . . . may serve the later historian as a historical source which, as I said, carries in itself surety for its daily truth. (49)

Heine emphasized so strongly the authenticity of photographic records in order to highlight his attempts at writing contemporary history as a reliable witness; and in this he was entirely *zeitgemäss*, of his time. A century later such direct equation of the purely and totally objective camera image with historiographical objectivity was suspect. (Note, however, that Heine had also mentioned the photographer's "ordering mind.") In historiography, concepts of attainable objectivity had become more realistic; but not, evidently, notions of what the camera could and would do. There had been misunderstandings from the beginning, and they had to do, as Kracauer pointed out fairly, with the properties of the medium which triggered the inevitable comparison with the traditional arts and with historical inquiry: "photography resembles the diverse branches of knowledge in that it calls certain properties its own which tend to condition work within its confines. As far back as the archaic days of the medium, discerning critics diagnosed them by marvelling at the camera's exceptional ability to record as well as reveal visible, or potentially visible, physical reality." Understandably, then, photography was seen above all as a marvelously accurate and complete reproduction technique. "Naïve" or "scientific-minded" nineteenth-century realists, as Kracauer called them, among them in this respect Heine, agreed that photography recorded nature "with a fidelity 'equal to nature itself.'" They adored the detailed clarity and precision of photographic images, which, "to paraphrase Ranke's dictum, seemed to them to show how things actually are" (50f.).

The attribute "naïve" does not contradict Kracauer's empathy with the midnineteenth-century excitement over photographic recovery of "things as they actually are." Rather, his critique is directed against later views of photographic images as showing "nothing but what actually was"–views that tend to emphasize the dehumanizing aspects of recorded chronological time. Proust is called up again: his negative contrast between significant "involuntary, completely subjective memories" and mere "external and objective memories deposited in photographic statements;" and his notion of the ideal photographer as an "indiscriminating mirror, the counterpart of the camera lens" (51). There is a more suggestive, complex version of this contrast in a text by V. S. Naipaul that makes me wonder how Kracauer would have responded to it. Reflecting on his experience of cultural distances, Naipaul describes his looking at rather blurred photographs taken years ago of the place (in England) where he lives now and with which he tries to become more familiar. Instructively, he brackets his remarks on the effect on him of these images in order to indicate his awareness of their self-indulgent, private subjectivity: "(Photographs–snapshots–melancholy in their effect: each snapshot, capturing a moment of time, with all its unconsidered details, forcing one to think of the tract of time that had followed, and being a kind of memento mori, in the way a good painting of the same occasion–charged with the spirit and labour of the painter–would never have been.)"[57] The contrast is explicitly between the randomness of the sloppily taken snapshot and the deliberateness of the good painting. Moreover, as the reader knows from the context, the viewer's response of melancholy and his invocation of the painter's orienting presence is linked to photo images only conditionally: in this place, where he still feels lost; at this time, when he is trying to gain some measure of control.

The emphasis is on the viewer's perception as directed by the image and on the kind of knowledge produced in this process. Snapshots by themselves do not pretend to discernible direction, or sustained knowledge, unless they are judged by the viewer (who can also be the selecting photographer) to be a particularly "good" or "true" picture of the pictured. When Kracauer criticized the frequently skeptical attitude of practising historians toward the contribution of photography, he tended to simplify their concerns regarding the historian's perception. In his account of Droysen's position, for instance, historical narrative "is not intended to 'photograph' past events but aims at conveying our conceptions of them from this or that point of view." But this puts a different emphasis on what Droysen actually said: "Historical narrative does not wish to give a picture, a photograph of what once was, even less to be a collection of items and notes, but our perception of significant events, from this position, from this point of view."[58] It is true, Droysen used the negative reference to photography in order to emphasize meaningful selectiveness in historical perspective. However, he also separated the photo image from mere (random) "collection" of data. The passage is about the positionality of the historian's perception, the peculiar temporal modifications, enriching and limiting, of his perspective. If anything, Droysen's argument here is centered on language rather than image.

In the case of Lewis B. Namier, Kracauer pointed out his distinction between the photographer and the painter and his comparison of the historian to the painter. The historian's aim is defined as "to discover and set forth, to single out and stress that which is of the nature of the thing, and not to reproduce indiscriminately all that meets the eye."[59] But if Namier, like Droysen, refers to photography when arguing against the reductionist notion of the historian as impassively recording instrument, Kracauer overemphasizes their use of attributes that echo reductionist definitions of photography. Especially in Droysen's case, he does not seriously consider the complexities of the issue.

Droysen's concept of historical narration as mimesis of the past in the process of becoming, his distinction between "the laws of objective History" and the "laws of historical investigation and knowledge," and his emphasis on the latter[60] show him to be keenly interested in the problems of historiographical representation. Not only for a midnineteenth-century historian, Droysen was "remarkably sensitive to the possibility of past historical facts being recounted, explained and interpreted in vastly different ways."[61] Defending a broader, more flexible concept of historiographical objectivity, he did not yet see the possible analogies to the then brand new medium of photography. Kracauer's view of Droysen as a "contemporary of the primitive 19th-century realists" (51), is curiously unfair—so much so, in fact, that one is tempted to read into it a deeper disappointment. Droysen's perceptive and eloquent defense, against Ranke's "artistic" historiography, of the open, indefinite beginnings and endings of historical narrative that would accommodate the past in flux might have seemed to echo for Kracauer some of the most suggestive, most promising properties of the photo image.[62] But the midnineteenth-century historian's sophistication in the matter of historical perspective could not reasonably be expected to extend to such a new medium. After all, Kracauer had had a century of photography to learn from.

Kracauer's disappointment seems more justified in the case of Namier and other twentieth-century historians "who should have known better" than to simply see the camera as a mirror of nature (51f.). Had they been better informed about the medium, they would have known that the notion of objectivity which they imposed on photography was profoundly unrealistic:

> Even Proust's ideal photographer is bound to transfer three-dimensional phenomena to the plane and sever their ties with the surroundings. More important, he cannot help structuring the inflowing impressions; the simultaneous perceptions of his other senses, certain perceptual form categories inherent in his nervous system, and not least his general disposition, compel him to organize the visual raw material in the act of seeing. This being so, there is no earthly reason why the photographer should suppress his formative urges in the interest of the necessarily futile attempt to achieve objectivity–that Simon-pure objectivity so coveted by Taine that he wanted "to reproduce the objects as they . . . would be even if I did not exist." In any case, all great photographers have felt free to select motif, frame, lens, filter, emulsion, and grain according to their sensibilities. (Was it otherwise with Ranke? His vision of universal history, for instance, did not seem to encroach on his desire to show things as they were. Perhaps it is possible to say of him that his formative strivings joined forces with his realistic designs.) The upshot is that photographs true to type may range from neutral renderings of physical reality to highly subjective statements. (52)

Instructively, Kracauer touches here on the significance of the various technical practices involved in the production (and in the viewer's analysis) of photo images. If Namier was not sufficiently conversant with the different kinds of photographic attitudes and styles, H.-I. Marrou was: "He draws attention to the prints of men like Nadar and Cartier-Bresson; and he judiciously argues that, thanks to the intervention of authentic photographers in the mechanical processes involved, their pictures have something personal about them and are profoundly informed" (52f.).

Looking at its practitioners, Kracauer concludes that photography as well as photographic film often has not differed from the established arts:

photography that uses "Rembrandt lighting," films that show similar "longings for emancipation from the outer world," avant-garde film artists of the twenties who "freely invented shapes instead of recording and discovering them, and made real-life shots illustrate contents and meanings which were anything but an implication of what the visuals actually showed" (53). The same forceful drive to construct is found in historiographical practices–a predictable situation "since history coincides with the camera crafts in challenging its adepts to capture a given universe. The challenge is strict enough to rouse the urge for discounting it."[63] In other words, the drive to impose structure has its source in a strongly felt need to react to the overwhelming presence of the visible world, contemporary and past: to orient oneself by making choices, to find one's way, to map the territory. Photography, in the words of John Szarkowski, is a "system of visual editing. At bottom, it is a matter of surrounding with a frame a portion of one's cone of vision, while standing in the right place at the right time. Like chess, or writing, it is a matter of choosing from among given possibilities, but in the case of photography the number of possibilities is not finite but infinite."[64]

This situation accounts for the anteroom status of both photography and historiography and calls for what Kracauer described in *Theory of Film* as the "basic aesthetic principle" of the photo image. Reminding the reader of this principle at this stage of his argument in *History*, he strings together a number of relevant self-quotes: the photographer comes into his own only if he goes to the limits of his medium, whose essence is "recording and penetrating physical reality." "Owing to the camera's revealing power," he resembles more "the imaginative reader bent on studying and deciphering an elusive text" than the "expressive artist." His "intensity of vision" ought to be rooted in a "real respect for the thing in front of him."[65] The photographer's traits, then, are those of "an explorer who, filled with curiosity, roams yet unconquered spaces." And it is only in submitting herself to these new spaces–at first unimaginable because they are inhabited and shaped by the lives of others–that the she can "keep intact and make transparent" both herself in the act of exercising her craft and those never completely yielding "real-life phenomena." And finally: "If photography is an art, it is art with a difference: unlike the traditional arts, it takes pride in not completely consuming its raw material" (54f.).

This is the most active version of that by now familiar distinction–"takes pride"–enlarged to make more room for the comparative meanings of the photographer's and the historian's role. Again, Ranke is brought in as a witness and interpreted in a manner that suggests Kracauer's own "historical approach":

> "The writing of history cannot be expected to possess the same free development of its subject which, in theory at least, is expected in a work of literature." (Somewhat vague as Ranke's theoretical observations usually are, they have the advantage of resulting not from pottering about with a set of abstractions but from his undiluted experience as a practising historian.) What he wants to convey is this: It is the historian's business adequately to render, and account for, human affairs of the past. (55)

"Adequately" means "the 'right' balance between the formative and 'material' (realistic) tendencies," construction and reconstruction, presentation and representation; but note that Kracauer brackets the word *right*. This balance which *is* "the 'historical approach'" can only be achieved "if the historian's spontaneous intuition does not interfere with his loyalty to the evidence but, conversely, benefits his emphatic absorption in it" (56). Kracauer hastens to point out that the "formula: Realistic Tendency ≥ Formative Tendency" covers a "diversity of cases" in both historiography and photography. If one arranges them along a continuum, one pole is occupied by a deliberately objective approach: "faithful," "fact-oriented," "impersonal," "straight," "artless" are the attributes Kracauer assigns to representations of events, acts, actors, and situations that show "only the the slightest possible interference of subjective preferences and formative designs." He thinks statements of this kind useful but limited in that they meet the "minimum requirement of their respective media," that is, reproductive accounting.

But all the attributes listed here are "loaded." Take for instance "impersonal." Erich Salomon's photos collected in his highly successful *Berühmte Zeitgenossen in unbewachten Augenblicken* (1931) were often praised for reflecting this quality. In his introduction to the collection, *Portrait of an Age* (1975), Peter Hunter-Salomon, wishing to sum up his father's achievement, quotes the testimony of Norman Hall, publisher of the British photo magazine *Photography*: "Salomon and Cartier-Bresson perceive human life and portray it impartially and almost impersonally. Their cameras see and report everything; they are unprejudiced and incorruptible."[66] Salomon's photos are unstaged–hence their description "candid camera," coined by the London *Graphic* in 1929–but they are not therefore impersonal or impartial, spontaneous, unprejudiced, or incorruptible. This is how Salomon liked the viewer to perceive the images. His notorious inventiveness and cunning in taking photos where he was not supposed to resulted in historically informative images, but their meanings were also controlled, indeed prejudiced, by Salomon's rapid (snap) decisions. Pithy descriptions of his approach abounded during the Weimar period: "Houdini of photography," "master of indiscretion," the "invisible cameraman," all of them stressing the disappearance of the man behind the photo. Salomon, who invented for himself the neutral term "*Bildjournalist*," much preferred the designation "historian with a camera." "Dr. Erich Candid Camera Salomon" would not have been allowed in the White House to photograph a meeting between President Hoover and European leaders in late 1931 if Premier Laval of France had not insisted on his presence. Like Mussolini, Ramsay MacDonald, and Chancellor Brüning, Laval had become convinced that Salomon's "spontaneous snapshots" were important historic documents–a view held by Salomon himself.[67] He was indeed an inventive, imaginative, and highly resourceful recorder of contemporary history, and by no means impersonal or unprejudiced, he shared all the historian's difficulties with spontaneity, fairness, and objectivity (fig. 23).

Importantly, the other pole in Kracauer's scenario is occupied not by deliberately subjective approaches but "by readings in which spontaneity and receptivity seem to be in a state of equilibrium, interpretation so perfectly matching the pertinent data that it neither overwhelms them nor leaves an undigested remainder" (56f.). The significance of this arrangement is clearer when we consider the two examples given: an Alfred Stieglitz photo of a "group of huddled trees" in which the viewer (Kracauer) finds "really existing trees and at the same time a memorable image–or should I say allegory?–of autumnal sadness," and the parallel in historiography, Panofsky's "principle of disjunction" with respect to form and theme in art works of the high and late Middle Ages.[68] Panofsky, so the implication, constructs a satisfying, elegant historiographical formula or principle for a certain stage in the development of Western art. Trying to fit the formula to the findings of detailed "straight" research, he puts before the reader also the known exceptions.[69]

Precariousness is in the nature of such equilibrium–as Kracauer admits, referring to László Moholy-Nagy's famous photograph "From the Berlin Wireless Tower": at first sight such images appear to be "nonobjective compositions, while on closer inspection they reveal themselves as renderings of natural objects from an unconventional camera angle. A light shift of emphasis in the same direction and the 'right' balance between reproduction and construction is upset. We enter the region where the historian's formative impulses get the better of his realistic intentions" (57). The dilemma is, as he emphasizes repeatedly, the historian's rather than history's, the photographer's rather than photography's. Though he does not explicitly separate the two questions–and, indeed, they cannot be separated–Kracauer's emphasis here is important: his concern is not the question of historical evidence as a given entity to be found but rather the question of the historian's loyalty to the task of finding it. How does she go about seeking it out? How does she test it and trust it? The availability and accessibility of evidence are achieved (made possible) processually, and these processes are inevitably guided by the observer's (historian's) perception. Both the photographer and the historian, Kracauer points out, look at the life-world and see

> inanimate objects, faces, crowds, people who intermingle, suffer, and hope; its grand theme is life in its fullness, life as we commonly experience it. Small wonder that camera-reality parallels historical reality in terms of its structure, its general constitution. Exactly as historical reality, it is partly patterned, partly amorphous–a consequence, in both cases, of the half-cooked state of our everyday world. (58)

The spatial-temporal, "half-cooked" life-world of contingencies and indeterminacies, then, is most fully represented in the "mixed" mode of historiography and photography. But if it is true that photographic and historiographical discourse call for a more consistent posing of the question of perception, this question also has become an increasingly difficult issue because the modern historian's vision is inevitably guided by the cultural reality of accumulated historical information. The field of history, as Kracauer pointed out rightly, is cluttered with "inherited habits of thought and themes of long standing which altogether render it nearly impenetrable"

(60). (Had he lived to see the emergence in Western culture of minority and women's histories, he would have pointed out their all too often mutually exclusive "theoretical" claims to validity that reflect so clearly the inherited habits of Eurocratic history.) The field of historiography is cluttered, too, with the inherited and developing intertextual dependencies of verbal representation, which often obscure rather than clarify the presences they wish to know and to make known. On the other hand, the modern photographer's vision is cluttered with photo images, which are notoriously omnipresent and controlling in late modernity. Kracauer examined this situation in essays in the twenties,[70] and it has become immeasurably more entangled. He knew already then that analyzing interdependencies of such magnitude makes sense only if gradations, hesitations, lacunae can be accommodated. How, given these reservations, can the analogy between two "impenetrable" activities be expected to produce useful knowledge? Photo images, Kracauer pointed out, speak directly to the sense of vision: "the photographer's universe is, in a way, more readily accessible."

> Not to mention that the analogy with photography helps defamiliarize habitual aspects in the historical field, the odds are that our understanding of certain issues with which the historian is grappling will greatly profit by recourse to corresponding issues in the photographic crafts. Here implications and solutions hidden from view in the historical dimension stand a fair chance of becoming visible at once. (61)

The sense of vision central to the Western tradition of knowledge, and therefore currently under some suspicion, still makes good use of the advantage of distancing and negotiating distances: plurality, relation, and orientation. Kracauer's comparison between photography and historiography draws attention to different ways of making knowledge possible, and he emphasizes certain advantages the image has in this respect over the sentence. There is, after all, the literally visual root of the term *evidence*, the Latin *videre*. The late eighteenth-century explorer and travel writer Georg Forster, remarkably troubled by the question of objectivity in observation and documentation, became interested in the self-deceptions that shaped representations of an event or *Eräugnis* (*Ereignis*) as evidence. He preferred the regional spelling because it stresses the etymological connection between event, occurrence, and perception: Old High German *(ir)ougen*, "vor Augen stellen" (to put before the eyes), Middle High German *eröugen, eröugnen.* The English term *event,* developed from Latin *evenire,* "to come out" (so that it can be seen), also suggests the link with perception. Such emphasis on the visual is important to Kracauer because it implies the primacy of presence (the pictured) in the *poesis* of representation (the picture), the authority of the world "out there" in the process of constructing it as evidence.

6 Susan Sontag's essays on photography during the 1970s were contemporary to the renaissance of (a high-cultural) interest in photography. With a Proust-derived Benjaminian sensibility, she saw photography mainly in its deadening, flattening, alienating instrumentality, which would inevitably impoverish a remembered reality. The renewed appetite for photography suggested to her the desire to dismiss the "mental exertions" demanded by abstract art.[71] Generically, then, photography is, or at least is threatened by, mere consumption of reality; and reality, in her scenario, can only be redeemed by high art. I am offering here a simplified version of Sontag's ingenious, openly self-contradictory argumentation in order to clarify Kracauer's perspective. In contrast to her critical concentration on the problems of photographic–the photographer's–seeing, his position is clearly viewer oriented: it explicitly includes multiple acts of viewing and thus emphasizes an, as it were, potential collective enrichment of modern visual experience. He is not interested, as Sontag is, in individual photographers' claims of what *their* photography does for the enlargement of *their* vision. She quotes Weston on photography as "a way of self-development, a means to discover and identify oneself with all the manifestations of basic forms–with nature, the source" and comments: "contrary to what Weston asserts, the habit of photographic seeing–of looking at reality as an array of potential photographs–creates estrangement from, rather than union with, nature" (97). However, Weston was not speaking about an existential union with nature but the photographer's fascination with natural *forms* whose particularity he sought to elucidate by *photographic* identification. Uninterested in the particularities of photographic practice, Sontag defines all photographic seeing as "mainly the practice of a kind of dissociative seeing, a subjective habit which is reinforced by the objective discrepancies between the way that the camera and the human eye focus and judge perspective" (97). This subjective habit then accounts for "one of the perennial successes

of photography," that is, "its strategy of turning living beings into things, things into living beings." She disapproves—as her examples clearly indicate: she thinks suspect the fact that Weston's peppers, alluringly suggestive of female bodies, are much more voluptuous than his pearly, delicately abstracted nudes (98; figs. 22, 23).

In his concern for the recording, preserving properties of photography, Kracauer was not concerned with a hierarchy of "things" and "living beings." Like Adams,[72] he thought problematic Weston's vegetable series because it exhibited too strongly an impulse toward abstraction. But he very much agreed with Weston's exploration of the camera's capacity to register and thereby make accessible the most delicate, the most various, the extraordinary visual details of familiar objects.[73] This capacity, he believed, could only enlarge and enrich, with the viewer's concrete experience of a world present or past, her visual (historical) imagination.

Sontag sees the main difference between painting and photography as lying in the fact that "paintings invariably sum up: photographs usually do not. Photographic images are pieces of evidence in an ongoing biography or history. And one photograph, unlike one painting, implies that there will be others" (166). Surely, this depends on the photographer, the painter, the sitter, the viewer. The most glaring omission here is the enduring presence of the painter in the painted portrait, especially in modernist painting, from which Sontag exclusively draws her notion of art. "Great portraits," as Wright Morris rightly points out, "may well sum up the painter, but they seldom sum up the sitter. What photographs usually do, more than anything else, is authenticate personal appearance and existence. Authentication, not enlargement or interpretation, is what we want."[74] This, arguably, is what we want from historiography as well—no matter how much we appreciate the individual historian's talent for interpreting and enlarging, for writing good historiography that is also "good literature."

In their interpretations, painter-portraitists differ from photographers in kind of authentication. Sontag, too, thinks that as observers we "crave" reality, but such craving carries connotations that differ distinctly from Morris's (and Kracauer's) affirmation of the authentication achieved by the photo image. Morris includes himself when he notes that we would adore having photographs of figures like Achilles, or Helen of Troy, or Attila the Hun, because the photo likeness, like the sitter, is a "piece of nature" (65). Its authenticating properties render it more independent of the photographer as viewer and, precisely for this reason, more accessible to plural and different acts of viewing. Sontag, in contrast, points out that for most people–herself excluded–a photograph of Shakespeare would be more desirable than his portrait painted by the most gifted painter of his day because "having a photograph of Shakespeare would be like having a nail from the True Cross" (154). It would be reification of the most rigid and vulgar sort: living beings are turned into things, things into living beings.

For Morris (and Kracauer), the overwhelming attraction of the photographic image is its "realness," which is in most cases so much more like what our eyes see and therefore so much more immediate and sharable. He points out the centrality for us of "representative objects"–for our use in so many different ways and on so many different levels–which therefore "are the source of our needs and affections."[75] This is most palpably true for the human face. Morris wishes to explore the imaginational energies alive in the peculiarly unmediated photo representation of that obvious and elusive, life-enhancing, time-defying sharedness of "our needs and affections." Sontag, however, thinks it most important to focus on the simultaneously narcissistic and depersonalizing properties of the medium (167). Since a photo image can never "transcend the visual itself, which is in some sense the ultimate aim of modernist painting," it is in bondage to reality. As long as it cannot be transcended, reality, in Sontag's scenario, inexorably imprisons, deadens the imagination; and it obliterates the spaces of memory. She does not, then, allow for photography to bear witness to real (political) events, over time and for different viewers: "And it is never photographic evidence which can . . . identify events; the contribution of photography always follows the naming of the event. What determines the possibility of being affected morally by photographs is the existence of a relevant political consciousness. Without a politics, photographs of the slaughterbench of history will most likely be experienced as, simply, unreal or as a demoralizing emotional blow."[76] This extreme rigidity regarding the hermeneutic circle says little about the knowledge potential of photo images but much about Sontag's doctrinal devaluation of others' acts of viewing.

Like Benjamin's,[77] Sontag's desire to have the "thing-in-itself" magically revealed beyond the visual resists exploration of the peculiar properties of photo images. And it denies the intimacy, both troubling and intriguing, between the challenges of authentication and interpretation. This intimacy encases the tension between the picture and the pictured that shapes photographic perspective. Seemingly inexhaustible, the modalities of reality originate also in the photographer's vision. There are those happy cases in portrait photography where the photographer's visual imagination, technical skill, and psychological thoughtfulness produce an image that "sums up" the subject effectively with minimal imposition of a specific photographical style. Gaspard Félix Nadar's photo portraiture provides good early examples (figs. 1, 2), among them the portrait of Jacques Offenbach. But from its beginning, photographic portraiture has also shown itself fragmented and diffused, as in the self-consciously composed photo likenesses produced by the commercially successful André Adolphe Eugène Disdéri.[78] Disdéri's portrait photos with their emphasis on pose and props are *kitsch* in that they so clearly, distortingly stress the type rather than the individual.

In all their diversity, the photographers' visions have to be accessible to the viewer's vision. (On a not so trivial level, the hypothetical photo images of Shakespeare or Attila would have to be sufficiently preserved to represent a recognizably human face.) The analogy between photography and historiography also touches on the relation of the viewer to the pictured when she judges visual representation, and the relation of the historically informed reader to the subject matter when he judges historical evidence. Kracauer's favorite metaphor for the ideal photographer as driven by "insatiable curiosity" to immerse herself in the "book of nature"[79] conjures up the image of himself, familiar to his friends, buried in piles of research material. When in the notes for *History* he described the historian as an "insatiable reader and curious explorer,"[80] the reference is of course literal though he quoted himself from *Theory of Film*, where he had used the phrase in a figurative sense. But the analogy between photography and historiography was established and greatly elaborated explicitly for the sake of the latter. How, then, did he use it where the conditions of historical knowledge, that is, of judging historical evidence, are at issue, when he has to deal with the revolving door of the hermeneutic circle: historical reality is created by historical evidence, which, in turn, is judged by the standards by which historical reality has been judged in the process of being established (reconstructed)?

Kracauer responded by pointing out the variable modalities of historical reality dependent on different judgments contributed by different historians with different views on (the modalities of) historical reality. He did not just acknowledge the hermeneutic circle as methodologically inevitable–what the art historian Panofsky has described as the "circulus methodicus:"

> The individual observation assumes the character of a "fact" only when it can be related to other, analogous observations in such a way that the whole series "makes sense." This "sense" is, therefore, fully capable of being applied, as a control, to the interpretation of a new individual observation within the same range of phenomena. If, however, this new individual observation definitely refuses to be interpreted according to the "sense" of the series, and if an error proves to be impossible, the "sense" of the series will have to be reformulated to include the new individual observation. This *circulus methodicus* applies, of course, not only to the relationship between the interpretation of motifs and the history of style, but also to the relationship between the interpretation of images, stories and allegories and the history of types, and to the relationship between the interpretation of intrinsic meanings and the history of cultural symptoms in general.[81]

This briskly sensible account of the formation of historical knowledge leaves unexplored the historicity of acts of observation, and thus the *circulus methodicus* moves on with fictitiously frictionless ease. (Note also the quotation marks surrounding the crucial term *sense.*) Kracauer, in contrast, emphasizes and explores the historicity of observation with respect to both the acts of observation and the response to them by a critical community of observers. This historicity of understanding, the cause for the knowledge status of historical inquiry as "intermediary area" (16) or "anteroom" (191), could be elucidated by analogies to the knowledge status of photo images. In Kracauer's view, the (pure) science and (pure) literature positions in historiography are indeed related, and they obscure rather than clarify the problem of historical knowledge.[82] His response to the issue of circularity was to focus on a special epistemological (and then also cultural) status of historiography. He was helped in this by the analogies to photography because he could use them as a kind of explanatory shortcut through the complicated intertextual entanglements that are inherent to historiography as narration of historical experience and knowledge and that exacerbate circularity.

In some of the more recent literature on historiography we find attempts to deal with that problem by borrowing from the natural sciences a covering-law model (CLM). As Peter Munz points out rightly in *The Shapes of Time*, the "generality of laws used by the historical sciences is strictly limited to a certain period. In other words, many of the general laws used are of limited universality,"[83] for instance the medieval linkage of the presence of saints' relics with the rise of dynasties or the belief in satanic possession–examples we drew on above. It is precisely in that limited universality that the historian can find a "practical" (if not in a strict sense "logical") solution to circularity. Unlike the scientist's, his position as inquirer is defined by historicity. There is, then, "no obligation on the historian to confine himself to those general laws he himself would employ. On the contrary: general laws are ready made for him and he need therefore not become involved in the hopeless tangle of the circular problem. . . . The historian as historian is not really concerned with the truth of these general laws. All he wants to know is whether people believed them to be true" (52).

Up to a point, Munz's distinction is useful. However, establishing the organizational function of general laws for the historian, he does not give consideration to a crucial problem I touched on in the preceding section, namely the time-traveling historian's attempts at negotiating her own acculturation. In his scenario, the "limited universality" of general laws seems to apply only to past, not to present, conventions. But how, settled so securely in her own culture, could the historian make historical sense of cultural arrangements directed by general laws no longer valid for herself? Munz's notion of a "limited universality" of general laws in historical inquiry might at first seem to echo Kracauer's notion of history as an epistemological "anteroom"–a field of inquiry where knowledge in the sense of objectivity is understood to be composite and fluid. If truth is equated with being in full possession of, trusting fully, the evidence, it is excluded from this "anteroom." But Munz seems to see no problems with the historian's access to truth. His lack of suspicion in this regard is linked to his overly clean separation between the "art" and "science" components of historiography, which happily coexist without getting in each other's way. Both assumptions sharply distinguish his position from Kracauer's.

It is not enough to have the information that at a certain time a certain group of people held certain beliefs, because this information does not equal knowledge of these beliefs.[84] Making such knowledge possible would require having access to these beliefs in terms of their cultural status and value. And this would require knowing what it *felt like* in that culture to have and live by specific beliefs. There are different degrees of difficulty for making knowledge possible in different cases of belief. In any case, and most importantly (and commonly), the modern secular historian has to enter cultures of believers–an undertaking fraught with obstacles and perhaps "really impossible."[85]

Granting the historical individuality of human events, Munz does not deal with the enormous temporal, that is, cultural, distances traversed by the historian who, he thinks, can still "assume that no matter how unique these events were, the human beings involved in them tried to understand them even as the modern historian does. And therefore we can assume that some kind of explanation of these events is to be found at the very source of these events."[86] Surely, this is true only in some cases. In many other cases no explanation offers itself, unless there is a great deal of interpretation. Munz's distinction between the historian who still shares the general laws accepted by the people he studies and therefore gives "historical explanations" and the historian who uses general laws not yet known to the subjects of her inquiry and therefore interprets (70) oversimplifies and thereby distorts the situation. In the first case, too, interpretation, and with it circularity, can never be completely avoided, as even those general laws still shared by the observer and the observed are shared only in part. Taking into consideration the passage of time, the slower or faster flow of many interconnected and interdependent changes, all historical explanation is to some degree shaped by the hermeneutic circle; it is interpretive. Curiously, Munz's concept of the shapes of time seems rather atemporal. For this reason, too, he does not consider the extraordinarily and increasingly difficult problem of intertextuality: the writing of history as representation of past reality by means of evidence established in processes of corroboration on the basis of previous inquirers' writings, who constructed their documentation with the help of earlier texts, and so on–a truly awesome entanglement of circularities, if we stop to think about it.

Kracauer was very much impressed by the uneven rhythms of the *circu-*

lus methodicus, which make for the hesitations, detours, and lacunae in the process of historical inquiry. They are the cause of many errors, and they circumscribe the "anteroom" status of historical understanding. Based on many acts of observation, judgments as to what makes possible or enables knowledge of historical reality by means of articulating and agreeing on historical evidence can only be selective, fragmentary, and provisional. If these judgments make sense to a community of (professional) readers, such sense cannot be fully determined or analyzed. As in the case of photographic likenesses, making sense depends on a shared recognition, stretched over time and cultural spaces, in which the activities of explanation and interpretation are closely intertwined. Explanation is shaped by interpretation, and both are guided by acculturation. Like the photographer, the historian can never be a "camera that does not lie," a mere, therefore "true," recorder, because the compositeness of her perspective worries the stability of "her" facts. The instability of historical judgment is rooted in the composite historicity of the life-world, which is different for the observer and the observed, causing the openness of all historical information to further interpretation.

7

The instability of historical judgment, the processual, composite, corroborative nature of historical evidence, makes nonsense of an ideally complete collection of historical facts. And here we come back to Kracauer's argument in chapter 5, "The Structure of the Historical Universe" (and eventually to the question of a hidden "theological" dimension in his understanding of history).[87] For a "paradigmatic instance of micro histories" Kracauer returned to Panofsky's "principle of disjunction," which he used in chapter 2 when describing the "'right' balance between reproduction and construction" (57). As he had done in that context, he enlisted in chapter 5 the analogy to photo images. An example of "interpretative small-scale histories," Panofsky's analysis of the uses that Western art made during certain periods of the "models" provided them by art from earlier times could be called a "close-up." Because this analysis resembled "film shots of this name which isolate and magnify some visual detail–a face, a hand, a piece of furniture–to familiarize us with its particular physiognomy" (105f.).

The choice of term here is important: *physiognomy* is a term used by Panofsky in the attempt to describe the coherent specificity of periods in art history. Kracauer explicitly borrowed the term—that is, he drew attention to his using it—in chapter 6, "Ahasverus or the Riddle of Time," which continues the argument presented in chapter 4, "The Historian's Journey" (152). In chapter 5, where he discussed the composite nature of the historical universe and the "'right' balance" of the historian's composite perspective, its presence is highly suggestive in terms of Kracauer's distinctions between different kinds of micro histories. Here is the Panofsky passage in which he found the term:

> a period—and this applies to "megaperiods" as well as to the shorter ones—may be said to possess a "physiognomy" no less definite, though no less difficult to describe in a satisfactory manner, than a human individual. There can be legitimate disagreement as to when a human individual comes into being (at the moment of conception? with the first heartbeat? with the severance of the umbilical cord?); when he comes to an end (with the last breath? with the last pulse? with the cessation of metabolism? with the complete decomposition of the body?); when he begins to be a boy rather than an infant, an adult rather than a boy, an old man rather than an adult; how many of his characteristics he may owe to his father, his mother, his grandparents, or any of his ancestors. Yet, when we meet him at a given moment within a given group, we shall not fail to distinguish him from his companions; to put him down as young or old or middle-aged, tall or short, intelligent or stupid, jovial or saturnine; and ultimately to form an impression of his total and unique personality.[88]

What, then, is the most helpful "historical approach" to a phenomenon as complex and temporally composite as the "physiognomy" of the lived lives of the past? Not, in Kracauer's view, micro history as "technical history" (136), straight, "artless," fact-oriented accounts, "that first yield of the historian's journey into the past." Close-ups, on the other hand, a "direct extension" of such accounts, explore their material "to the full," instead of limiting themselves to "neutral stock-taking." They desire "to supplement, refine, or indeed invalidate notions and explanations which have been unquestioningly accepted by generations of macro historians" (106).

"Interpretive small-scale" histories were very appealing to Kracauer's empiricist temperament. He clearly sympathized with historians like Tolstoy and Lewis B. Namier, who were impressed by "historical reality as an endless continuum of microscopic incidents, actions, and interactions which, through their sheer accumulation, produce the macroscopic upheavals, victories, and disasters featured in the run of textbooks" (107). But how to cope with this viscous mass of facts? Kracauer's example from the visual medium, Fernand Léger's dream of a monster film that would record the "infinitesimal continuum" of the life of a man and woman over a twenty-four-hour period, emphasizes the difficulties encountered by a micro historical account of that kind. No detail in the lives of these two people who are unaware of the camera would be omitted; everything would be open to the viewer, who would be shocked by this "normally hidden whirlpool of crude existence" and would strain to escape from the inexorable rush of images (108).

Because we do not experience the process of living that way. But, then, how do we experience it? or, rather, how can the historian, herself involved in this elusively and inexorably temporal process, gain access to its past actuality? Not, in Kracauer's view, by following Tolstoy's "poor" philosophy of (nineteenth-century) determinism, which drowns the observer in an infinitude of facts, but by considering the fictions he created within and out of this infinitude: the shape of his narrative created by his choices. Even if "Tolstoy's fixation to the mechanistic notions of his time asserts itself" throughout *War and Peace*, "this does not impinge on the truth, embodied by his Kutuzov, that really creative action is inseparable from intensive passive observation." The implication here is that the historical *and* fictional character of the Russian field marshal Mikhail Larionovich Kutuzov could serve as an allegory of the never ideal but sometimes successful historian. He manages to drive Napoleon into retreat because of his "capacity for listening to, and interpreting, the chorus of confused voices from root regions. . . . His sole ambition is to bring to fruition the formless thoughts and desires he finds inscribed in millions of Russian hearts" (110).

The most advantageous route to take for the historian does not end in total immersion in the minutiae of the past but passes through it to choice, judgment, interpretation. The question is how "exactly" that happens. Like Tolstoy's, Namier's judgment was that "collective micro studies" have to supersede "macro historiography" (114). From a position influenced by Marxian materialist debunking of ideational autonomy, Namier showed that Marxian historiography, too, just exchanged one macro conception for another. And, clearly indebted to Freudian uncovering of the "psychological springs" behind political thought and action, in his role of historian he still rejected Freudian orthodoxy. Such a "mixed" position was deeply appealing to Kracauer, who pointed out the unmistakable presence of an "artistic strain" in Namier's work. The historian, in this scenario, belongs to the membership of artistic modernity–"those painters, poets, and musicians" desiring to dissolve, with the help of Marx and Freud, the conventions of perception: "They proceed throughout from the big wholes and overarching compositions of old to, in a way, fragmentary statements which, perhaps, will never again jell into wholes. The (provisional) result is an adjustment of our senses to what remains of the web of used-up conventions once it is undone. (What remains is at least uncontestable)" (112). Clearly, Kracauer saw himself in their company; and the "anteroom" of historical inquiry appears expanded by their tolerance for the fragmentary.[89]

Yet–and here Kracauer's explicit sympathy for the artistic skepticism regarding macro compositions was as important as his stated skepticism regarding an artistically constructing approach in historiography: there *were* historical developments of longer duration, especially in the realm of ideas. Enduring ideational conflicts *were* real; they had "a peculiar substance, an irreducible content. And any historian treating them merely as derivatives of psychological processes misses part of what really happened and made people tick" (115). Thus he found it impossible to deny or sanitize the reality of Weimar intellectual experience: the vivid play of ideas, their seductive pull, explosive conflicts, and, finally, their destructive power.

Not unexpectedly, Kracauer's suggestion to "discerning historians aspiring to history in its fullness" was an "interpenetration of macro and micro history" (121). Many historians have practiced this mixed approach more or less successfully (Kracauer was impressed by Marc Bloch's *Feudal Society*) (124). But it will always be a question of degree. The historian willing to go that way will encounter many and quite difficult adventures en route requiring her to prove herself as a level-headed and imaginative, a sensitive and resilient time-traveler. Significantly, the concrete examples of such mobility and flexibility are taken from *Theory of Film.* Trying to illustrate the composite nature of perspective in negotiating different (temporal) distances, Kracauer quoted Vsevolod Pudovkin's argument that the combined analysis and interpretation of a (in visual terms) large-scale event involved a constant movement between different levels of generality, that is, between the macro and micro dimensions:

> "In order to receive a clear and definite impression of a demonstration, the observer must perform certain actions. First he must climb upon the roof of a house to get a view from above of the procession as a whole and measure its dimension; next he must come down and look out through the first-floor window at the inscriptions carried by the demonstrators; finally he must mingle with the crowd to gain an idea of the outward appearance of the participants."[90]

If Kracauer used cinematic analogies in order to present the historian's need for mobility in the strongest, most literal terms, he used (imaginary) historiographical examples to point out its risks. The historian "must be in a position freely to move between the macro and micro dimensions." But does the structure of the historical universe in fact allow that? Is it sufficiently homogeneous for the historian to negotiate the different levels? "Substance and validity of macro history–its reality character–depend upon unhampered two-way traffic" (122). But the "law of perspective," that is, the increasing importance of perspective with increasing scope of historical inquiry, streamlines, as it were, the evidence. If one imagines three historical narratives working on different levels but all containing a portrait of Luther–a history of the German people, of the Reformation, a biography of Luther–it is clear that they most probably "involve different sets of meanings and therefore are in a measure incommensurable" (124).

If Kracauer was here again reminded of a filmic phenomenon, the analogy is ambiguous. He quoted observations he made in *Theory of Film* of the "paradoxical relation between close-ups and long shots (shots of ensembles) in the cinematic narrative." The big close-up of Mae Marsh's hands in the trial episode of Griffith's *Intolerance* makes the viewer see them differently, that is, as differing from ordinary hands: "Isolated from the rest of the body and greatly enlarged, the hands we know will change into unknown organisms quivering with a life of their own. Similarly, the historian's close-up is apt to suggest possibilities and vistas not conveyed by the identical event in high-magnitude history" (126).

The "paradoxical relation" between the different components of a composite visual perspective enhances the viewer's visual experience by triggering "disclosures of new aspects of physical reality" as richly suggestive, puzzling image shifts and associations.[91] But a similar expansion of the historian's experience may result in troubling rather than enhancing indeterminacy. Questioning the meanings for the historian of time as a function of space, and impressed by the obstacles he found on his route, Kracauer responded with images of journeying, terrain, and mapping, of motion and resistance:

> The traffic between the micro and macro dimensions is subject to severe restrictions. Because of the "law of perspective" part of the evidence drops out automatically. And because of the "law of levels" part of the virtually available evidence reaches its destination in an incomplete state. This means that the historical universe is of a nonhomogeneous structure. It comprises fields of varying density and is rippled by unaccountable eddies. Radically speaking, the resultant traffic difficulties are unsurmountable. (127)

"Radically speaking," however, is a stage of the argument that needs to be traversed. Kracauer knew that he could not afford to stay with that insight too long because the "anteroom" of history is built of many attempts at writing history that cannot and should not be discounted. At the end of chapter 4, "The Historian's Journey," which focuses on the advantages of the historian's flexible, mobile self, Kracauer states that he had

> deliberately omitted two difficulties confronting him en route. He moves about in a universe which, because of its nonhomogeneous structure, makes it necessary for him to negotiate many hurdles. And he travels through Time–a medium whose complexity further obstructs his advance. These difficulties call for close attention [he deals with them in chapters 5 and 6]. Did history not exist, one might almost say that it is an improbable undertaking. (103)

But the point is that he did not say it. Instead he showed the unsolvable conflictedness in the historiographical approaches of highly respected, successful historians: between "formative desires" and "realistic passion," small-scale and large-scale narration. He also showed conflict in their filmic analogies, for instance "Griffith's admirable non-solution" in combining close-ups and extreme long shots, a composition of perspectives that both underlines and diffuses meaning.[92] The frequent references in this portion of Kracauer's argument to the handling of visually composite perspective in film suggest, if anything, the comparative severity of the terrain crossed by the time-traveling historian. Sensibly, he pointed out that some interpenetrations of micro and macro history were more helpful than others and, most importantly, that many have contributed to the increase of historical knowledge: "One will now better understand the peculiar truth value of ideas and their oblique relation to factual accuracy" (129).

The goal of factual accuracy is the touchstone of the historian's responsibility to past experience and crucial to the expanding spaces of modern cultural memory. Again and again, Kracauer came back to the serious methodological problems of micro histories; again and again, he asserted their contribution to the capaciousness of memory that had meant so much to him. As he had known (and argued) all along, factual accuracy can never be fully realized since the historian's historicity prevents the gathering of facts from being complete–with respect to both their quantity and their "facticity" (quality). What, then, *is* the cultural meaning of "technical history," an approach that explicitly embraces the historiographical goal of complete, unbiased collection of all, even the smallest available, facts? Is not the serious proposal of this ideal goal positively counterproductive in an area of inquiry in which evidence must be judged, from a position of critical realism, in terms of probability? The question is answered indirectly but clearly in the "Anteroom" chapter. At the end of chapter 5, however, Kracauer presents us with an "admirable non-solution," a "theological" argument in support of a methodologically impossible completeness of historical knowledge. Here once more is the passage from which I took off in section 4:

> So the question as to the meaningfulness of "technical history" would seem unanswerable. There is only one single argument in its support which I believe to be conclusive. It is a theological argument, though. According to it, the "complete assemblage of the smallest facts" is required for the reason that nothing shall go lost. It is as if the fact-oriented accounts breathed pity with the dead. This vindicates the figure of the collector."[93]

8

Pity with the dead because time has flushed them away and obliterated them. Kracauer took care to put in quotation marks the ideal of metaphysically complete collection: the qualifying "though" after "theological argument," the distancing effect of the quote, the "as if" mode of the connection between "pity" and "fact-oriented." Still, he left the reader with the sense that, if not a solution for the conundrum of historical perspective, this particular "theological argument" carries its own justification because it offers the living the solace of pity with the dead. However, we are clearly concerned here with a dimension of cultural memory that, for the sake of his inquiry, the historian cannot or should not enter, even if he is temperamentally drawn to it. Among the unpublished notes for *History* is one that echoes and questions this dimension:

> In defense of detached curiosity about the past–a curiosity not aroused by the historian's concern with the situation in which he finds himself. At the bottom of this curiosity may be a desire to collect all and everything no matter whether it is important or not. A day may come when our judgment about good and bad may be reversed and it is for this day that the genuine *collector* assembles things and aims at completeness. The curious collector resembles the collector of stamps and seashells and like him he may be driven by a desire to gather all historical material available for use by the highest Court of Appeal (= theology lurking around the corner).[94]

The connection between the two passages is the historian's attitude toward the enforced passivity of the past, which has become that upon which judgment is passed. The historian-as-collector's desire for an impossible completeness may be motivated by the possibility that in time "all historical material" could–should the occasion arise–be judged differently. Her pity with the dead is her informed empathy with the concrete substance of their lives lost in the flux of time. But her collecting against obliteration can only be realized within the historicity of modern culture, which acknowledges the instability, that is also the temporality, of historical judgment. Collecting under these circumstances may call up the possibility of redeeming ("*einlösen*") the past. This, however, will not happen in that one impossibly complete history but in incomplete alternate histories that might reclaim, for a time and precariously, the presence of the dead for the living. The "genuine collector" is closer to the poet than the historian. Like Orpheus, he desires to regain and retain the past fully.[95]

Here we come back again to the argument that *History* as a whole is strongly resonant of redemption in the religious terms of Benjamin's work, especially the "Theses on the Philosophy of History," and that the particular passage we have been concerned with was "taken almost directly from Benjamin."[96] In a sense, I have used the larger portion of my last chapter to prepare for the refutation of such resonances because their assumed presence gravely distorts the meanings of Kracauer's concept of history and thus the contribution of his work to cultural modernity. Unless one sets out deliberately to read Kracauer "against himself," one would be hard put to hear "Benjamin's voice" in Kracauer's texts. (This disarmingly frank proposition has been made by several critics bent on constructing a Benjaminian version they think more easily marketable.)[97] To go back to the unpublished note with which most readers are unfamiliar: to equate the "highest Court of Appeal" with "theology lurking around the corner," clearly suggests reservations against the former rather than affirmation of the latter because the attribute "lurking" is negative, therefore cautionary. But beyond agreeing on this reading of a particular passage, it should be clear from Kracauer's argumentation in *History* generally, and in chapter 5 particularly, that the authority of the "highest Court of Appeal," though possibly a directive for the collector with a yearning for metahistorical, poetic completeness, is too absolute for the "anteroom" secularity of historical inquiry. To invoke it would not help the time-traveling historian to act on her pity with the dead; it might actually hinder her.

Kracauer's concern was not a final "redemption ['*erlösen*'] of the power and specificity of historical thought."[98] Much more modest, it was a reclamation, in the terms of a modern culture, of the conflicted ongoing practice of historical inquiry. In practice, if not in theory, arguments for or against this or that historiographical approach are taken to be provisional and temporary—not least because history is the realm of unpredictable new beginnings. (Instructively, the result of reading Kracauer "against himself" has been the construction of yet another existentially exiled authentic intellectual removed from the contingencies, the surprises, of history.) But can there be progress in historiography if the ideal of complete historical collection appears more and more impossible while cultural recollection is expanding? Kracauer closed his discussion of the structure of the historical universe with two sentences that, taken out of context, might seem ambiguous: "It is difficult to imagine that Thucydides will ever be surpassed. The belief in the progress of historiography is largely in the nature of an illusion" (138). In the context of his argument, "surpassed" has to be understood in terms of the historian's historicity: Thucydides' cultural contribution made then and there as reflected in the contributions of others made from the position of *their* then and there. The importance his work has had for historiography may indeed never be surpassed. However, it is not the "progress of historiography" that is an illusion but the "belief" in it, for instance in that impossible ideal of completeness. It is probable that there will be progress (though of an unpredictable nature) because there has been progress, however halting and erratic. Beyond that we cannot tell.

History, then, is not the place for "theological" arguments, even when they seem to hold seductive promises. A perceptive reader of *History* has suggested an explanation for Kracauer's use of the attribute "theological" by linking it with Jewish understanding of tradition located in *Gemara*.[99] *Gemara* is a collection of the explanatory and critical contributions to the discussion of *Mischna*. The record of a dialogical culture, it is guided by the principle of complementarity, which supports the collecting of *all* statements made in the debate of a specific issue. There is also the question of original materials not included in *Mischna* (ca. A.D. 200) but collected in a work accompanying *Mischna* called *Tossefta*, "addition." Not only do quotes from *Tossefta* play an important complementary role in the Talmudic debates, but the issue of additional materials that relax an already codified law is explicitly discussed in *Tossefta*. Gathering in Jawne after the destruction of Jersualem, the wise men decided to collect and preserve by name all opinions, also minority positions, so that they could be drawn on for support "when perhaps their hour comes."[100]

Kracauer may have been familiar with *Gemara* and he may have associated the collector's drive for completeness with the exhaustive collecting of contributions to theological discussion, that is, with the *form* of theological debates in the Jewish tradition. Such conjectural connections may or may not explain the way in which he introduced a "theological argument" into the discussion of historiographical methodology. There is also a suggestive association between the marginal annotations printed as additional commentary, *Tossafot*, in Talmud editions and Kracauer's repeated references, especially in *History*, to writing something in the margins–instead of incorporating it into the main text and thereby claiming (a higher) authority for it. These references emphasize the "in-between" status of human knowledge and judgment, the secular contingencies of truth. In an "open" letter written on the occasion of Bloch's eightieth birthday in 1965, when he was intensely involved with the problems of historiography, Kracauer reminded his old friend and adversary of his "fearful mistrust in grand dreams that are not marginal annotations but allowed to interfere to the extent of making so radically transparent what is closest to us in experience that we are almost left incapable of seeing what and how it is."[101]

For the sake of seeing, as clearly as humanly possible, what and how it is, Kracauer's historian does not dream the grand dreams of philosophy or poetry because these hide rather than reveal whatever version, part, of historical truth may be accessible. "The difficulty of deducing the truths in the interstices from the high-level statements, principles, or doctrines under whose rule they fall does not imply that they were sheer mirages. Sometimes that which is buried under an imposing either-or may shine forth from a casual apercu, written in the margin of a close-up" (216).

Kracauer's concern in *History* is not a coming upon truth as a moment of revelation, of certainty. The knowledge on which human judgments are based can be neither that instantaneous nor that complete. "Judgment Day," which figures so importantly in "Theses on the Philosophy of History," has a very different meaning for him than it does for Benjamin. Here is the passage from the third thesis that some readers have found echoed in *History*:

> A chronicler who recites events without distinguishing between major and minor ones acts in accordance with the following truth: nothing that has ever happened should be regarded as lost for history. To be sure, only a redeemed mankind receives the fullness of its past–which is to say, only for a redeemed mankind has its past become citable in all its moments. Each moment it has lived becomes a *citation a l'ordre du jour*–and that day is Judgment Day.[102]

The published passage in *History* contains no reference to "Judgment Day"; the unpublished note clearly qualifies the notion of the day before "the highest Court of Appeals" with the bracketed reference to "(= theology lurking around the corner)." Kracauer distanced himself from the believer's desire that his collection be complete on Judgment Day, at the end of human time. He was not interested in a final, irrevocable Judgment passed by higher authority from beyond the secular life-world. Rather, he imagined a judgment that one day, at some point in human time, might reverse a cultural status quo and and give new energy to the reclamation ("*Einlösung*") of heretofore marginal histories that would enrich, by questioning it, history. If the historian's collecting realized within our life-world is motivated by that possibility, it also is prevented by it from reaching completeness–as is the project of history.

For Kracauer the cultural contribution of history is located precisely in its open-ended secularity. Written in very dark times, Benjamin's "Theses" were exclusively concerned with the salvation-as-completion of history. It will be fulfilled only after the redemption ("*Erlösung*") of mankind is completed. But the moment of the fullness of the past is the moment of transcending human time–a transcendence to which the "genuine collector" would have contributed significantly. For Benjamin, the writing of history required a poetic-theological dimension. Temperamentally drawn to thinking in images of transcendence and transhistoricity, he had always cast epistemological questions in aesthetic or religious terms, that is, outside life-world contingencies. His desperately difficult situation in 1940 only exacerbated this tendency. Redemption, especially where it concerned history, meant quite literally completing by dissolving, "*erlösen*": the alchemic release of potent substances; the crossing of existential borders; the magic of setting free. If Kracauer's focus was on clearly marked points in human time, the there and then of other lives, Benjamin's was on mapping the past with a seductively suggestive, mysterious web of personal correspondences and significances.

Writing in a time and place dramatically different from that of Benjamin's "Theses," Kracauer came to confront most directly the meanings of the historical universe as a cultural challenge that for him included preeminently the historian's personal responsibility to and for the past. The intelligent and shrewd self-restrictions crucial to his concept of historiography were supported by his insistence on keeping the past open as past lifetime, extending into its future–the historian's present–unresolved problems, unsolved puzzles, unanswered questions. For Kracauer, the "has been" dimension of past events, acts, and actors is essential to the writing of history. This, too, was the reason for his establishing and frequently drawing on the analogy between historiography and photography. The cultural contribution of history, which held such profound attraction for him, is the creation of historical time–time that is not empty flux in need of poetic-religious redemption but defined by the shapes of past living, which the historian traces in acts of (re)construction. The "infinite" gain of this constructing is the secular redemption of lived time, and the photo image serves as a powerful metaphor, in the literal sense, between time and space.[103] The suggestive contrast that Peter Munz set up in *The Shapes of Time* between the experience of the passage of time as diminishing and depriving and the experience of "spatial extension" as enriching—hence, perhaps, his solid concept of story shapes[104]—fits the photo image most literally. Where the passage of time as the "accumulation of differences in the same space" signifies the experience of a series of disappearances, of loss, the experience of space as "differences that take place at the same moment of time" signifies the experience of gain.

> One of the strongest impulses for the conversion of time into history is based on this asymmetry between time and space. We can combat the depressing experience of deprivation through time by trying to assimilate the passage of time to the extension of space. And this is precisely what we are doing when we are writing history. When we see the past as a story, we give shape to time. And since there is no absolute shape that we could give to time, it might be more appropriate to think of the transformation of time as a process of putting sets of masks over the face of time.[105]

Munz's healing thought-image of layered masks that might still the inexorable flux of time calls up Kracauer's terrifying vision of Ahasver's face, decomposed and recomposed by the ravages of this flux over many lifetimes. It was one of Kracauer's deepest desires to give shape to time. But though he admired other historians' attempts to do so, he was concerned about the validity, that is, the authority, of the stories that make up history—or of which history is made. When he reflected on the conditions of historiographical discourse, he was impressed by the "uncertain light" in which the historian gathers "fragments" of the past and the "uncertain ends" they might serve.[106] Yet he sought to clarify for himself the possibility rather than impossibility of historical knowledge because he pursued such clarification in the company of others. Their contributions had shaped, after all, his own historicity; moreover, this shape, in all its puzzling compositeness, was the most important guiding influence on his own historical inquiry.

History exhibits a remarkable perceptiveness to the different times, places, and ways in which to write history. Kracauer did of course select, and he was most strongly attracted to historians devoted to the documentary dimension of historiography.[107] Granted the unavoidable errors and the inevitable distortions of their perspective, they are trying to penetrate, with the "insatiable curiosity" that they share with the maker of photo images, that once concrete presence, the thick, tenacious flow of the everyday life of the past. The shapes of its reconstruction (ought to) resist rigid patterns of emplotting,[108] especially of the ideological kind. In tracing these shapes, historian and photographer alike have to be sensitive to their capaciousness, fluidity and changeability, as present and past lives are "made up of moments within everybody's reach, moments as common as birth and death, or a smile, or 'the ripple of the leaves stirred by the wind.'"

> Small random moments which concern things common to you and me and the rest of mankind can indeed be said to constitute the dimension of everyday life, this matrix of all other modes of reality. It is a very substantial dimension. If you disregard for a moment articulate beliefs, ideological objectives, special undertakings, and the like, there still remain the sorrows and satisfactions, discords and feasts, wants and pursuits, which mark the ordinary business of living. Products of habit and microscopic interaction, they form a resilient texture which changes slowly and survives wars, epidemic earthquakes, and revolutions. Films tend to explore this texture of everyday life, whose composition varies according to place, people and time. So they help us not only to appreciate our given material environment but to extend it in all directions. They virtually make the world our home.[109]

Such familiarizing, extended in space and in time, called up strong resonances in the exile Kracauer; it is both a challenge of modernity and, in the modern expanding world, a task that can not be completed. As both time and space are accessible to her only insofar as they are her own and others' cultural constructs, the traveler will, in time, come to the end of her imagination. A notoriously patient observer of worldly contingencies, Kracauer was of course aware of these limitations. He acknowledged them in the last chapter, "The Anteroom," the most incomplete and potentially most important chapter of the book. Kracauer would be the last to assign a particular poignancy to this coincidence. He just happened to die while working on a difficult portion of his argument meant to describe history in terms of the modern experience of personal and cultural temporality. Death as the both ultimate and inevitable limit was very much present in the argument. An old man, who had always been sharply aware of the significance of contemporaneity and of time passing, experienced with increasing urgency the achievements and challenges of history. Striving to become more familiar with the past lifetime of others also meant considering their–and his own–precarious and poignant striving for a future. In the introduction to *History* there is an uncharacteristically personal observation, offered characteristically within parentheses. It refers to the dead as historical reality, and to historical reality as the dead looking back at us–like the portraits of August Sander (figs. 5–10): "(I sometimes wonder whether advancing age does not increase our susceptibility to the speechless plea of the dead; the older one grows, the more he is bound to realize that his future is the future of the past–history)" (6). And, like the women and men and children in Sander's images, this future both offers itself and retreats into strangeness.

Epilogue

Modernity, Poetry, and the Writing of History

1

The "postmodernist" fascination with the notion of a self-generating and self-perpetuating textuality reflects a general contemporary impatience with the intricacies of what Friedrich Schleiermacher in 1819 described as the "art of understanding" or "the art of interpretation."[1] It is true, the reluctance on the part of the critic to get involved with the historicity of the reader, the text, and the act of reading, with reading as a culturally shared activity, has been centered in literary studies. Literary texts with their high degree of complexity tend to elicit readerly responses that themselves are highly complex and, when written down, depend on *their* readers' complex interpretive practices. On the whole, this problem has not presented itself quite so dramatically in historiography, where questions of textual complexity and of interpretation are posed in a different context regarding questions of referentiality, truth status, evidence. But here, too, the notion of an omnipresent textuality is now more often considered for its promised redefiniton of problems posed by the past as a depository of entangled conflicts between often self-contradictory voices that question the historian's authorship and authority.

Kracauer's consistently social and temporal conception of history–the time-traveling historian's "tact"–neutralizes these questions. "Art with a difference" and "science with a difference," historiography presents a situation in which authorship and authority are relative and partial, even self-consciously provisional. But do most historians practicing this hybrid art-science in the last decade of the twentieth century see it that way? The current heated debate of the "objectivity question,"[2] which clearly indicates a sense of methodological "unrest," may suggest otherwise.

The most radical questioning of modern historical understanding has focused on the complex linguistic issue of unstable fluid signification. Derrida-influenced scenarios propose a radical disjuncture of sign and signified rather than interpretive exploration of historically established (and changing) connections. In his 1989 essay "Intellectual History and the

Return of Literature," which provoked some instructive responses, David Harlan showed himself much impressed by a general "triumph of literary theory" in the human sciences in general, and historiography in particular.[3] Signs, he discovered, were no longer "bonded to signifieds; they merely point to other signifiers." And he assured his readers that after Derrida's attack on Saussure they were left with an "endless chain of signifiers in which meaning is always deferred and finally absent." Embracing Derrida's rejection of a "transcendental signified"[4] as authorized guarantor of meaning, Harlan delighted in the "incessant and unremitting play of signifiers." And he agreed with the Master that "this, strictly speaking, amounts to destroying the concept of 'sign' and its entire logic." Historians should therefore overcome their notorious skepticism regarding theory and accept the superior intellectual power and jouissance of an authorless "textuality."[5]

Bolstered by the very solid authority of one author's dictum, Harlan cast a glance at the epistemological foundations of predeconstructionist historiography and declared them ripe for demolition. His celebrations of the authorless text suggest a comfortably abstract and general concept of author, authorship, and authority–an, as it were, remote diffuse energy whose declared absence should not really have much influence on the ways in which history is done or talked about. Of course, neither Derrida nor, for that matter, Harlan are absent from *their* texts; their voices are not indistinct, nor their intentions unrecoverable. But the intended meanings of other authors' texts (other historians' writings) appear distinctly malleable in Harlan's readings. Thus he can construct their general deep-rooted naïveté regarding epistemological problems, singling out especially contextualist historians whose work focuses explicitly on the recovery of authorial intentions.[6]

The rhetorical exuberance of Harlan's stance against contextualism can easily detract from the fact that his argument raises serious questions regarding the historian's use of language in the construction of historical meaning. His scenario in which (all) modern historians are irredeemably hung up on "fixed and determinable meanings"[7] is exaggerated to the point of silliness. As a group, modern historians have of course questioned each others' readings of historical documents precisely out of their awareness of the historicity of language, that is, the positionality of language use. Yet they have also exploited the ambiguities inherent in language use to fashion their own temporarily "fixed" versions of historical meaning. Thus the concern, more widespread in the last decades, over the problems of historiographical method has rightly focused on the historian's use of language as reader and writer; and in this context Harlan's essay may have had some shock value. Many historians are indeed still working with an inflated notion of historiographical objectivity. Their professional training has been to get it right: not "more than less," just right–as physicians are trained to preserve life and lawyers to win cases, both at any cost. But though objectivity and authority are interdependent and need to be consistently questioned, Harlan's transferring the whole problem to the level of historians' preoccupation with "chaining" signs to structural schemata is of little help. Even less so is his asserting their existential (not just professional) dependence on the idea of a supra- or transhistorical guarantor of meaning. Instructively, the early Derrida, on whom radical critics of historical understanding like Harlan or LaCapra base their liberation from historiographical conventions, projected such dependence onto his philosophical contemporaries because he wished to define his own *philosophical* position against them.[8]

Harlan is clearly not concerned with specific problems in contemporary historiographical practice. Notably absent from his argument are the indeed very important epistemological difficulties encountered by historians in our increasingly polarized and confused intellectual culture when they try to balance their contemporaneity with the implications of their literal "interest" in the actuality of past experience. He seems to think that these difficulties are simply solved once and for all if historians follow literary critics in declaring the ascendancy of transhistorical textual free play over the search for historical authorial strategies and textual meanings.

To be fair to Harlan's attraction to such radical shortcuts through the entanglements of historical understanding, the issue of interpretation in the recovery of past meanings has been so complicated and troubling that many historians have tended to suppress it. The implications of this attitude show up nicely where the historiographical uses of literary texts (in contrast to theories) are concerned. The argument here is usually that literary texts do not yield "reliable" access to past actuality, implying that such access is otherwise no problem for the conscientious historian for whom corroboration seems the most "natural," that is, self-evident, procedure.[9] To the historically oriented literary critic who is impressed by the current methodological confusion, such unambiguous loyalty to "reliable" access to past actuality seems exotically refreshing, if not useful. It also does not help much to uphold, on principle, the accuracy of historical meaning and at the same time concede the "mixed" nature of historical scholarship: "as artistic as it is scientific," relating "both the real and the imagined," it is "part memory, part imagination."[10] The problem–and the reason for our well-advised openness to methodological doubts–is that these "parts" are not neatly separate but symbiotically entwined and that it is precisely this symbiosis that fuels language use. The ability to speak is rooted in the fact that memory is sharable imagination and imagination is sharable memory.

Time-traveling investigative reporters and documentarists, historians have combined fact finding and puzzle solving with conceptual and narrative patterning. Historiography has always been located at the intersection of different discourses, and many of its most talented practitioners have been aware of the promises as well as the problems that come with a mixed mode of inquiry, which they nevertheless have seldom questioned rigorously. Yet the multivocal, mediating, "impure," unfinished, self-transforming discourse of historiography is in need of critical examination precisely because of its significance for a contemporary culture dominated by science and technology.

2 Harlan's provocation, however, is his professed love affair with the idea of a global liberation from the constraints of historical meaning to be achieved by a "return of literature" into intellectual history. By "literature" he does not mean literary texts in the conventional sense but a certain brand of current literary theory which, like its (German) Romantic precursor, is indeed a kind of poetry of thought. This heady mixture would gloriously deconstruct all the erroneous assumptions underlying all dedication to the goal of a greater accuracy of historical meaning. Because the "endless chain of signifiers in which meaning is always deferred and finally absent" (583) must inexorably frustrate the belief reigning among historians that language can hold down historical meaning long enough for them to permanently seize it. Under the right literary "pressures" texts will, as it were, liquify and merge with other texts, submerging, with their boundaries, authorial presences.

This liquidation, in Harlan's account, is not just a possibility to speculate about; it has already happened across a broad range of disciplines. Especially intellectual historians who feel responsible "for keeping our cultural memory alive and our intellectual traditions relevant" had better watch out as they stand "to lose the most from the postmodern analysis of representation and narrative" (583). Harlan is happy to speed up this process by seriously misrepresenting the early nineteenth-century hermeneutical positions on which modern intellectual history has drawn. The historiographical recovery of past meaning was of central importance to Schleiermacher, but he did not therefore believe that meaning could be recovered fully and in all cases. Schleiermacher saw quite clearly the difficulties involved in this enterprise when he pointed out the (almost infinite) regress of readings, given a certain degree of textual complexity. Consider the first aphorism in his compendium of statements on hermeneutics (1805): "As soon as the *subtilitas explicandi* becomes more than the outside of understanding, it becomes itself an object of hermeneutics and belongs to the art of presentation." This crucial insight is followed immediately with the observation of "two divergent maxims for understanding. (1) I am understanding everything until I encounter a contradiction or nonsense. (2) I do not understand anything that I cannot perceive and comprehend ["*construieren*"] as necessary. In accordance with this second maxim understanding is an unending task."[11] Throughout the compendium and his lecture notes are explicit references to historical understanding as an always unfinished, unending, open-ended process because of the extraordinarily complex reality of language use as a (on different levels) temporal phenomenon: "Each person represents one locus where a given language takes shape in a particular way, and his speech can be understood only in the context of the totality of the language. But then too he is a person who is a constantly developing spirit, and his speaking can be understood as only one moment in this development in relation to all others" (98).

Language use occurs at a particular moment in the development of the user–to which language contributes–and a particular moment in the development of language–to which the user contributes. Interpretation has to accommodate the fullness of that moment, that is, to acknowledge that (historical) understanding is (no more than) a utopian direction for the interpreter.[12] The life of the language and the life of the person using it connect in the moment of speech (which for Schleiermacher is also the moment of thought) into an infinite horizon to which the interpreter is inevitably drawn and which inevitably defeats him. The indeed almost infinite interpretive regress is the central epistemological problem in the history-based human sciences. It is for this reason that Schleiermacher's hermeneutic explorations–and Dilthey's rethinking of them–have become so important to attempts to understand the theoretical foundations of knowledge in this area of inquiry.

Hermeneutics is the discipline of the text–no more, no less. In his 1900 essay, "The Rise of Hermeneutics," Dilthey stressed the fact that understanding can attain general validity only in relation to *written* documents because only they can be shared–presupposing their availability through durability and distribution–and thus are not in danger of becoming the exclusive property of one or the other interpreter. Dilthey located Schleiermacher's importance precisely in his conceiving the analysis of understanding as a general encompassing process and making it the groundwork for codifiying (biblical) exegesis. Basing himself on Schleiermacher's insights and extrapolating from them, Dilthey stated:

> Individual differences are not in the last analysis determined by qualitative differences between people, but rather through a difference in the degree of development of their spiritual process. Now inasmuch as the exegete tentatively projects his own sense of life into another historical milieu, he is able within that perspective to strengthen and emphasize certain spiritual processes in himself and to minimize others, thus making possible within himself a re-experiencing of an alien form of life.[13]

If that sounds rather too hopeful, it does not preclude Dilthey's understanding–following Schleiermacher's–of the incomplete, partial, unfinished nature of all (historical) understanding. This is not, to be sure, because of an infinite play of signifiers independent of writers and readers, but because individual writers and readers, users of language, are, as Dilthey put it, "*ineffabile.*" The interconnection of textual complexity and the complexity of readerly activities, fed by a symbiosis of memory and imagination, produces yet another textual complexity and so on *ad* (almost) *infinitum.* The analysis of historical understanding, then, does not aim to generalize about the nature of understanding but

> to preserve the general validity of interpretation against the inroads of romantic caprice and skeptical subjectivity, and to give a theoretical justification for such validity, upon which all certainty of historical knowledge is founded. Seen in the context of the theory of knowledge, of logic and the methodology of the human studies, the theory of interpretation becomes an essential connecting link between philosophy and the historical disciplines, an essential component in the foundation of the human studies themselves. (244)

It is not, for Dilthey, a question of a more philosophical historiography but of an *analysis* of historical understanding that would be valid for all inquiry in the human sciences. In his scenario there would be no need for "literature" as self-aware interpretive praxis to "return" to intellectual history because it would never have been absent. The questions to be asked, then, do not concern the intrinsically interpretive nature of historiography but the kind of interpretive historiographical praxis.

When Schleiermacher defined "the art of interpretation" in 1819, he saw it "develop its rules only out of a positive formula and this is: the historical *and* divinatory, objective *and* subjective reconstructing of a given utterance" (111). Understanding is never nonpositional but always stands at a given point in history, bound by the writer's and the reader's (verbal) historicity. Hermeneutics, the reading and understanding of the text in the dialogical mediation between text and reader, was for Dilthey liberation of (biblical) exegesis from dogma precisely because it bases interpretation on linguistic usage and historical circumstance. It is the *written* and *read* text that has been and continues to be adaptable to new insights that cannot be limited to or exhausted by a particular reading (for a particular reason) at a particular time.

3 Despite his neoromantic version of Pyrrhonism, Harlan shares this idea–in the case of certain texts. Emphatically if inconsistently, he wants to save "the great books" worthy of the attention of the intellectual historian from the deconstruction of understanding in intertextuality. For this salvaging enterprise he enlists the help of Barthes, LaCapra, Kermode, and Iser, suggesting, curiously, that the notion of the (relative) inexhaustibility of a very complex text is a brand-new, postmodernist insight. Thus he celebrates the "plenitude of meanings and interpretations" available in Barth's "writerly texts," Kermode's "canonical works," their "multidimensionality," "omnisignificance," and "indeterminacy," which enable

continuously surprising new readings. Notwithstanding the frictionless flow of intertextuality and the liquidation of (all) authors, "great books" emerge as indisputably distinct from, let's say, comic books: "By drawing on Barthes, LaCapra, and Kermode, we can patch together provisional, working criteria for identifying the books with which intellectual history might concern itself" (598). But who are the "we" Harlan speaks for? If his celebration of the absence of (historical) meaning is so totalizing as to be inaccessible to–and therefore unassailable in–rational discourse, his advocacy for the distinctive greatness of great works is not. Whether deconstructionists like it or not, understanding *is* positional; the conditions for reading, for establishing meaning, vary a great deal depending on both the text and its reader. In view of the proliferation of conflicting canons in late twentieth-century (Western) culture, Harlan's "we" is indefensible. "Canonical," "readerly" texts that *he* thinks inexhaustible, that is, perpetually open to new interpretations, may not seem so to other readers (for instance, women) and may indeed be "thrown on the rubbish heap," notwithstanding Iser's protestations. On the other hand, texts that neither he nor Barthes nor Iser may think worthy to be included in their canon may be used to establish other canons precisely because they enable different readers to articulate their different positions.

Iser's concept of the indeterminacy of a text is notoriously transhistorical and translinguistic, predicated on the curiously combined notion of a reader whose mind is a *tabula rasa* and who will yet read new, unforeseen ideas into or out of the recognized indeterminacy of a text.[14] But Iser and Harlan, both of them intellectual readers at the end of the twentieth century, have their own historically grounded reasons for celebrating the plenitude of textual indeterminacy. And historians who think that it is possible, up to a point, and worth their while to recover the historical meanings of texts do not come to them in a paradisaical state of innocence. To varying degrees they are aware of the positional nature of understanding; they realize at least some of the implications of their own historicity.

It is from this position that historians will attempt to open historical texts to a past intellectual linguistic actuality in which their writers shared, both receiving and giving. This opening process is fraught with difficulties, even fallacies. But it has to be undertaken as long as historians agree that language is a social-historical phenomenon that reflects the contributions, through the ages, of a very great plurality of language users, including themselves. Harlan's argument, interesting for its symptomatic character, is based on a both eclectic and totalizing concept of language which he perceives to be authorized by writers like Derrida, Foucault, and de Man. Working with an impossibly clean dichotomy between language as "a play of unintended self-transformations and unrestrained self-advertisements" and as "a set of stable meanings and external references," Harlan simply denies the historicity of language use. True, the historian's task would be immeasurably easier if authors remained absent, audiences unknown and the "unruly text" just went on "spewing out its manifold significations, connotations, and implications" (585).

But even this postmodernist scenario calls for the interjection of a postmodernist reader into those infinite "self-transformations." If we agree that we can know about them only when they are written down–that is, by professional readers who are also writers–the question of the omnifertile unruly text poses itself in quite different terms. It appears that the subversive joy of self-creating infinite and infinitely playful textuality by its postmodernist readers/writers is a matter of high seriousness to them and very much a question of *their* authorial ingenuity. In fact, their highly subjective readings/writings are very effective in terms of name recognition. In their indebtedness to the erotic dissolution by German Romantic poet-critics of all discourse into "*Transzdentalpoesie*," "*progressive Universalpoesie*,"[15] practitioners of deconstructionism like Derrida, de Man, and the later Foucault have been notorious for their narcissistic linguistic preciousness and hermeticism, which, in turn, have had profound influence on their disciples.

Bemused readers have indeed wondered about the implications of deconstructionist writing style for deconstructionist arguments. The implications of deconstructionist practice of authorship and authority, however, have seemed less obvious. While the author of a text subjected to a deconstructionist reading may indeed be dead, the writer of the new reading is by no means dead. Rather, in rewriting that now unresisting, authorless text, the deconstructionist critic has become the author of–and therefore assumed the authority for–that new text. Celebration of the infinite play of textuality is predicated, in deconstructionist discourse, on the postmodernist critic's individual playful literariness, which relies on recognizably *his or her* authorial intentions and strategies. Removing authorship and authority in the case of the historical author but asserting it in the case of the late twentieth-century reader/writer of this author's text is no playful matter. It suggests a radical revision not only of historical understanding but also of the critical community of historical inquiry developed over time, in both cases with profound implications for cultural modernity to which historiography is of crucial importance.

4 What meanings, what audiences are intended in Harlan's text published by the eminently respectable *American Historical Review* (which "disclaims responsibility for statements, either of fact or of opinion, made by contributors")? Did its author expect that his historian readers would hold *him* to the implications of the "protean and uncontrollable"[16] nature of (his) words? I will draw here briefly on one published response to Harlan that eloquently and instructively poses these questions. Sensitive to the significant temptations of "cutting edge" methodology, this response also takes seriously the troubling epistemological problems central to the history-based human sciences that are partly responsible for the attention given to the deconstructionist challenge.[17] However, when she argues against the disappearance of the author, the respondent is not sufficiently clear about the significance of the historicity of language use for historical understanding. Pleading for the importance of recoverable human agency in the construction of texts, which would nurture the historian's desire to escape imprisonment in the present (1332), she misjudges the energies and direction of deconstructionist rejection of linguistic historicity.

Despite her awareness of Harlan's motivations in making his case for "the new ahistorical historian," who would be liberated from the burden of historical understanding (1328), Appleby also embraces methodological pluralism. Since our current cultural situation does not present us with a unified theory of knowledge (has there been one in modernity?), she encourages willingness to be open to the playful intellectual fullness of late twentieth-century culture with one crucial caveat: contextualism is not to be excluded from this plethora of options because the grounds for its dismissal, the essential elusiveness and ultimate absence of (historical) meaning, are simply unacceptable to her; they are, as she says, "meaningless."

> Words are totally inert. If they change meaning, it is because some sentient human being has embedded them in a new context that another human being has

> discerned. Whatever happens to words happens through the imaginative processes of their human inventors and users. Words are protean because human beings use them to explain, encode, describe, mask, obscure, obfuscate, deny, exclude, abbreviate, express, reveal, and tease. (1328)

Of course they do. But it does not, therefore, follow that other users of words will agree to protect the (possible) presence of historical meaning. Asserting his newly found liberation, Harlan will most probably not do so, though, disagreeing, he will indeed use words to exclude other historians, or deny the need for rational discourse, or express his desire to be free of the burdensome challenge to historiography to get it (more than less) right.

For Appleby as reader and writer, intertextuality signifies a resource for meaning rather than its absence: "present meaning is not deferred, it stops with every satisfied reader. Only meanings that others in the future might find can be described as deferred" (1330). This statement, unaggressive and conciliatory in tone, inexorably excludes a reader and writer like Harlan from an acceptable methodological pluralism–as his argument excludes her. But if he does not present "logical arguments" to support his position, neither, as she explicitly acknowledges, does Appleby. She appeals to (her) experience, pointing to the problem of proof for the historian, which, in contrast to the physical scientist's externalization of the "validation process through experimentation and demonstration," involves "the assent of a knowing subject" (1331).

I think this distinction is too sharp and weakens rather than helps her argument. The question is not such an assent–which, in any case, is also true for the scientist. The question is, rather, the professional community of knowing subjects and their cultural self-awareness and self-articulation as a group. Appleby stresses the dependence of communality in judging on "shared participation in a complex intellectual practice." This notion leads to her expectation, surprisingly firm under the circumstances, that other historians, out of their common experience, will agree with her insistence on subjectively intentional language usage and will therefore reject claims that "language is an autonomous play of unintended transformations" (1331). Unwilling to take seriously Harlan's refusal to do so, Appleby praises what she sees as a postmodernist challenge

> to that philosophical tradition that asserts the existence of objective truths, considers language a vehicle for the discovery and articulation of those truths, and

depends on the stable passage of words from author to reader to spread them. No one reading Derrida or Richard Rorty or Foucault could fail to appreciate the seriousness of their effort to dispose this reigning epistemological tradition. The importance of their work, exhilarating, liberating, and cautionary, cannot be exaggerated. However, there is insufficient agreement among these thinkers to undermine our confidence in communication. (1330)

Would Appleby, on these thinkers' authority, accept the proposed absence of meaning if they *did* agree? Would she then be prepared to follow Rorty in embracing an absolutist cultural primacy of the discourse of poetry–more precisely, a kind of poetry represented by the later work of Derrida? In Rorty's scenario of a "thoroughly Wittgensteinian" approach to language,[18] poetic discourse is placed above other cultural activities like philosophy or historiography precisely because it undermines–"deconstructs"–the "idea of languages as representations." He seems to think that all (other) philosophy has been based on such an idea and that it is therefore essential that we have "no prelinguistic consciousness to which language needs to be adequate, no deep sense of how things are which it is the duty of philosophers to spell out in language. What is described as such a consciousness is simply a disposition to use the language of our ancestors, to worship the corpses of their metaphors." Rorty's stated intention is to "de-divinize the world" (21f.), that is, free it from the obligation to articulate that "deep sense of how things are" and from bondage to the "corpses" of others' metaphors. Here he finds most helpful the more and more elaborately auto-fictive, playfully fantastic–or fantastically playful–discourse of the later Derrida, who "privatizes his philosophical thinking, and thereby breaks down the tension between ironism and theorizing." Derrida has now simply dropped theory as "the attempt to see his predecessors steadily and whole." Instead he has chosen to "fantazise" about and play with them, "giving free reign to the trains of associations they produce."[19]

Rorty sees this choice as "the only solution to the self-referential problem which such theorizing encounters, the problem of how to distance one's predecessors without doing exactly what one has repudiated them for doing." He is partly right about the problem, which concerns the difficulties of mediating between subject and object, self and world–in Rorty's extrapolating juxtaposition: the "private and the public." But the Derridian solution, as he presents it, is curiously simplistic and mechanical. Rorty praises Derrida for "having had the courage to give up the attempt to unite the private and the public, to stop trying to bring together a quest for private autonomy and an attempt at public resonance and utility."[20] But what does Derrida's "solution" mean in the case of an intellectual to whose authority readers appeal in their own writings? The "private autonomy" automatically becomes "public resonance," and the question is indeed one of utililty–to Derrida and his followers.

What Rorty celebrates as the "incredible richness of texture" (129), as consummate playfulness in a late Derrida text like "Envois," appears to other readers as the consummation of fantastic ritualistic self-absorption. For the reason of this total self-centeredness, too, they would think it quite unlike Proust's *Remembrance of Things Past*–in contrast to Rorty's assertions of a similar, and similarly total, authorial autonomy in both texts (136f.). The difference lies in the presence of other voices. In remembrance, Proust yields to their otherness because it is that otherness that enriches memory and it is memory that enriches and opens the self. Fantasizing them, Derrida appropriates the voices of others into the sameness of his private autonomy, his poetic authorship. Taken as a whole, Appleby's argument does not at all suggest approval of such appropriation. A glorification of autonomous sameness, it threatens to shut down, with a plurality of voices, the diversity of discourse, which is palpably important to her. Yet, unquestioning, she has accepted the assertion of a "reigning epistemological tradition" based on a "transcendental signified" in need of deconstruction. Notwithstanding the claims of her "authorities," as a part of cultural history, the history of epistemological positions, too, shows a record of many and contradictory voices. In their dealings with this past, writers like Derrida, Foucault, or Rorty have simply suppressed its diversity.

The historian at the end of the twentieth century has to deal with the issue of an indeed infinitely entangled intertextuality that includes intersubjectivity and is a potent obstacle to historical understanding. If Appleby suggests a "shared practice of doing history at a particular time and place rather than from our commitment to a set of standards abstracted from experience" (1331), she does not seem to consider that the time and place of our present are deeply troubled by a perceived cultural crisis of meaning. There is an exhilarating but also paralyzing chaotic proliferation of signs responsible for conflicting interpretive practices and of competing segregationist discourses, which we have to confront in an environment where the cultural primacy of science and technology goes largely unquestioned. This fertile chaos is by no means new. Central to the Weimar period, it provoked discussions among intellectuals about the meanings of their cultural contribution which were in certain important ways close to what is thought vanguard intellectual discourse today. This does not make it any easier for the late twentieth-century intellectual to understand her own contemporaneity. The challenges here are formidable, perhaps most urgently in the case of the historian.

5 In his 1963 "Cogito and the History of Madness," Derrida put to Foucault the problem of other, different betrayals intrinsic to his enterprise of releasing in *his* voice the heretofore unheard voices of past madness. Foucault's rational discursive language was inadequate to the challenge of articulating and thereby releasing from silence these trans- or extrarational languages.[21]

Derrida's suggested remedy for the historian's difficulties in articulating temporal-cultural differences was his ontological concept of "*différance*." An expanding of language into the future in order to accommodate, by infinite deferral, such voicing of what heretofore had been cultural silences ostensibly undercut the pathos of Foucault's utopian attempts to construct an alternate redemptive history. But Derrida's thought-image (rather than concept) of "*différance*" developed under Heidegger's influence, especially in late texts like "Time and Being," is itself predicated on utopian yearnings. Circumventing the difficulties of a complex and confusing contemporary culture, it stretches toward the being present, in the future, of an alternate language as prelapsarian completeness and fullness. It is precisely the desire of the late twentieth-century intellectual for the future return of a nonsymbolic, nonambiguous immediacy of meaning which attributes significance to a present infinite deferral of meaning. In its neo-Romantic nostalgia for the oldest, the Adamitic language of naming, "*différance*" holds in a paradoxical suspense the dichotomy of prelapsarian total identity and postlapsarian total rupture of sign and signified. Untainted by the hesitations and lacunae of the (many different) languages of postlapsarian (historical) experience,

Adamitic language, regained in some indefinite future, pictures paradise instantaneously and fully.[22]

This nostalgia has been widespread among German intellectuals since the turn of the century. But in Derrida's work–and this is the reason for its influence on current literary theory–the regaining of the fullness of origin is not just reflected or desired. Rather, such fullness is reenacted in the critic's rewriting of others' texts as the endless play of textuality. The elaborate autofictionality of Derrida's late work, then, presents one "logical" development of such reenacting. The endless circling around himself as author or originator of his texts holds both the promise of their fullness, which originally includes authorship, and the absence of such fullness. In order to distinguish the later Derrida from Heidegger, Rorty asserts that Derrida helps us to "cleanse Romanticism of the last trace of German idealism" by "letting us think of poets as themselves *ursprünglich* rather than recipients of the gifts of Being."[23] But it is precisely the celebration of the poet's *Ursprünglichkeit* that is troubling–and here the symbiotic relationship between German philosophical Idealism and poetic Romanticism cannot be denied. At issue is the claim to the highest cultural significance of the poet's "autonomous" creation of new words, new languages, new worlds–a claim located in the *ursprünglich* Adamitic language of naming and creating. "Logically," Rorty expands Shelley's claim that "poets are the unacknowledged legislators of the world."[24] "A sense of human history as the history of successive metaphors would let us see the poet, in the generic sense of the maker of new words, the shaper of new languages, as the vanguard of the species" (20). A species on its way back to a future paradise, drawn into the spiral of the Romantic triad (the Hegelian dialectic) by its poetic vanguard. What are the implications of the late twentieth-century philosopher-critic's desire to reenact the Romantic poet-critics' elevation of poetic over all other discourses?

The distance between Foucault's and Derrida's positions has considerably decreased over the last decades. In his later work Foucault, too, seeks out the energies emanating from the presence, in the distant future as well as the distant past, of linguistic fullness, immediacy, and purity. A clear example is the first volume of his *History of Sexuality* with its literally mimetic, not symbolically mediated cross-temporal and cross-cultural invocations of an encircling power, which then is said to incite and control an ever-increasing, all-consuming discourse of sexuality. In these acts of, as it were, performative language use, the terms *power, discourse, sexuality, systemicity* are assigned considerably expanded meanings that diffuse their conceptual specificity. Arguably, such "counterhistory" is directed against not so much the distortion or falsification as the historicity itself of the concrete past experience and articulation of sexuality. "Reading," and then writing, the past is predicated here on the assumption that an omnipresent web of signs or hieroglyphs is spread out before the historian whose transtemporal position is secure in newly made words. Arguably, such practice with its radically simplifying language centricity has other goals than that of contributing to a more reflective, self-critical concept of historical understanding as a processual, culturally shared enterprise.

6 Self-critical historical understanding is concerned with the difficulties of gaining access to past actuality in the reading of historical documents. This also means the difficulties of making the access accessible, that is, the difficulties of writing (in response to) that reading which brings out more clearly the hermeneutic circle. It is a circle in which historians–whether they acknowledge it or not[25]–are inevitably caught but which varies from reader to reader and from text to text. In considering it, the useful approach has been to keep open, clarify, and refine an admittedly difficult, often elusive process rather than stage inexorable ruptures. Especially where such staging is done in imitation of literary theorists who themselves are imitating philosopher-critics whose metaphysical concept of language ignores the rich pluralities of language use and is thus inimical to modern historiography.

Significantly, the seductive floating of signifiers that Derridian literary theorists have passed on to some historians reveals a seriously abridged and confused notion of signification and an instructive misunderstanding of Saussure's position. The issue for Saussure was the arbitrariness of the sign in connection with its historicity: language use as convention both upheld and circumvented by individual speakers, as continuity and rupture, sameness and change, concealment and disclosure. Historians as readers have to be interested in the specificity as historicity of language use, including their own. They need to consider the implications of the fact that as readers they do and do not share—and to varying degrees—the language use of historical texts. Their challenge is mediation, and trying to meet it, they will have to reflect on their own language use. This "mixed" linguistic practice is central to the "mixed" discourse of historiography, and it, too, needs to be critically explored.

But historians like Harlan or LaCapra are not interested in detailed shared critique. LaCapra's "problematization" of the "nature and import of reading texts in history" leaves no room for questions in the interest of that "greater degree of historiographic self-understanding" that he himself proposes.[26] Like Harlan's, his approach is both eclectic and totalizing, and therefore exclusive. It may not have been clear to either Harlan or LaCapra that in their reliance on the Derridian concept of textuality, they were assuming precisely that "transcendental position outside of language" for which they have erroneously blamed other historians. But it has been clear to Rorty that this concept echoes and confirms the philosophical solipsism of Wittgenstein's position in the *Tractatus*, which emphatically denies the historicity of the philosophical self: "Was geht mich die Geschichte an? Meine Welt ist die erste und einzige!" (What do I care about history? My world is the first and only one!)[27]

Wittgenstein's concern that we cannot say anything about the world as a whole had its source in that solipsism, which, in its yearning for a paradisaically clear and complete language, excludes other speakers. From his position of "logical atomism," projection or portrayal of the facts ("*Tatsachen*") that constitute the world was possible only through the sign-facts of language based on the assumption of a logical form shared by world and language. Wittgenstein was not interested in understanding the existence of objects ("*Dinge*"), that is, ontological questions. He wanted to understand, rather, the existence of facts ("*Tatsachen*") by understanding the determinate way in which objects ("*Dinge*") are connected in a state of affairs ("*Sachverhalt*"), that is, the structure of a state of affairs (proposition 2.032). The way to understand such structures was to use models that Wittgenstein described in subpropositions to proposition 2 (2.1, 2.14, 2.141, 2.151). But these models did not solve the problem that was so profoundly disquieting to him at the time: we cannot portray the form itself—language itself—of the world. This is impossible, because to do so we would have to assume a position outside the world–or language–and then the world would cease to be the whole world–or language–for us. Wittgenstein's attempts at solving this problem led him to propose 2.171, "The picture can represent every reality whose form it has" ("Das Bild kann jede Wirklichkeit abbilden, deren Form es hat"), and 2.172, "The picture, however, cannot represent its form of representation; it shows it forth" ("Seine Form der Abbildung aber kann das Bild nicht abbilden; es weist sie auf"). The form itself of the world, then, can only *reveal* itself in the logical structure of its portrayal, which cannot portray itself. There is an obvious tension, then, between the stretching of the philosophical "I" to the world's boundary and its receptive attention to what might be revealed concerning the form of the whole world.

This tension moves the ostensibly philosophical discourse of the *Tractatus* toward poetic discourse. Wittgenstein was aware of that situation, as is clearly indicated in his letters about his intentions in the *Tractatus* to Ludwig von Ficker in 1919 and to Paul Engelmann in 1918.[28] More conclusively than his much quoted statement in the letter to Engelmann that philosophy really ought to be written like poetry ("Philosophie dürfe man eigentlich nur dichten"), proposition 4.121 points to Wittgenstein's understanding of philosophy as embedded in an essentially neo-Romantic poetic discourse: "Propositions cannot represent the logical form: this mirrors itself in the propositions. That which mirrors itself in language, language cannot represent. That which expresses *itself* in language, *we* cannot express by language. The propositions *show* the logical form of reality. They exhibit it." ("Der Satz kann die logische Form nicht darstellen, sie spiegelt sich in ihm. Was sich in der Sprache spiegelt, kann sie nicht darstellen. Was *sich* in der Sprache ausdrückt, können *wir* nicht durch sie ausdrücken. Der Satz *zeigt* die logische Form der Wirklichkeit. Er weist sie auf.")

For the Wittgenstein of the *Tractatus*, "language itself" exists in a mysteriously creative connection with a world that it significantly reveals by concealing it. Wittgenstein was to develop misgivings regarding the paradoxical silences imposed by such rigorously pure language, which he later understood to be caused by its independence of the (historical) specificity and diversity of language use. If the assumption of such independence has posed problems for the philosopher, it certainly has done so for the historian. There is the serious threat that it will lead to the usurpation of others' language use and deny the past actuality not only of the plurality of voices but also of their complexity, their contradictory and elusive nature, which are the historian's concern.

The awareness of postlapsarian language use, which reflects the role of diversity and contingency in human affairs, has been one of the great challenges to modern historiography. With the increasing fragmentation, incompleteness, ambiguity, and obscurity of modern cultural knowledge, the complete stories that make up "counterhistory" have had a strong poetic appeal for many intellectual readers. But whether focused on dismantling the power of language or debunking the language of power, they have tended to be remarkably authoritative in mistrusting the responsiveness of other voices as complementary clarification. For their radical revision of the ongoing enterprise of a critical community of inquiry, they have invoked the negative authority, so to speak, of a curiously abstract and all-embracing suspicion of power as violence inherent in all rationally organized discourse. But the indeed formidable problems of historical understanding cannot be contained in that Manichean grid of bad instrumental and good critical reason that encourages the private autonomy of the reader as rewriter. "Fantazising" about the stories of others, playing with them, and "giving free reign to the trains of associations they produce,"[29] such a reader assumes authorship vis-à-vis his predecessors, exercising an authority much more absolute and powerful than that of the deauthorized texts. The bewildering rich diversity of language use in a long and complex tradition of writing, which makes historical understanding such a difficult task, needs to be acknowledged and accommodated–from case to case, from culture to culture, from one past to the other. This presupposes the willingness and ability to understand other voices on their own terms, especially where they appear shifting and unexpected. It presupposes, too, the modern responsibility to seek out shared areas of experience and locate in them an admittedly fragile, provisional, relative communality of speech.

Notes

PREFACE. TIME TRAVEL

1. Gabriele Annan, "Cautionary Tales," *New York Review of Books* 38, no. 15 (1991): 3ff., esp. 4.

2. Siegfried Kracauer to Arnold Hauser, Nov. 26, 1962 (Literaturarchiv Marbach, Kracauer papers 72.1408/5).

CHAPTER 1. TIME AND KNOWLEDGE

1. Siegfried Kracauer, *History: Last Things before the Last* (Oxford: Oxford University Press, 1969).

2. Martin Jay, "The Extraterritorial Life of Siegfried Kracauer," *Salmagundi* 31–35 (1975–76):49–106, and "Adorno and Kracauer: Notes on a Troubled Friendship," in *Permanent Exiles: Essays on the Intellectual Migration from Germany to America* (New York: Columbia University Press, 1985), 217–36. D. N. Rodowick, "The Last Things before the Last: Kracauer and History," *New German Critique* 41 (Spring-Summer 1987):109–39. On my disagreement with Jay's and Rodowick's readings see chap. 6, secs. 4, 7, 8 of this study.

3. J. H. Hexter, Report to Oxford University Press, June 29, 1966, on the first four chapters of *History* ("*History* six folders," Literaturarchiv Marbach, Kracauer papers 72.3525/8).

4. June 4, 1962 (quoted in Ingrid Belke and Irina Renz, "Siegfried Kracauer 1889–1966," *Marbacher Magazin* 47/1988, 118).

5. Theodor W. Adorno, "Der wunderliche Realist: Über Siegfried Kracauer," in *Noten zur Literatur, Gesammelte Schriften* 2, ed. Rolf Tiedemann (Frankfurt: Suhrkamp, 1984 [1974]), 388–408, esp. 393.

6. On the similarities between *Dialectic of Enlightenment* and Derrida-influenced "philosophical" scepticism regarding historical understanding, see the Epilogue to this study.

7. See Dagmar Barnouw, *Weimar Intellectuals and the Threat of Modernity* (Bloomington: Indiana University Press, 1988), 156.

8. See Kracauer's discussion, especially with Bloch, of what he considered a harmful abstractness of Hegelian thought, chap. 2, sec. 3 of this study.

9. Kracauer would have agreed–up to a point and in certain cases–with Kurt Tucholsky's "Ein Bild sagt mehr als 1000 Worte," *UHU* (Ullstein Magazin) 3 (1926/27), Heft 2. See the critical remarks in his film criticism during the Weimar period on the transition from silent movies to talkies, chap. 4, sec. 5 of this study.

10. This is not to say that the lament for meaning was central to Simmel's cultural philosophy, which, especially in such texts as *The Philosophy of Money*, was provocatively ambiguous in this respect: see chap. 2, sec. 1 and the relevant n. 6 of this study.

On the role of Marxism during this period see Eckhardt Koehn, "Die Konkretionen des Intellekts: Zum Verhältnis von gesellschaftlicher Erfahrung und literarischer Darstellung in Kracauers Romanen," *Text + Kritik* 68 (1980):41–54, esp. 48f. Kracauer did not, as Koehn and others have argued, develop this interest under the influence of Bloch in 1925: there was no contact between them during that period, and, as shown in chap. 2 of this study, Bloch's "Marxism" differed profoundly from Kracauer's.

11. Siegfried Kracauer, *Die Angestellten: Aus dem neusten Deutschland, Schriften I* (Frankfurt: Suhrkamp, 1971), 205–304. See the discussion of this 1929 "documentary," chap. 3, sec. 6 of this study.

12. See Barnouw, *Weimar Intellectuals*, pt. 1, "Tempted by Distance."

13. See Kracauer's letter of December 8, 1923, to Leo Lowenthal complaining humorously about Adorno's "literary style [which] is, as you probably know, of such a quality as to make Benjamin's . . . scurrilous language sound like . . . baby talk" (quoted in Leo Lowenthal, *An Unmastered Past: The Autobiographical Reflections of Leo Lowenthal*, ed. Martin Jay [Berkeley: University of California Press, 1987], 206 [Lowenthal's ellipses].) See also Kracauer to Bloch, July 5, 1934 (*Briefwechsel Siegfried Kracauer–Ernst Bloch 1921–1966*, ed. Inka Mülder, vol. 1 of *Ernst Bloch Briefe 1903–1975*, ed. Uwe Opolka et al. [Frankfurt: Suhrkamp 1985]), 257–406, esp. 381f.: "He [Benjamin] has left for Denmark to see his God, and Hamlet should now have an occasion for some remarks on the two of them. . . . Perhaps in the meantime he has sent you his essay on Kafka, of which he is very proud. The treatise is really profound and beautiful, though there is, of course, that extreme eccentricity with which you are familiar. Kafka certainly would be astonished were he to be informed of his close neighborly relations with Brecht and Communism. This much entre nous."

14. See Allan Megill, "Recounting the Past: 'Description,' Explanation, and Narrative in Historiography," *American Historical Review* 94 (June 1989): 627–53, esp. 632, on the hermeneutic naïveté of logical positivists among historians. It also applies to the diverse cultural Marxisms in their relation to history. See also the recent attempt to rescue Adorno's Marxism for the postmodern experience in Frederic Jameson, *Late Marxism: Adorno or the Persistence of the Dialectic* (London: Verso, 1990), especially pt. 1, "Baleful Enchantment of the Concept" and the concluding "Adorno in the Postmodern."

15. See E. P. Thompson's argument in *The Poverty of Theory* (New York: Monthly Review Press, 1978) and in the foreword to *The Making of the English Working Class* (New York: Vintage, 1963).

16. References to *History* in the critical debates concerning historiography are confined to the contributions of literary historians: see Hans Robert Jauss, "Geschichte der Kunst und Historie," in Reinhart Koselleck and Wolf-Dieter Stempel, eds., *Geschichte Ereignis und Erzählung* (Munich: Fink, 1973), 175–209, esp. 195: in the con-

text of discussing the exclusionary tendencies of tradition, Jauss draws attention to Kracauer's "Geschichtsphilosophie" in *History*, which, he writes, "justifies in many ways the desire . . . to 'undo the injurious work of tradition'" (Jauss quotes from *History*, 7). See also Lionel Gossman, "History and Literature Reproduction or Signification," in Robert H. Canary and Henry Kozicki, eds., *The Writing of History* (Madison: The University of Wisconsin Press, 1978), 3–39, esp. 24–26. Gossman uses *History* to argue the emergence of some "correspondences between developments in historiography and certain developments in modern fiction–among them the repudiation of realism, the collapse of the subject or character as an integrated and integrating entity and an increasingly acute awareness of the fundamental logic or syntax of narrative and of the constraints and opportunities it provides." Thus he emphasizes Kracauer's statement that "harmonizing" tendencies in early twentieth-century historiography "flagrantly conflict with those of contemporary art: the modern novels of Proust, Woolf and Joyce resolutely decompose (fictitious) continuity over time" (*History*, 182). But Kracauer's concept of the cultural and epistemological "anteroom" status of historiography has nothing to do with such literarily resolute decomposition. The problems of historiographical representation, which are indeed rooted in the "contingent and indeterminant" (*History*, 181) nature of (past) reality, cannot be understood (much less solved) through analogies with modern fiction. The analogies that Kracauer thinks helpful in this context are those with the photo image. Significantly, Gossman bases his appreciation of *History* on chap. 7, "General History and the Aesthetic Approach," which is least important for the overall argument of the study. For this context see also George Levine, "Scientific Realism and Literary Representation," *Raritan* 10, no. 4 (1991): 18–39.

17. Hannah Arendt, "A Reply to Eric Voegelin," *Review of Politics* 15 (Jan. 1953): 76–84, esp. 77.

18. *History*, 16, 191–95. Historical narrative is the form of representation best suited to this kind of inquiry: see chap. 5, sec. 3 of this study. See also Megill's argument in "Recounting the Past" for an epistemologically valid status of historical narrative (637f.) and his thorough discussion of the different positions on that issue, which establishes a useful context for my critical description of Kracauer's project. For a discussion of historical versus fictional narrative, see chap. 6, sec. 1 of this study.

19. This is also true–if for different reasons–for Arendt's view of exile. See my *Visible Spaces: Hannah Arendt and the German-Jewish Experience* (Baltimore: Johns Hopkins University Press, 1990), esp. chap. 3, "The Silence of Exile."

20. Christian Meier, "Die Entstehung der Historie," in Koselleck and Stempel, *Geschichte*, 251–305, esp. 252.

21. Aristotle, *Poetics*, 9:1451b, *The Basic Works of Aristotle*, ed. Richard McKeon (New York: Random House, 1941), 1463f.

22. Eric Partridge, *Origins: A Short Etymological Dictionary of Modern English* (New York: Macmillan, 1959), 427f.

23. Attempting to clarify the contribution of modern historiographical narrative, Megill points out that poetry has "dropped out of the circle of universal knowledge" now defined by mathematics-based natural and social sciences ("Recounting the Past," 634). True; but there is also the late twentieth-century doctrinal celebration of poetry which, coming from German Romanticism via late Heidegger, underlies deconstructionist positions and asserts a general "postmodern" status of knowledge: see my argument in chap. 5 and in the Epilogue to this study.

24. Francis Bacon, *Advancement of Learning*, in *Works of Francis Bacon*, ed. James Spedding, T. E. Ellis, and D. D. Heath, 7 vols. (London: Longman and Co., 1857–59) 3:343.

25. Bacon, *De Augmentis Scientiarium, Works* 4:302.

26. See the editor's useful introduction to Francis Bacon, *The History of the Reign of King Henry the Seventh*, ed. F. J. Levy (Indianapolis: Bobbs-Merrill, 1972), 32f.–though Levy does seem to suggest an awareness on Bacon's part of the difficulties the compiler encounters in making decisions about evidence.

27. In chap. 1, "Nature," Kracauer discussed the relations between historiography and science, arguing for the overriding validity of the principle of indeterminacy in human affairs being reflected in historiography. Here he drew on the representation of indeterminacy in film, a montage sequence Eisenstein had wanted to insert into a planned screen adaptation of Dreiser's *An American Tragedy* in order to show with filmic means the complex interaction of factors not to be "grasped" logically in Clyde's decision to drown Roberta. Kracauer used this example in support of his statement: "If history is a science it is a science with a difference" (*History*, 28–30). See also chap. 6, sec. 1 of this study.

28. To Hans Kohn, Feb. 4, 1964 (Kracauer papers 72.1514/5); there were other complaints in this matter during that year, e.g., to Adorno on the occasion of his birthday essay "Der wunderliche Realist" (Apr. 1, 1964; Kracauer papers 72.1122/6). Kracauer also habitually implored all the critics who reintroduced postwar German audiences to his work not to mention his birthday: see his letter to Wolfgang Weyrauch, June 4, 1962 (excerpt in Belke and Renz, "Siegfried Kracauer," 119). On the *Fragebogen* (questionnaire) sent out in 1957 by the Deutsche Akademie für Sprache und Dichtung in an effort to record personal and professional data from the exiles, Kracauer, though very thorough in his bibliographical information, repeatedly "forgot" to supply the date of his birth (Deutsche Bibliothek Frankfurt, Nachlass W. Sternfeld EB 75/177).

29. Feb. 24, 1963 (Kracauer papers, Adorno correspondence folder 4, 72.1121/12). On the meanings of such extraterritoriality for the historian's negotiation of historical time and her own historicity see chap. 5, sec. 2 of this study.

30. This also concerned the places of exile: on his return from a long trip to Europe, Kracauer wrote to Leo Lowenthal on Oct. 27, 1958: "When we . . . came back to our apartment, I had an attack of claustrophobia. It really is unnatural to have a permanent residence, a so-called home; the best thing is to live like a vagabond. The next day

I was reconciled with my existence here. It is good for working and I have the feeling of being, so to speak, extraterritorial" (Literaturarchiv Marbach, Kracauer papers 72.1571/7).

31. Adorno made this claim for *History* in "Der wunderliche Realist," 407. However, the general tenor of this deeply ambivalent and curiously self-centered piece is to stress the friend's distance from philosophy, which Adorno held responsible for the "dilettantish" quality of Kracauer's cultural critique. He also thought significant Benjamin's calling Kracauer "an enemy of philosophy . . . once, around 1923" (ibid.).

32. Feb. 10, 1961 (Kracauer papers 72.1571/20); italicized words are in English.

33. On Kracauer's choice between the different meanings of *redemption* see chap. 6, sec. 8 of this study.

34. Kracauer writes about that significant moment when, coming across an early essay on photography, he realized that decades ago he had already "compared historism with photography." It was an important discovery because it "confirmed the legitimacy and inner necessity of my historical pursuits; and by the same token it justified . . . the years I had spent on *Theory of Film.*" Conceived "as an aesthetics of the photographic media, not less and not more," the film book now appears to him "in its true light: as another attempt of mine to bring out the significance of areas whose claim to be acknowledged in their own right has not yet been recognized" (*History,* 4). Significantly, Kracauer does not mention here—or anywhere else in the copious preparatory notes to *History*—the early essay's ambivalent attitude toward the cultural meanings of both historism and photography: see chap. 3, sec. 1 of this study.

Kracauer had asked a student engaged in research for a dissertation on his work to look for early essays in which history played a role. She found six, among them "Die Photographie" (*Frankfurter Zeitung,* Oct. 28, 1927, now in Siegfried Kracauer, *Das Ornament der Masse: Essays* [Frankfurt: Suhrkamp, 1963], 21–39), with its comparison between nineteenth-century interest in historiography and the nineteenth-century development of photography. The student's letter to Kracauer of Feb. 2, 1962, is quoted in Jay, "The Extraterritorial Life," 90. See also Kracauer's entry in his compendium of notes for *History,* "Guide (original) (complete)": "With Ranke's writings, historicism gains momentum simultaneously with the rise of photography" (Kracauer papers 72.3525/1, 9).

35. "Guide," 9; for a definition of "found story" see Siegfried Kracauer, *Theory of Film: The Redemption of Physical Reality* (New York: Oxford University Press, 1960), chap. 14, "The Found Story and the Episode."

Chapter 2. Contemporaneity and the Concept of History

1. Letters to Adorno of Apr. 1, 1964, and Feb. 24, 1963 (Literaturarchiv Marbach, Kracauer papers 721122/6 and 721121/12).

2. In contrast to most professional readers of Kracauer's work, I think it useful to emphasize its continuity: see n. 26 below.

Since the rediscovery of Kracauer's Weimar texts in (West) Germany, critics have tended to stress his intellectual kinship with Adorno, Bloch, and Benjamin, despite clear textual evidence to the contrary: Gerwin Zohlen, "Text-Strassen: Zur Theorie der Stadtlektüre bei Siegfried Kracauer," *Text + Kritik Siegfried Kracauer* (Oct. 1980), 62–72, esp. 64, 68; Stefan Oswald, "Die gebrochenen Farben des Übergangs: Zum Essay Band 'Das Ornament der Masse,'" ibid., 76–81, esp. 77–79. More useful are the distinctions drawn in Michael Schröter, "Weltzerfall und Rekonstruktion: Zur Physiognomik Siegfried Kracauers," ibid., 18–40, esp. 23, 25, 37–40.

3. Dec. 13, 1929, "Briefwechsel Siegfried Kracauer–Ernst Bloch 1921–1966," ed. Inka Mülder, *Ernst Block: Briefe 1903–1975*, ed. Uwe Opolka et al. (Frankfurt: Suhrkamp, 1985, 2 vols.), 1:257–406, esp. 329. The literal translation would be "as deep as an abyss."

4. Adorno, "Der wunderliche Realist," *Noten zur Literatur, Gesammelte Schriften* (*G.S.*), ed. Rolf Tiedemann (Frankfurt: Suhrkamp, 1984 [1974]) 2:388–408, esp. 393. First published in *Neue Deutsche Hefte* (Sept. 1964), 17–39, the essay was included in *Noten zur Literatur 3* (Frankfurt: Suhrkamp, 1965). The phrase "erbittliches Nachdenken" ("exorable reflection": *NDH*, 20) was eliminated here and not reinserted in *G.S.*

5. In "Der wunderliche Realist," Adorno claims that Benjamin "invented" this "mixed" approach, as if Kracauer then "owed" it to Benjamin (*G.S.* 2:396). However, Benjamin, who wrote for *Frankfurter Zeitung* on a freelance basis, was clearly influenced by Kracauer. This is not so much to argue influences as to point out Adorno's attempts to set up cultural hierarchies on the basis of authorities; Benjamin, promoted by Adorno, was just beginning to become one.

6. See the disagreement between Adorno and Bloch over the latter's review, "Revue Form in Philosophy" (1928), of Benjamin's *Einbahnstrasse* (Ernst Bloch, *Erbschaft dieser Zeit Gesamtausgabe* 4 [Frankfurt: Suhrkamp, 1962], 368–71; *Heritage of Our Times*, trans. Neville and Stephen Plaice [Cambridge, U.K.: Polity Press, 1991], 334–37). Bloch's suggestion of Benjamin's affinities in *Einbahnstrasse* to Simmel's "questioning-questionable impressions" (*Erbschaft*, 369; *Heritage*, 335) had led Adorno to accuse him of hostility toward Benjamin because, for the Frankfurt School, Simmel's "impressionism" amounted to original (intellectual) sin. Bloch sensibly rejected this insinuation, defending Simmel and his (indeed unquestionable) influence on Benjamin: Bloch to Adorno, December 1934, "Briefe an Theodor W. Adorno 1928–1968," ed. Inka Mülder, *Briefe*, 2:423–28, esp. 424f.

In his *Soziologie als Wissenschaft Eine erkenntnistheoretische Untersuchung* (1922) Kracauer vacillated in his evaluation of Simmel's contribution to social philosophical thought. This in many ways confused "philosophical" critique of sociology is centered in a rejection of theoretical systems (idealism) from a phenomenological position that, like Husserl's, combines metaphysical and empirical impulses. Husserl pointed out the differences between them in an informal evaluation of the text in a letter of Jan. 14, 1934: "Auf anthropologischem Boden fand ich darin fruchtbare Gedanken entwickelt, die (oder mit denen verwandte) ich im systematischen Zusammenhang meiner Phänomenologie aus transzendentalen Quellen (und entsprechend gewandeltem Sinn) durchzuführen versucht hatte. Meine diesbezügliche Publication steht noch aus." Husserl saw rightly that Kracauer did not share his interest in "transcendental sources"–the only "solution" of the arch problem of how to make valid general statements concerning individual perspectives on the phenomenal world: see chap. 5, sec. 7 of this study. Trying to establish himself in Paris, Kracauer had asked Husserl to write in his support and included Husserl's letter, together with two recent references from Thomas and Heinrich Mann, in his application to the American Guild of June 8, 1938 (Deutsche Bibliothek Frankfurt, Kracauer American Guild EB 70/177).

7. For a detailed discussion of Kracauer's reaction to Adorno's intellectual portrait of him in "Der wunderliche Realist" see chap. 5, sec. 1 of this study.

8. "Georg Simmel," *Das Ornament der Masse* (Frankfurt: Suhrkamp, 1963), 209–48, esp. 247. This 1920 evaluation of Simmel's "mixed" philosophical-essayistic discourse is influenced, to a degree, by the student's intellectual dependence on the teacher, but it does stress those aspects that were to become important for Kracauer's own attempts in that direction.

9. "Der wunderliche Realist," 393–94.

10. "Das Ornament der Masse," *Ornament*, 50–63, esp. 50. The essay was first published in *Frankfurter Zeitung*, June 9 and 10, 1927.

11. For a discussion of the concept of distraction see chap. 3, sec. 4 of this study.

12. See Kracauer's 1947 "Jean Vigo" in Lewis Jacobs, ed., *Introduction to the Arts of the Movies* (New York: Noonday Press, 1960), 223–27. Kracauer admired Vigo for his method of composition because it revealed an "original relation to the screen." His plots were light and very loosely knit, his emphasis was on the imaginative presentation of objects in their spaces. But praising the results of this technique in *Zero de conduite*, Kracauer expressed reservations about the degree to which the filmmaker's fascination with objects had taken over in *Atalante*: "Responding to the overwhelming appeal of material phenomena, Vigo, however, more and more withdrew from social criticism. In *Atalante* it appears, indeed, as if he actually had wanted to affirm an attitude hostile to intellectual awareness. Could it be, then, that Vigo's career had taken a retrogressive course? But in *Zero de conduite* satire still manifested itself, and perhaps he indulged in the magic of mute objects and dark instincts only in order, some day, to pursue more thoroughly and knowingly the task of disenchantment" (227).

13. "Das Ornament der Masse," 58.

14. See Dagmar Barnouw, *Weimar Intellectuals and the Threat of Modernity* (Bloomington: Indiana University Press, 1988), pt. 1.

15. See Epilogue, sec. 4, of this study; Richard Rorty's recipe for being competently postmodern is to mix cultural utopianism, cultural despair, and estheticism: see his *Contingency, irony, and solidarity* (Cambridge: Cambridge University Press, 1989).

In "Das Ornament der Masse," 56–59, Kracauer affirms Max Weber's concept of disenchantment.

16. See chap. 4, sec. 5 of this study.

17. For a critique of the Frankfurt school's critique of Enlightenment culture see Dagmar Barnouw, "Modernity and Enlightenment Thought," *The Enlightenment and Its Legacy Studies in German Literature in Honor of Helga Slessarev*, ed. Sarah Friedrichsmeyer and Barbara Becker-Cantarino (Bonn: Bouvier, 1991), 1–14. See also the Epilogue of this study.

18. "Die Photographie," *Ornament*, 21–39, first published in *Frankfurter Zeitung*, Oct. 28, 1927; "Zu den Schriften Walter Benjamins," *Ornament*, 249–55, first published in *Frankfurter Zeitung*, July 15, 1928.

19. Walter Benjamin, "The Work of Art in the Age of Mechanical Reproduction" and "On Some Motifs in Baudelaire," both originally published in the Frankfurt Institute's *Zeitschrift füer Sozialforschung* 1936 and 1939, now in *Illuminations*, ed. Hannah Arendt (New York: Harcourt, Brace and World, 1968). On the ambiguities and contradictions of Benjamin's argument here see Barnouw, *Weimar Intellectuals*, 187–90.

20. Letter of Mar. 18, 1936, *G.S.* 1 (1972): 1000–1006, esp. 1002f.

21. See also a suggestive passage in the first version of the essay, *G.S.* 1:440.

22. For the discussion between Adorno and Benjamin concerning the publication of this first version of the essay on Baudelaire, a part of the book project on the Paris Arcades, see *G.S.* 1:1065–1136.

23. "On Some Motifs in Baudelaire," *Illuminations*, 157–96, esp. 189f.

24. Kracauer's use of the term *Transparent*, "transparency," plays on the double meaning of shining through and being displayed; see chap. 5, sec. 3 of this study.

25. Siegfried Kracauer, *Theory of Film: The Redemption of Physical Reality* (New York: Oxford University Press, 1960), 14–16; *History: Last Things before the Last* (Oxford: Oxford University Press, 1969), 160–63.

26. Inka Mülder-Bach, whose *Siegfried Kracauer: Grenzgänger zwischen Theorie und Literatur: Seine frühen Schriften 1913–1933* (Stuttgart: Metzler, 1985) provides a useful introduction to Kracauer's Weimar texts, insists in a more recent article on a distinct and far-reaching split between Kracauer's prewar and postwar work: "Schlupflöcher: Die Diskontinuität des Kontinuierlichen im Werk Siegfried Kracauers," in Michael Kessler and Thomas Y. Levin, eds., *Siegfried Kracauer: Neue Interpretationen* (Tübingen: Stauffenburg, 1990), 249–66. She is unfamiliar with Kracauer's work on photography (published and unpublished), which is centered precisely in the exploration of the seemingly insignificant, easily obscured "surface" phenomena of modern life which she sees sacrificed to allegedly totalizing tendencies in the exile texts. For a similar if more interesting argument see Helmut Lethen, "Sichtbarkeit. Kracauer's Liebeslehre," *Siegfried Kracauer*, 195–222.

27. See Barnouw, *Weimar Intellectuals*, 161–67.

28. "Zu den Schriften Walter Benjamins," *Ornament*, 251–55, esp. 251.

29. See chap. 6, sec. 8 of this study.

30. This pressure could have come from Adorno, and it did come from Bloch; see Ernst Bloch to Kracauer, Feb. 4, 1928, *Briefe* 1:295–97, esp. 296.

31. See the many sketches of urban scenes, written for *Frankfurter Zeitung* during the Weimar period and later collected in *Strassen in Berlin und anderswo* (Frankfurt: Suhrkamp, 1964).

32. "Zu den Schriften," 255; Kracauer here quotes Benjamin on Kraus.

33. "Zu den Schriften," 254. See also Kracauer's letter to Adorno of Aug. 1, 1930, concerning Adorno's assertion that Kracauer had accepted Benjamin's "formula of buidings as the dreams of the collective": "This is not the case at all. I referred to certain spatial images as society's dreams because they represent a level of this society's existence which has been concealed from its consciousness. That is, I meet Benjamin–who, by the way, is of the same opinion–only in the word *dream*. It is like meeting at a street crossing and then continuing in different directions. The view of the city as a dream of the collective still seems to me romantic" (Kracauer papers 72.1119/6).

34. See Lowenthal's instructively contradictory celebration of this status of the exile as central to the intellectual's authenticity and integrity in his "In Memory of Walter Benjamin: The Integrity of the Intellectual," in *An Unmastered Past: The Autobiographical Reflections of Leo Lowenthal*, ed. Martin Jay (Berkeley: University of California Press, 1987), 216–34. The reader is not told that the essay was written for the publisher Suhrkamp's celebration of the complete edition of Benjamin's work, which, with its literally fantastic devotion to annotation, was exactly what is called in German a *Klassikerausgabe*, that is, an edition fit for the culturally most established, the canonical writer–an edition, too, that belongs to a period of religious belief in high culture.

35. In an early essay, "Die Gruppe als Ideenträger" ("The Group as Transmitter of Ideas"), *Ornament*, 123–56, first published in *Archiv für Sozialwissenschaft und Sozialpolitik* 1922, Kracauer tried to clarify such connections, which are esssential for intellectual cultural politics.

36. For an instructive counterexample see Bloch's epistolary style in *Ernst Bloch–Arnold Metzger "Wir arbeiten im gleichen Bergwerk," Briefwechsel 1942–1972*, ed. Karola Bloch, Ilse Metzger, and Eberhard Braun (Frankfurt: Suhrkamp, 1987): Bloch relied on Metzger in practical matters in exile, responding to his appeals for intellectual intimacy with formulaic and largely impenetrable reiterations of his, Bloch's, philosophical position.

37. The complexity of cultural processes to which the dynamics within intellectual groups contribute significantly is frequently lost in the streamlining memories of the former participants: see Leo Lowenthal's highly selective, admiring, and harmonizing 1979 "Theodor W. Adorno: An Intellectual Memoir" and his 1983 "Recollections of Theodor W. Adorno," *An Unmastered Past*, 183–200, 201–15. In the context of stating his skepticism regarding the accuracy of historiography in general, and on the subject of the Frankfurt Institute for Social Research in particular, he writes: "This experience

has led me to reflect on the question of documentation. One may reconstruct history from documents, or one may rely on memory; I, however, have the great fortune to possess both documents *and* a memory, and these serve mutually to correct each other" ("Recollections," 202). Having survived the other members of the Frankfurt Institute, Lowenthal wrote these pieces for celebratory occasions, emphasizing that "Adorno was a genius" ("Adorno," 183, 189) and "brotherly" friend to Lowenthal as a member of the "inner circle" (188, 190) of the Institute. This memory might have been corrected by the letters he wrote when Adorno and Horkheimer were alive and difficult: see Lowenthal to Kracauer, Dec. 13, 1963 (English original):

> The most traumatic event of my whole life which I probably will never overcome and which literally makes me suffer at some hour every day and every night is the estrangement from the old group. . . . It is not a nice story and it is quite possible that I committed more mistakes and acted more wrongly than MH. The provocations, however, defy description. I have little respect for Teddie's so-called solidarity which led him to break off any connections with me and has led to such absurdities as the complete silence for my name and work in the circles of the Institute. I must frankly say that I find it rather degrading for them and not for me to use the occasion of private fights for intellectual defamation. I have never talked to anybody about it but I think it is time that you are at least aware of this cauldron. (Kracauer papers 72.2642/15)

For additional documentation of L.L.'s difficulties with Adorno and Horkheimer see also his letters to S.K. of Jan. 20 and Apr. 28, 1958, and S. K.'s answer of May 3, 1958 (ibid., 72.2641/16, 18 and 72.1571/3).

The Frankfurters' vanguard status was always central to their intellectual politics–a situation that seemed problematic to Kracauer in the Weimar period and increasingly so in exile. But that status continued to be important to Lowenthal. If he celebrated "this genius" Adorno as "Germany's most prominent academic teacher and outstanding citizen of the Western European avant-garde," he responded to the fact that for several decades Adorno had dominated the intellectual scene in West Germany. There was no reason to question now Adorno's "merciless, but always theoretically founded, indictment of the social phenomena themselves as well as their faulty, distorted, and manipulated pseudo-interpretations in bourgeois philosophy, social research, and literary criticism" ("Adorno," 189f).

38. "Prophetentum," *Frankfurter Zeitung*, Aug. 27, 1922. See Bloch's letter of Sept. 1, 1922 (*Briefe* 1:265–68, esp. 266). Among other things, Bloch had argued that his language was not, as Kracauer thought, "*zügellos*" (undisciplined) and had referred him to his "Arbeiten zur Sprachlogik." But Bloch's language in his "serious," "public" texts was often, as Kracauer pointed out, dysfunctionally "creative." See also Bloch's refusal, compounding his difficulties in exile, to consider his readers' desire to understand at least partly what they were reading: Peter Zudeick, *Der Hintern des Teufels: Ernst Bloch–Leben und Werk* (Moos: Elster Verlag, 1985), 177–80. On similar tendencies in Benjamin see my *Weimar Intellectuals*, 164–67.

39. Leo Lowenthal quotes from a letter Kracauer wrote him on Aug. 31, 1923: "As a thinker he [Rosenzweig] is and remains an idealist . . . and even his star won't redeem

him from that–just as I don't believe that his book will have great success in the future, in spite of Scholem and his brother Benjamin" ("Recollections of Adorno," 205).

40. Siegfried Kracauer, "Die Bibel auf Deutsch," *Ornament*, 173–86, esp. 173–74, first published in *Frankfurter Zeitung*, Apr. 27–28, 1926. See Stephané Moses, "Walter Benjamin and Franz Rosenzweig," *Philosophical Forum* 15, nos. 1–2 (1983): 188–205. Martin Jay, "Politics of Translation. Siegfried Kracauer and Walter Benjamin on the Buber-Rosenzweig Bible," *Yearbook of the Leo Baeck Institute* 21 (1976): 3–24, does not do justice to Kracauer's arguments.

41. Kracauer's phrase is "aus dem mythologischen Betrieb," the implication being that such *Betrieb*, a term meaning both "enterprise" and "hectic activity," may be a contemporary but not a contemporaneous phenomenon. On the issue of *Ungleichzeitigkeit*, "noncontemporaneity," see this chapter, sec. 5.

42. "Die Bibel auf Deutsch," 183–86. See too, Kracauer's comments on Lowenthal's resolve to study Hebrew in a letter to L. of Apr. 12, 1924 (quoted in Ingrid Belke and Irina Renz, "Siegfried Kracauer 1889–1966," *Marbacher Magazin* 47/1988, 40). It would be a pity, Kracauer writes, if Lowenthal distanced himself from intellectually accessible European philosophy and turned himself into a Hebraist. Like Kracauer, Lowenthal is a "hybrid," a modern intellectual to whom the "brilliance of the authentic" is not becoming. Though he might very well be seduced by "buberisieren" or "scholemisieren," the existentially "positive" word is not his. Going back to the roots is not an option.

43. May 20, 1926, *Briefe*, 1:269–71, esp. 269.

44. In the most directly political of the essays in *History and Class Consciousness*, "Toward a Methodology of the Problem of Organisation," Lukacs assigned, in philosophically "objective" terms, extraordinary intellectual power and leadership to the party, but the Communist party, directed from Moscow, did not perceive such exalted claims as politically advantageous.

45. May 27, 1926, *Briefe*, 1:272–74.

46. See *Weimar Intellectuals*, 167f.

47. See Lee Congdon, *The Young Lukacs* (Chapel Hill: University of North Carolina Press, 1983), 76–78, esp. 78. See Eva Karadi, "Bloch und Lukacs im Weber-Kreis," in Arno Münster et al., eds, *Verdinglichung und Utopie: Ernst Bloch und Georg Lukacs zum 100. Geburtstag* (Frankfurt: Sendler, 1987), 30–47.

48. See here the astonishingly untroubled entelechy that Lukacs, with hindsight, imposed on his life: Istvan Eoersie, ed., *Georg Lukacs: Record of a Life. An Autobiographical Sketch* (London: Verso Editions, 1983), esp. chap. 3, "In Exile."

49. Georg Lukacs, *History and Class Consciousness Studies in Marxist Dialectics* (Cambridge: MIT Press, 1971 [1962]), xxiii.

50. "Aktualität und Utopie Zu Lukacs' Philosophie des Marxismus," *Der Neue Merkur* 7 (1923/24): 457–77.

51. "The Marxism of Rosa Luxemburg," *History and Class Consciousness*, 27–45, esp. 27.

52. On reactions to Karl Mannheim's suggestions along these lines in *Ideology and Utopia* (1929), see *Weimar Intellectuals*, 2–5.

53. "Rosa Luxemburg," 34 (my emphasis).

54. "Toward a Methodology of the Problem of Organisation," *History and Class Consciousness*, 323.

55. "Briefwechsel Georg Lukacs–Ernst Bloch 1910–1971," ed. Arno Münster, *Briefe*, 1:25–208: Apr. 30 and July 2, 1965 (206–7). See also Bloch's congratulatory note of Apr. 9, 1965, sent through Lukacs's West German publisher (205). For the development of their friendship between 1910 and 1917 see *Briefe*, 1:28–192.

56. *Briefe* 1: 194–205.

57. In contrast to the politically ambitious Lukacs, Bloch was interested in cultural power: see his delighted description of his privileged position in East Germany, which echoes descriptions of utopian existence in *The Principle of Hope*, quoted in Zudeick, *Der Hintern des Teufels*, 206–17.

58. See Lowenthal, "Recollections of Adorno," about Adorno's charmed existence ("protected beautiful life"), which gave him his enduring self-centered "confidence" that the world would adapt itself to him (203f.). His fin-de-siècle precociousness and preciousnes, powerfully attractive to the young Lowenthal, and for a while also to Kracauer, would not be tainted by experience. For an example of Kracauer's fond irony regarding the young Kierkegaardian's high seriousness, see his letter of Dec. 8, 1923, to Leo Lowenthal (quoted Lowenthal, *An Unmastered Past*, 206).

59. See *Weimar Intellectuals*, 154f.

60. *Theodor W. Adorno und Ernst Krenek: Briefwechsel*, ed. Wolfgang Rogge (Frankfurt: Suhrkamp, 1974), 220; see Susan Buck-Morss, *The Origin of Negative Dialectics: Theodor W. Adorno, Walter Benjamin, and the Frankfurt Institute* (New York: Free Press, 1977), 28–30.

61. See for instance Lukacs, *Essays on Thomas Mann* (New York: Grosset and Dunlap, 1965); see also Bloch's congratulatory letter to Lukacs of June 11, 1955, on his "masterful" essay on *Felix Krull* (later the third part of *Essays on Thomas Mann*) in *Aufbau* 11 (1955), in which Lukacs "protected Mann against himself and against the advice of Adorno-Wiesengrund" (*Briefe*, 1:202–5, 203). Here Bloch also points out the profound and genuine links between them: they have the same friends and the same enemies; together they are "considered to demonstrate to the intelligentsia most uniquely the high level and the perspectives, the wealth of knowledge and the humaneness of Marxism" (203f.).

62. Buck-Morss, useful in outlining Adorno's reception of *History and Class Consciousness*, is not sufficiently clear on (or interested in) these priorities (36–38).

63. *Adorno und Krenek: Briefwechsel*, 215.

64. June 6, 1926, *Briefe*, 1:275–78, esp. 277f. 276. *Selbstergreifung*, literally "self-grasping," signifies Bloch's attempt at emphasizing the active, concrete energy in the proletariat's becoming self-conscious. *Volk Gottes*, Bloch explains, is a Benjaminian term that, for unspecified reasons, he thinks useful in "this difficult area."

65. June 29, 1926, *Briefe*, 1:280–85, esp. 280.

66. It was Kant, not Hegel, to whom Kracauer, in the role of mentor, had introduced the younger Adorno in the early 1920s: "Der wunderliche Realist," 388f.

67. See Bloch to Kracauer, Mar. 22 and Aug. 5, 1928, *Briefe*, 1:299f., esp. 309.

68. Dec. 11, 1929, *Briefe*, 1:322–28, esp. 323.

69. "Briefe an Theodor W. Adorno 1928–1968," ed. Inka Mülder, *Briefe*, 2:407–56, esp. 421f. The context is Bloch's rejection of an accusation Lukacs had made from Moscow about his concept of economics.

70. Dec. 13, 1929, *Briefe*, 1:328–30, esp. 329; the review essay had been submitted for publication in *Frankfurter Zeitung*. See also Siegfried Kracauer, "Betrachtungen zu Greens Leviathan," *Frankfurter Zeitung*, Dec. 1, 1929, Literaturblatt nr.48.

71. Mar. 13, 1930, *Briefe*, 1:332f.

72. Apr. 29, 1931, *Briefe*, 1:353–56.

73. *Briefe*, 1:356, n. 6; 362, n. 5.

74. May 25, 1932, *Briefe*, 1:357f. For information on the film and an analysis of Kracauer's review, see chap. 4, sec. 5 of this study.

75. May 29, 1932, *Briefe*, 1:358–62, esp. 358: Kracauer points out that his protest against the censor had been more thorough than others and that his concrete, detailed argumentation would have contributed substantially to the lifting of the ban. The decision against publishing Benjamin's piece concerned most probably the indeed very problematic "Was ist das epische Theater?" (see *Briefe* 1:355, n. 2).

76. Bloch was not impressed by the fact that Kracauer had changed his mind on Tretiakev's work, now praising his method of production and his documentary style in two articles in *Frankfurter Zeitung* (Feb. 17 and Apr. 17, 1932).

77. June 1, 1932, *Briefe*, 1:363f.; on Adorno's critique thirty years later of Kracauer's enduring empiricism, see chap. 5, sec. 1 of this study.

78. On Bloch's self-centeredness, see especially the voluminous, detailed correspondence with Lukacs from 1910 to 1917 (*Briefe*, 1:28–192) on Bloch's financial difficulties, caused largely by establishing himself and his new wife in high bourgeois style. Bloch presented these difficulties in terms of Lukacs's bourgeois lack of emotional warmth and financial generosity, in particular, and as indicative of the religiopolitical corruption of the world in general (see especially *Briefe*, 1:126–31, 153–55). The correspondence also documents Bloch's curiously exploitative relationship with his first wife, whose aristocratic elegance and blondness he adored (see *Briefe*, 1:42, 49, 102, 112–16). Intellectual temperament, responsible for intellectual choices,

is intimately connected with such attitudes. In exile he did on occasion see his own considerable problems in the context of the even greater difficulties of others: see his letters to the American Guild in 1938 and 1939 concerning support. Deutsche Bibliothek Frankfurt, American Guild EB 70/177.

Sending Lukacs an essay and anticipating some reservations as to its "conceptual acuity," Bloch insisted that it was there, "but often only in an adjective, and that is why you have to read well" (June 6, 1915, *Briefe*, 1:158). However, these adjectives, no doubt fraught with profound meaning, tend to resist even the reader who is willing to cross-reference attributive connotations for the relatively few and then still unrelated key notions that make up Bloch's "philosophy."

79. The Ur-form of this circle was the relationship with Lukacs, which Bloch, in a letter to Lukacs of Aug. 16, 1916 (*Briefe*, 1:166–71, esp. 167), described as a "realm in which, excepting us, no living soul can breathe and of which nobody has any notion." See also Lowenthal's enthusiastic evaluation of the cultural significance of an elite group in his "I Never Wanted to Play Along: Interviews with Helmut Dubiel," (*An Unmastered Past*, 15–159). Lowenthal explains the formative influence of the Institute for all its members (58) and especially for him, who belonged to the "hard core that determined the Institute's theoretical orientation": "My first years there were a sort of anticipated utopia: we were different, and we knew the world better" (77). To Lowenthal, the history of that group seems "quite extraordinary." One of the reasons is the *Zeitschrift für Sozialforschung*, which he compares with Kraus's *Fackel* in terms of importance and univocal editorial position, "although written not by one person but by a group working closely together." He finds extraordinary, too, the fact that the group had built in the United States "an island of German radical intellectuals. This in itself was rather significant. If I were to elaborate on all of this in detail it would add up to a unique fusion of intellectual talent, worldwide political perspectives, and a far-ranging imagination molded by an upper-class Jewish lifestyle. None of us believed that all this would be confirmed by the reputation earned by the Frankfurt group" (59). See also his explicit pride in the group's intellectual isolation in exile and their distinctness from other emigré groups: "We were completely isolated; ours was a singular story. . . . We did not wish to be typical" (65).

80. It is precisely this quality that has made him enduringly attractive to many West German intellectuals—young and not so young, radical and not so radical—whereas Adorno, whose position of significant negativity profoundly influenced a whole generation of West German intellectuals after the war, was openly criticized by radical students during the cultural revolution of the 1960s.

81. July 12, 1911, *Briefe*, 1:39–43, esp. 41. See Zudeick's official Bloch biography, *Der Hintern des Teufels*, which documents this fact, inadvertently and convincingly.

82. June 4, 1932, *Briefe*, 1:365–68, esp. 368.

83. June 29, 1926, *Briefe*, 1:280–85, esp. 281.

84. See Oswald, "Die gebrochenen Farben des Übergangs," 76–77, and Schröter, "Weltzerfall und Rekonstruktion," 18–20.

85. Dec. 1934, *Briefe*, 2:423–34, esp. 423, 429–31.

86. Adorno's letter no longer exists. His objections have to be inferred from Bloch's answer (especially *Briefe*, 2:424–26, 430) and his letter to Benjamin of Dec. 18, 1934 ("Briefe an Walter Benjamin 1934–1937," ed. Burghart Schmidt, *Briefe*, 2:649–68, esp. 658–61). Here Bloch refers to the "disciple Wiesengrund's" objections to the essay collection, *Heritage of Our Times*, in general but particularly to his reprinting the review of Benjamin's 1928 *Einbahnstrasse*, "Revueform in der Philosophie." Bloch wants to impress on Benjamin that the revised version of the original review emphasizes the "surrealistically most important point of your approach," assuring him of his "*profound* collegiality" (*Briefe*, 2:658f.). But he also acknowledges enduring disagreements on both sides. In the important letter to Kracauer of June 1, 1932, he complained of Benjamin's "cold and insolent language"; in contrast, there had never been any unkindness in *their* relationship (*Briefe*, 1:364).

87. See his protest to his old friend Metzger regarding his prior rights to the phrase "Transzendieren ohne Transzendenz," asserting, at the same time, that ultimately, of course, he was for abolishing mine-thine distinctions ("*Wir arbeiten im gleichen Bergwerk*," 112–17, esp. 113).

88. *Briefe*, 2:426: "wie ein endloses Nachtgespräch."

89. Bloch to Adorno, Mar. 18, 1934, *Briefe*, 2:434–37, esp. 435.

CHAPTER 3. REPRESENTATION AS RECLAMATION

1. D. N. Rodowick, "The Last Things before the Last Kracauer and History," *New German Critique* 41 (Spring-Summer 1987): 109–39, conjures up a Benjaminian spirit in *History* (see chap. 6, sec. 8 of this study), using references to *Theory of Film* in order to juxtapose Benjamin and Kracauer quotes (112f., 120f.) that put falsifying mystico-Freudian hues into Kracauer's interest in the visual dimension of "physical reality."

2. Siegfried Kracauer, *Theory of Film: The Redemption of Physical Reality* (New York: Oxford University Press, 1960), 16.

3. May 31 and Sept. 25, 1959 (Literaturarchiv Marbach, Kracauer papers 72.1571/10,12).

4. See Erwin Panofsky, "Style and Medium in the Motion Pictures," *Critique* 1, no. 3 (1947): 5–28, revised version of a 1937 essay of the same title, now in Gerald Mast and Marshall Cohen, eds, *Film Theory and Criticism* (New York: Oxford University Press, 1985), 215–33, esp. 216: "Today there is no denying that narrative films are not only 'art' . . . but also, besides architecture, cartooning and 'commercial design,' the only visual art entirely alive. The 'movies' have reestablished that dynamic contact between art production and art consumption which . . . is sorely attenuated, if not entirely interrupted, in many other fields of artistic endeavor." In *Theory of Film* Kracauer draws repeatedly on this intelligent and shrewd essay. See also Alfred Stieglitz's memories of the positive reactions of painters to his early (in some ways "pictorial") photos in the 1880s and their regret that they were just photos: "'If they had been made by hand, they would be art.' . . . I found it difficult how, with society supposed to be 'in

the hands of engineers,' machine-made objects were looked down upon. In a sense, a camera and lens are mere mechanical objects. Nonetheless, without my being one with them, what aroused admiration for my pictures could not have existed. I developed a natural respect both for well-made machines and for whatever they produce that is beautifully created" (Dorothy Norman, *Alfred Stieglitz: An American Seer* (New York: Random House, 1973 Aperture]), 30f.

5. "*Theorie des Films* Vorfassung" 1940 Marseille (Kracauer papers 72.3557/6).

6. The comparatively recent Kracauer renaissance in Germany has stressed the Weimar Kracauer and exaggerated a break in his work after he went into exile, especially with reference to *Theory of Film* and *History*: see chap. 2, n. 26 of this study.

7. Kracauer to Bloch, June 29, 1926, "Briefwechsel Siegfried Kracauer–Ernst Bloch 1921–1966," ed. Inka Mülder, in *Ernst Bloch Briefe 1903–1975*, ed. Uwe Opolka et al. (Frankfurt: Suhrkamp, 1985, 2 vols.), 1:257–406, esp. 281: "Nothing may be forgotten and nothing remembered may remain unchanged. The motive of transformation plays a decisive role for me."

8. See chap. 5, sec. 4 of this study.

9. In *Theory of Film*, chap. 3, "The Establishment of Physical Existence," where he focuses on the reclamation of seemingly insignificant, inconspicuous details of the life-world in the filmic representation of "physical reality," Kracauer not only does not distinguish between the still and the moving image, but he also seems to give credit (and responsibility) for such reclamation to the camera rather than the photographer or director.

10. See Kracauer's letters to Panofsky of Dec. 12, 1948, Jan. 23, 1949, and Nov. 6, 1949 (Kracauer papers 72.1686/22–24), thanking him for his support of Kracauer's (successful) application for a Bollingen Foundation Fellowship (23) and for his advice regarding the history of photography (24).

11. See *Theory of Film*, chap. 3, "The Establishment of Physical Existence," where Kracauer gives a number of examples for the capacity of photo images to retain information both crosstemporally and crossculturally: for instance, the anecdote about rural African viewers noticing a chicken that appeared momentarily in the corner of a frame and that had been overlooked by the European filmmaker.

12. *Theory of Film*, chap. 10, "Experimental Film," 188: Kracauer here quotes Deren's critique of "the concept behind the usual abstract film" as denying the "special capacity of film to manipulate real elements" and substituting "exclusively the elements of artifice (the method of painting)" (*An Anagram of Ideas on Art, Form and Film* [Yonkers, N.Y., 1946], 46).

13. Maya Deren, "Cinematography: The Creative Use of Reality," *Daedalus* 89, no. 1 (1960), now in Mast and Cohen, *Film Theory and Criticism*, 51–65, esp. 54, 56.

14. See Panofsky, "Style and Medium," 218.

15. Deren, "Cinematography," 61.

16. To Lowenthal, Feb. 10, 1961 (Kracauer papers 72.1571/20); italicized words in English.

17. *Theory of Film*, 300.

18. See Kracauer to Lowenthal, Oct. 31, 1959: "If everything goes well–*cross the fingers*–the book will come out in October 1960. I am sure it will be violently attacked because especially the last chapter is very *subversive, but I for one don't mind*," and Nov. 29, 1959: "*Of one thing I am sure: it will arouse violent controversies, and the art-minded will, all of them, be against it*" (Kracauer papers 72.1571/13, 14); italicized words in English.

19. *Theory of Film*, 300.

20. See Pauline Kael, "Is There a Cure for Film Criticism? Or, Some Unhappy Thoughts on Siegfried Kracauer's *Theory of Film: The Redemption of Physical Reality*, *Sight and Sound* 31, no. 2 (1962), now in P.K., *I Lost It at the Movies* (Boston: Little Brown, 1965), 243–63. See the list of reviews at the end of the German text: Siegfried Kracauer, *Theorie des Films*, *Schriften* 3, ed. Karsten Witte (Frankfurt: Suhrkamp, 1975).

21. "Die Photographie," *Das Ornament der Masse* (Frankfurt: Suhrkamp, 1963), 21–39. As Kracauer states in the 1962 introduction to his *History*, this early essay draws a connection between the nineteenth-century phenomena of historism and photography (*History: The Last Things before the Last* [Oxford: Oxford University Press, 1909], 4). But he had to be reminded of the existence of the essay by a research assistant checking his papers for previous references to historiography. *Ornament* appeared after he had written the introduction to *History*, which he did not rework. Whether he noticed it or not, his understanding of historism and of photography in *Theory of Film* and *History* differs dramatically from the Weimar essay: see chap. 6, sec. 4 and "Die Photographie," 23f.

22. On the instructive fallacies of the two Benjamin essays see chap. 2, sec. 2 of this study and Dagmar Barnouw, *Weimar Intellectuals and the Threat of Modernity* (Bloomington: Indiana University Press, 1988), 187–90. See also Miriam Hansen, "Benjamin, Cinema and Experience: 'The Blue Flower in the Land of Technology'," *New German Critique* 40 (Winter 1987): 179–224, esp. 207f. Hansen rightly mentions the influence of Kracauer's essay on Benjamin's writings on the photo image. With her Benjaminian perspective, however, she stylizes Kracauer's suggestive but fragmented and contradictory argument into a "great essay" that accommodates her reading into it Benjamin's problematic notion of an "optical unconscious," developed in his "Short History of Photography" (1931). But this notion, like Benjamin's *Aura*, is deeply alien to Kracauer's intellectual temperament. Sprouting up around the Benjamin cult, such willful misreadings of Kracauer obscure his particular contribution to modernity and with it the diversity of Weimar culture. See also chap. 6, n. 97 of this study.

23. "Die Photographie," 25–28. Especially those passages that argue the sitter's fragmented identity in the photographic portrait are syntactically entangled and seman-

tically obscure because the contrast with the painted portrait is so forced. In his 1930 review essay, "Die Biographie als neubürgerliche Kunstform" on the occasion of Leon Trotzki's *Mein Leben: Versuch einer Autobiographie* (Berlin: Fischer, 1930), Kracauer argues against a bourgeois biographical concept of the individual's reality as a solidly enduring construct. His attempt here to develop a concept of modern knowledge interdependent with the concept of an open self anticipates his position in *Theory of Film* and in *History* (*Ornament*, 75–80). Instructive attacks on him in this respect by political Marxists connected with *Linkskurve* are quoted in Anton Kaes, ed., *Weimarer Republik: Manifeste und Dokumente zur deutschen Literatur, 1918–1933* (Stuttgart: Metzler, 1983), 341.

24. Kracauer's use of this term, which plays on the double meaning of shining through and being displayed, does not help things, nor does his syntax: "allein das Transparent des Gegenstandes aber wird von dem Kunstwerk vermittelt." Notwithstanding his skeptical attitude toward the neo-Hegelian vacuities characteristic of much cultural Marxism of the 1920s (see chap. 2, sec. 3 of this study), he shared in them whenever he resorted to a Hegelian "mediation" ("*Vermittlung*").

25. Lászlό Moholy-Nagy, *Malerei, Photographie, Film* (Munich: Albert Langen, 1925), 32 (quoted in Ute Eskildsen, "Innovative Photography in Germany between the Wars," *Avant-Garde Photography in Germany 1919–1939* [San Francisco Museum of Modern Art, 1980], 35–47, esp. 40).

26. Albert Renger-Patzsch, "Ziele," *Das Deutsche Lichtbild* 1 (1927): xviii (quoted in Beaumont Newhall, *The History of Photography* [New York: Museum of Modern Art, 1982 (1949)], 195).

27. Albert Renger-Patzsch, "Das Photographieren von Blüten," *Kamera Almanach* (1924): 106 (quoted in Eskildsen, "Innovative Photography," 40).

28. The publisher's advertisement of the book quoted Mann's phrase to emphasize the extraordinary visual experience. Also instructive is the quote from a review of the book in *Frankfurter Zeitung*: "One cannot hold back (*sich entziehen*) from this new way of seeing; one is thrilled–critique falls silent." These images, Mann implies, are more powerful than language (quoted in David Mellor, ed., *Germany: The New Photography, 1927–33* [London: Arts Council of Great Britain, 1978], 8).

29. Thomas Mann, "Die Welt ist schön," *Berliner Illustrirte Zeitung*, no. 52 (1928), 2262f. (quoted in Newhall, *History*, 192).

30. Quoted in Eskildsen, "Innovative Photography," 46, n. 29; my translation.

31. Albert Renger-Patzsch, *Die Welt ist schön; einhundert photographische Aufnahmen* (Munich: Kurt Wolff, 1928), pls. 11, 43, 44, 37. See *Ansel Adams*, ed. Liliane De Cock (Boston: New York Graphic Society, 1972), pl. 95; Martha A. Sandweiss, *Laura Gilpin: An Enduring Grace* (Fort Worth: Amon Carter Museum, 1986), pls. 46, 47, 59; Sarah Greenough, *Paul Strand: An American Vision* (National Gallery of Art, Washington, D.C., in association with Aperture Foundation, 1990), pl. 65.

32. See also the images reproduced in Renger-Patzsch, *Die Welt ist Schön*, pl. 77, and Theodore E. Stebbins, Jr., and Norman Keyes, Jr., *Charles Sheeler: The Photographs*

(Boston: Museum of Fine Arts, 1987), pl. 48 ("Blast Furnace and Dust Catcher," 1927). See *Paul Strand*, pl. 60 ("Lathe," 1923).

33. See his statement on photography and art in *Das Deutsche Lichtbild* (1929). Because color photography is still in its infancy, the photographer is limited to the following phenomena: "all shades of light from the brightest to the deepest shadow, line, plane and space. In order to fashion these into vital form and shape he has the media of light (natural or artificial), lens, plate, developer, copying paper, his eyes and his photographic taste. These tools open up to him–within the limitations placed on photographic technique–a thousand creative forms" (quoted in Mellor, *The New Photography*, 15f.). Eskildsen's assignation "idealistic" is much too simplistic ("Innovative Photography," 40).

34. Ulrich Keller, "Sander and Portrait Photography," *August Sander: Citizens of the Twentieth Century, Portrait Photographs 1892–1952*, ed. Gunther Sander (Cambridge: MIT Press, 1986), 1–62, esp. 17.

35. Alfred Döblin, Introduction to August Sander, *Antlitz der Zeit* (Munich: Kurt Wolff, 1929) (quoted in Mellor, *The New Photography*, 55–59, 58).

36. See the photographs collected in *August Sander: Citizens of the Twentieth Century*. The English translation of the original German title, *August Sander: Menschen des 20. Jahrhunderts* (Munich: Schirmer/Mosel, 1980), is misleading: the point of these portraits was to record and show differences, including class differences. When Sander tried to fill the gaps in his *Menschen des 20. Jahrhunderts* project after the end of the Nazi dictatorship, the search for "types" that would clearly articulate the differences had become much more difficult (see *August Sander*, 21).

37. John Szarkowski, *Photography Until Now* (New York: Museum of Modern Art, 1989), 9, 232. In "*Theorie des Films* Vorfassung," in the context of emphasizing film's capacity for handling a "plurality of perspectives" that could stimulate the limited conventional imagination to expand, Kracauer also notes his plan to include a "history of the technical means" (Kracauer papers 72.3557/6, Heft I, 19f.).

38. See chap. 4, sec. 5 of this study.

39. Quoted in Constance Rourke, *Charles Sheeler: Artist in the American Tradition* (New York: Harcourt, Brace, 1938), 120; Kracauer found the quote in Newhall, *History*, 178.

40. Quoted in Theodore E. Stebbins, Jr., and Norman Keyes, Jr., *Charles Sheeler: The Photographs* (Boston: Museum of Fine Arts, 1987), 4.

41. See *Sheeler: Photographs*, 12f.; see also Carol Troyen and Erica E. Hirshler, *Charles Sheeler: Paintings and Drawings* (Boston: Museum of Fine Arts, 1987), 69, 89. For photos and paintings of industrial sites on which Sheeler worked at a later stage of his career, see *Sheeler: Paintings and Drawings*, 186–93.

42. Both quotes in *Sheeler: Photographs*, 8, 9.

43. Quoted from Henry McBride's review of the show, "New Light on Cubism," *New York Sun*, Dec. 10, 1917, 7 (*Sheeler: Photographs*, 8).

44. Interview July 6, 1975, quoted in Naomi Rosenblum, "Paul Strand: The Early Years, 1910–1932" (Ph.D. diss., City University of New York, 1978), 67. For examples see Strand's "Abstraction, Porch Shadows, 1916" (*Paul Strand*, Aperture Masters of Photography 1 [New York: Aperture Foundation, 1987], 9) and "Ranchos de Taos Church, New Mexico, 1931" (Sarah Greenough, *Paul Strand: An American Vision* [Washington, D.C.: National Gallery of Art, in association with Aperture Foundation, 1990], 42).

45. Rourke, *Charles Sheeler*, 67 (quoted in *Sheeler: Photographs*, 11).

46. *Sheeler: Photographs*, 11, pl. 21.

47. Edward Weston, "Seeing Photographically," *The Complete Photographer* 9, no. 49 (1943): 3202 (quoted in *Theory of Film*, 8).

48. See art critic Sadkichi Hartmann's remarks on "straight photography" as the source for the aesthetic value of pictorial photography in his review of a 1904 exhibition of Stieglitz's Photo-Secession at the Carnegie Institute: "Rely on your camera, on your eye, on your good taste and your knowledge of composition, consider every fluctuation of color, light and shade, study lines and values and space division, patiently wait until the scene or object of your *pictured vision* [my emphasis] reveals itself in its supremest moment of beauty, in short, compose the picture which you intend to take so well that the negative will be absolutely perfect and in need of no or but slight manipulation" ("A Plea for Straight Photography," *American Amateur Photographer* 16 (1904): 101–9, quoted in Newhall, *History*, 167). See also Hartmann's distinction in a later article between the photographer and the painter: "The painter composes by an effort of imagination. The photographer interprets by spontaneity of judgment. He practices composition by the eye" ("On the Possibility of New Laws of Composition," *Camera Work* 30 [1910]: 23–26, quoted in Newhall, *History*, 167).

49. Sarah Greenough points out a curious discrepancy regarding Stieglitz's work at the turn of the century: although he organized the Photo-Secession around symbolist pictorial photography, published many statements on symbolist aesthetics in *Camera Notes*, associated with critics and photographers who had direct links with symbolism, and collected German symbolist painting, Stieglitz produced images that did not show much symbolist influence ("How Stieglitz Came to Photograph Clouds," *Perspectives on Photography: Essays in Honor of Beaumont Newhall*, ed. Peter Walch and Thomas F. Barrow (Albuquerque: University of New Mexico Press, 1986), 151–65, 154–57). Throughout the 1910s Stieglitz was concerned explicitly with "pure" or "straight" photography, emphasizing the medium-specific properties of photo images. The quotation is from Newhall, *History*, 172 (photogravure in *Camera Work* 49–50 [1917]); Newhall juxtaposes the quote with the image of the blind woman (*History*, 173). "Portrait–Washington Square, New York 1916" is reproduced in *Paul Strand*, pl. 15.

50. Newhall, *History*, 171. Newhall quotes John A. Tennant, owner and editor of *Photo-Miniature*, who reviewed the exhibition enthusiastically: "What sort of photo-

graphs were these prints, which caused so much commotion? Just plain, straightforward photographs. . . . They offered no hint of the photographer or his mannerisms, showed no effort at interpretation or artificiality of effect; there were no tricks of lens or lighting . . . so perfect were these prints in their technique, so satisfying in those subtler qualities which constitute what we commonly call 'works of art.'"

51. Paul Strand, "Photography," *Seven Arts* 2 (1917): 524f., quoted in Newhall, *History*, 174. See also Charles H. Caffin's review of Paul Strand's exhibition at "291," *Camera Work* 48 (Oct. 1916): 57f. Caffin thought Strand's early work demonstrated the "unassailable possibilities" of the photographic medium, namely a kind of objectivity not accessible to drawing or painting. These straight photographs, products of abstention from any "tampering with the negative," "are in the strictest sense records of actual objectivity. . . . They are, in fact, an unanswerable witness to the pleasure and interest that the objective holds for us" (quoted in James B. Colson, "Stieglitz, Strand, and Straight Photography," *Perspectives on Photography*, ed. Dave Oliphant and Thomas Zigal [Austin: Humanities Research Center, University of Texas, 1982], 103–23, esp. 109).

52. *Theory of Film*, 16; see chap. 6, sec. 4 of this study.

53. Paul Strand, "The Art Motive in Photography," *British Journal of Photography* 5 (Oct. 1923): 57f.; and Lou Stettner, "A Day to Remember: Paul Strand Interviewed by Lou Stettner," *Camera* 35 (Oct. 1972): 75 (both statements quoted in Colson, "Stieglitz, Strand," 117).

54. Ansel Adams, *An Autobiography* with Mary Street Alinder (Boston: Little, Brown, 1985), 109f. See also Walker Evans's 1974 statement to James B. Colson that Strand was the only photographer who had influenced his own development (Colson, "Stieglitz, Strand," 118).

55. Quoted in Adams, *An Autobiography*, 110f.

56. Szarkowski, *Photography Until Now*, 285.

57. Edward Weston, "Amerika und Fotographie," in Karl Steinorth, ed., *Internationale Ausstellung des Deutschen Werkbunds Film und Foto Stuttgart 1929* (Stuttgart: Deutsche Verlagsanstalt, 1979), 13f. Weston asks photographers to consider van Gogh's statement: "Ein Gefühl für die Dinge als solche ist viel wichtiger als ein Sinn für das Malerische" (13; "A feeling for things themselves is much more important than a sense for painterly qualities").

58. *The Daybooks of Edward Weston*: Vol. 1, *Mexico*, ed. Nancy Newhall (Millerton, N.Y.: Aperture, 1973), 55.

59. See Kracauer's use of Weston as an example for the dual formalist/realist nature of photography. See also the ensuing conflict for the photographer, and the exchange between Adams and Weston on Weston's vegetable series, chap. 4, sec. 1 of this study.

60. Quoted in *Theory of Film*, 8 (from László Moholy-Nagy, Vision in Motion [Chicago, 1947], 210).

61. Quoted in *Theory of Film*, 11.

62. See *Theory of Film*, 12–23; also see chap. 4, sec. 2 of this study.

63. Walter Benjamin, "Kleine Geschichte der Photographie," in *Gesammelte Schriften* (*G.S.*), ed. Rolf Tiedemann and Hermann Schweppenhaeuser (Frankfurt: Suhrkamp, 1977), vol. 2, pt. 1, 368–85. See Benjamin to Gershom Scholem, Oct. 1931: "You have guessed it right, the study on photography has come out of the prolegomena to the *Passagenarbeit*" (quoted *G.S.*, vol. 2, pt. 3, 1130).

64. "Kleine Geschichte," 376. Characteristically, this sentence deliberately both sets up and fudges an interactive relation between aura and gaze: "Es war eine Aura um sie, ein Medium, das ihrem Blick, indem er es durchdringt, die Fülle und Sicherheit gibt" (literally: "There was an aura around them, a medium that lends their gaze, through its [the medium's] penetration by it [the gaze], its fullness and certainty").

65. "Kleine Geschichte," 380–81; see also Szarkowski's statement on that influence (this chap. sec. 2 and n. 38).

66. See Rudolf Arnheim, *Art and Visual Perception: A Psychology of the Creative Eye* (Berkeley: University of California Press, 1969), 288–92 on the perception of space in De Chirico.

67. "Cultural Crossroads," *Los Angeles Times Magazine*, June 23, 1991: 26. Robert Hughes, "Art, Morality and Mapplethorpe," *New York Review of Books* 39, no.8 (1992): 21–27.

68. "Kult der Zerstreuung," *Frankfurter Zeitung*, Mar. 4, 1926 (*Ornament*, 311–17); my references to "Cult of Distraction," trans. Thomas Y. Levine, *New German Critique* 40 (Winter 1987):91–96. See also Siegfried Kracauer, "Die kleinen Ladenmädchen gehen ins Kino," *Frankfurter Zeitung*, Mar. 1928 (*Ornament*, 279–94), an exploration of dominant themes in film at the end of Weimar yielding (some) evidence of massive escapism in troubled times. This essay series got much attention: see for instance Alfred Schutz in a letter from Paris to Eric Voegelin of Mar. 3, 1939, about having met Kracauer, who he assumes is known to Voegelin as "the author of the excellent book on the *Angestellten* and of the *Frankfurter Zeitung* essay series 'Die kleinen Mädchen gehen ins Kino'" (Voegelin papers, box 34/10, Hoover Institution, Stanford). The text foreshadows in certain ways *From Caligari to Hitler*, published two decades later.

See the uncritical, simplistic discussion, indebted to Miriam Hansen, of the concept of *distraction* in Richard W. Allen, "The Aesthetic Experience of Modernity: Benjamin, Adorno, and Contemporary Film Theory," *New German Critique* 40 (Winter 1987): 225–40, esp. 235–38.

69. Kracauer to Lowenthal, Feb. 16, 1957 (Kracauer papers 72.1570/36).

70. Lowenthal to Kracauer, Jan. 28, 1960 (Kracauer papers 72.2642/1); Kracauer to Lowenthal, Feb. 15, 1960 (72.1571/15).

71. Rudolf Arnheim, "Melancholy Unshaped," *Journal of Aesthetics and Art Criticism* 21 (1963): 21–29; my references are to *Toward a Psychology of Art* (Berkeley: University of California Press, 1966), 181–91, esp. 181.

72. *Theory of Film*, 72.

73. "Melancholy Unshaped," 184; *Theory of Film*, 116.

74. *Theory of Film*, 255, 303. For my reading of this passage see chap. 4, sec. 2 of this study.

75. Arnheim's position was less judgmental in his "classic" *Film als Kunst* (1932), to which Kracauer refers twice in chap. 7, "Language and Sound," concerning technical details (nn. 23, 30). However, in the first edition of *Art and Visual Perception* (1954), to which Kracauer refers once for a technical detail, there is a clear sense that photo images, still and moving, belong to the "secondary arts" because they differ from painting or sculpture in their relation to physical reality. In the second edition Arnheim mentions *Theory of Film* when trying to distinguish artistic from organic shape: "Kracauer has pointed out that in photography highly defined compositional form falsifies the medium, which is the joint product of the organizing mind and physical reality" (*Art and Visual Perception*, 52). But the issue for Kracauer was that photography is "art with a difference," a mixed medium (see below, sec. 4). The secondary status of photo images emerges repeatedly when Arnheim discusses painterly illusionism, playing with lifelikeness: "This use of pictures cannot be called an artistic response, if art is considered an interpretation rather than a duplication of reality" (114). Instructive for our context is also his linking the discovery of central perspective with the printing of the first woodcuts in Europe, which "establishes for the European mind the almost completely new principle of mechanical reproduction" and thereby undermines "reproduction (as) a product of creative imagination." The print as a "mechanical replica of the wooden matrix" "creates a new scientific criterion of correctness," which Arnheim thinks "a dangerous moment in the history of Western thought. The discovery suggested that the product of successful human creation was identical with mechanical reproduction and, in consequence, that the truth about reality was to be obtained by transforming the mind into a recording device. The new principle did away with the creative freedom of both perception and representation" (279). Arnheim finds particularly disturbing the drawing machines constructed by Albrecht Dürer: "in theory" they mean the "capitulation of the human mind to a standard of mechanical exactness" (280). To this standard Arnheim attributes "an all-time low of popular visual culture in the nineteenth century" and in the twentieth century "a violence of dissension that diverted much creative energy to the cult of extravagance" (281).

76. "Melancholy Unshaped," 188; *Theory of Film*, 17.

77. The context for his remarks, neglected by Arnheim, is statements made by Beaumont Newhall in his *History of Photography*, to which Kracauer refers and on which he elaborates: *Theory of Film*, 16–17.

78. *Theory of Film*, 17f.; see also *History*, 57.

79. "Melancholy Unshaped," 188f.

80. *Theory of Film*, vii–xi, 300–311. See also Kracauer's observation, noted in "*Theory of Film* Vorfassung," of the "Hic et Nunc-Charakter" of film which accommodates

the principle of accident (Kracauer papers 72.3557/6, Heft II, 25; he later marked this entry with the comment, "eminently important"). In contrast to the novel, Kracauer wrote here, film signified a further step in the process of the secularization of knowledge.

81. On Kracauer's use of Alfred Schutz's essay, "The Stranger" (1944), for his description of the historian's (and photographer's) perspective and the interrelated question of Schutz's critique of Husserl's "life-world" concept, see chap. 5, secs. 5 and 7 of this study.

82. See *Theory of Film*, x, 303.

83. With the exception of one piece, they were all written for *Frankfurter Zeitung*. For Kracauer's preexile work see Inka Mülder, *Siegfried Kracauer Grenzgänger zwischen Theorie und Literatur: seine frühen Schriften 1913–1933* (Stuttgart: Metzler, 1985); see also Genia Schulz, "Traum und Aufklärung: Die Stadtbilder Siegfried Kracauers," *Merkur* 36 (1982): 878–88; Gerwin Zohlen, "Text-Strassen: Zur Theorie der Stadtlektüre bei Siegfried Kracauer," *Text + Kritik* 68 (Oct. 1980): 62–72. The first two texts are useful. The last one imposes on Kracauer's perspective the equation city = text, which is distinctly misleading; even more misleading is the fictitious intellectual closeness to Adorno, Bloch, and especialy Benjamin which Zohlen tries to establish: see chap. 4, n. 4 of this study.

84. Siegfried Kracauer, *Strassen in Berlin und anderswo* (Frankfurt: Suhrkamp, 1964); *Die Angestellten: Aus dem neuesten Deutschland* (Frankfurt: Frankfurter Societäts-Druckerei, 1930).

85. Siegfried Kracauer, *Jacques Offenbach und das Paris seiner Zeit, Mit einem Vorwort von Siegfried Kracauer* (Frankfurt: Insel, 1980), 9.

86. On the discussion between Adorno and Benjamin concerning the publication of this essay, a part of the book project on the Paris Arcades, see *G.S.* 1:1065–1136.

87. In *Zeitschrift für Sozialforschung* 6, no. 3 (1937): 697f.

88. See here chap. 5, sec. 1 of this study.

89. On the mixed discourse of his two "philosophical novels" see Mülder, *Siegfried Kracauer– Grenzgänger*, 125–45, and Hans G. Helms, "Der wunderliche Kracauer: Zu seinen Schriften," *Neues Forum* 1 (1971): 27–29, 2 (1971): 48–51, 3 (1971): 27–30, 4 (1972): 55–58.

90. July 5, 1934, *Briefe* 1:381.

91. Nov. 3, 1934 (quoted in Karsten Witte, "Nachwort," *Jacques Offenbach und das Paris seiner Zeit*, 361–69, esp. 361).

92. Ernst Erich Noth, "Le romancier Kracauer devient l'historien du Second Empire, du Boulevard et d'Offenbach, *Nouvelles Littèraires* no. 765, June 12, 1937 (quoted Witte, "Nachwort," 366).

93. Kracauer to Lowenthal, Apr. 3, 1956 (Kracauer papers 72.1570/29). Kracauer suggests cutting those passages in which Lowenthal claims for literary works of high

art an instantaneous reflection of social change that actually happened over a longer period and advises against disguising the necessarily fragmentary nature of his selection of texts.

94. *History*, 4f.

95. Kracauer to Adorno, Oct. 24, 1936: "I will never ask for admission where three or four times I have been kicked out or treated in an uncivilized manner. I'll enter here only through the *wide-open main entrance* and if received with full honors" (Theodor W. Adorno Archive, quoted in *Marbacher Magazin*, 84).

96. See Kracauer's letters to Adorno, May 25, 1930, objecting to Horkheimer's complaint that he had not been sent a copy of *Die Angestellten* and to Horkheimer's demonstrated lack of interest in the work, and Jan. 21, 1933, complaining about Horkheimer's sulking because Kracauer had not arranged for a review: "Dialectic behavior seems to be directed only toward issues that are of no personal concern. Therefore: let's not forget it (*keinen Schwamm darüber*)" (Kracauer papers 72.1119/4, 13).

97. *Marbacher Magazin*, 84, 90.

98. John E. Abbott to Kracauer, June 19, 1939 (quoted in *Marbacher Magazin*, 94).

99. Letters, May 3 and May 13, 1937 (quoted in *Marbacher Magazin*, 91).

100. Walter Landauer to Kracauer, Feb. 4, 1938. Landauer sent Kracauer a preliminary contract for the film book and reassured him: "In spite of all difficulties and reservations, I believe it is the right thing for you to do and that it will be to your advantage" (quoted in *Marbacher Magazin*, 92).

101. See Rolf Wiggershaus, "Ein abgrundtiefer Realist. Siegfried Kracauer, die Aktualisierung des Marxismus und das Institut für Sozialforschung," in Michael Kessler and Thomas Y. Levin, eds., *Siegfried Kracauer: Neue Interpretationen* (Tübingen: Stauffenburg, 1990), 285–95. Wiggershaus speculates that Kracauer never saw Adorno's evaluation of his piece, which stated all the "weaknesses" of his position: his "*outsiderhafte Position*," "*individualistische Reserven*" against Marxist methods, dilettantism, and what Wiggershaus sums up as the accusation of "*Warenschriftstellerei*," commodity writing. Adorno had conceded a certain quality of observation and formulation and "a certain ability for structuring the materials that occasionally balances out what the piece lacks in actual theoretical power" (293f.). In his letter to Adorno, however, Kracauer pointed out precisely these prejudices, which must have become clear to him from Adorno's letter–Horkheimer, according to Wiggershaus, was shocked by its tone when he saw it later (ibid.)–and also Adorno's extraordinary editorial arrogance vis-à-vis Kracauer's manuscript.

102. See Dagmar Barnouw, "'Beute der Pragmatisierung': Adorno und Amerika," *Wechselseitige Spuren in der Literatur der Gegenwart*, ed. Wolfgang Paulsen (Bern: Francke, 1976), 61–83, and "Modernity and Enlightenment Thought," in Barbara Becker-Cantarino, ed., *The Enlightenment: An Era and Its Critique. Studies in Honor of Helga Slessarev* (Bonn: Bouvier, 1991), 1–14. Jürgen Habermas, "The Entwinement of

Myth and Enlightenment: Rereading *Dialectic of Enlightenment*," *The Philosophical Discourse of Modernity* (Cambridge: MIT Press, 1987), 106–30. See also Theodore W. Adorno, "Freudian Theory and the Pattern of Fascist Propaganda (1951)," in Andrew Arato and Eike Gebhardt, eds., *The Essential Frankfurt School Reader* (New York: Continuum, 1985), 118–37.

103. The unpublished manuscript of "Totalitäre Propaganda" 1937–38 (85 pp.) is among the Kracauer papers in Literaturarchiv Marbach; see also Kracauer's later summary of this paper, "Zur Theorie der autoritären Propaganda" (Kracauer papers 72.3579).

104. Kracauer to Adorno, Aug. 20, 1938 (Kracauer papers 72.1119/20, 1f.).

105. Kracauer papers 72.1119/20, 2f. Leo Lowenthal in his conversations with Helmut Dubiel described the Institute's theoretical position as evolving "informally": " . . . it came through more in the preliminary editorial work and in the conferences over the studies to be published in the Zeitschrift. . . . There you would hear such phrases as, 'you cannot put it that way,' or 'we mean this in a different sense,' or 'we do not use such an expression,' or 'this expression we employ differently,' and so forth. This is how the language of Critical Theory began. In common theoretical work a collective opinion emerged within our group." Leo Lowenthal, "I Never Wanted to Play Along: Interviews with Helmut Dubiel," *An Unmastered Past: The Autobiographical Reflections of Leo Lowenthal* (Berkeley: University of California Press, 1987), 17–159, 71. Adorno's editorial style and Lowenthal's complaints about the Institute's power politics in unpublished letters to Kracauer (see chap. 2, n. 37 of this study) suggest that such harmonious intellectual cooperation and integration were fictitious.

106. "Ideenskizze zu meinem Buch über den Film" (Kracauer papers 72.3532).

107. "*Theorie des Films* Vorfassung" 1940 Marseille (Kracauer papers 72.3557/6).

108. Kracauer, who acquired English in middle age, worked very hard to gain a certain ease in speaking and writing it, because he did not want to be isolated in his new cultural and intellectual environment. When *Theory of Film* was in press, he wrote to Lowenthal (Nov. 29, 1959): "and the English remains almost unchanged [in the process of copy editing]–I am proud of this achievement as a writer." (Kracauer papers 72.1571/14).

109. Exile archive, Deutsche Bibliothek Frankfurt, American Guild EB 70/177.

110. Kracauer to H. and G. Levin, Feb. 28, 1943 (quoted in *Marbacher Magazin*, 104).

111. Kracauer draws attention to the fact that the first film shown was the 1895 *Lunch Hour at the Lumière Factory*. See Erik Barnouw, *Documentary: A History of the Non-Fiction Film*, rev. ed. (Oxford: Oxford University Press, 1983 [1974]), 6–13: the beginning of cinematography is rooted in the documentary impulses of "catching life on the run" (6). The Lumière brothers' early success was very much connected to their filming of local events so that people could see themselves (their former selves) in their environment (7, 11).

112. “Notes on the Planned History of the German Film” (Kracauer papers 72.3714/16, 2f.).

113. Siegfried Kracauer, *From Caligari to Hitler: A Psychological History of the German Film* (Princeton: Princeton University Press, 1947), v.

114. *Theory of Film*, x.

115. This position is of course true of much of the criticism and history of photo images: see Gisèle Freund, *Photography and Society* (Boston: David R. Godine, 1980), the explicit topic of which is the interaction of “artistic expression and social forms” (3–5). But instead of exploring this interaction, Freund treats it largely as a given, avoiding all difficult questions about the interdependencies of “artistic” representation and social knowledge.

116. Kracauer papers 72.1686/21; italicized words originally in English.

117. Paul Rotha, “*From Caligari to Hitler*,” *Film To-Day* (Summer 1947): 41 (quoted in *Marbacher Magazin*, 106f.). Two decades later, one of the (few) German obituaries for Kracauer criticized *Caligari*: “The underlying conceptual grid, extracting Nazism as latent potentiality from German intellectual and art history, seems antiquated today: a product of the immediate postwar years.” But this critic, too, praised the sociological approach (“Zum Tode Siegfried Kracauers,” *Die Welt*, Nov. 30, 1966).

118. *Caligari*, 9–11. See Hans Staudinger, *The Inner Nazi: A Critical Analysis of MEIN KAMPF* (Baton Rouge: Louisiana State University Press, 1981) and Wilhelm Roepke, *The Solution of the German Problem* (New York: G. P. Putnams' Sons, 1947).

119. *Caligari*, 272.

120. “Künstliche Mitte,” in *Erbschaft dieser Zeit Gesamtausgabe* 4 (Frankfurt: Suhrkamp, 1962), 33–35. “Artificial Centre (1929),” in *Heritage of Our Times*, trans. Neville and Stephen Plaice (Cambridge, UK: Polity Press, 1991), 24–26. In contrast, Bloch's review of Benjamin's *Einbahnstrasse*, resented so much by Adorno and Benjamin, is more focused on the text it deals with.

121. Feb. 7, 1935, *Briefe* 1:384–87, esp. 385f.

122. *Erbschaft*, 104–26; *Heritage*, 97–116.

123. *Erbschaft*, 108–22; *Heritage*, 101–13.

124. Siegfried Kracauer, *Die Angestellten Schriften* 1, ed. Karsten Witte (Frankfurt: Suhrkamp, 1971), 215.

125. See the current critical discussion, more than half a century later, of the witnessing quality of randomly shot photographs and videotapes and my “Seeing and Believing,” *Common Knowledge*, Oct. 1994.

126. See contemporary evaluations of the achievement of *Die Angestellten*, which stress precisely the new subject matter: “a sensation,” “this topic has never been dealt with before,” “a discovery” (quoted in *Marbacher Magazin*, 51, 57, 58). See also Kracauer to Bernard von Brentano, his predecessor at *Frankfurter Zeitung*, Dec. 21, 1929,

about reactions on the left: "The KPD [Communist party of Germany] students, at least in Frankfurt, don't know what to do with the study; but these people who will be absolute philistines in ten years, whether they are right or left, never know where the really radical will to change has to set to work." The Belgian social psychologist Hendrik de Man, a former socialist who later was interested in Nationalsocialism but was respected for his work on labor, wrote Kracauer on Jan. 10, 1930: "I think your work *by far* the best available social and psychological monograph of a group. And I have a good conscience when I say that my judgment has not been influenced by agreement with the basic social position that is evident everywhere in your work–it is borne out by purely scientific, methodological criteria" (quoted in *Marbacher Magazin*, 51, 58).

CHAPTER 4. THE SHAPES OF OBJECTIVITY

1. Siegfried Kracauer, *History: Last Things before the Last* (Oxford: Oxford University Press, 1969), 191f.

2. Siegfried Kracauer, "Guide (original) (complete)," 9 (Literaturarchiv Marbach, Kracauer papers 72.3525/1).

3. Siegfried Kracauer, *Theory of Film: The Redemption of Physical Reality* (New York: Oxford University Press, 1960), 19, x.

4. Gerwin Zohlen, "Text-Strassen: Zur Theorie der Stadtlektüre bei Siegfried Kracauer," *Text* | *Kritik* 68 (Oct. 1980): 62–72, makes much of Benjamin's influence on Kracauer in terms of reading the world like a text. But where Benjamin does indeed use the text–and the act of reading–as an allegory for looking at the visible world, Kracauer uses a simile pointing to the degree of concentration with which the photographer looks at the information yielded by images and the historian at the information yielded by historical evidence.

5. See Charles Sheeler's statement in connection with the 1917 exhibition of his Doylestown photographs, chap. 3, sec. 2, of this study.

6. Weston to Adams, Jan. 28, 1932, *Ansel Adams: Letters and Images 1916–1984*, ed. Mary Street Alinder and Andrea Gray Stillman (Boston: Little, Brown, 1988), 48; see "Pepper No. 30. 1930" (ibid., 49) and Beaumont and Nancy Newhall, eds., *Masters of Photography* (New York: Braziller, 1958), 123. For Adams's "mixed" attitude vis-à-vis these crucial issues, see his remarks on what he perceived to be the artistic shortcomings of his friend Cedric Wright's photography, *Ansel Adams: An Autobiography* with Mary Street Alinder (Boston: Little, Brown, 1985), 34: It was precisely Wright's "disregard for many of the basic technical principles of photography" that had made him vulnerable to the position of pictorialists like Nicholaz Haz that "the formula for creativity was freedom from rules and technique. Cedric's photography never entirely recovered from the self-indulgence this fostered." See also Wallace Stegner's "Foreword" to *Ansel Adams: Letters* pointing out Adams's "favorites, particularly Weston and Strand, and his anathemas, particularly Edward Steichen, 'the Antichrist of photography.' He did not much like the documentarians, with the exception of Dorothea

Lange and Walker Evans, and he liked *them* not because they were documenting social significance but because they were artists" (viii): see chap. 6, sec. 2.

7. *Adams Letters*, 49.

8. *Theory of Film*, x.

9. *Theory of Film*, x, 302: "Indeed, along with photography, film is the only art which exhibits its raw material. Such art as goes into cinematic films must be traced to their creators' capacity for reading the book of nature. The film artist has traits of an imaginative reader or an explorer prodded by insatiable curiosity."

10. Weston to Adams, Jan. 28, 1932, *Adams Letters*, 48f.

11. See here Arnheim's advice to the film maker not to "rest content" with the "shapeless reproduction" of the visible world by the mechanically recording camera: "In order that the film artist may create a work of art it is important that he consciously stress the peculiarities of his medium. This, however, should be done in such a manner that the character of the objects represented should not thereby be destroyed but rather strengthened, concentrated and interpreted" (*Film as Art* [Berkeley: University of California Press, 1957 (1932)], 35).

12. Chromogenic color print (Museum of Modern Art, New York), *New Yorker*, June 22, 1992, 59. See also Susan Kismaric, *Jan Groover* (New York: Museum of Modern Art, 1987) and Jan Groover, *Pure Invention–The Table Top Still Life: Photographs* (Washington, D.C.: Smithsonian Institution Press, 1990).

13. See Gordon Wood's review of Simon Shama's *Dead Certainties (Unwarranted Speculations)*, "Novel History," *New York Review of Books* 38, no. 12 (1991): 12–16. Justly disturbed by the epistemological naïveté of Shama's "fictionalized history" (14), Wood uses the representation of historical events in a historical novel–Fabrizio's bewildering experience of the battle of Waterloo in Stendhal's *Charterhouse of Parma*–to point out the fallacies inherent in the "basic premise" of Shama's book: "that participants have a privileged access to knowledge of the events they are involved in. The opposite is in fact true: it is the historian removed from the events who is in a better position to put together the confused, disparate, and sometimes contradictory accounts by the participants into a plausible whole." Wood may be a bit too certain of historical knowledge; still, he nicely exposes Shama's unreflected and self-indulgent despair of it. See also chap. 5, n. 51 of this study.

14. Siegfried Kracauer, "Die Photographie," *Das Ornament der Masse* (Frankfurt: Suhrkamp, 1963), 21–39, esp. 23; *History*, 4.

15. *Theory of Film*, 245f.; for the quotes to follow that describe the properties of found stories see *Theory of Film*, 247–51; for the role of found stories in historiography see also this chap., sec. 3.

16. The term–and Kracauer's praise for Flaherty–does not deny the fact that Flaherty "cooked" his documentary images, especially in his most most famous film, *Nanook of the North*, which established the genre of the documentary. The question is not the

fact but the manner of the "cooking." For a discussion of Flaherty's decisions regarding his filmic narrative see chap. 6, sec. 2 of this study.

17. "*Theorie des Films* Vorfassung": "Der Anschluss an die Oberwelt, die der Film sucht, scheint sich im 'Film d'Art' zu realisieren. De facto ergreift im 'Film d'Art' das Theater vom Film parasitär Besitz im Akt der Beschlagnahmung, durch den der Film aus seiner ihm eigentümlichen Bahn gedrängt wird. Zunächst thesenhaft ausgesprochen: *der Film hat mit dem Theater nichts gemein*" (Kracauer papers 72.3557/6, Heft I, 10–16, esp. 10).

18. "Der Film kann materielle Phänomene in *jeder beliebigen materiellen Bewegung* aufnehmen und dabei selber jede beliebige Bewegung vollführen" and, underlined in red, "Die Vielheit [multiplicity] der Perspektiven" ("Vorfassung," 18–19).

19. "Vorfassung," 21–22: "Kein Einzelner kann alle materiellen Elemente und Bezüge einkalkulieren." He did not go into the difficulties involved in such collective calculation and construction.

20. *Theory of Film*, chaps. 12, "The Theatrical Story," and 13, "Interlude: Film and Novel."

21. See the critical discussion of this equation in Michael Geisler, *Die literarische Reportage in Deutschland: Möglichkeiten und Grenzen eines operativen Genres* (Königstein/Ts: Scriptor, 1982), pt. 1, chap. 4, "Abbildung in der Reportage."

22. A recent development in the manipulation of photographs by the computer, however, raises important questions (beyond the issue of personal perspective) about the documentary value of photographs. In art, this has been seen as an exciting opportunity; in photojournalism, historiography, and legal practice it poses enormous problems. Andy Grundberg in a piece titled "Ask It No Questions: The Camera Can Lie" (*New York Times*, Aug. 12, 1990, sec. 2: 1, 29), points out that "even historically important photographs can be refashioned to provide a new version of the past." He refers to an eerily altered photograph of the Yalta conference (1) in which Stalin is replaced by Groucho Marx and Sylvester Stallone (Rambo) is added. See Fred Ritchin, *In Our Own Image: The Coming Revolution in Photography* (New York: Aperture, 1990) and William J. Mitchell, *The Reconfigured Eye* (Cambridge: MIT Press), 1992.

Even a filmmaker like David Lynch, who stresses the fantastic dimension of his films, refers to the importance of "real life" experience as a matter of course. "The reigning master of locating the bizarre, the surreal and the disturbing in American life" in films like *Blue Velvet* and *Wild at Heart* and a hit television series, *Twin Peaks*, Lynch explains, "Well, I'm an American, and this is what I see out there. . . . Every little neighborhood, every little back yard has a certain feel to it, and I'm just letting real life be my guide" (Larry Rohter, "David Lynch Pushes America to the Edge,"*New York Times* Aug. 12, 1990, sec. 2:1). Though he guides more than he is guided, it is significant that he puts the issue in these terms. See also the implications of the Mapplethorpe controversy, chap. 3, sec. 4.

23. See especially *Theory of Film*, pt. 3, "Composition," which starts with the observation: "The two most general film types are the story film and the nonstory film, the

latter comprising the bulk of *experimental* films and all the varieties of the *film of fact*" (175).

24. See Imre Lakatos's more flexible alternative to Kuhn's concept of "paradigm": a research program is "*theoretically* progressive" if it "predicts some novel, hitherto unexpected fact." It is "*empirically* progressive if this excess empirical content is corroborated" ("Methodology of Scientific Research Programmes," in Imre Lakatos and A. Musgrave, eds., *Criticism and the Growth of Knowledge* [Cambridge: Cambridge University Press, 1970], 91–195, esp. 118). See also Ian Hacking, "A Surrogate for Truth," *Representing and Intervening: Introductory Topics in the Philosophy of Natural Science* (Cambridge: Cambridge University Press, 1983), 112–28, esp. 114, 118, 128, and George Levine, "Scientific Realism and Literary Representation," *Raritan* 10, no. 4 (1991): 18–39.

25. *Theory of Film*, ix. Kracauer lists here several questions inherent in this assumption: "How is it possible for films to revive events of the past or project fantasies and yet retain a cinematic quality? What about the role of the sound track? If films are to confront us with our visible environment, a good deal obviously depends on the manner in which the spoken word, noises and music are related to the pictures. A third question bears on the character of the narrative: Are all types of stories indiscriminately amenable to cinematic treatment or are some such types more in keeping with the spirit of the medium than the rest of them?"

26. *Theory of Film*, 303; the self-quote is taken from "The Found Story and the Episode" (255); the examples given here are Jean Renoir's *La Règle du Jeu* and *La Grande Illusion*.

27. *Die Angestellten, Schriften* 1, ed. Karsten Witte (Frankfurt: Suhrkamp, 1971), 216.

28. See chap. 2, sec. 2, and chap. 3, sec. 1 of this study, also the dicussion of this passage in *History*, 160–63.

29. Alfred Eisenstaedt, *Remembrances* (Boston: Little, Brown, 1990), 67, 60. For further discussion of Lange's documentary style see chap. 6, sec. 2 of this study.

30. Siegfried Kracauer, *From Caligari to Hitler: A Psychological History of the German Film* (Princeton: Princeton University Press, 1947), 182f.

31. *Caligari*, 184f. See also Siegfried Kracauer, "Der heutige Film und sein Publikum," *Frankfurter Zeitung*, Dec. 1, 1928 (quoted in *Caligari*, 187f.).

32. *Frankfurter Zeitung*, Nov. 17, 1927 (*Von Caligari zu Hitler*, "Anhang 2," "Filmkritiken 1924–1939," *Schriften* 2 [Frankfurt: Suhrkamp, 1979], 397–582, esp. 407–9).

33. The expectations implicit in such an equation make the documentary vulnerable to political and ideological exploitation: see Sigrid Schneider, "Von der Verfügbarkeit der Bilder Fotoreportagen aus dem Spanischen Bürgerkrieg," *Fotogeschichte* 8/29 (1988):49–64, 50–52. Schneider shows how documentary photo images were used regardless of the photographers' (political) intentions in making them: a photograph taken for and published in a leftist journal was also printed in propaganda material for the Right.

34. See chap. 1, sec. 2 of this study.

35. See David Lynch's remarks about his TV series, *Twin Peaks*: being attracted to the "abstractions, absurdities, surprises" inherent in this medium made it easier for him to include "what is going on beside the story." One of his leading actresses in the series explained its attraction in terms not so much of significant indeterminacy as of the victory, beyond all the carefully orchestrated confusion, of "the good" or "love" (National Public Radio, *Morning Edition*, Aug. 16, 1990).

36. "Ein Bild sagt mehr als 1000 Worte," *UHU* (Ullstein Magazin) 3 (1926–27), Heft 2.

37. Quoted in Karsten Witte, "Nachwort," *Caligari, Schriften* 2, 607.

38. See Louis O. Mink, "Philosophical Analysis and Historical Understanding," in *Historical Understanding* (Ithaca, N.Y.: Cornell University Press, 1987), 118–146, esp. 137. Mink thought such projection of "future pasts" not uncommon in historiographical practice despite the obvious flaws and distortions.

39. See here the instructive review of a film of Gerhart Hauptmann's "naturalist" drama, *Die Weber*, "Die verfilmten Weber," *Frankfurter Zeitung*, May 30, 1927 ("Filmkritiken 1924–1939," 402–4). Kracauer emphatically denies the film's alleged similarity to Eisenstein's *Potemkin*, stressing, in contrast, its anachronism. He clearly distinguishes here between the screen version of the play and the play itself. The drama was very much of its time; the film is not: "A decent historical film. No more" (404).

40. See, however, Kracauer's use of the film to argue a general cultural fascination with street life in the Germany (Berlin) of that time, clearly making his interpretation fit his overall argument (*Caligari*, 158f.).

41. "Asphalt," *Frankfurter Zeitung*, Mar. 28, 1929 ("Filmkritiken," 413f.).

42. "Ein Zirkusfilm," *Frankfurter Zeitung*, Jan. 18, 1928 ("Filmkritiken," 405–7, esp. 406).

43. See, however, Erwin Panofsky's thoughtful remarks on the meanings of the invention of the sound track in 1928. More sanguine than Kracauer (though sharing some of his concerns), he was convinced that the sound track would not be able to diminish the "unique and specific possibilities" of film, namely the "*dynamization of space* and, accordingly, *spatialization of time*." The addition of speech will not "change the basic fact that a moving picture, even when it has learned to talk, remains a picture that moves and does not convert itself into a piece of writing that is enacted." He thinks entirely misleading Eric Russell Bentley's statement "The potentialities of the talking screen differ from those of the silent screen in adding the dimension of dialogue—which could be poetry" and suggests instead: "The potentialities of the talking screen differ from those of the silent screen in integrating visible movement with dialogue which, therefore, had better not be poetry" ("Style and Medium in the Motion Pictures," in Gerald Mast and Marshall Cohen, eds., *Film Theory and Criticism* [New York: Oxford University Press, 1985], 215–33, 218–20).

44. See the discussion of Adorno's essay, "Transparencies on Film," chap. 5, sec. 1 of this study.

45. Siegfried Kracauer, "Zur Frage der Internationalität des Tonfilms" (Kracauer papers 72.3577, 2): The silent film

> ging im Grossen und Ganzen nicht von der Internationalität der visuellen Impressionen aus, er ging auf sie zu. . . . Die Grenze der Verständlichkeit beginnt erst mit dem Einsatz der Worte. Kaum hatten sie die Herrschaft an sich gerissen, so war es mit dem internationalen optischen Austausch vorbei, und man wird noch heute das bittere Gefühl nicht los, nach den paradiesischen Zeiten einer alle Völker vebindenden Bilderrede wieder in das Chaos der babylonischen Sprachverwirrung zurückgeworfen zu sein.

See also "*Theorie des Films* Vorfassung": "Der *Stummfilm* ist von Anfang an nur eine *Etappe.* Vordeutend: eine besonders glückliche Etappe, weil er die Sprache in Quarantäne setzt, die die grösste Verführung des Films zur Unterwerfung unter die Intentionen der *Totale* darstellt" (Heft I, 16). Here, as in other remarks on *Tonfilm*, Kracauer speaks of language intruding on filmic images in terms of usurpation, subjugation, domination. In "Zur Frage der Internationalität des Tonfilms" he links such domination with the fascist concept of power, nationalism, and capitalism (2).

46. *Frankfurter Zeitung*, Oct. 12, 1928 ("Filmkritiken," 409–11). The term, instructive in its emphasis on the *symbiosis* of sound and image, was soon to change to *Tonfilm.*

47. See also "*Theorie des Films* Vorfassung": "Zwischenbemerkung: die ganze Welt in jedem Sinne: von Anfang an zielt der Film auf die Einbeziehung von Ton, Sprache, Farbe ab" (Heft I, 16). The context for this remark is the filmic reclamation of the "whole world."

48. See also Kracauer's insistence in "Zur Frage der Internationalität des Tonfilms" on the importance of using the universal, collective, anonymous, involuntary properties of sound in *Tonfilm* which would thereby contribute to a transcending of national borders: "Sie liegen im wörtlichen Sinne auf der Strasse" (4). In this unpublished text of 1930 Kracauer was clearly ambiguous about the potential of *Tonfilm.*

49. "Filmkritiken," 410f.; note the semantically and grammatically idiosyncratic use of the verb *erlösen*, which cannot be fully rendered in English: "Das unbeabsichtigte Getöse der Strasse zum Eingreifen in unsere Welt zu erlösen."

50. A practising journalist, Kracauer was much less certain about a general cultural decline inherent in all mass democracies than other Weimar intellectuals, especially his Marxist friends whose exclusive concern was the preservation of high culture on their terms. See for instance his 1926 essay "Kult der Zerstreuung," *Ornament*, 311–17, esp. 313.

51. "Über den musikalischen Tonfilm," *Frankfurter Zeitung*, Nov. 1, 1930 ("Filmkritiken," 446–48, esp. 447).

52. *Frankfurter Zeitung*, Nov. 25, 1930 ("Filmkritiken," 454–56, esp. 455f.).

53. "Westfront 1918," *Frankfurter Zeitung*, May 5, 1930 ("Filmkritiken," 430–32, esp. 431f.). See also *Caligari*, 232–35.

54. "Im Westen nichts Neues," *Frankfurter Zeitung*, Dec. 12, 1930 ("Filmkritiken," 456–59, esp. 459, 457). Kracauer's argumentation here differs remarkably from his usual level-headed approach. The film and "of course the book, too," he claims, present war as "mythical fate"—an assertion that is blatantly untrue. This alleged neutrality is "hostile to knowledge"; it does not explicitly examine the roots of war—Kracauer did not ask such examination of Pabst's film—but remains arrested in "petty bourgeois [a term he usually avoided] eruptions of discontent" (458). The reason for this spurious attack may have been the huge (and therefore, to high-minded Kracauer, somehow suspicious) success of the novel, which arguably was supported by Remarque's focus on the experience of individual characters. The review is not only unfair but also noticeably disconnected: there is the leftish ideological part with its "correct" stance against the film's focus on the individual instead of the collective, and then there is the film expert's quite positive description of the effective use of technical know-how in the service of presenting the "individual figures with incomparable clarity without neglecting the course of general events" (458).

55. "Der blaue Engel," *Neue Rundschau* 1930 ("Filmkritiken," 418–21).

56. See Anton Kaes, *Kino-Debatte: Texte zum Verhältnis von Literatur und Film 1909–1929* (Tübingen: Max Niemeyer, 1978), 30.

57. Siegfried Kracauer, "Literarische Filme," *Die Neue Rundschau*, 1931 ("Filmkritiken," 466–69, esp. 467) and "Berlin-Alexanderplatz als Film," *Frankfurter Zeitung*, Oct. 13, 1931 ("Filmkritiken," 508–10, esp. 510).

58. See the analysis of that novel in my *Weimar Intellectuals and the Threat of Modernity*, pt. 2, chap. 3.

59. *Frankfurter Zeitung*, Feb. 13, 1931 ("Filmkritiken," 480–83, esp. 482). See also his remarks on this film in *Caligari*, 251–53, where he voices some reservations, especially with regard to the actors' declamatory style carried over from the silent film. But here, too, he stresses the visual as the centrally cinematic dimension: "But the visual part is not yet reduced to a mere accompaniment of the dialogue, and at least in one instance Ozep combines sounds and pictures in a truly cinematic way" (252).

60. "Filmkritiken," 483. Kracauer's use here of terms like *language* and *syntax* is metaphorical. He does not argue a structural analogy between the composition of the filmic image and a sentence, as Eisenstein seems to do in a suggestive, if problematic, passage: "Now why should the cinema follow the forms of theatre and painting rather than the methodology of language, which allows wholly new concepts or ideas to arise from the combination of two concrete denotations of two concrete objects [how are these signs (images) 'concrete'?]. Language is much closer to film than painting is. For example, in painting the form arises from the abstract elements of line and colour [how is paint 'abstract'?], while in cinema the material concreteness of the image [?] within the frame presents—as an element—the greatest difficulty in manipulation. So why not lean towards the system of language, which is forced to use the same mechanics in inventing words and word-complexes" (quoted in Alan Trachtenberg, *Reading American Photographs* [Toronto: Hill and Wang, 1989], 259).

61. On the influence of expressionist concepts of perception on German aesthetics of film developed during the twenties, see Kaes, *Kino-Debatte*, 23–34.

62. "Film-Hochsaison," *Frankfurter Zeitung*, Feb. 23, 1931 ("Filmkritiken," 484–87, esp. 484).

63. "Filmkritiken," 484; Kracauer's use of *aufheben* imitates the Hegelian pun but does not claim Hegelian significance.

64. "Zweimal Wildnis," *Frankfurter Zeitung*, Oct. 6, 1931 ("Filmkritiken," 503–5, esp. 504).

65. "Geschichte eines Grosstadthauses, *Frankfurter Zeitung*, Nov. 29, 1932 ("Filmkritiken," 559f., esp. 560).

66. There is, of course, no such thing as "pure" sensation where complex organisms are concerned. I am overstating the distinction to make my point.

67. "Einige Filme: Abstrakte Kunst," *Frankfurter Zeitung*, Mar. 19, 1932 ("Filmkritiken," 533f., esp. 533).

68. "'Kuhle Wampe' verboten!" *Frankfurter Zeitung*, Apr. 5, 1932 ("Filmkritiken," 536–41, esp. 538); see also his analysis of the film in *Caligari*, 243–47, esp. 246f. In contrast to Adorno, Horkheimer, Bloch, and Benjamin, Kracauer, who knew much more about the realities of lower-middle-class life during the Weimar Republic, did not have much use for the concept and the term. See his review in *Frankfurter Zeitung*, June 5, 1932 (quoted in Michael Schröter, "Weltzerfall und Rekonstruktion: Zur Physiognomik Siegfried Kracauers," *Text + Kritik* 68 [Oct. 1980]: 18–40, esp. 34): "A person's characterization would have to yield her petty bourgeois qualities; but a person must not be characterized by simply being referred to as petty bourgeois in a tendentious manner."

Chapter 5. Orpheus and Ahasver: The Strangeness of Things Past

1. See chap. 2, n. 88 of this study.

2. Apr. 1, 1964, and Feb. 24, 1963 (Literaturarchiv Marbach, Kracauer papers 721122/6 and 721121/12).

3. Aug. 20, 1938 (Kracauer papers 721119/20); see chap. 3, sec. 6 of this study.

4. Theodor W. Adorno, "Der wunderliche Realist: Über Siegfried Kracauer," *Noten zur Literatur, Gesammelte Schriften* (*G.S.*) 2, ed. Rolf Tiedemann (Frankfurt: Suhrkamp, 1984 [1974]), 388–408, 393.

5. Jürgen Habermas, "The Entwinement of Myth and Enlightenment: Rereading *Dialectic of Enlightenment*," *New German Critique* 26 (Spring/Summer 1982): 13–30, esp. 13. See also the revised version of the text, "The Entwinement of Myth and Enlightenment: Max Horkheimer and Theodor Adorno," *The Philosophical Discourse of Modernity*, translated by Frederick Lawrence (Cambridge: MIT Press, 1987), 106–30, esp. 106: "their blackest book." My references are to the earlier, less guarded version.

6. Max Horkheimer and Theodor W. Adorno, *The Dialectic of Enlightenment* (New York: Continuum, 1986), xi; see Dagmar Barnouw, "The Power of Paradox: *The Dialectic of Enlightenment* in Postwar Germany," in Dieter Sevin, ed., *Die Resonanz des Exils: Gelungene und misslungene Rezeption deutschsprachiger Exilautoren* (Amsterdam: Rodopi, 1992), 218–30.

7. *Dialectic of Enlightenment*, xvi. For a critique of the Frankfurters' critique of Enlightenment thought see Dagmar Barnouw, "Modernity and Enlightenment Thought," in Sarah Friedrichsmeyer and Barbara Becker-Cantarino, eds., *The Enlightenment and Its Legacy: Studies in German Literature in Honor of Helga Slessarev* (Bonn: Bouvier, 1991), 1–14.

8. Leo Lowenthal, "I Never Wanted to Play Along: Interviews with Helmut Dubiel," in Martin Jay, ed., *An Unmastered Past: The Autobiographical Reflections of Leo Lowenthal* (Berkeley: University of California Press, 1987), 15–159, esp. 77.

9. See Dagmar Barnouw, "'Beute der Pragmatisierung': Adorno und Amerika," in Wolfgang Paulsen, ed., *Wechselseitige Spiegelungen in der Literatur der Gegenwart* (Bern: Francke, 1976), 61–83.

10. Siegfried Kracauer, *Das Ornament der Masse* (Frankfurt: Suhrkamp, 1963). See Lowenthal to Kracauer, Dec. 13, 1963, about the republication of his early essays: "*Ornament der Masse* arrived a few weeks ago and I was deeply moved to relive this period of our lives, which probably will never be surpassed in intellectual sophistication" (Kracauer papers 72.2642/15).

11. See chap. 2, sec. 2 of this study.

12. Mar. 18, 1936, *G.S.* 1:1001–6, esp. 1003f. In this context, Adorno also refers Benjamin to his discovery that the allegedly progressive elements of jazz are truly reactionary.

13. Miriam Hansen in her lengthy introduction to this slight text thinks "this essay seems to suspend some of the major fixations of Adorno's theory on Culture Industry. Moreover, it encourages a reading against the grain of Adorno's writings on film and mass culture" ("Introduction to Adorno, 'Transparencies on Film' (1966)," *New German Critique* 24–25 [Fall/Winter 1981–82]: 186–98, esp. 186, 192f). "Reading against the grain" is a practice common among critics who wish to preserve a particular cultural significance rather than the meaning potential of a text. Adorno's position on mass culture is really untenable in the late twentieth century: rereading him in this situation requires rewriting him.

14. Originally published in *Die Zeit*, Nov. 18, 1966, "Filmtransparente" was collected in Theodor W. Adorno, *Ohne Leitbild* (Frankfurt: Suhrkamp, 1967). My references are to "Transparencies on Film," trans. Thomas Y. Levine, *New German Critique* 24–25 (Fall-Winter 1981–82): 199–205, esp. 202f.

15. Mar. 3, 1965 (Kracauer papers 72.1122/12).

16. See Kracauer's remarks to Leo Lowenthal in letters of Oct. 26, 1955, Oct. 27, 1958, and Feb. 15, 1960 (Kracauer papers 72.1570/24; 72.1571/7; 72.1571/15). In these pri-

vate letters to a friend who shares his grudges against the brilliantly successful and prolific Adorno, Kracauer's judgment is colored by resentfulness: much of Adorno's work is "shallow on a high level," "tired profundities." But his critique of Adorno's frictionless dialectics and aridly abstract concept of utopia is of long standing and well taken.

17. "Der wunderliche Realist," *Neue Deutsche Hefte* (Sept. 1964): 17–39, 20. The phrase was eliminated in the book publications (see chap. 2, n. 4 of this study). I cite the journal pages in addition to the *G.S.* reference when quoting Kracauer's annotations or underlinings.

18. *G.S.* 2:390; *Neue Deutsche Hefte*, 20.

19. *G.S.* 2:391–93; *Neue Deutsche Hefte*, 21–23.

20. *G.S.* 2:394–400, 403; *Neue Deutsche Hefte*, 24–28, 33: "no."

21. *G.S.* 2:396; *Neue Deutsche Hefte*, 26.

22. Oct. 15, 1964 (Kracauer papers 72.1122/9).

23. "Nachtrag" to "Guide (original) (complete)," 1 (Kracauer papers 72.3525; quoting from this manuscript I have let stand Kracauer's errors in grammar and punctuation). Martin Jay oddly labels Kracauer's thought "ontologist"–connoting (negative) Heideggerian qualities–on the basis of this conversation ("Adorno and Kracauer: Notes on a Troubled Friendship," *Permanent Exiles: Essays on the Intellectual Migration from Germany to America* [New York: Columbia University Press, 1985], 217–36).

24. Jürgen Habermas, "The Entry into Postmodernity: Nietzsche as a Turning Point," in *The Philosophical Discourse of Modernity*, 83–105, esp. 96f; see also 97–100.

25. See sec. 7 below on the exchange of letters between Karl Loewith and Eric Voegelin in the winter of 1944–45 about Nietzsche's meanings for the philosophical historian in the midtwentieth-century situation of cultural crisis.

26. See chap. 6, sec. 7 of this study.

27. *G.S.* 2:394; *Neue Deutsche Hefte*, 24.

28. *G.S.* 2:402; Nov. 21, 1964 (Kracauer papers 72.1122/11): "Meine Beanstandung bezieht sich rein auf den nachweislich falschen kausalen Zusammenhang, den Du zwischen meinem Erfolg und meinem 'Glücksgelöbnis' herstellst, *nicht* auf Deine Anpassungstheorie. Ich halte sie zwar aus guten Gründen für eine Entstellung der Realität–meiner Realität–aber Du siehst mich eben wie Du mich siehst."

29. Nov. 3, 1964 (Kracauer papers 72.1122/10). Adorno's formulation to which Kracauer's letter refers echoes a rapid, hard-hitting conceptual motion, dialectic, of which Kracauer was suspicious because he thought its distinctions simplistically clear and its solutions too eagerly anticipated: "den Gedanken aus dem ihm Widerspenstigen zu extrapolieren, das Allgemeine aus dem Extrem der Besonderung" (*G.S.* 2:394).

30. Siegfried Kracauer, *History: Last Things before the Last* (Oxford: Oxford University Press, 1969), 201.

31. Kracauer is not fair here to Loewith–though he points out rightly Loewith's tendency, especially in his later work, to search for higher orders of (historical) being and meaning (*History*, 201). For more on Loewith's position, see this chap. secs. 4, 7.

32. *History*, 201. See also Kracauer's letter to Lowenthal of Feb. 15, 1960, which repeats almost verbatim the statement about Adorno's use of utopia (see n. 16 above).

33. See the "inexorable" solipsism of *Minima Moralia: Reflexionen aus dem beschädigten Leben* (Frankfurt: Suhrkamp, 1951), arguably the bible of West German intellectuals who were young in the fifties and sixties.

34. Nov. 21, 1964 (Kracauer papers 72.1122/11); for "middle distance" see chap. 3, sec. 6 of this study.

35. Now in Siegfried Unseld, ed., *Ernst Bloch zu ehren: Beiträge zu seinem Werk* (Frankfurt: Suhrkamp, 1965), 145–55, esp. 145.

36. Kracauer is clearly playing here with the literal meaning of *Erfahrung*, "experience," which suggests such mobility. In this context he speaks about the storyteller's (Bloch's) desire to invoke in his story what cannot be said so that it can be experienced ("*erfahren*"), however insufficiently (*Bloch zu ehren*, 146).

37. Mar. 16, 1966 (Kracauer papers 72.1624/1).

38. See my argument in the Epilogue, sec. 4, of this study.

39. "Guide (original) (complete)," 10 (Kracauer papers 72.3525).

40. See the curiously uncritical evaluation of this atttitude in Habermas's 1981 "Leo Lowenthal–A Felicitation," *An Unmastered Past*, 9–14, esp. 12. Habermas praised the exiled Frankfurters' decision to continue the *Zeitschrift für Sozialforschung* in German, pointing out that this decision meant isolation from "the culture of their immediate environment" and therefore "required an already deep certitude in fundamental values." Habermas is not troubled by the possibility that such "certitude" might lead to orthodoxy and parochialism. Acknowledging that value judgments might become rigid "if their validity is not also confirmed by the very critique such judgments guide," he thinks "this confirmation was realized"–because we are dealing with "Critical Theory." See here also Adorno to Lowenthal, Dec. 2, 1954, on the certain and enduring value of their work because it is centered in "Critical Theory" ("The Correspondence of Leo Lowenthal with Theodor Wiesengrund Adorno," Leo Lowenthal, *Critical Theory and Frankfurt Theorists*, New Brunswick: Transaction, 1989, 127–49, esp. 145).

41. Sept. 5, 1955 (Kracauer papers 72.1120/15). See also Kracauer to Leo Lowenthal, Oct. 26, 1955 (Kracauer papers 72.1570/24) on Adorno's repeated exhortations that "*das 'Eigenste'*" (the intellectually most intimate and authentic) could only be said in German. See Karl Loewith, "Vorwort," *Weltgeschichte und Heilsgeschehen: Die theologischen Voraussetzungen der Geschichtsphilosophie* (Stuttgart: Kohlhammer, 1953): Loewith explains here to his German readers certain peculiarities of his study, which had been originally published as *Meaning in History* (Chicago: University of Chicago

Press, 1949): "He [the author] has found it useful to find his way into a language which does not yield to conceptual subtleties and verbal profundities, but which is, in its own way, precise and rich." There is also the survival value of English for the intellectual exile, to which Adorno and Horkheimer, protected by the independent wealth of the Institute, were notoriously superior. See Brecht's shrewd remarks on the Frankfurters' obtuseness in his *Arbeitsjournal* (Frankfurt: Suhrkamp, 1973), 1:13. In 1940 Horkheimer complained about the overeager adaptability of many exiles who were less fortunate than members of the Institute: "That the German intellectuals don't need long to change to a foreign language as soon as their own bars them from a sizeable readership, comes from the fact that language already serves them more in the struggle for existence than as an expression of truth"–a curious distinction for an adult person of his generation (quoted in Martin Jay, *The Dialectical Imagination* [Boston: Beacon Press, 1973], 114). See Barnouw, "'Beute der Pragmatisierung,'" 66–73.

42. "Der Essay als Form, *Noten zur Literatur, G.S.* 2:9–33, esp. 25. On this concept of the essay see Dagmar Barnouw, "Literat und Literatur: Robert Musil's Beziehung zu Franz Blei," *Modern Austrian Literature* 9 (1976): 168–99, esp. 174–76.

43. Kracauer to Adorno, Aug. 27, 1955, criticizing Adorno's large generalizing about music as commodity ("*musikalische Warenanalysen*"): "I would like more history than construction here, or rather, more construction in the material of history" (Kracauer papers 72.1120/14). See also Kracauer to Lowenthal, Oct. 28, 1963, on his having to read so much for *History*, "because I have to state my thoughts in the material" (72.1571/30).

44. See Kracauer to Lowenthal, Oct. 28, 1956, on his return from a three-month stay in Europe (the entire letter is in English though Kracauer usually wrote to Lowenthal in German interspersed with English phrases). Europe had been "a unique, wonderful and in some respects redeeming experience." The evening spent with "Horkheimers" and the lunch shared with "the Teddies" had been "interesting;" Rome, Florence, Paris marvelously beautiful; "and yet we are happy to be home again, for it is home for us here [New York] now that we have definitely ceased to be immigrants. And one more thing: it is as if people in Europe had lost the power of assimilating the new. Somehow it is suffocating over there" (Kracauer papers 72.1570/33).

45. See Lili Kracauer to Lowenthal, Feb. 25, 1967, with a list of Kracauer's descriptions of his experience of time: "Exterritorialität in der chronologischen Zeit," "chronologische Fatalität," the "Skandalon" of the flow of chronological time and of the end of consciousness (Kracauer papers 72.3242/1).

46. See chap. 6, sec. 1 of this study.

47. See Kracauer's review, "Prophetentum" (*Frankfurter Zeitung*, Aug. 27, 1922), of Ernst Bloch's *Thomas Münzer als Theologe der Revolution*, a highly critical analysis of Bloch's characteristic mixture of Marxian arguments and chiliastic mysticism (see chap. 2, sec. 3 of this study).

48. “Der wunderliche Realist,” *G.S.* 2:399.

49. For More’s ingenious use of fictitious dedications and comments and his use of the traveler’s mobility in setting up an intricate interplay of perspective in book 1, see Dagmar Barnouw, *Die versuchte Realität Utopischer Diskurs von Thomas Morus zur feministischen Science Fiction* (Meitingen: Corian, 1985), chap. 1.

50. The reality (practice) of historiographical justice is obscure because it is predicated on the recognition that it is largely impossible. Hayden White’s *Metahistory: The Historical Imagination in Nineteenth-Century Europe* (Baltimore: Johns Hopkins University Press, 1973) has been most successful in literary studies in which the issue of justice can be blissfully ignored. But it has had at least shock value for many historians who reject the usefulness of his historiographical typology and, most importantly, insist on distinguishing historical from other kinds of narration: see *Metahistory: Six Critiques, History and Theory, Beiheft* 19 (Middletown: Wesleyan University Press, 1981); see also chap. 6, sec. 1 of this study.

51. See Gordon Wood’s review of Simon Shama’s *Dead Certainties (Unwarranted Speculations)*, “Novel History,” *New York Review of Books* 38, no. 12 (1991): 12–16. In his useful critique of Shama’s “experiment in fictionalized history” (p. 14), Wood points out the fallacies inherent in Shama’s rather melodramatic despair of historical knowledge. In his afterword Shama laments the fact that historians are left “forever chasing shadows, painfully aware of their inability ever to reconstruct a dead world in its completeness, however thorough or revealing their documentation. . . . [They are] doomed to be forever hailing someone who has just gone around the corner and out of earshot.” Shama does not deny that a past reality exists, but he works with what he calls “the rather banal axiom that claims for historical knowledge must always be fatally circumscribed by the character and prejudices of its narrator” (quoted 15f.). Rightly, Wood objects to the “fatally.” If he does not, as does Kracauer, seem to think inevitable the incompleteness of historiographical recovery of the past, he at least accepts it as a possiblity. For Wood, as for Kracauer, the potential for recovery is relative–more rather than less complete, correct, honest, objective. See also chap. 4, n. 13 of this study.

52. *History*, 31; for Kracauer’s use in *History* of the attribute “theological” see also chap. 6, secs. 4, 8 of this study.

53. This passage in particular–in a more general way the whole argument concerning the historian’s story–echoes the characterization of photography in *Theory of Film*: it “tends to stress the endless” in its “emphasis on fortuitous complexes which represent fragments rather than wholes.” Film as a photographic medium gravitates “toward the expanses of outer reality–an open-ended, limitless world,” a “flow of random events,” which clearly differs from the “finite and ordered cosmos set by tragedy” (*Theory of Film: The Redemption of Physical Reality* [New York: Oxford University Press, 1960], 19, x).

54. See chap. 6, secs. 7, 8 of this study.

55. Hans Jonas, “Heidegger and Theology,” in *The Phenomenon of Life: Towards a Philosophical Biology* (New York: Dell, 1966), 235–61, 258.

56. See Kracauer’s reservations in his letter to Adorno, Mar. 3, 1965 (Kracauer papers 72.1122/12), regarding Adorno’s critique of Heidegger’s philosophical style as “Jargon der Eigentlichkeit” (jargon of authenticity). He had liked the original article but thought the book-length version belabored the obvious. Himself addicted to this jargon, Adorno had turned it against Heidegger to accuse him of making the distinction between the authentic private and the inauthentic public and then trying to overcome it through illegitimate discourse and political (fascist) affiliations.

57. Karl Loewith, *Mein Leben in Deutschland vor und nach 1933: Ein Bericht* (Stuttgart: J.B. Metzler, 1986), 27f., 45. See also Loewith’s quotes from a letter Heidegger wrote to him in 1921 (30).

58. *History*, 201; see also Kracauer to Adorno, July 4, 1951 (Kracauer papers 72.1120/11), criticizing his dialectic as blind in important ways to the contemporary situation, relying on old familiar concepts, and to Lowenthal, Oct. 27, 1958 (72.1571/7), criticizing the self-congratulatory radical style of Adorno’s cultural politics in postwar Germany (“a radicalness that is having a fine time”). He complains here, too, about Benjamin’s “Messianic dogmatism,” which seems “abstruse” and “arbitrary” to someone working with a broader concept of culture.

59. *History*, 199; the context is his critique of Gadamer’s “smooth fusion of major immanentist motifs” in *Wahrheit und Methode* (1960; *Truth and Method*, 1975).

60. Johann Gustav Droysen, *Vorlesungen über Enzyklopaedie und Methodologie der Geschichte, Historik* (Darmstadt: Wissenschaftliche Buchgesellschaft, 1972), 1–316, esp. 133–44. This edition also contains the shorter, programmatic *Grundriss der Historik* (317–428) published by Droysen himself, first in 1858. References to *Grundriss* to this edition.

61. *Historik*, 284f.; on Kracauer’s overly critical reaction to Droysen’s reference to the (then very new) medium of photography see chap. 6, sec. 5 of this study.

62. Feb. 27, 1962 (Kracauer papers 72.1571/25). See also the argument in chap. 6, sec. 5 of this study.

63. For a contrasting comparison between the “genuine collector” and the historian that raises the same questions see chap. 6, sec. 8 of this study.

64. *History*, 83f. Alfred Schutz, “The Stranger,” *American Journal of Sociology* 49, no. 6 (1944): 499–507, now in Alfred Schutz, *Collected Papers* 2, ed. Arvid Brodersen (The Hague: Martinus Nijhoff, 1971), 91–105. In a footnote attached to this statement, Kracauer made a general reference to his friend’s essay; for the portion of the argument on which he actually drew, see “The Stranger,” 95–100.

65. Alfred Schutz, “The Homecomer,” *American Journal of Sociology* 50, no. 4 (1945): 363–76, now in *Collected Papers*, 106–19.

66. *History*, 83f.; “The Stranger,” 104.

67. "The Homecomer," 115; *History*, 91–92.

68. *History*, 86f. See, in contrast, Lowenthal's remarks on the same issue in his "Recollections of Theodor Adorno" (*An Unmastered Past*, 201–15) and chap. 2, n. 37 of this study.

69. *History*, 89; the first phrase is a quote from Herbert Butterfield's "Moral Judgments in History," in Hans Meyerhoff, ed., *The Philosophy of History in Our Time* (Garden City, N.Y.: Doubleday, 1959), 228–49, esp. 229. Whenever the historian "probes the sources to check the truth-to-fact of some inclusive narrative, some broader historical construction, he is likely to happen upon generalizations or macro-units which call for a fresh look at the diverse materials they allegedly cover" (*History*, 89).

70. "Moral Judgments in History," 244; *History*, 91. See chap. 4, sec. 2 of this study.

71. Ingrid Sischy, "Good Intentions," *New Yorker*, Sept. 9, 1991, 89–95, esp. 92.

72. "Good Intentions," 91. *An Uncertain Grace: Photographs by Sebastiao Salgado* (New York: Aperture in Association with the San Francisco Museum of Modern Art, 1990).

73. John Szarkowski, *Photography Until Now* (New York: Museum of Modern Art, 1989), 224. See also the informative documentation in Glenn Gardner Willumson, *W. Eugene Smith and the Photographic Essay* (Cambridge: Cambridge University Press, 1992).

74. *History*, 91. Strauss disagrees in this respect with Collingwood: "On Collingwood's Philosophy of History," *Review of Metaphysics* 5, no. 4 (1952): 559–86, esp. 583.

75. Schutz, "The Homecomer," 115.

76. See chap. 3, secs. 1, 4, and chap. 4, secs. 1, 2 of this study.

77. See chap. 2, sec. 5 of this study.

78. See my *Weimar Intellectuals and the Threat of Modernity* (Bloomington: Indiana University Press, 1988), pt. 2, chap. 2, "Ulrich, a Life: Robert Musil and the Experiment of the Real."

79. *Theory of Film*, 162; these images are collected in Helmar Lerski, *Verwandlungen durch Licht*, ed. Ute Eskildsen (Freren: Luca Verlag, 1982): see the informative "*Vorwort*" by Andor Kraszna-Kraus, 6–13. See also Helmar Lerski, *Köpfe des Alltags: Unbekannte Menschen* (Berlin: H. Reckendorf, 1931), 50; *Helmar Lerski, Lichtbildner: Photographien und Filme 1910–1947* (Essen: Museum Folkwang, 1982).

80. See for instance D. H. Mellor, *Real Time* (Cambridge: Cambridge University Press, 1981). For more on the poetic (religious) nature of such reconciliation see chap. 6, sec. 8 of this study.

81. See chap. 2, secs. 3, 5 of this study.

82. See Barnouw, *Weimar Intellectuals*, 2–5, 31f.

83. There is not much sense in assigning, from a late twentieth-century perspective, the labels "left" or "right" to these positions, since both were radically reactionary in cultural terms.

84. Eric Voegelin, *Order and History*, 5 vols. (Baton Rouge: Louisiana State University Press, 1956–87).

85. Voegelin papers, Hoover Institution, Stanford, Calif., correspondence Eric Voegelin/Alfred Schutz, box 34/10.

86. Aug. 12, 1943. For the work-in-progress, "The Stranger," see *Philosophers in Exile: The Correspondence of Alfred Schutz and Aron Gurwitsch 1939–1959*, ed. Richard Grathoff (Bloomington: Indiana University Press, 1989), chap. 2, "The Strange and the Stranger (November 8, 1941–July 16, 1944)."

87. Schutz wrote, "Ich glaube, dass die Entdeckung der vorprädikativen Sphäre, die Blosslegung des Intersubjektivitätsproblems, die Rückführung der Logik, Mathematik, der Naturwissenschaften auf den Boden der Lebenswelt, die Beiträge Husserls zur Analyse des inneren Zeitbewusstsseins und zur Raumkonstitution . . . in der Tat philosophische Fundamentalprobleme berühren" (Nov. 11–Dec. 13, 1943, Voegelin papers, box 34/10). His concession, of course, would have been unacceptable to Husserl. Searching for a firm basis of human knowledge and taking to heart Gottlob Frege's accusation that he was confusing psychology and logic, Husserl tried to distinguish clearly between psychology and phenomenology in his 1910 *Logos* essay "Philosophie als strenge Wissenschaft." His concept of philosophical science underwent changes, but he held fast to the (problematic) concept of science as a body of indubitable and objective truths.

88. At the end of the Weimar period, in a situation of extreme social and political upheaval, Husserl's *Formale und transcendentale Logik* (1929) asserted that the transcendental ego exists "absolutely" and all other things exist only relative to it. This is the position criticized by Schutz. There is, however, a signal for a change in direction in the 1935 lectures Husserl published in Belgrade one year later under the title, *Die Krisis der europäischen Wissenschaften und die transcendentale Phänomenologie*, on which Schutz in this letter to Voegelin does not elaborate: it concerns Husserl's belief now in an intersubjectivity of transcendental egos and the primary importance, for our understanding of scientific knowledge, of "*Lebenswelt*." However, the projected intersubjectivity still involves transcendental egos, and the world of science is still sharply separated from the world of daily life.

89. Voegelin underlined these passages of Schutz's letter and wrote question marks in the margins.

90. Voegelin, searching for a more "objective," comprehensive position, marks this passage with "unfortunately!"

91. "Der Philosoph versteht sein Problem . . . immer nur unvollständig. Es steht für ihn immer in einem wesentlich uneinsichtigen Sinnzusammenhang von ungeklärten, weil leer antizipierten Implikationen, es hat seine offenen Horizonte, die nicht ausgelegt werden können, weil sie unerfüllt sind und alles dahinsteht. Erst im Rückblick kann manchmal der Philosoph, häufiger der philosophische Zeitgenosse, immer aber die in seiner Tradition stehende Nachwelt die vordem leeren Horizonte

auslegen, weil sie inzwischen erfüllt und ihre Implikate sichtbar geworden sind. Dies ist die vitale Funktion der Kritik in allen ihren Formen für den Fortgang der philosophischen Tradition. . . . Die Kritik, die natürlich eine unendliche und in jeder Generation neu erwachsende Aufgabe bleibt, stellt die Sinnzusammenhänge zwischen ihrem Gegenstand und seinen erst jetzt einsichtig gewordenen Implikationen her. Alles was an der Theorie des Historizismus gesund ist, scheint in diesem Satz enthalten zu sein" (Voegelin papers, box 34/10).

92. July 16, 1944, *Philosophers in Exile*, 69–72, esp. 70.

93. *Philosophers in Exile*, 71. On the philosopher's animosity toward the public sphere see Dagmar Barnouw, *Visible Spaces: Hannah Arendt and the German-Jewish Experience* (Baltimore: Johns Hopkins University Press, 1990), chaps. 1, 5. Arendt's attitude toward the experience of exile was quite similar to that of Kracauer and Schutz, and her emphasis on the importance of the public sphere was centrally informed by it. But like Leo Strauss in *Natural Right and History*, and like Voegelin (from whom she otherwise differed dramatically) in *The New Science of Politics* and in *Order and History*, in *The Human Condition* and in "What is Authority?" she looks to Greek antiquity for norms by which to define and to order, in certain ways also to anchor and authorize political thought and behavior.

94. *Philosophers in Exile*, 71f.

95. See Gurwitsch's and Schutz's reactions to *The New Science of Politics*. Gurwitsch, sending Schutz a copy of his letter to Voegelin (*Philosophers in Exile*, 184f.), emphasizes, to Schutz if not to Voegelin, his closeness in this work to phenomenology: "What is it for the most part, if not a phenomenology of historically active societies! The entire method is phenomenological, making use of the concept of motivation, which he just doesn't call by that name. But as you will see, I haven't written him that, or at least not emphasized it. The language which I speak with him is that of the historian and archheretic" (Nov. 2, 1952, 183). This is not a correct description of Gurwitsch's attitude in the letter to Voegelin, which praises precisely those arguments that appear problematic for the modern historian: " . . . a *science of order* is such an important desideratum. If one takes your book as an historical study, then it is something we have been awaiting for a long, very long time." Instructively, Schutz does not see any kinship to phenomenology (letter to Gurwitsch, Nov. 10, 1952, 186). His letter to Voegelin (27 pages, Nov. 1952) is much more critical, focusing on Voegelin's idiosyncratic and carry-all use of the term, *gnosticism*, in order to explain the destructive power of twentieth-century ideologies (published, together with Voegelin's answers of Jan. 1 and 10, 1953, in Peter J. Opitz and Gregor Sebba, eds., *The Philosophy of Order: Essays on History, Consciousness and Politics* [Stuttgart: Klett-Cotta, 1981], 434–48, 449–62). See also Rudolf Bultmann's critical reaction to Voegelin's use of the term: letters to Voegelin of July 19, 1957, and Mar. 4, 1960 (Voegelin papers, Hoover Institution, Stanford, Calif., correspondence Eric Voegelin/Rudolf Bultmann, box 8/55).

See also Voegelin's 1949 Guggenheim project, which would eventually become *The New Science of Politics*: "The over-all aim of the work will be the restoration of the classic, that is, of the Platonic-Aristotelian range of a theory of politics. The realization of this aim entails the elaboration of (1) a philosophical anthropology, a theory of the nature of man, (2) a theory of political society as the field in which the nature of man actualizes itself, (3) a theory of the dynamics of political forms in the historical cycles, (4) a theory of ideas (political myths) as a constitutive factor of political reality" (Voegelin papers, box 15/25).

96. Eric Voegelin, *Order and History*. IV. *The Ecumenic Age* (Baton Rouge: Louisiana State University Press, 1974).

97. Eric Voegelin, "Historiogenesis," *Philosophisches Jahrbuch* 48 (1960): 419–46.

98. Eric Voegelin, "Reason: The Classic Experience," *Published Essays 1966–1985, Collected Works*, ed. Ellis Sandoz (Baton Rouge: Louisiana State University Press, 1990) 12, 265–91.

99. "Reason," 265; the term *luminous* in Voegelin's usage carries the connotation "grounded existence or expanded consciousness of the connection between the human and the divine."

100. See *Dialectic of Enlightenment*, xi; see sec. 1 above.

101. See n. 93 above.

102. Loewith to Voegelin, Nov. 14, 1944; Voegelin to Loewith, Dec. 17, 1944 (Voegelin papers, Hoover Institution, Stanford, Calif., correspondence Eric Voegelin/Karl Loewith, box 24/4).

103. See "Reason," 273: "there would be no existential unrest moving toward the quest of the ground unless the unrest was already man's knowledge of his existence from a ground that he is not himself."

104. Voegelin to Loewith, Mar. 21, 1949; Loewith to Voegelin, Mar. 26, 1949 (Voegelin papers, box 24/4).

105. Eric Voegelin, *In Search of Order, Order and History V* (Baton Rouge: Louisiana State University Press, 1987), 21.

106. Karl Loewith, *Meaning in History*, 19.

107. Karl Loewith, *Permanence and Change: Lectures on the Philosophy of History* (Cape Town: Haum, 1969), 11.

108. *Permanence and Change*, 24, 33; discussion of the historical-philosophical tradition, 18–33.

109. *History*, 167. See also 199, under the heading "*Historical relativity*": "We live in a cataract of times."

110. *History*, 179.

111. Quoted in *History*, 211; Jacob Burckhardt, *Weltgeschichtliche Betrachtungen: Gesamtausgabe* 7 (Stuttgart: Deutsche Verlagsanstalt, 1929), 1–208, esp. 1.

112. Quoted in *History*, 211; Burckhardt, *Weltgeschichtliche Betrachtungen*, 3.

113. Louis O. Mink, "Philosophical Analysis and Historical Understanding," in *Historical Understanding* (Ithaca: Cornell University Press, 1987), 118–46, esp. 137.

CHAPTER 6. IMAGE, IMAGINATION, AND HISTORICAL EVIDENCE

1. See chap. 1, sec. 2 of this study.

2. Siegfried Kracauer, *History: Last Things before the Last* (Oxford: Oxford University Press, 1969), 16, 191.

3. Siegfried Kracauer, *Theory of Film: The Redemption of Physical Reality* (New York: Oxford University Press, 1960), 300.

4. See Inka Mülder-Bach, "Schlupflöcher. Die Diskontinuität des Kontinuierlichen im Werk Siegfried Kracauers," in Michael Kessler and Thomas Y. Levin, eds., *Siegfried Kracauer: Neue Interpretationen* (Tübingen: Stauffenburg, 1990), 249–66. Mülder-Bach postulates a profound break in Kracauer's work connected with the irreversible absence of his "magic gaze" in exile. But she can do so only because in her discussion of his Weimar texts she selects those which enable her to claim its presence (*Siegfried Kracauer, Grenzgänger zwischen Theorie und Literatur: seine frühen Schriften 1913–1933* [Stuttgart: Metzler, 1985]). For a more instructive discussion of Kracauer's focus on the seemingly insignificant see Klaus Koziol, "Die Wirklichkeit ist eine Konstruktion. Zur Methodologie Siegfried Kracauers," *Neue Interpretationen*, 147–58.

5. John Clive, *Not by Fact Alone: Essays on the Writing and Reading of History* (New York: Alfred Knopf, 1989), 15.

6. *Not by Fact Alone*, 34; the novelist is V. S. Pritchett. Clive, who is very much aware of the uses of "good" literary strategies in historiography, makes this statement against absolutist positions concerning the omni-importance of the literary dimension, for instance Hayden White, *Metahistory: The Historical Imagination in Nineteenth-Century Europe* (Baltimore: Johns Hopkins University Press, 1973). See the essays collected in *The Representation of Historical Events: History and Theory Beiheft* 26 (Middletown, Conn.: Wesleyan University Press, 1987); almost all the essays in the latter issue at least refer to White, if only to refute or to modify his assertions.

7. See George Levine, "Scientific Realism and Literary Representation," *Raritan* 10 (Spring 1991): 18–39. Arguing for the need to arrive at a clearer understanding of the status of literary representation, Levine refers to the current popularity among literary theorists of Cifford Geertz's notion of "thick description." Geertz's use of the concept, *fiction*, for both anthropological and literary description, Levine points out, does not obliterate the fact that "in the novel 'the actors are represented as not having existed and the events as not having happened,' while in anthropology they are represented as actual" (23). Curiously, this crucial distinction has indeed been obliterated in the practice of many literary theorists today.

8. Louis O. Mink is not sufficiently clear on this crucial point since he does not clarify the status of "narrative form" in its relation to evidence ("Narrative Form as a Cognitive Instrument," in Robert H. Canary and Henry Kozicki, eds., *The Writing of History* [Madison: University of Wisconsin Press, 1978], 129–49, esp. 141–48). See also John

Passmore, "Narratives and Events," *The Representation of Historical Events*, 68–74. Acknowledging the ubiquity of stories, Passmore distinguishes events from "event-descriptions." He advises juxtaposition of "event-descriptions" and "narratives," disputing in both cases claims to "correctness" since both are influenced by the perceptual conventions and individual temperaments that guide language use (71). But he then retreats into asserting "correctness" in some cases, referring to "events" originating in his own activities that are therefore "ontological," namely removed from the distorting perception of others. His argument is symptomatic of the current situation of uncertainty: he both grants the semantic refractions of historiographical representation and pleads to refrain from taking the "liberties" of the novelist (73).

9. The epistemological emphasis on perception does not eliminate or stabilize that fluid connection. C. Behan McCullagh holds that the historian in his search for historical truth needs to assume the existence of the world as independent of what he believes about it (*Justifying Historical Descriptions* [Cambridge: Cambridge University Press, 1984], 1). Leon J. Goldstein argues that this "entirely vacuous" assumption plays no role at all in the "disciplined endeavor" to acquire historical knowledge ("Impediments to Epistemology in the Philosophy of History," *Knowing and Telling History: The Anglo-Saxon Debate* in *History and Theory Beiheft* 25 [Middletown, Conn.: Wesleyan University Press, 1986], 82–100, esp. 92). But in a largely imponderable psychological sense, McCullagh's kind of naïve realism has played a fairly important role in most of historiographical practice. See also his equally unchic straight belief in a "fair overall representation of the central subject" as the "organizing principle . . . peculiar to history and not found in fiction" ("The Truth of Historical Narratives," *The Representation of Historical Events*, 30–45, esp. 31). Goldstein, here close to Kracauer's position, thinks Peirce's concept of *abduction* (in contrast to *deduction* and *induction*), with its emphasis on the possible and the plausible, a most fitting description of how historical knowledge is formed (93). But in contrast to Kracauer's historian, he does not use this greater epistemological flexibility for greater mobility toward and within past actualities.

10. On the epistemological problems with the "covering-law model" in historiography, see sec. 4 below. On the in some ways alienating function of history–the historian as exile or stranger–see chap. 5, secs. 4, 5 of this study.

11. F. R. Ankersmit critizes in detail problems associated with the role of the "governing-law model" in Anglo-American historiography, but his own "solution" of concentrating on the exploration of language use in historiography is not helpful because it circumvents the issue of historical evidence. Ankersmit claims with some justification that in the case of historiography it is "particularly difficult" to "distinguish between what is said and how it is said." However, his argument that "that which *seems* to be a debate on reality is *in fact* a debate on the language we use" both states the obvious–the inevitable interdependency of language and (historical) knowledge–and neglects to deal with important differences in focus ("The Dilemma of Contemporary Anglo-Saxon Philosophy of History," *Knowing and Telling History*,

1–27, 16). More useful is L. B. Cebik's warning that the current skepticism regarding covering-law epistemology makes historians "ignore epistemology's more general concerns in which science, explanation, objectivity, proof and reference begin as problemata, not as presuppositions. In addition, they fail to notice epistemology's function to formulate what theories may and must contain. If we ignore history's regulative commitment to telling the truth (however we analyze the term) and to being bound within the limits of reliable evidence, then of course history becomes no more than a variant of literature rather than being a disciplined investigation" ("Understanding Narrative Theory," *Knowing and Telling History*, 58–81, esp. 59). In order to be at all useful to historians, narrative theory has to deal with the "epistemic dimensions" of narratives, namely what these narratives actually do with respect to questions of truth and falsity. He suggests therefore not to begin (as does Hayden White) with the finished, highly refined, sophisticated story (60) but to "distinguish between what demarcates certain uses of language and what demarcates certain uses of things built from language" (62). See also John Passmore, "Explanation in Everyday Life, in Science, and in History," *Studies in the Philosophy of History*, ed. George H. Nadel (New York: Harper Torchbooks, 1965), 16–34.

12. Clive, *Not by Fact Alone*, 35.

13. See Peter Novick, *That Noble Dream: The "Objectivity Question" and the American Historical Profession* (New York: Cambridge University Press, 1988).

14. Wright Morris, "The Camera Eye," in *Time Pieces: Photographs, Writing and Memory* (New York: Aperture, 1989), 11–22, esp. 13.

15. See "Walker Evans on Himself": "Nobody knows what art is, and it can't be taught. It's the mind and the talent of the eye of the individual who is operating this machine that produces what comes out of it. He selects, whether consciously or not, what he is doing; and that really leads to the question of style. One really doesn't associate a machine—a little box with glass in it—with the personal imprint of the operator, but it is there, and it's a kind of magic, inexplicable quality" (*Images of the South: Visits with Eudora Welty and Walker Evans. Southern Folklore Report 1* [1977]: 35.

16. See Maria Morris Hambourg's description of Atget's photographic goals: "Atget never considered his purpose or his production to be primarily artistic. His job, he said, was documentation, a discipline combining description, classification and cataloguing. It demanded a judicious selection of the facts to be describecd, a program for their gathering, and a periodic consideraton of the profile and range of the pictorial catalog as a whole. The approach was typical of nineteenth-century documentary photography, and its method kept Atget from the digressions of artistic self-consciousness that characterized the work of so many of his contemporaries in Europe and America" (*The Work of Atget.* Vol. 2. *The Art of Old Paris* [New York: Museum of Modern Art, 1982], 15). These perceived documentary qualities support certain analogies between photography and historiography and are the cause for the attraction of Atget's photography to late twentieth-century viewers.

17. Gisèle Freund, *Photography and Society* (Boston: David R. Godine, 1980), 93.

18. Quoted in William Stott, *Documentary Expression and Thirties America* (Chicago: University of Chicago Press, 1986 [1973]), 319f. In *Images of the South* (32) we can find a notably different statement on the cooperation with Agee, made to a different interviewer in a different context.

19. *Photography until Now* (New York: Museum of Modern Art, 1989), 215. See also my argument in chap. 3, sec. 2 of this study.

20. "I Saw" was the title of the lecture on European fascism with which John Spivak toured the United States in 1936 for *New Masses.* See his memories of his work in the thirties in *A Man in His Time* (New York: Horizon, 1967). More than half a century later, listeners' letters to radio programs that, like National Public Radio's "All Things Considered," emphasize "in-depth" investigative reporting, frequently single out for praise the fact that these reports had transported them to the scene of the action; that, listening, they felt (as if) they had been *there* to *see* it.

21. Roy E. Stryker, "Documentary Photography," in Willard D. Morgan, ed., *The Complete Photographer* (New York: National Educational Alliance, 1942–43, 10 vols.), 4:1364.

22. See Stott, *Documentary Expression*, chap. 3, "The Two Persuasions."

23. See chap. 3, sec. 6 of this study.

24. Erik Barnouw, *Documentary: A History of the Non-Fiction Film*, rev. ed. (Oxford: Oxford University Press, 1983 [1974]), 313.

25. Dorothea Lange, *Photographs of a Lifetime* (New York: Aperture, 1982), 122.

26. Szarkowski, *Photography Until Now*, 216. See also Stott, *Documentary*, 61f., on Lange's selective "stories." Stott considerably simplifies the situation, but some of his observations on the selection of poses are helpful precisely because they point out so "innocently" the extraordinary difficulties of the documentary (and, by extension, of historiography): "In Lange's photograph the Okie girl nurses her son. Why does she not spank him or yell at him for having thrown his food on the ground? . . . And she must laugh enormously too, hug her son roughly and dance him about. . . . And she yawns and scratches and giggles and cleans her nose. But these things are not shown. All her life, everything she is, gets reduced to the instrumental, to the pitiable, to a poignant helplessness and wan despair. When Lorentz claimed that Lange's one desire was to record poor people "as they are, not as they should be, not as some doctrine insists they should be," he exaggerated. Lange's people were treated according to a doctrine, and the doctrine was documentary."

27. Wright Morris, "Time Pieces," *Time Pieces*, 37–45, esp. 40.

28. *Photographs of a Lifetime*, 46 (quoted from Daniel Dixon, "Dorothea Lange," *Modern Photography* 16 [Dec. 1952], 69); see chap. 1, sec. 2 of this study on Bacon's praising the documentary efforts of the historian.

29. Bourke-White's *You Have Seen Their Faces* (1937), a collaboration with Erskine Caldwell, outraged FSA photographers because of what they perceived to be a largely

fictitious, often simply staged, prettifying depiction of migrant laborers. See Szarkowski's assessment in *Photography Until Now*, 224. Her well-known "At the Time of the Louisville Flood 1937," reproduced by Szarkowski, shows a breadline of blacks underneath a huge poster advertising the "World's Highest Standard of Living": a white, middle-class family complete with kids and dog on an outing in the family car. Bourke-White was struck by the sharp visual signification of a well-known social contrast. But both sides–the blacks wait in an orderly line (partly of her making)–seem to be particles assembled for the purpose of that poster.

30. *Ansel Adams: An Autobiography* with Mary Street Alinder (Boston: Little, Brown, 1985), 269; see chap. 4, n. 6 of this study.

31. Reproduced in Szarkowski, *Photography until Now*, 192.

32. Ansel Adams, *Born Free and Equal: Photographs of the Loyal Japanese-Americans at Manzanar Relocation Center, Inyo County, California* (New York: U.S. Camera, 1944); John Armor and Peter Wright, *Manzanar Commentary by John Hersey, Photographs by Ansel Adams* (New York: Times Books, 1988), 86.

33. Quoted in Barnouw, *Documentary*, 36. There were other incidents when Flaherty accepted great risks to himself and the Eskimos, for instance an unsuccessful "polar bear aggie"–they found no bear–that almost cost them their lives. See also the "cooking" of the celebrated igloo sequence: since their usual igloo proved too small for interior photography, the Eskimos built an outsized "aggie igloo" that promptly collapsed and then, rebuilt, was still too dark for the camera. One half was sheared away, forcing Nanook and his family to sleep unprotected from the cold–for the sake of the recording photo images (38).

34. *Born Free and Equal*, 7, 9; see the instructively abridged quote of this paragraph in Armor and Wright, *Manzanar*, xvii: focused on the victim status of Japanese-Americans, they cut out Adams' references to his "creative" interests and his understanding of the importance of human interaction with nature.

35. Morris, "Photography in My Life," *Time Pieces*, 111–40, esp. 114f.

36. See Dagmar Barnouw, *Weimar Intellectuals and the Threat of Modernity* (Bloomington: Indiana University Press, 1988), 167–82.

37. *Die Angestellten, Schriften* (Frankfurt: Suhrkamp, 1971) 1:216; see chap. 3, sec. 6 of this study.

38. See Koziol, "Die Wirklichkeit ist eine Konstruktion," 154f.

39. Michael Schröter, "Weltzerfall und Rekonstruktion," *Text und Kritik* 68 (Munich, 1980): 18–40, esp. 33.

40. See Mark Singer's letter to the *New Yorker*, Mar. 30, 1989, giving a postscript on the fate of Adams in response to readers' questions after his profile of the filmmaker Errol Morris (*New Yorker*, Feb. 6, 1989).

41. Errol Morris in an interview with Bill Moyers, broadcast together with the film, KPBS, San Diego, May 10, 1991.

42. See the review, "True Detective," *New Yorker*, Sept. 5, 1988, 76–78.

43. See Kracauer's sketch of a film script, "Dimanche," a study of visual perspective and knowledge. He projects two accounts of a Sunday excursion by means of two image sequences, the first produced by a small child whose spatial perception is defined by the child's size and degree of visual acculturation, the second by an adult's "normal" perspective, which transforms the child's fantastic spaces into familiar ones. Such repeated recording of the excursion, Kracauer writes, should have the effect of solving a visual puzzle. Importantly, the images do not tell a story. The point of this short film would be a film-specific exploration of the interpretive character of perception. Such exploration might also shed light on epistemologically interesting discrepancies between the child's verbal and visual acculturation–a possibility implied here by Kracauer rather than stated explicitly (Literaturarchiv Marbach, Kracauer papers 72.3513).

44. Morris, "Photographs, Images, and Words," *Time Pieces*, 53–65, esp. 64.

45. See chap. 2, sec. 1 of this study: Adorno's dismissive term for Kracauer's empiricist attitude in intellectual matters.

46. Martin Jay, "Adorno and Kracauer: Notes on a Troubled Friendship," *Permanent Exiles: Essays on the Intellectual Migration from Germany to America* (New York: Columbia University Press, 1985), 217–36, esp. 225.

47. Martin Jay, "The Extraterritorial Life of Siegfried Kracauer," *Salmagundi* 31–35 (1975–76): 49–106, esp. 89, 93. For different aspects of Kracauer's argument against aesthetic reconciliation see chap. 5, secs. 5, 6, 7 of this study. I will come back to Jay's reading in sec. 8 below.

48. Jay, "Extraterritorial Life," 93f.; *History*, 136. See also *History*, 31, for equating *theological* with *doctrinaire* and chap. 5, sec. 4 of this study. Kracauer makes repeated use of Herbert Butterfield's term, *technical history*, drawing attention to Butterfield's insistence on the historian's "act of self-emptying" when working in that "limited and mundane realm of description and explanation, in which local and concrete things are achieved by a disciplined use of tangible evidence" (quoted in *History*, 89; Herbert Butterfield, "Moral Judgments in History," *The Philosophy of History in Our Time*, ed. Hans Meyerhoff [Garden City, N.Y.: Doubleday Anchor, 1959], 228–49, esp. 228f.). See also *Man on His Past: The Study of the History of Historical Scholarship* (Boston: Beacon, 1960), 139; see chap. 5, sec. 5 of this study.

49. Theodor W. Adorno, "Der wunderliche Realist: Über Siegfried Kracauer," *Noten zur Literatur, Gesammelte Schriften* 2, ed. Rolf Tiedemann (Frankfurt: Suhrkamp, 1984 [1974]), 388–408, esp. 407.

50. See Steven Weinberg's comments on the role of critical consensus in cosmology, the most speculative science: "Scientific practice is not really in danger from a false consensus. It *needs* a consensus, in order for us to have something to talk about with each other, in order that our work adds up. Without a consensus you don't have any way of knowing even if the consensus is wrong" (quoted in Daniel J. Kevies, "'The

Final Secret of the Universe,'" *New York Review of Books* 38, no. 9 [May 16, 1991]: 27–32, esp. 32).

51. Kracauer to Lowenthal, Mar. 18, 1961, Feb. 27, 1962, and Oct. 28, 1963 (Kracauer papers 72.1571/21, 25, 30).

52. *History*, 105; see also: "The diverse histories may also be arranged along a continuum one pole of which is occupied by syntheses of extreme generality–universal histories, that is–while the opposite pole would have to be assigned to investigations of atom-like events" (104).

53. See here Alfred Schutz's Husserl critique in his correspondence with Eric Voegelin, chap. 5, sec. 7.

54. *History*, 46. Edmund Husserl, *Die Krisis der europäischen Wissenschaften* (The Hague: Martinus Nijhoff, 1962), 448: "die Wissenschaft schwebt so wie in einem leeren Raum über der Lebenswelt."

55. Peter Munz, *The Shapes of Time: A New Look at the Philosophy of History* (Middletown, Conn.: Wesleyan University Press, 1977), 84f. For the concept of "enactment" see R. G. Collingwood, *The Idea of History* (London: Oxford University Press, 1967 [1946]), 171–76, 282–302. For Munz's critique of this concept see sec. 5 below.

56. *Shapes of Time*, 85. On Munz's view of the role and function of general laws in historical inquiry see sec. 5 below; for other positions on the covering-law model see n. 83 below.

57. V. S. Naipaul, *The Enigma of Arrival* (New York: Viking, 1987), 173.

58. *History*, 51. Johann Gustav Droysen, *Historik: Vorlesungen über Enzyklopädie und Methodologie der Geschichte*, ed. Rudolf Hübner (Darmstadt: Wissenschaftliche Buchgesellschaft, 1972), 285.

59. Quoted in *History*, 51. See in contrast Oscar Handlin on the historian's encounter with pictorial representations in his *Truth in History* (Cambridge, Mass.: Belknap Press, 1979), chap. 9 "Seeing and Hearing," esp. 234–37, 239–45.

60. Johann Gustav Droysen, *Outline of the Principles of History*, trans. E. Benjamin Andrews (Boston: Ginn, 1893), Appendix 2, "Art and Method," 118 (trans. of *Grundriss der Historik*, 3d ed. 1881 [1858]).

61. Allan Megill, "Grand Narrative and the Discipline of History," ms., 14. I am grateful to Allan Megill for giving me access to his stimulating argument. I tend to be more impressed than he by Droysen's remarkable modernity, for instance his awareness of the problems posed by these differences. He insisted on the need for a working principle that would guide historical knowledge: "Even the narrow, the very narrowest of human relations, strivings, activities, etc., have a process, a history, and are for the persons involved, historical. So family histories, local histories, special histories. But over all these and such histories is *History*," as an in some ways agreed on working concept of historical inquiry (*Outline*, sec. 73, 44). See also Hans Robert Jauss, "Geschichte der Kunst und Historie," in Reinhart Koselleck und Wolf-Dieter Stempel, eds., *Geschichte–Ereignis und Erzählung* (Munich: Fink, 1973), 175–209, esp. 183–93.

62. See chap. 5, sec. 4 of this study.

63. *History*, 54. Droysen in his critique of Ranke dealt with precisely this issue: see chap. 5, sec. 4 of this study.

64. Quoted in Susan Sontag, *On Photography* (New York: Noonday Press, 1989 [1973]), 192.

65. Quoted in *History*, 55; the quote is taken from Paul Strand, "Photography," *Seven Arts* 2 (Aug. 1917), 524f. Significantly, Kracauer refers here to a photographer known for his remarkable sensitivity to the qualities of the "world out there." See chap. 3, sec. 2 of this study.

66. *Berühmte Zeitgenossen in unbewachten Augenblicken* (Stuttgart: J. Engelhorns Nachfolger, 1931); Peter Hunter-Salomon, *Portrait of an Age* (New York: Collier Macmillan, 1975), xiv.

67. *Erich Salomon* (New York: Aperture History of Photography Series 10, 1978), 5, 11f.

68. Erwin Panofsky, *Renaissance and Renascences in Western Art* (New York: Harper & Row, 1972 [1960]), 84: "the 'principle of disjunction': wherever in the high and later Middle Ages a work of art borrows its form from a classical model, this form is almost invariably invested with a non-classical, normally Christian, significance; wherever in the high and later Middle Ages a work of art borrows its theme from classical poetry, legend, history or mythology, this theme is quite invariably presented in a non-classical, normally contemporary, form."

69. *History*, 57; I come back to Kracauer's use of Panofsky's "principle of disjunction" in sec. 7 below.

70. See "Die Photographie," and "Film 1928," both in *Das Ornament der Masse*; also "Photographiertes Berlin," *Frankfurter Zeitung*, Dec. 15, 1932.

71. Sontag, *On Photography*, 130.

72. See chap. 4, sec. 1 this study.

73. *Theory of Film*, Introduction, 8.

74. Morris, "Photographs, Images and Words," *Time Pieces*, 64.

75. Morris, "Structures and Artifacts," *Time Pieces*, 141–48, esp. 147.

76. *On Photography*, 19. Sontag's skepticism here is motivated by ideological considerations rather than information about the rapidly developing technology of the medium that led Fred Ritchin to warn us about its implications for the evidence status of photo images: *In Our Own Image: The Coming Revolution in Photography* (New York: Aperture, 1990), esp. chaps. 3, 5, 6.

77. See *Weimar Intellectuals*, 187–90.

78. For illustrations see Freund, *Photography and Society*, 42, 60f.

79. *Theory of Film*, 16; see "Walker Evans on Himself": "I have a theory that seems to work with me that some of the best things you ever do sort of come through you. You

don't know where you get the impetus and the response to what is before your eyes, but you are using your eyes all the time and teaching yourself unconsciously really from morning to night" (*Images of the South*, 34).

80. "Guide (original) (complete)," 10 (Kracauer papers 72.3525/1).

81. Erwin Panofsky, *Meaning in the Visual Arts: Papers in and on Art History* (Garden City, N.Y.: Doubleday Anchor, 1955), 35, n. 3.

82. See Clive, *Not by Fact Alone*, 35; sec. 1 above.

83. Munz, *Shapes of Time*, 50. Kracauer used similar examples in *History*, chap. 2, "The Historical Approach," 225–27. See Munz's discussion of different historians' understanding of general or covering laws, *Shapes of Time*, 306–11. For the "covering-law model" (CLM) see Carl G. Hempel, "The Function of General Laws in History," *Journal of Philosophy* 39 (1942): 35–48. On the role played by CLM in English and American historiography see Ankersmit, "The Dilemma of Contemporary Anglo-Saxon Philosophy of History," 1–27.

84. See chap. 5, secs. 4, 5 of this study.

85. On some of the difficulties of access–different in each case–see V. S. Naipaul, *Among the Believers: An Islamic Journey* (London: André Deutsch, 1981); Van A. Harvey, *The Historian and the Believer* (Philadelphia: Westminster Press, 1966).

86. Munz, *Shapes of Time*, 64f. He argues here against Collingwood for a greater rationality of these processes (66), rejecting his (partly Dilthey-derived) concept of "reenactment" (Collingwood, *The Idea of History*, 171–76, 282–302; for Kracauer's comments on Dilthey's concept of empathy see chap. 5, sec. 4 of this study). But if Collingwood's concept is indeed too cloudy, Munz, too, fails to provide clarity for these messy problems. Acknowledging the importance for historiography of an artistic sense of judgment and "power of intuition," he does not examine their significance: "Insofar as history is art, it is difficult to think critically and philosophically about it and insofar as we are thinking critically and philosophically about it, we are really trying to deal with that area and those aspects of history that are capable of rational method" (67). The challenge is to think critically about historiography as a *composite* mode of inquiry.

87. See secs. 4 above and 8 below.

88. Panofsky, *Renaissance and Renascences*, 4.

89. The explicit preference for the *Kleinform* (small form) in the performing arts (one-act drama, variété) around 1900 was influenced by the increasingly fast pace of urban life, including the new medium of cinematography: Anton Kaes, ed., *Kino-Debatte Texte zum Verhältnis von Literatur und Film 1909–1929* (Munich: Deutscher Taschenbuch Verlag, 1978), 5.

90. Vsevolod Pudovkin, *Filmregie und Filmmanuskript* (Berlin, 1928) 1:68f., quoted in *History*, 122, *Theory of Film*, 51. Kracauer used this instruction for filming a demonstration in chap. 3, "The Establishment of Physical Existence," which deals with the

camera's potential for experimenting with perception. See also Heinrich Mann's lecture "Der Film," *Volksverband für Filmkunst*, Capitol film theater Berlin, Feb. 28, 1928: he emphasized film's image-centeredness and advised against basing films on works of literature. Mann praised the artistry of filmmakers like Pudovkin (*The Last Days of St. Petersburg*) in letting "life itself pass by once more": "He stands next to the camera waiting till the peasant's face looks just right, genuine (*echt*). Then he gives the sign" (*Kino-Debatte*, 166–72, esp. 171). The photographer's (historian's) "intensive passive observation" (*History*, 110) is not possible without, is indeed shaped by, judgment.

91. See Kracauer's comments on Griffith's use of close-ups for cinematic narration. The famous close-up shot of the brooding face of a woman waiting for her husband's return in *After Many Years* (1908), usually seen as part of a remarkable montage sequence that takes the viewer inside the woman's mind (images of her husband stranded on a desert island), can also be viewed differently: "But is this really its only function? Consider again the combination of shots with the close-up of Annie's face: the place assigned to the latter in the sequence intimates that Griffith wanted us also to absorb the face for its own sake instead of just passing through and beyond it; the face appears before the desires and emotions to which it refers have been completely defined, thus tempting us to get lost in its puzzling indeterminacy" (*Theory of Film*, 46f.).

92. *History*, 120; *Theory of Film*, 231.

93. *History*, 136. The quote is from John Bagnell Bury, "The Science of History," *The Varieties of History: From Voltaire to the Present*, ed. Fritz Stern (New York: Meridian, 1956), 210–23, esp. 219. See also n. 49 above.

94. "Guide," 34; this section of the notes is entitled "Present and Past." See here also "Guide," *Contents*, no. 14: "Theological (and philosophical) views–lurking around the corner."

95. On the contrasting comparison between Orpheus and the historian see chap. 5, sec. 4 above.

96. Jay, "The Extraterritorial Life," 93f. See sec. 4 above.

97. D. N. Rodowick, "The Last Things before the Last: Kracauer and History," *New German Critique* 41 (Spring-Summer 1987): 109–39, 111, n. 4 and 136–39. The purpose of this strategy is to hear more clearly "Benjamin's voice . . . echoing against the influence of Dilthey and Husserl." But the informed reader cannot find such influence. On Kracauer's imprecise use of Husserl's term, "*Lebenswelt*" see sec. 4 above. Dilthey's presence in his argument is diffuse and ambiguous (see chap. 5, secs. 4, 7 of this study). Rodowick nicely complains that his Benjaminian Kracauer did not himself draw attention to the parallels authored by Rodowick (124, n. 31). See also chap. 3, nn. 1, 24, and chap. 5, n. 15 of this study.

98. Rodowick, "The Last Things," 110.

99. Michael Kessler, "Entschleiern und Bewahren: Siegfried Kracauer's Ansätze für eine Philosophie und Theologie der Geschichte," *Neue Interpretationen*, 105–28.

100. Kessler, "Entschleiern und Bewahren," 127, n. 79.

101. "Zwei Deutungen in zwei Sprachen," *Ernst Bloch zu ehren: Beiträge zu seinem Werk*, ed. Siegfried Unseld, (Frankfurt: Suhrkamp, 1965), 145–55, esp. 145; see chap. 5, sec. 2 of this study.

102. Walter Benjamin, "Theses on the Philosophy of History," *Illuminations*, ed. Hannah Arendt (New York: Schocken, 1973), 254.

103. See chap. 3, sec. 1 of this study on the spatial-temporal compositeness of photo images.

104. See the context of his discussion of covering laws in sec. 5 above.

105. Munz, *Shapes of Time*, 37f.

106. "Guide," 9.

107. The situation, then, is seen not in terms of building an "agreed and cumulative body of facts" (Clive, *Not by Fact Alone*, 293)–a process supported by Butterfield's concept of "technical history"–but rather of going on to question whether and how that could actually be done. See also Kracauer's analogy between the "sensitive historian" engaged in the gathering of detailed evidence and the maker of a documentary film, both searching for an "(unattainable) objective truth." That search itself assumes significance–for the sake not of the searcher but of the subject matter, granting their entangled relation (*History*, 89–91).

108. See *Theory of Film*, chap. 14, "The Found Story and the Episode."

109. *Theory of Film*, 303f.

EPILOGUE

1. Friedrich Schleiermacher, *Hermeneutics: The Handwritten Manuscripts*, ed. Heinz Kimmerle, trans. James Duke and Jack Forstman (Missoula, Mont.: Scholars Press, 1977), ms. 3, 95–151. Interpretation is not, for Schleiermacher, necessarily limited to the written text: "The necessity for the art of interpretation is not based on the difference between oral and written statements" (109). My argument here concerns only written texts.

2. See Peter Novick, *That Noble Dream: The "Objectivity Question" and the American Historical Profession* (New York: Cambridge University Press, 1988); Allan Megill, ed., *Rethinking Objectivity* 1 and 2, *Annals of Scholarship* 8, nos. 3, 4 (1991) and 9, nos. 1, 2 (1992).

3. David Harlan, "Intellectual History and the Return of Literature," *American Historical Review* 94 (June 1989): 581–609, esp. 583.

4. Jacques Derrida, *Of Grammatology* (Baltimore: Johns Hopkins University Press, 1976 [1967]), 49. On Derrida's taking off from from Husserl and Peirce in his moving toward the "deconstruction of the transcendental signified" see Jeffrey Barnouw, "Peirce and Derrida: 'Natural Signs' Empiricism versus 'Originary Trace' Deconstruction," *Poetics Today* 7, no. 1 (1986): 73–94, esp. 73–85.

5. Harlan, "Intellectual History," 582f.

6. For a useful critique of Harlan's "method" in attacking contextualism see David A. Hollinger, "The Return of the Prodigal: The Persistence of Historical Knowing," AHR Forum, *American Historical Review* 94 (June 1989): 610–21, esp. 612–14. See also Allan Megill, "Recounting the Past: 'Description,' Explanation, and Narrative in Historiography," *American Historical Review* 94 (June 1989): 627–53.

7. Harlan, "Intellectual History," 582.

8. Dominick LaCapra, "Chartier, Darnton, and the Great Symbol Massacre," *Soundings in Critical Theory* (Ithaca: Cornell University Press, 1989), 67–89. For the influence on Derrida of the late Heidegger, especially in "Time and Being" (Martin Heidegger, *On Time and Being*, trans. Joan Stambaugh [New York: Harper & Row, 1972], 1–24), see sec. 5 below.

9. See Gary D. Stark, "Vom Nutzen und Nachteil der Literatur für die Geschichtswissenschaft: A Historian's View," *German Quarterly* 63 (1990): 19–31, esp. 19. "Literate" in the latest views on the troubled sign-signified relations, Stark thinks them fine for soft-core literary studies but irrelevant for historical inquiry (22f.).

10. Ibid., 29.

11. Schleiermacher, *Hermeneutics*, 41.

12. See *Hermeneutics*, 99–104; see also Schleiermacher's remarks on the different combinations of what he calls "grammatical" and "psychological" interpretations suitable for different kinds of texts.

13. Wilhelm Dilthey, "The Rise of Hermeneutics," *New Literary History* 3 (1971–72): 229–44, esp. 243.

14. See Dagmar Barnouw, "Critics in the Act of Reading: Jauss, Iser and Eco," *Poetics Today* 1 (1980): 213–22.

15. Friedrich Schlegel, "Athenäums-Fragmente" (1798), *Kritische Schriften*, ed. Wolfdietrich Rasch (Munich: Hanser, 1964), 25–88, esp. 38.

16. Harlan, "Intellectual History," 582.

17. Joyce Appleby, "One Good Turn Deserves Another: Moving beyond the Linguistic; A Response to David Harlan," *American Historical Review* 94 (Dec. 1989): 1326–32, esp. 1327, 1330. I am grateful to Joyce Appleby for drawing my attention to the Harlan essay and for discussing with me its implications. I have learned a great deal from our disagreements.

18. Richard Rorty, "The Contingency of Language," *Contingency, Irony, and Solidarity* (London: Cambridge University Press, 1989), 3–22, esp. 21. On Wittgenstein's statements on the relation of philosophical and poetic discourse in the *Tractatus*, see sec. 6 below.

19. Richard Rorty, "From Ironist Theory to Private Allusions: Derrida," *Contingency*, 122–37, esp. 125.

20. Ibid., 125. Derrida's indebtedness to Heidegger is indeed most harmful in his denial of the public sphere with its plurality and diversity of speakers, that is, language *use.*

21. Jacques Derrida, "Cogito and the History of Madness," *Writing and Difference*, trans. Alan Bass (Chicago: University of Chicago Press, 1978), 31–63, 33–39.

22. On the presence of this concept of language in Wittgenstein's *Tractatus* see sec. 6 below.

23. Rorty, "Ironist Theory," 123, n. 4.

24. Percy Bysshe Shelley, *Defense of Poetry*, in *Selected Poetry and Prose*, ed. Kenneth Neill Cameron (New York: Holt, 1951), 490.

25. See here Hollinger, "The Return of the Prodigal," 613.

26. LaCapra, *Soundings*, 68, 77. In his Derridian critique of Chartier's and Darnton's readerly strategies, LaCapra praises Chartier's essay for acknowledging "the value of Darnton's undertaking even while he questions it. In my own questioning of Chartier's questions, as well as in the critical discussion of Darnton's book that follows, I too insist on the value of both Chartier's and Darnton's endeavors, particularly in the difficult effort to acquire a greater degree of historiographic self-understanding with implications for the practice of research." This declared goal, however, does not prevent his negative summary evaluation of Darnton's hermeneutic naïveté (79f.). See also LaCapra's reading of Rousseau under the influence of Starobinski's *Jean-Jacques Rousseau: La transparence et l'obstacle* and Derrida's *Of Grammatology*, which he sets against Darnton's account of an earlier reader's access to Rousseau (82–89). I am not interested in supporting Darnton's account of an "ideal" reading but rather in pointing out LaCapra's anachronistic assumptions as to the general validity of his own late twentieth-century approach to Rousseau's *La nouvelle Héloise.*

27. Ludwig Wittgenstein, *Notebooks 1914–1916*, ed. Georg Henrik von Wright and G. E. M. Anscombe (Oxford: Blackwell, 1961), 82, 82e.

28. See my "Loos, Kraus, Wittgenstein and the Problem of Authenticity," in Gerald Chapple and Hans H. Schulte, eds., *The Turn of the Century: German Literature and Art, 1890–1915* (Bonn: Bouvier, 1981), 249–73, esp. 267–71.

29. Rorty, "Ironist Theory," 125.

Index

Barnouw, Dagmar.

There and then : history, photography, and the critical realism of Siegfried Kracauer / Dagmar Barnouw.

p. cm. – (Parallax)

Includes bibliographical references and index.

ISBN 0-8018-4753-2 (hc : alk. paper). – ISBN 0-8018-4754-0 (pbk. : alk. paper)

1. Motion pictures–Philosophy. 2. Visual communication. 3. Motion pictures and history. 4. History–Methodology. 5. History–Philosophy. I. Title. II. Series: Parallax (Baltimore, Md.)

PN1995.2.B37 1994

791.43′01–dc20 93-42710